One Nation Under Law

One Nation Under Law

America's Early National
Struggles to Separate

CHURCH AND STATE

Mark Douglas McGarvie

NORTHERN ILLINOIS UNIVERSITY PRESS

© 2004 by Northern Illinois University Press

Published by the Northern Illinois University Press, DeKalb, Illinois 60115

Manufactured in the United States using acid-free paper

All Rights Reserved

Design by Julia Fauci

Library of Congress Cataloging-in-Publication Data

McGarvie, Mark D. (Mark Douglas), 1956–

One nation under law : America's early national struggles to separate church and state / Mark Douglas McGarvie. — 1st ed.

   p.   cm.

Includes bibliographical references and index.

ISBN 0-87580-333-4 (hardback : alk. paper)

1. Church and state—United States—History. I. Title.

KF4865.M35 2004

322'.1'0973—dc22

2004004281

History, as a disciplined way of thinking about the past,

is one of the many efforts to erect bastions of meaning in our perennial

war against chaos, hopefully to overcome it and create a secure island

of meaning and discourse in the midst of surrounding meaninglessness—

to forestall the experience of nothingness which

threatens to overwhelm us.

—Sidney E. Mead

Contents

Illustrations

Acknowledgments

DURING MY WORK ON THIS PROJECT, I lost three friends who had contributed mightily to my understanding of the subject matter addressed in this text. Students of Sidney Mead will recognize the tremendous debt that I owe this brilliant scholar, former president of the American Society for Church History, and longtime professor at the University of Iowa. I was fortunate enough to meet Professor Mead and his wife, Mildred, and to spend several weeks visiting them at their home in Tucson, Arizona, as I was beginning this project. We lost Professor Mead a few years ago, just short of his hundredth birthday. While I was an undergraduate at Northwestern University, Professors Richard Leopold, Timothy Breen, and Robert Wiebe reawakened a long-standing love for history nearly destroyed by high school history courses. Professors Wiebe and Breen met with me years after my college graduation to encourage and advise me in my pursuit of a new career. In early 2001 I learned of Professor Wiebe's sudden passing, just weeks after receiving a last letter from him. Professor Paul Lucas, the man who introduced me to the study of religious history at Indiana University and embraced me as a returning student and a friend, died of a heart attack in 1996. I cannot imagine how different both I and this text would be without the tremendously positive influences of these three gentlemen.

In addition, Professor Larry Friedman, Professor Michael Grossberg, Professor Stephen Conrad, and Professor Bernard Sheehan, all at Indiana University, were instrumental in helping me as I formulated the ideas and perspectives expressed in this text. I wish also to thank a host of other scholars who read all or parts of this text and offered me support and guidance through their comments: Professor Robert Gross of the University of Connecticut, Professor Charles Hobson of the Marshall-Wythe School of Law at the College of William and Mary, Professor Fred Konefsky and Professor Betty Mensch of State University of New York at Buffalo Law School, Professor Richard Bernstein of New York Law School, Professor John Phillip Reid of New York University School of Law, Professor Fran Flavin of University of Texas at Dallas, Professor Robert Hay of Marquette University, Professor John Robinson of Notre Dame University Law School, Professor Marion Winship of Virginia Commonwealth University, Dr. Brent Tarter at the Library of Virginia, Professor Mark Valeri of Union Theological Seminary, and my colleagues at the University of Richmond—Professors Doug Winiarski, Terri Halperin, and Ed Larkin.

Thanks are also due to the wonderful people at the Presbyterian Historical Society Library in Philadelphia, the New York Historical Society, the Episcopalian Church Library in New York, the South Carolina Library in Columbia, the South Carolina Historical Socity in Charleston, and the Special Collections Room in the Portland, Maine, public library. Portions of chapters 3 and 7 have been published previously; I appreciate both Cambridge University Press (publisher of *Charity, Philanthropy, and Civility in American History,* a piece I co-edited with Lawrence J. Friedman) and the National Association of College and University Attorneys in conjuction with Notre Dame University Law School (publishers of the *Journal of College and University Law*—vol. 25, no. 3 of which contains my essay) for permitting me to publish revised versions of those texts here.

I am tremendously indebted also to Professor Bill Nelson at New York University School of Law for his most generous guidance and support when I was revising the text as a Golieb Fellow in legal history at NYU.

Of course, my wife, Blythe, has contributed to this project in ways that can only be appreciated by others who have shared the experience. She has provided hope, love, and support while serving as my primary source of inspiration.

One Nation Under Law

Introduction

WHEN AMERICANS living in the twenty-first century think about the legal basis for separation of church and state, they may mistakenly turn to the First Amendment, which, as part of the Bill of Rights, protects American citizens from governmental interference with their private rights. The First Amendment secures religious freedom, protecting the right to religious belief as a matter of private conscience. It does not separate church and state. This distinction is frequently used by theologians and scholars who argue that the Constitution did not separate church and state. Some of these people then further assert that the Founders never even desired a separation of church and state, and that governments in the United States may support religion in nondiscriminatory or at least nonexclusionary ways.

Yet the legal basis for separating church and state does exist in the Constitution, in article 1, section 10, in the "contract clause." In this provision, the supreme law of the land protects all matters of private interest expressed in contract from interference by government. During the early republic, consistent with the ideology that spawned the First Amendment, Americans reconceived of churches as private voluntary associations, legally recognized as private, not public, corporations. This transformation of the churches from public to private entities arose in the midst of contentious debate over American values, rooted in different conceptions of man and different understandings of religious truths. Constitutional language and the ideology it expressed served as the basis for separating church and state in the early republic as Americans formed civil institutions consistent with Revolutionary-era ideals.

This is not to imply that law acted on its own accord to restructure American society. Changes in Americans' beliefs and values precipitated the Revolution and significantly influenced the nature of the new republic's institutions. By the end of the eighteenth century, the dominant American worldview was no longer rooted in the providential Christianity of the colonial era, but rather in the libertarianism of the Enlightenment. Law, as an expression of ideas, had to change to reflect this ideological transformation. Ideas, not law, were the prime movers of social change. Yet law, as an expression of ideas, became the means of accomplishing this change and determined the form or structure of civil society.

Three themes are presented and developed in this work. First, the process of disestablishment in the early republic involved Americans in their greatest ideological debate prior to the Civil War. Conflicting groups of people dis-agreed over the values and goals of American society and the design of the in-stitutions in which they would be reflected. Second, law provided the means by which disestablishment would occur by imposing principles of liberal re-publicanism, expressed in common law and judicial interpretations of con-stitutions. New contract-law doctrine forced churches to accept a corporate form, repositioning them as private entities rather than public institutions. But, while law determined the process of disestablishment through the sepa-ration of private and public institutions, it could not resolve the substantive issues at the heart of America's ideological debate. This conflict then per-sisted with private associations and corporations able to offer visions of American society that were alternative to those expressed through the public sector. Third, while law could command the separation of church and state through the delineation of public and private spheres, American society struggled for decades to remove religion from public policy and the churches from roles of public responsibility.

In the spring of 2001 President George W. Bush expressed a desire for the federal government to rely more heavily on America's churches to feed, clothe, shelter, and educate the poor. He did not suggest merely that private charity take the place of government programs, as his father advocated in his reference to "1,000 points of light" a decade earlier, but proposed a new integration of church and state to address society's needs. During the debate spawned by this proposal, many people have questioned the historical rela-tionship between religion and the government, the meaning of what is re-ferred to as "separation," and the flexibility of the legal prescriptions that created the American system.

Eleven of the original thirteen colonies established a church prior to the Revolution. Most frequently these religious establishments imposed duties upon the citizens to support a prescribed local church with tax dollars and to attend worship services. Establishment also provided the legally recog-nized church or churches with the special status required to take and hold property, perform public ceremonies, and hold public meetings. Perhaps even more significant, established churches played important roles in influ-encing early American culture through the performance of their responsibili-ties for education, poor relief, and record keeping.

In their cultivation of established churches, the American colonies continued practices prevailing in England and throughout western Europe. When as part of a new nation the states pursued disestablishment, the process of separating the churches from the state governments, Americans acted on ideas that were also part of a broader Western development. Historian Peter Gay describes the Enlightenment as a time when the doctrines of Christianity fought to survive against the onslaught of critical thinking. Gay properly identifies societal efforts to resolve ideological conflict as chief contributors to cultural change in the age of Enlightenment.[1] The process of disestablishment in America brought two conflicting worldviews into sharp disagreement over the nation's future and significantly altered American culture.

Those who contended over the role of the church in the early republic derived their differing conceptions of society from their different conceptions of man.[2] Consistent with these differing conceptions, each group understood law to serve vastly different purposes. If man is weak and inclined to evil, as proponents of perpetuating a Christian commonwealth espoused, then strict laws and enforcement of deference to authority are essential to restrain him. Established religion arose as a product of this perspective. Ministers functioned as the societal alternative to lawyers and judges, best able to discern what was good and just and to develop law to serve these ends. Liberty was subordinated to concerns for the general welfare. But Enlightenment humanism regarded man as rational, reasonable, and free. Laws, enforced through limited state authority, preserved a realm conducive to man's exploration and development. In this realm, laws protected rights of individuals from the power of the state; lawyers and judges assumed authority to enforce the law recognizing private rights. Law and religion served as contrasting means of understanding man's place in the world.

Alexis de Tocqueville was perhaps the first observer of American culture to note the duality of its philosophical inheritance: "it is the result of two distinct elements, which in other places have been in frequent hostility, but which in America have been admirably incorporated and combined with one another. I allude to the spirit of Religion and the Spirit of Liberty." Most subsequent writers found greater tension in America over this duality. Writing in 1986, political scientist Anne Norton postulated that intermittent challenges to the dominant social and political themes of American history were explained by the cultural inheritance of conflicting ideologies derived from the Reformation and the Enlightenment. Ten years before Norton, Henry May had identified two prevalent idea systems in early America: Calvinist Protestantism and the Enlightenment. He argued that these idea systems overlapped but asserted they were distinct enough that by 1800 Americans were compelled to adopt one or the other. In 1983 historian John Thomas asserted that America's belief structure is a product of Enlightenment tradition that has been Christianized by the powerful forces unleashed by an evangelical movement after 1800.[3]

Religious historian Sidney Mead spent most of his career analyzing the tension inherent in America's dual intellectual inheritance. In 1963 he asserted only that it was "commonly accepted" that rationalism and pietism constituted two intellectual movements in eighteenth-century Western thought and that "their differences which were real, are stressed to the point of making them appear to have been completely separate and even mutually exclusive developments."[4] Over time Mead sharpened his own perception of this inconsistency and its importance to American culture. In 1975 he wrote in an introduction to a series of three essays: "One motif permeates these essays: that there is, and always has been, an unresolved tension between the theology that legitimates the constitutional structure of the republic and that generally professed and taught in a majority of the religious denominations of the United States. . . . I have dwelt for a long time with the problems it suggests because I thought them important not only for the future health of the religious and national lives of the Republic, but also for the well-being of the individual who is trying to be both a good citizen and a good church member."[5] Finally, in 1977, Mead wrote:

> I have concluded that the two stand in a relation of mutual antagonism and are perhaps logically mutually exclusive. This is to say that practically every species of traditional orthodoxy in Christendom is intellectually at war with the basic premises upon which the constitutional and legal structures of the Republic rest. And if this *is* the case, then every convincing defense of the one tends to undermine belief in the other. It follows that every ardent defense of a sectarian orthodoxy tends at best to confuse the citizen's understanding of the basic premises of his country's ideals, at worst to undermine his belief in them, in either case to muddle his identity.[6]

The ferocity of this ideological conflict has largely escaped historians who have studied America's disestablishment. For many years the idea that disestablishment occurred as an almost inevitable product of religious pluralism, colonial religious toleration, and the growth of dissenting sects has served as the dominant historiographical paradigm.[7] No less a religious historian than Martin Marty of the University of Chicago has endorsed this school of thought, adding, "the change [disestablishment] was made as if with a sigh of relief, in a spirit of tidying up, and with only whimpers of reaction." Louis Hartz, relying upon this interpretation, asserted that the American Revolution did not have to destroy the church to replace a Christian worldview with a humanistic one. From this perspective, religious diversity led to religious freedom. But advocates of this position do not recognize that, at the time of the Constitutional Convention, religious diversity existed largely within a range of Christian belief, establishment was a state, not a federal, matter, and models existed for multiple or Protestant Christian establishments.[8]

The extent of the ideological debate has also been minimized by those historians who view disestablishment as constituting something less than what Thomas Jefferson described as "a wall of separation" between church and state. During the 1980s and 1990s a number of works presented the constitutional proscription of any "law respecting an establishment of religion, or prohibiting the free exercise thereof," as intending nothing more than a prohibition of the government favoring one Christian denomination over another.[9] Writers of this perspective have relied upon the work of William McLoughlin and others who have captured the important role of dissenters (that is, Protestant Christians belonging to nonestablished churches) in spearheading the disestablishment battle. As McLoughlin has documented, dissenting clergy supported the idea of religious freedom as a means of rendering their own existence more secure and of lessening the competition posed to them by state-supported denominations.[10] Yet most of these dissenters never envisioned that disestablishment would lead to Christian doctrine being excluded from the nation's laws and Christian churches being excluded from the authorized performance of societal duties. Arguing that these dissenters sought only an equal playing field on which to pursue the dissemination of their message, neoconservatives such as Richard Neuhaus, Glenn Miller, Christopher Mooney, and Robert Cord contend that the idea that government cannot assist religion is a latter-day development that defies the Founders' intents. Yet, in support of their argument that America was founded as a Christian nation, these writers largely ignore the ideological contest of the early republic and look instead to judicial and policy pronouncements of the late nineteenth century, hardly a relevant era for the point they wish to make.[11]

Most recently, Philip Hamburger has asserted that the Constitution did not even address the separation of church and state but was concerned only with the protection of religious liberty. He argues that separation arose only from fears of the growing strength of Catholicism in the late nineteenth century. Hamburger's attention to the early republic, like that of others who build upon McLoughlin, is focused predominately upon the role and arguments of dissenters who endorsed religious liberty.[12] But this is only part of the story.

I contend that this scholarship minimizes the extent of ideological conflict over disestablishment. This conflict emanated, in part, from different conceptions of God as well as of man. The humanistic philosophy composing a major thread of Enlightenment thought may conceive of God as a distant creator, rendered benign by his own unobtrusiveness; or even as an anachronism, irrelevant in a society of human construction in which one's contractual obligations had come to replace the Ten Commandments as a guide to behavior. People of this perspective tolerated a republican education reflecting both the changed conception of morality from piety to virtue and the elevation of individual over community as the primary social unit. Yet for many individuals religion remained a matter beyond human reason and rationality, rooted in a mystical spiritual world that forever would exceed human comprehension. In this world, God as a living spiritual entity did unceasing battle with Satan for human souls. The need to design institutions to preserve public order against human tendencies to sin, incorporating the teaching of God's laws as moral absolutes, derived from these beliefs. These individuals included many Baptist and Methodist dissenters who may have won a victory for religious liberty but would lose the war over the separation of church and state.

People holding opposing beliefs of God and his relevance to society feared that their ideological adversaries threatened the creation and perpetuation of a proper republic. Religiously conceived voluntary associations reflect the degree of Christian concern, even hostility, toward the mainstream culture. In 1814 the founders of the American Tract Society, committed to publishing pamphlets and books expressing Christian doctrine and morals, conceived of secularists as "the enemy" and expressed their contest with the "satanic press" in terms of war: "there is in this direction an invasion of the private virtue and public morals of the nation, more insidious, but not less formidable, than the approach of a foreign army, with all the demoralizing influence of war."[13] Defenders of a Christian state perceived and depicted the advocates of a secular state as divorcing the nation and its people from God and therefore frequently equated the rationalism of Enlightenment thought with depravity. Timothy Dwight, a Congregational minister who led "the standing order" in Connecticut during the 1790s and early 1800s, attacked "modern infidels" devoted to "pleasure" and "liberty" and the American worship of the "Goddess of reason." Ministerial attacks on "liberals" frequently focused on their harshness and insensitivity.[14]

This conflict in Americans' worldviews was temporarily masked by broader agreement on political issues.[15] Gordon Wood writes that the Revolution created an opportunity for Americans to express their "republican tendencies." This necessarily involved how people thought about both themselves and their relationships to the community. Wood notes that "adopting republicanism was not simply a matter of bringing American culture more into line with the society. It meant as well an opportunity to abolish what remained of monarchy and to create once and for all new, enlightened republican relationships among people." Part of this transition involved the transformation of "subjects" into "citizens." Wood identifies three components of this new citizenship.[16] First, the Revolutionary era abolished "artificial distinctions" such as rank or title and recognized all men as equal in liberty and station. Social and economic distinctions would be attributable to merit, not privilege. Access to property and the legal protection of it, like the exercise of political autonomy, were rights derived from nature and secured in citizenship. Second, the liberal-minded revolutionary did not define his citizenship parochially. Loyalty to the Revolution and to the emerging republic was easily integrated with cosmopolitanism, through which Americans believed themselves participants in a transatlantic Enlightenment culture.[17] Last, but most significant to the republican conception of citizenship, was the valuation of civic virtue. Late eighteenth-century Americans recognized two forms of virtue. Private virtue involved the voluntary limitation of one's own exercise of liberty in recognition of the rights of others. Public virtue required the sacrifice, by men of special talent, of the opportunity of more lucrative endeavors in order to serve the public.[18] Perhaps most important of all, Americans reconceived morality as civic virtue rather than Christian piety. The inculcation of civic virtue was a prerequisite to the maintenance of a citizenry capable of self-government. Republican education would have to reflect this change in the public's conception of morality.

Postrevolutionary America, in constructing its early institutions, had to address the issue of man's nature. Both parties arising within the Washington administration accepted the classical republican reliance upon virtue, but they differed in their confidence in the degree to which the American people were possessed of virtue. The old constitutional-era divide between federalists and antifederalists expressed itself in the 1790s, as the Federalist party of Hamilton and Adams sought to restrain the democratic excesses they perceived as emanating from the Jeffersonians in the Democratic-Republican (Republican) party.

Classical republicanism had tempered liberty with virtue, the social recognition that liberty is not license and that the good of the commonwealth required voluntary restraints. The tenuous reliance on virtue to prevent anarchy seemed to many Federalists to have been overwhelmed by Jeffersonian liberalism after 1800. Wood writes: "All they [the Federalists] and their Republican successors had was the assumption, attributed in 1806 to Jefferson, 'that the public good is best promoted by the exertion of each individual seeking his own good in his own way.'"[19] Joyce Appleby recognizes this developing liberalism as the expression of Adam Smith's Enlightenment doctrine that political and economic freedoms, both naturally derived, must go hand in hand to realize economic efficiency and political self-determinism.[20]

In the early 1800s Americans did their best to realize this social ideal as private pursuits tended to take priority in the national consciousness. Common-law judges used the law to redefine the roles of people in society. In the process they helped to supplant a communitarian republican ideal with an individualistic ideal rooted in contract as an expression of legal independence and equality.[21] At the same time, spurred by the religious enthusiasm of the Second Awakening, Americans who sought a greater role for Christian morality and communitarianism in society launched an aggressive campaign to save America from the dangerous excesses of liberalism.[22]

The ideological debates of the early republic have been minimized by those historians who have focused their attention on the question, To what degree would the doctrine of religious liberty restrict governmental support of religious institutions? For early Americans the greater question was, To what degree would the churches be prohibited from leadership roles in American society? This question addressed not only political ideology but the validity of religious belief. It was at the heart of successful efforts to separate church and state in the early republic. Recognition of this issue helps us to see the disestablishment struggle as proceeding through two different steps. First, the primary laws of the nation and the states eliminated public support for religion. This was comparatively easy. Second, the states removed the churches from their traditional role of public service. This second step involved the community in a debate over the influence of Christian doctrine upon secular institutions. In some states this debate was resolved through the political process. Yet in most instances no public consensus could be gained, and courts had to inform the states of the prevailing legal principles in order to bring about social change. In this, the courts relied on new conceptions of public and private realms.[23]

This new legal conception derived from the political ideology that came to dominate the society of the early republic. During the last twenty-five years intellectual historians have shown the early republic to be a period of tremendous ideological contention over the design of American society.[24] The development of the two-party system in the late 1790s represents only the tip of the proverbial iceberg, elucidating Americans' differing images of democracy, economic growth, and civic duty. The value of this recent literature, addressing what has come to be known as the republican synthesis, has been not only to correct the more reductionist historiography of the consensus school scholars of the postwar era but also to revitalize the role of ideologies as systems of belief in American history.

Those founders who espoused a classical republicanism professed a sincere respect for liberty as a natural right, yet in their conception of civic virtue they also recognized the duty of all citizens to voluntarily subordinate their individual self-interest to the good of society. Liberals, on the other hand, embraced liberty as a social and political goal. Government, in the liberal worldview, should serve to protect individuals in their private pursuits of self-fulfillment. The new appreciation of the value of individual economic activity in a free market went hand in hand with the growth of liberal doctrine.[25]

The adoption of a liberal program for the design of American society after 1790 required the resolution of questions regarding the nature of man, specifically the degree to which his virtue was innate or required cultivation. While Americans generally recognized the dependence of a democratic republic upon a virtuous citizenry, they differed in the extent to which governing institutions might be required to foster virtue. The writings of Gordon Wood, Joyce Appleby, Bernard Bailyn, John Pocock, Drew McCoy, Lance Banning, Pauline Maier, and others address the transformation of a classical republican America at the time of the Revolution to a liberal America some time in the early republic. In the process of this transformation the attainment and practice of virtue became a matter of individual personal development rather than a product of social prescription and proscription. In every Western polity prior to American independence, the church worked in conjunction with the state to foster virtue. Churches assumed responsibility for moral leadership. In working with civic governments, churches encouraged their partners to reflect a religious morality in their laws and policies. America moved to disestablish its churches at the same time it redefined morality as civic virtue distinct from Christian piety. The intellectual history of disestablishment is an integral part of the growing historiography on the republican synthesis.[26]

The conflict within the early republic over the role of the church in American society must also be placed in the context of the tremendous social change of the era. The growth of market capitalism in the early nineteenth century certainly concerned more people than just evangelical Christians. Many Federalists, and others of a classical republican perspective, perceived free markets as a threat to civic virtue, disrupting established community hierarchies and the values of deference and responsibility that accompanied them. The idea of selling one's labor to the highest bidder, and the implicit rejection of community relationships that such an attitude entailed, was anathema to these social conservatives. The marketplace could be a source of corruption, embodying unrestricted self-interest, that could prey on human weakness. However, liberals saw in the free market a chance at self-fulfillment and the realization of dreams for prosperity, social status, and personal growth.[27]

American law came to express a liberal perspective in the early 1800s as it embraced contract-law theory. Liberalism conceived of law serving an essentially "negative" function as a means of protecting individuals from each other and from the state. Contract-law theory, recognizing parties to any contract as reasonable, rational, and equal, became the basis of all social relationships.[28] It vested social responsibility within private individuals. Even while the Founders were drafting the public law that would be the foundation of the new nation, tensions arose between individual liberties and the public welfare, and private law was used to resolve disputes in a way that would shape the new society. Between the 1780s and 1840 common-law judges enunciated a legal doctrine recognizing individuals as free and independent actors, able to control their own destinies. The developing law of "contract," recognizing individuals as bound solely by their commitments as expressions of their own wills, embodied this legal doctrine and governed a myriad of personal and economic relationships, from marriage to trade to labor. Courts further perceived the unrestricted use of individual initiative, which contract law facilitated, both to conform to liberal republican models of natural law and political right and also to hold the most promise for serving the public good.

The agreement of legal historians on this doctrinal development of American law up to 1840 distorts the real disagreement among them concerning the role of law within society. From the 1950s through the 1980s the prevailing historiographic school, known as "instrumentalist," followed a Gramschian approach, in which the actions of social leaders are understood to derive from social interests, especially class consciousness, rather than from intellectual activity. Ideology is perceived as a rationalization for social interests, and thinkers are subordinated to secondary historical roles. In this model, law served simply as a tool or instrument of a governing elite.

Many recent historians have taken issue with the instrumentalist models developed by James Willard Hurst, Morton Horwitz, Kermit Hall, and Lawrence M. Friedman.[29] This more recent examination of law has looked at diverse historical actors in a greater variety of behaviors. Latter-day historians have found that changes in the law were not merely reflections of social or economic interests of an elite. Sometimes legal change appears to predate social change rather than vice versa. Instead of functioning as a tool of its creators, American law tended to operate as if it had a life of its own, shaping society to conform to legal values by directing the actions of individuals. Recognizing law's relative autonomy, scholars such as Michael Grossberg,

Christopher Tomlins, and Mark Tushnet contend that law acted to infuse the new society—including the judges—with a system of rules and principles derived from liberal ideology.[30] Many authors have noted the incremental pace of legal change. Law's structural dependence on the Constitution, common-law precedent, and the procedural dictates of pleading recognizable legal arguments mitigated any societal tendencies toward rapid transformation. Instrumentalism, as a theory of understanding law, fails to fully appreciate its institutional inertia, the multiplicity of forces involved in its creation, and its hegemonic role as a relatively autonomous body of values, beliefs, and doctrine that provides the means of "discourse" in a nation of law.[31]

The current study of the separation of church and state, more closely aligned with the Nelson-Reid school of thought than to either of the more contentious historigraphic schools, nonetheless provides further evidence of the weakness of the instrumentalist school of thought. I argue that ideas—not social interests—were the prime movers of both legal principle and social policy in the early republic. Law came to express a liberal republican ideology as the embodiment of man's rationality.

These early findings suggest further research is needed regarding some long-standing historical assumptions. Grossberg, Tomlins, and Tushnet accept the Republican judges in the state trial courts as expositors of Jeffersonian liberalism. In enforcing contract law, these judges reconfigured American society into a polity of presumably equal and autonomous economic and political actors—ridding it of any vestiges of privileged hierarchies. Yet, in arguing that the federal appellate courts contributed to this transformation, I implicitly put Federalist judges, most significantly those on the Marshall Supreme Court, in roles of allies to the Jeffersonians.

In a series of cases during the second decade of the nineteenth century, the Marshall Court relied upon the contract clause to eviscerate state regulations of private enterprise. Traditionally these decisions have been seen as testaments to the Federalists' preference for national authority over state powers. Yet they also parallel the coterminous development of contract-law doctrines in the common law, and they endorse the Jeffersonian vision of free and autonomous economic actors acting independently of government control. Central to all of these decisions, and absolutely crucial to the resolution of the church-state relationship, was the use of the contract clause to delineate public and private actions. The primary case in these Marshall Court decisions is the *Dartmouth College* case (discussed in chapter 7). In this decision the Court used the contract clause to prevent New Hampshire's legislature from interfering with the activities of a private Christian school.

The Marshall Court's use of contract law to resolve a variety of public law disputes supports those who argue for law's relative autonomy. If social interest served as the prime mover of legal policy, certainly John Marshall, Joseph Story, and other Federalist Party members of the Supreme Court would not have used judicial discretion to further the ideological goals of their political rivals. Yet, in enforcing the law derived from governing idcological premises shared by members of both parties, they gave voice to the supremacy of that law. Politics was subordinated to law.

Implicitly, then, I also argue that substantive law, rooted as it was in liberal republican ideology, transcended important constitutional questions regarding federalism. State and federal courts, in private and public law cases, applied a contract-law doctrine to protect individual action from interference by people or governments that argued for the preeminent concern of the public good. Whether this consequence was intended by the Founders is best answered by their inclusion of the contract clause in the Constitution.

This text should make clear that the U.S. Constitution did not separate church and state. Several states after 1787 continued to recognize established churches and to support them with tax dollars, and nearly every state relied on its churches to provide vital public services. The process of disestablishment, removing the churches from their roles as public institutions, required nearly fifty years and involved the American people in perhaps the greatest ideological debate of the early republic. Through this debate, various groups of Americans with sharply contrasting images of the ideal society came to a tenuous resolution concerning the forms of the new nation's civil institutions.

The Constitution did not separate church and state, but it did endorse a conception of society that made separation inevitable. The protection of private rights from public action required the delineation of private and public activities. Once law separated public and private realms, churches could not continue in their historic roles of public service. While the separation of church and state was essentially a state matter, states that relied on the political process to effectuate this separation encountered tremendous difficulty in doing so. Politics could not determine the form that educational and welfare institutions would take in the early republic because no political consensus existed. The law could—and when state and federal courts turned to consider this issue, their decisions were informed by the same legal doctrine. Ultimately the Supreme Court did impose a model of privatization on all of the states, but its effect was more to redirect political debate than to resolve political tension.

No less a scholar than G. Edward White has begun a reconsideration of the old assumptions regarding the Marshall Court. He contends that it relied on a number of "first principles" derived from the Constitution and the prevailing intellectual character of the nation, an integration of republicanism, liberalism, and American exceptionalism, to form its jurisprudence. Every decision was an attempt to be consistent with these first principles, and every opinion was infused with them. The Marshall Court conceived of law as a way to give the first principles that prevailed at the time of the nation's founding a permanence that would withstand cultural change. William Nelson confirms the apolitical nature of the Marshall Court by finding that it separated legal from political issues and relied on consensual values in addressing the former.[32]

Although the study of legal history is experiencing a revitalization, the study of intellectual history seems to have stagnated after the enthusiasm expressed in the republican synthesis debates of earlier decades. Postmodernist schools of thought tend to undervalue ideas as historical forces. Both the predispositions and the methodologies of recent historians have contributed to the tendency to minimize the ideological conflict involved in the process of disestablishment. Ideology itself is oftentimes seen as a means of justifying self-interest. For instance, in a 1991 essay Michael Zuckerman notes that most historians studying religion and economics follow Marx's understanding that religion is used by the owners of the means of production to maintain order through rationalizing subordinance to a group of elites. Contemporary historians also tend to perceive "truths" as multiple and relative. For example, Leonard Levy contends that "Freedom of speech [implicitly also of religion] could not become a civil liberty until the truth of men's opinions, especially their religious and political opinions, was regarded as relative rather than absolute." But an acceptance of relative truths implies a judgment that what is true for one may not be true for another, and it implicitly asserts that cultural or psychological conditions may engender proclivities to belief that one is better to accept than to challenge.[33]

By this perspective, truth is relative only because it is nonexistent. Relative truth is a fungible creation to be utilized for social good and personal well-being. It does not exist apart from the believer in any universal guise. The historical actors on both sides of the disestablishment controversy rejected such an understanding of truth. Instead, doctrinal adherents in each party expressed a hopeful confidence that the darkness enveloping the other party would lift so that their countrymen could perceive the truth. This confidence in the power of truth, rather than in its denial, allowed each party to embrace the concept of a free marketplace of ideas as a temporary means of gaining universal understanding.

Other scholars have argued that religion accommodated liberalism by adapting to social rather than to ideological truths. Reinhold Niebuhr implies this compromise in contending that toleration is essential in any pluralistic society. Henry F. May asserts that the ideas of the Enlightenment and Protestant Christianity could not exist together after the 1790s, but neither could either one dominate the other. The resolution came not in persistent tension but in amalgamation. Religion became rational and socially oriented, moralistic and flexible. American Christianity came to embody much of the thought of Scottish Moralism. While Michael Kammen notices a persistent tension in American society, he identifies its source less in ideological doctrine than in social necessity. Diversity required liberty, and legitimacy necessitated authority. For Kammen the push and pull between freedom and control results not from America's dual intellectual heritage but from the need to build one society from a diverse population. More recently Peter Field, preferring a materialist to an idealist approach, has asserted that an affinity for and identification with the accoutrements of elite Boston society were responsible for the liberal Brahmin departure from traditional Congregational doctrine into Unitarianism. Disestablishment came to New England only after social forces had fragmented the standing order.[34]

Although all of these works contribute significant insights to our historical understanding, they also tend to minimize the extent of the ideological conflict that underlay social and political change. Sidney Mead not only identified the tension between Christian and modernist ideologies, he also proposed a thesis for explaining how, in the midst of conflict, Americans came to codify the separation of church and state in their primary law. He identified three dominant worldviews in the constitutional era: Enlightenment rationalism, liberal Christianity, and pietistic evangelical Christianity. The rationalists largely doubted the Bible as a source of truth, understood religious belief as a matter of individual conscience, and accepted religion primarily for its service in inducing moral behavior and preserving social order. Liberal Christians controlled many of the established churches and integrated new understandings of scientific truth and man's free will into the traditional Christian message. Jesus Christ provided in his message the means by which man could secure his salvation. Those defined by Mead as pietists were members of the fast-growing dissenting sects who eschewed the more esoteric Christian teachings of the established churches for an emotional religion rooted in Calvinist precepts. Mead postulates that in order to secure their own autonomy the pietists formed a temporary alliance with the rationalists to secure the constitutional protections of religious freedom. Yet, upon realizing the effects of making religion a matter of individual conscience rather than of societal prescription, the pietists broke from the rationalists and united with their Christian brethren to undo the damage caused by their earlier alliance. It was too late—as the primary law, already drafted, would be used to resolve issues over the role of religion in the new society. Mead also recognizes, though he does not develop the argument, that churches adapted to the new legal environment after 1790 by reforming themselves as private voluntary associations assuming a corporate form. In this form, on the periphery of American public institutional society, they served to express dissent to the prevailing modernist liberal doctrine.

Breaking slightly from Mead, I assert that the Constitution, far from being the final word regarding the role of religion in the republic, served mainly as a declaration of war between two groups of Americans harboring contesting worldviews. The real battle over disestablishment involved the removal of both the churches and Christian doctrine from entrenched social institutions on which the social good had come to depend (see chapter 4). This was a state-by-state struggle, in which the history and culture of each state combined with more generally understood legal concepts to contribute to that state's own unique resolution.

Liberalism met its greatest test from those who sought to sustain their Christian communities (involving the subordination of individual interests and freedoms to the values of the group) by asserting man's dependence upon God. When divided public opinion could not bring about a political solution, the courts imposed the liberal contract-law doctrine to resolve the debate. The Supreme Court's decision in the *Dartmouth College* case of 1819 was the crucial national pronouncement that repositioned the churches as private entities distinct from institutions of public governance. The decision expressed a new model of civic organization conceived with the Constitution. However, the legal model considered form rather than substance, imposing a private-public distinction and designating separate forums in which the two worldviews would hold sway. In this resolution, law perpetuated the contest between the two worldviews that form the intellectual basis of American culture.

Disestablishment was both a national and a state issue. Most of the existing work on disestablishment has centered on two states, Virginia and Massachusetts. No effort will be made here to go over this well-trodden ground, other than to present basic factual outlines that indicate how these states' actions are accommodated by the proposed thesis.

Virginia established the Anglican Church in 1624 and nineteen years later created vestries in each parish for raising taxes to support the church and its functions. This religious establishment persisted up to the Revolution, despite a laxity among Virginians in religious attitudes. Jefferson wrote in his *Notes on the State of Virginia* that by the eve of Revolution, two-thirds of Virginians were dissenters of one kind or another, either non-Christians or adherents of a sect other than Anglicanism. At the end of the war a traveler from Europe observed: "If the Virginians themselves did not freely and openly admit that zeal for religion, and religion generally, is now very faint among them, the fact might easily have been divined from other circumstances."[35] Evidence of religion's decline is apparent by 1749, when Anglican clergy sought legislative support because the gentry of the state, largely disinclined to religion of any type, failed to support the ministers. The Virginia Assembly responded with what was referred to as the Two Penny Act, setting a ridiculously low level of support, lampooning the clergy and further eroding its stature. In 1776 the Revolutionary-era legislature passed the Declaration of Rights recognizing religion as a private matter of individual conscience. The next year the legislature suspended the Act for the Support of the Clergy and banned all clergymen from elected office. Yet Thomas Jefferson as governor of the state failed to secure passage of his "Bill for Religious Freedom" during the war years. Only when Patrick Henry introduced new legislation to support "a Christian Church" did Virginians come together, in opposition to Henry's proposal, to pass Jefferson's bill. James Madison led the movement for passage of the bill in the 1780s while its drafter was in France. Madison himself wrote his famous "Memorial and Remonstrance," expressing his republican sentiments on religious freedom, to garner support for his friend's proposal. During this campaign, rationalists, agnostics, and deists joined with evangelical dissenters to win the battle over legal establishment. Yet, as many writers have noted, their goals differed.[36] Madison,

Jefferson, and their supporters desired to create a secular state in which religion was nothing more than a private belief and not subject to state consideration. Jefferson is quoted during this debate as saying, "America is not and ought not to be a Christian country." The dissenting sects sought freedom to practice, as Isaac Backus said, "the essential rights of Christianity" free from government control.[37]

Backus's Baptists provided essential support for the passage of Jefferson's Bill for Religious Freedom. Yet the form that religious freedom took in Virginia differed greatly from that desired by Backus. Disestablishment was secured through the political process, but law determined what form disestablishment would take. Consistent with liberal legal doctrine, Virginia's legislators and judges interpreted religious freedom as the separation of religion from state processes, not as a doctrine of religious toleration. If religion was truly the concern of each man, the state had no right to intrude into that domain.

Constitutional disestablishment served as an introduction to a long debate between evangelicals and rationalists over the values and institutions to be cultivated in Virginia.[38] This conflict presented itself after 1784 as evangelicals petitioned the legislature, with very little success, for Sabbath protection laws, a series of blue laws, and multiple enactments to "punish the vices and immoralities of the times," and to "favor Christianity [by] supporting those laws of Morality which are necessary for Private and Public happiness." As the battle over the values and institutions of Virginia persisted into the nineteenth century, the liberals reacted by moving to secularize what were previously church functions and to confiscate church lands. In an early case concerning the status of formerly "public" churches now legally viewed as private entities, Virginia's churches scrambled to find protection through incorporation. In 1802 the legislature found Episcopal landholdings (accrued during the long period of establishment) to be ill-gotten gains and ordered them sold by public overseers and the proceeds used to care for the poor "or any other non-religious purpose [upon] which a majority of the voters might decide."[39] This action was tested in the courts. Legal definitions of "private" and "public" were used to protect incorporated private assets from state action. In order to preserve their property, churches were forced to adopt a private corporate form. Contract law enforced the separation of church from state by dictating that churches' institutional integrity (that is, their ability to hold property and present opinions free from governmental action) depended upon their assertion of rights as legal individuals.

Existing accounts of disestablishment in Massachusetts provide similar evidence of a long-standing ideological conflict eventually resolved by law. The disestablishment action of the legislature in 1833, fourteen years after the *Dartmouth* case resolved the disestablishment issue in New Hampshire, merely recognized the legal dictates with which Massachusetts begrudgingly complied. Opponents of establishment never gained a majority in Massachusetts; law determined the need for change when politics would not.

Massachusetts held a constitutional convention in 1820, in which it considered eliminating a religious test oath for officeholders, control of Harvard, and public support for religion. Just months after the *Dartmouth* decision precluded New Hampshire's interference with a private corporation serving that state's need in higher education, Massachusetts addressed whether it should fund a private institution controlled by the Unitarian Church or start a public school subject to the control of the state. Despite the clear legal precedent diminishing the state's rights to control a private religious school, Massachusetts voters rejected the chance to fund a state school and retained the test oath and an established church by a vote of twenty to eleven thousand. The issues were framed in terms of preserving the traditional "community" of the state. Religion was depicted as the glue that held society together and formed its values. An editorial asked "whether Infidels and Nothingarians shall enjoy the blessings of a government that derives its stability and equity from Christianity?"[40] This position stood in abject contradiction of liberal republican concepts of political equality. Yet, in 1820, it held sway in Massachusetts.

While the voters in 1820 could reject the prevailing ideological and legal context, the court could not. Massachusetts churches faced a schism in the second and third decades of the nineteenth century, in which Congregational churches were being taken over by Unitarian ministers. Traditional Congregational doctrine conceived of a church as composed of its members, an autonomous political body united in pursuit of a godly society. The idea that a minister not of their liking could be imposed upon them was inconceivable to most Congregationalists. Yet this is precisely what happened after 1810. As traditional Congregationalists sought to leave these churches, the issue of ownership of property arose. In 1821, the Massachusetts Supreme Court, in a holding consistent with the *Dartmouth* case, ruled that only corporations could hold property, not amorphous societies of believers.[41] Unitarians, in control of the legally recognized charters, retained the churches and their funds as Congregationalists departed. Only in response to these court decisions did the citizens support disestablishment, putting all the churches on equal footing in 1833. Contract law succeeded where politics would not, in overcoming public support of religion.[42]

Three states, which proceeded with disestablishment at different times and in different regions, are examined here. In each case, the legal separation of private and public actions was inextricably related to church-state separation. New York, from the mid-Atlantic region, involves the disestablishment of the Anglican Church during the war (see chapter 5). As one of the states drafting a Revolutionary-era constitution, New York reacted to the republican spirit of the times to cast aside the church as a vestige of social privilege and archaic ideals. Most of the mid-Atlantic states acted on disestablishment during the Revolution and encountered relatively little opposition. However, the prohibition of state support of religion was only the first step in the process. As the New York legislature considered the design of postwar society, it was forced to recognize the property rights of churches as private "corporate citizens." After divorcing its churches from the realm of public governance, New York struggled for decades to secularize its social institutions.

South Carolina, from the southern region, disestablished its church in the 1780s, during the constitutional era. The church in South Carolina served a traditional role of legitimizing social order with comparatively little influence over beliefs and programs for societal improvement. Chapter 6 addresses the difficulties South Carolina faced in disestablishment. The case study reflects the South's difficulty in accepting contract-law theory while preserving its social system. Slavery, even in the early republic, significantly influenced South Carolina's political actions. When slaveholders feared that evangelical condemnations of the institution might gain authority as expressions of "the church," they sought to weaken that church as an institution that might curtail their power. South Carolina's unique republicanism expressed itself in law as churches were made private at the same time that the government was weakened. Public institutions remained weak, even after disestablishment, as private citizens refused to delegate power to their governments.

New Hampshire's established Congregational Church, like that of most New England states, persisted into the third decade of the nineteenth century. Disestablishment resulted only after a long and bitter conflict between churchmen and republicans prompted the Supreme Court to intercede in a matter of state governance. Chapter 7 addresses the reappearance of the Federal Constitution in the issue of disestablishment. In the *Dartmouth College* decision (1819), the Supreme Court clarified the preeminence of liberal contract-law principles and the dependence of government initiatives upon public funding, while also protecting the rights of churches as private corporations to offer dissent to the prevailing liberalism of the secular society.

After *Dartmouth,* law prescribed the public-private relationship in which all the states would ultimately have to comply. In this, law functioned to impose a new system of values and rules to replace that of the colonial era. While some states made political decisions to separate church from state, contract law determined the design of the civil institutions that would arise after those separations occurred.

The irony of the new status of Christian organizations in American society was that they were protected in their rights to attempt to convert the nation to Christianity only because they assumed the form of private entities divorced from the institutions of public political power. They all became "dissenters" to the prevailing secular ideology rooted in liberal humanism. Protected as dissenters, the achievement of their goal—a Christian nation— became inconsistent with their continued viability to pursue it. Disestablishment occurred as a process of social change, reconciling the republic to a new set of values and beliefs. This reconciliation involved the maintenance of social harmony through the perpetuation of the tension between opposing ideological factions. Rather than resolving the ideological dispute, the legal compromise perpetuated it. The law, addressing form rather than substance, merely carved out different realms for each of the disputants instead of addressing the merits of their arguments.

While neither side could claim total victory in the culture wars of the early republic, the opponents of establishment were able to impose their structural model upon the design of the society. Not only were churches redefined as private corporations but religion was largely excluded from schools and statehouses. Many children's books and other materials used for teaching from 1790 to 1820 were rewritten to substitute republican virtues for Christian pieties and to foster attitudes of individual advancement over the communal good. While the Bible may still have rested on many an American's bookshelf, law became the ultimate authority and served as a better guide to American values and behaviors.[43] Under the law, churches enjoyed no special privileges in the political forum. As recently as 1970, the Supreme Court reiterated the doctrine it had announced in the *Dartmouth College* case over one hundred fifty years earlier: "Adherents of particular faiths and individual churches frequently take strong positions on public issues, including . . . vigorous advocacy of legal or constitutional positions. Of course, churches as much as secular bodies and private citizens have that right."[44] Churches retained the right to express dissenting opinions but only as private institutions peripheral to the government.

American political society in the early republic adopted a decidedly secular tone. The subsequent increase in the popularity of Christianity in the Victorian Age has distorted many Americans' perceptions of the nature of American culture in the early republic. The closing of businesses and the cessation of mail delivery on Sunday did not become commonplace until much later in the nineteenth century, after the "Social Gospel" had redefined much of America from the Founders' vision. Coins did not contain the words, "In God We Trust" until very late in that century, and paper money did not bear the motto for several additional decades.[45] These Victorian-era developments should not be used to characterize America as a Christian nation at the time of its founding.

The fluctuating influence of religion upon American culture reflects the perpetual tension inherent in the nation's attempt to integrate two conflicting ideological tenets. During the 1920s, the Supreme Court used the Fourteenth Amendment to preclude state interference with First Amendment rights, including the free exercise of religion. Yet in 1983, nearly two hundred years after the drafting of the Constitution, President Reagan boldly declared the "Year of the Bible" in America. More recently, Kansas has limited the teaching of evolution in its public schools, and a justice for the Supreme Court of Alabama has refused to remove the Ten Commandments from his courtroom despite being instructed to do so by the U.S. Supreme Court. Perhaps most reminiscent of an earlier era of American history is the call in 2003, by Alabama governor Bob Riley, for reform of that state's tax policies, calling them "immoral" and citing peoples' "Christian duty" to help the poor. In perpetuating tension, the legal design of the early republic accommodated temporary ascendancy of one worldview or another, while denying to both any real hope of dominance.[46]

1 Toleration versus Freedom

Colonial Society and the State Church

> If they [those holding false beliefs] be infectious, and leprous, and have
> plague sores running upon them, and think it their glory to infect others;
> It is no want of mercy, and charity, to set such at a distance: It is a merci-
> less mercy, to pity such as are incurably contagious, and mischievous, and
> not to pity many scores or hundreds of the souls of such, as will be in-
> fected and destroyed by the toleration of the other.
>
> Joseph Cotton, from *The Bloody Tenent, Washed, and Made White in the Bloud
> of the Lambe* (1624).

TO FULLY UNDERSTAND THE DEGREE to which the churches were marginalized during disestablishment, it is necessary to appreciate the roles they
assumed prior to the Revolution. Despite tremendous differences among the
English colonies, all of them utilized religion to support a social hierarchy, an
intolerance of dissent, and a communitarian emphasis premised at least in
part on concepts of moral duty and Christian brotherhood. Colonial laws supported the maintenance of a Christian ethic by respecting the institutional integration of religion and government and subordinating individuals, and of
course their rights and interests, to the concerns of the community.

Communitarianism, reflecting an ethic of concern for one's fellow man,
served as the backbone of Protestant conceptions of society. John Winthrop
made communitarianism the focal point of his society when he encouraged
the members of the Massachusetts Bay Company to

> Delight in eache other, make others condicions our owne, reioyce together,
> mourne together, labor and suffer together, allwayes having before our eyes our
> commission and community in the worke, our community as members of the
> same body. . . . [We must] worke as one man, wee must entertaine each other in
> brother[ly] affeccion, wee must be willing to abridge our selves of our super-
> fluicties, for the supply of others necessities.[1]

It may be tempting to dismiss Winthrop as a religious radical from the earliest
days of English colonialism, but his invocation to Christian communitarianism

is more representative of the entire colonial era than it is at odds with it. Certainly, Protestant Christianity transformed itself during the colonial era in response to the individualistic influences of Enlightenment thought, the growth of market capitalism, and the increased stability of colonial settlements. Various interpretations of American Calvinism spawned multitudinous sects, each with its own doctrinal beliefs and further distinguished from the others by differences in regional affiliation, ethnicity, and social status. Given both the changes and the diversity in colonial Christianity, generalizations concerning colonial Americans' practice of religion must be hazarded with great caution. Yet one bold statement is incontrovertibly true—throughout England's colonial America, Protestantism influenced perceptions of social needs and the design of institutions to address them.

The significance of religious establishments in the American colonies cannot be measured only in the functional support provided by governments through church taxes and laws requiring church attendance. In sanctioning particular religious bodies, colonies premised social order upon cultural homogeneity. More important, establishment promoted Christian values that came to permeate colonial laws and social norms. Protestant Christianity provided the ideological basis of a colonial American worldview, and colonial churches served as the institutional vehicles of its dissemination. Established churches further functioned to integrate Christian values, beliefs, and traditions with colonial social behavior. Through the practices of preaching, teaching, caring for the poor, and maintaining community records, churches built communities consistent with Protestant Christian values. In providing these community services, churches depended upon the support of civil governments. The symbiotic relationship between church and the civil order that had existed in Europe persisted throughout English America in the colonial era.

Religion has long provided a means of understanding that which man struggles to comprehend. It offers absolute answers to questions regarding mankind's beginnings and ends, the reasons or purposes for existence, and the ways people should behave themselves while on earth. The importance of religious belief in early colonial America derived not only from the piety of those who came to the new land as religious refugees but also from the uncertainty and fear that confronted all English settlers. They faced starvation, extremes in heat and cold, loneliness and isolation, disease, wild animals, Indian attacks, and back-breaking labors without promise of success in a realm that offered rudimentary housing, minimal medical care, limited military defenses, and an economic and social structure lacking the sophistication and effectiveness to be found in England. In this context, religion offered some certainty amidst uncertainty.

In the cultural and religious maelstrom that was seventeenth-century America, many prominent religious spokesmen argued for religious absolutism. This became a dominant perspective among New Englanders. Meanwhile, religious establishments in the southern colonies are better understood as expressing the societal need for intellectual comfort and social integrity that could be provided by religion. Yet, in both New England and in Virginia, uniformity of belief strengthened the confidence of the early colonists and the bonds of their communities. In this context there was little room for tolerating deviance. As New England minister Nathaniel Ward stated: "He that is willing to tolerate any religion, or discrepant way of religion, besides his own, unless it be in matters indifferent, either doubts his own, or is not sincere in it."[2] In relying upon religion to build communities, colonists had little motivation to equivocate from strict doctrinal positions. Spiritual error could not only fragment communities but also bring down the wrath of God upon them. Plagues, wars, fires, and droughts were frequently perceived by colonists as divine sanctions for sin.

In colonial America, though less than in Europe, the concept of community implicitly accepted the existence of a social hierarchy in which the church played a key role. All social hierarchies designate privilege while accepting inequality. The church served as great a role as wealth in colonial hierarchies. Ministers taught their adherents to obey public as well as moral authorities and to assume their proper place in society. Calvinism accepted government as "an ordinance of God," proclaiming it the duty of governors to regulate the moral as well as the civil life of the citizenry.[3] Individual self-interest, including personal economic activity, had to be subordinated to the common good.[4] Civil governments relied upon the churches to imbue the people with sufficient piety to humbly defer to their betters and forgo personal gain for the sake of communal order. The form of colonial communities reflected the general social acceptance of patriarchal theory, which asserted that some people could and should be responsible for others.[5]

Calvinist doctrine itself reinforced colonial communitarianism, encouraging adherents to accept existing social stratifications. The great chain of being, at which God was the head, recognized hierarchies as persisting with God's blessing. People were taught to accept the status God afforded them. In this context, laws readily subordinated individual desires or inclinations to Christian teachings and public concerns. For instance, nearly all colonial communities proscribed wastefulness, idleness, and selfishness as much for their detrimental effects upon the community as for their violation of Jesus' moral exhortations. Attempting to distinguish reasons for such laws would be not only futile but inconceivable to colonial Americans.

Christian morality was infused into a variety of laws and social duties. Ministers from Massachusetts to South Carolina preached that God had created human society with rich and poor, and that the rich had an obligation to assist the poor. Many sermons explained the presence of the poor as a gift from God that allowed those at the top of the community to exhibit their Christian love. Nevertheless, civil laws enforced this Christian duty. Throughout the colonies, people in need could make claims to their communities for aid. In New England, these requests were heard in town meetings; in New York and Virginia they were put before the parish vestry. In all cases, the authorities called upon those with means to help, invoking Christian duty in the process. The integration of church and state, Christian values and civic duties, is evident in all the colonies in their handling of poverty.[6]

Throughout the colonies, law imposed duties upon the wealthy to privately support dependent workers, orphans, and the indigent. When social position is believed to be derived from God rather than from one's own talent or effort, the wealthy more readily assume an obligation incumbent with their status to alleviate the sufferings of those beneath them. This charitable obligation, frequently written into law and institutionalized, reaffirmed colonial hierarchies. Colonial communities depended upon each group of people performing its sanctioned roles. Early Virginia court records document the prosecution of a "runaway master" who "fled from his servants" to evade supporting them, and the assignment by the parish of poor boys to labor for wealthy individuals, whether or not they were needed.[7] In those early Virginia laws, in which the church and its value system influenced the southern worldview, are seeds of the ironic positions later taken by the Anglicans and other southern clergy in justification of slavery as a paternalistic institution embodying Christian love and charity. Religious values and church authority reinforced premodern understandings of social hierarchy and deference.[8] In the North and the South, religiously sponsored charity for the poor and the sick was intended to relieve immediate suffering rather than to transform lives and social order.[9]

In New England, early civil magistrates perceived themselves as arms of God, enforcing his law through the enforcement of man's laws. Not only were biblical proscriptions on lying, idleness, and sexual license administered, but criminal penalties were imposed for failing to attend church or for engaging in such pursuits as playing cards, sports, or music or for kissing one's wife on the Sabbath. In colonial Connecticut, the law required every home to have a Bible. Although governors in the South may have held more secular understandings of their authority, the laws they passed still evince a strong religious influence. In Virginia as well as in New England, criminal statutes referred to the punishment of "sin" and prescribed public ceremonies so that the community could stand in witness to the criminal's punishment. The purpose of public punishment was to teach a lesson necessary to preserve communal order—to induce wayward sheep to return to the flock. The community itself acted in the process of preventing and punishing sin, exercising and encouraging a Christian pattern of redemption consisting of scorn, humiliation, and forgiveness.[10]

The churches did not limit their social goals to communal order. As religious historian Robert Handy noted: "From its earliest days, Christianity in America had a world-vision, a dream of a world won to Christ." No religion offers itself to possible devotees as one of several possible truths. Religions profess to certainty in adherence to doctrines of absolute truth—at once gaining for believers assurance of salvation after death and a moral code for behavior during life. This exclusionary absolutism, as much as the desire for social conformity, encouraged the establishment of religion throughout the colonies.[11]

Colonial religious establishments took various forms. Colonists were characteristically required to support a church with tax payments, attend it for worship, and profess conformity in belief to its doctrines in order to vote or hold public office. Established churches alone could promulgate the creeds that could be taught in schools or perform wedding ceremonies and baptisms. In the later colonial period, the established church could more easily incorporate and gain the right to hold property.[12]

Yet, especially after the 1720s and in New England, colonies generally permitted multiple establishments of the Protestant Christian religion.[13] Typically the colonial legislatures compelled towns to maintain ministers and teachers of Protestant doctrine within their boundaries. Each town was free to select for itself the Protestant sect with which its minister would be affiliated. While multiple establishment did increase the variation of religious expression within the colony as a whole, it also helped to promote a town-by-town sense of homogeneity. In addition, the ready availability of land allowed dissenters to move away from established towns to pursue their own opportunities in accordance with their own beliefs. In the process, each community could afford to become even more parochial.

Economic and ideological factors account for multiple establishment. By the middle 1600s, colonial entrepreneurs recognized the economic advantages of recruiting diverse peoples to work and live in the colonies. They fostered at least a minimal religious toleration. Religious diversity quickly became commonplace, and colonial legislators had to accommodate it. In the later decades of the seventeenth century, English laws commanded toleration, imposing it upon those colonies that did not grant it of their own volition.[14]

Earlier historians have seen religious pluralism as a necessary condition precedent to religious freedom.[15] Yet it is a mistake to regard the religious pluralism of seventeenth-century America as indicative of an unusually high degree of toleration among the colonists themselves. First, only Protestant Christian sects benefited from the "liberality" of multiple establishment laws. Second, subtle differences in interpretation of scripture became the basis for discrimination among a proliferation of different sects, each offering its own particular doctrine. The flogging and hanging of Quakers as well as the banishment of dissenters led by Anne Hutchinson and Roger Williams have taken on legendary qualities in the story of early New England's Puritan establishment. But during the seventeenth century, nearly all American colonies enacted laws to deter deviant religious practices or beliefs. Laws enforcing religious conformity resulted in criminal prosecutions for blasphemy, heresy, sedition, contempt, passion, the breaking of Sabbath day laws, or the offering of diverse new and dangerous opinions. These laws continued to be passed and enforced well into the eighteenth century. In 1703, South Carolina made blasphemy a crime, defining it as "defaming any person of the Trinity, denying the truths of Christianity, or denying the divine authority of the Bible." New York prosecuted a blasphemy case pursuant to an already existent statute during that same year. Delaware brought a blasphemy suit in 1705, Maryland in 1710, and North Carolina in 1717. As late as 1757, Massachusetts found a farmer guilty of blasphemy for saying "God was a damned fool for ever making a woman" and sentenced him to a public whipping. During the Great Awakening, Connecticut passed a law prohibiting all itinerant preaching in an attempt to stifle the growth of evangelical dissenters.[16]

Colonial laws relating to economic activity, premised on Christian ethics and morals, further reinforced communitarianism. Business laws subordinated individual interests to communal considerations, defining social values and appropriate behavior consistent with Christian teachings. In the seventeenth century, laws restricted and regulated economic activities up and down the eastern seaboard.[17] Towns constructed marketplaces, limited the days and hours of business operations, and regulated the quality, size, and price of the products sold. Prices were determined by societal concern, not market demand. Governing bodies assumed the authority of determining just prices for goods and services and prosecuting any who exceeded them in attempting to profit at the expense of the public.[18] Laws provided for rewards for any person providing information as to the "unjust" sale or distribution of regulated goods. The effect of these laws was to promote social stability rather than growth or change. As legal historian William Nelson has noted, these laws "impeded opportunities for economic change and discouraged competition" up to the time of the Revolution. The clergy helped to check economic ambition not only by admonishing greed and encouraging communal sentiments but also by its support for and endorsement of the colonial laws restricting commerce.[19] In New England, it was regarded as "sinful" to charge more than a just wage or price. Moral justice, as expressed in civil laws against "oppression," determined the cost of goods and labor.[20]

Throughout the colonial era, the primary goal of criminal law was to preserve communal morality. Both written texts of substantive law and trained lawyers were scarce. Accordingly, magistrates, lawyers, and juries relied on community values largely shaped by religious and moral sentiment. The nature of this sentiment is reflected in the colonial records of criminal prosecutions. In Massachusetts, between 1760 and 1774, over one-half of all the criminal prosecutions were for sexual offenses or offenses against God and religion, including biblically proscribed activities such as adultery, fornication, working on the Sabbath, missing church, blasphemy, or swearing. As late as the 1740s, judges in that colony charged their juries "to use law to create a 'Civil and Christian state'" so as to eliminate "all profaneness and immorality" in order to reform mankind "with a Due Regard to God."[21]

While colonial judges were strongly influenced by Christian doctrine in the performance of their functions, colonial ministers actually assumed the functional roles of magistrates, serving as an alternative to judges and lawyers. Several colonies, including Pennsylvania, Connecticut, New Jersey, and South Carolina, allowed defendants in civil or criminal suits to choose to have their cases heard by the clergy in the church or by a panel of arbitrators (frequently ministers) rather than in secular courts. These options presumed the Christian influence upon colonial law and the communitarianism of the colonial era. A panel of five ministers, chosen to arbitrate a business dispute in 1675, counseled the disputants regarding the goals of the proceedings, "that upon mutual forbearing and for guiding each other in love you may retain the spirit of unity of spirit in the bond of peace and returne to the enjoyment of communion with crist and one another in all his ordenances."[22]

Established churches served as essential components of community order and governance through English America. The Anglican or Episcopalian Church was established in Virginia by charter prior to the landing at Jamestown.[23] Church attendance and the maintenance of orthodoxy were compulsory in Virginia as they were in New England. By the second half of the seventeenth century, elected vestry managed the parochial and local government affairs of the parishes, including census and record keeping, collecting religious taxes for the payment of the parish minister, and enforcing church discipline.[24] As in New England, laws recognized an integrated church and civil government to provide for Christian education, the proper care of children and the poor, and the preservation of social tranquillity. The General Court "took cognizance of all causes whatsoever, both Ecclesiastical and civil, determining everything by the standard of Equity and good conscience."[25]

Like New Englanders, colonial Virginians attempted to use law to impose moral standards of equity and fairness upon commercial activity. Even after the widespread cultivation of tobacco as a cash crop fragmented Virginia society in the second decade of the colony's existence, laws restricted the hours people could work, the prices that could be charged, and the number of economic ventures that could be pursued by anyone at the same time. A communitarian ethic also infused the colony's decision to encourage silk production by growing mulberry trees as food for silkworms. In 1614, all Virginia landowners were required to plant ten mulberry trees for every hundred acres of owned property, and fines were imposed for nonperformance.[26]

Even in those colonies frequently described as religious refuges, Rhode Island, Pennsylvania, and Maryland, religiously-inspired worldviews recognized vital roles for Christianity in forming communities. None of these colonies required church membership and support. Still, law encouraged communitarianism through the imposition of Christian values.

Roger Williams's commitment to religious freedom was derived not from the rights of man to be free from state interference but from a belief in the supremacy of God and the depravity of man's created churches. Rhode Island, like the other colonies, continued to impose moral restraints on human behavior, legislating in accordance with the scripture, believed by

Williams to be the source of saving knowledge. The relative toleration provided in Rhode Island's legal code has diminished the historical appreciation for the intensity of Williams's own convictions about the "true religion." While welcoming Quakers to Rhode Island, he nonetheless referred to them as "Anti-Christians," who seemingly denied Christ's own humanity in their acceptance of a mystical Jesus, their focus on invisibilities, and their belief in an indwelling Christ. He regarded it as blasphemous to suppose that God and Christ dwelled within man.[27]

Perhaps in no other colony is it easier to see how religion shaped settlement patterns, as each Rhode Island community sought to maintain its religious homogeneity. Dissenters were welcome—just so long as they did not move in across the street. Anne Hutchinson and William Coddington settled in Portsmouth rather than challenge Williams's authority in Providence. Samuel Gorton, calling himself "Professor of the Mysteries of Christ," moved from Massachusetts to Portsmouth, where he was whipped and banished for espousing doctrines of Christian anarchy. Subsequently banished from Providence, he and his followers founded the town of Warwick. Absent any colony-wide laws before 1647, each community was able to write its own regarding property distribution, crime, education, voting, and religious practice. When Rhode Island enacted its first Code of Law and established a superior court, it looked to the New Testament for legitimacy, basing the law on that described in 1 Timothy, 9–10. Consistent with general colonial desires for community, Rhode Island in 1647 gave striking attention to crimes against social order—drafting separate proscriptions of rioting, rebellion, disturbing the peace, contempt, slander, and defamation. Notably absent from the code were restrictions on trade, such as fair price prescriptions and market regulations. Even after creation of the code, Rhode Island struggled to preserve its legal protection of religious liberty in cases between residents with different beliefs. In one especially poignant case, the town of Providence brought suit against a man for whipping his wife whenever she attended Williams's religious services, which expressed doctrine with which he disagreed. He argued it was his "religious duty" to correct her errors, if for no other reason than to save her soul. When the court ruled against him, he took his wife back to Massachusetts, leading her by a rope. The law, based on biblical expressions of a husband's authority, was powerless to control this imposition of his religious perspective over hers.[28] Regardless of the colony's relative endorsement of religious freedom, in Rhode Island, as elsewhere in colonial America, individual liberty was limited by prevailing religious sentiments expressed in law.

It is similarly wrong to extrapolate from religious diversity and recitals of religious toleration the absence of a de facto Christian establishment in Pennsylvania. Despite all of his relative liberality, William Penn reflected a traditional Christian cosmology in writing: "The great business of man's life is to answer the end for which he lives; and that is to glorify God and save his own soul." Penn asserted that religious liberty implied the duty to "exercise of ourselves in a visible way of worship."[29] Between roughly 1680 and 1720, Penn governed Pennsylvania as a Quaker oligarchy. Quakers assumed roles of business and political leadership, and their early successes in both realms solidified their control of the colony. Penn himself asserted that business success was God's reward for hard work. This providentialism attributed the Quakers' success to the will of God and fostered philanthropic activities reflecting appreciation of God's beneficence through the practice of Christian charity.

Pennsylvania law protected freedom of conscience (since God alone is, as Penn claimed, Lord of Conscience), but only for those who believed in God. Agnostics and atheists could not participate fully in society, being restricted in voting and property ownership. Only Christians could hold office, and blasphemy, profanity, and breach of the Sabbath were criminal offences. The law also prohibited the usual sexual offenses, drunkenness, card playing, and other "harmful games." Floggings, ear croppings, and other forms of corporal punishment attended conviction for moral offenses. The colonial code also provided for government to administer poor relief as an expression of Christian "kindness, goodness, and charity."

While Quakerism was never established, it exercised tremendous control over people's lives. No personal concern was too private to be addressed by the community. Monthly meetings heard cases concerning excessive ornamentation, prideful speech, untender childrearing, harsh treatment of servants, and fostering wayward children (those who were not practicing the faith). In addition, the meetings assessed a couple's level of spirituality before permitting marriage.

Ultimately, Quakers could not sustain their control of Pennsylvania in the face of an increasing majority of non-Quakers. True to their doctrinal tenets that the spirit of God lives in all people, who are therefore equal in the eyes of God and men, the Quakers retreated from diversity rather than persecuted it. Quaker domesticity became a substitute for Quaker community. The household became the primary moral and economic social unit. Domesticity encouraged a further emphasis on privacy, individuality, and self-sufficiency, all characteristics of a more modern eighteenth-century American society.[30] However, rather than Pennsylvania being viewed as an example of an early colonial rejection of religious or Christian communitarianism, it must be seen as a unique expression of Quaker doctrine in forming community. Pennsylvania's economic success, religious diversity, philanthropic progress, and political democracy in the colonial era are not so much expressions of postrevolutionary liberalism as they are expressions of Quaker beliefs. In Pennsylvania, as in other colonies, the Christian sectarian beliefs of the founders and early settlers controlled the formation of civil society.

Maryland's religious toleration was due largely to its being imposed by English authorities. Yet the absence of laws addressing the practice of religion resulted not in communal harmony but rather in social strife over religious difference. Ultimately, Maryland too turned to religious establishment to rebuild its communities. James I intended to give the colony to George

Calvert, a devout Catholic, the first Lord Baltimore, and trusted servant of the King. When Calvert died, his son, Cecil, inherited the title, and in 1629 Charles I gave him Maryland. Representatives of the failed Virginia Company, fearing further land devaluation, immediately protested the grant to a Catholic as violation of English law and an invitation to Spanish or French intervention. The protest delayed settlement until 1633 and shaped the religious character of the colony. The new Lord Baltimore, knowing his estate was precarious, tried to minimize the influence of religion altogether. He insisted Catholics preserve unity and peace by refraining from public discussion or practice of religion. This policy precluded not only Catholic establishment but even construction of Catholic churches. Catholics nonetheless retained social power, as Baltimore awarded choice lands and high offices to Catholics, even though they were a minority among the settlers. This fact fed resentment of the Catholic oligarchy.

Maryland suffered from various religious uprisings during the 1600s, during which one group (Catholic or Protestant) would gain control of the government and author highly discriminatory laws in favor of its chosen beliefs. In each instance, action from England revoked these laws and imposed the toleration needed to encourage business. These policies of toleration attracted dissenters to the colony.

Religious diversity, however, did not mean acceptance so much as separation: each religious enclave exercised its own rules regarding conformity with a sectarian defensiveness that stemmed from the precarious state of any religion in Maryland. Only one Anglican minister preached in the colony before the late 1650s, and most Protestants could not afford to support a minister, build a church, or maintain a school. For three generations, most people in Maryland did not attend a single church service. Responsibility for public services, which usually fell to churches, vested instead in the gentry. As a result, prior to 1700 almost no schools, practically no poor relief, and few records existed in Maryland. The colony lacked the usual signs of community—churches, town squares, schoolhouses—and the public life they foster. Before 1670 vacant country homes served as jails, but every town had stocks, pillory, and whipping post.

In 1692 a predominantly Anglican assembly passed an "Act of Establishment" that would have given legal support to the Anglican Church. The Lords of Trade under King William and Queen Mary refused to accept it. When Queen Anne succeeded King William in 1702, she confirmed the 1692 act and revoked orders securing freedom of religion for Catholics. As in other colonies, Queen Anne's reign represented a period of intensified Anglicanism, embraced by the Maryland Assembly because of its implicit anti-Catholicism. When Anne's royal governor John Seymour arrived, his first action was to arrest and threaten Catholic proselytizers. Seymour also urged adoption of criminal laws to address the problems that he perceived to be caused by the Romish Clergy. These laws resulted in the prohibition of Catholic worship in public and severe penalties for Catholic proselytizing.

Legally, the Anglican establishment was relatively weak. It permitted practice of any Protestant religion and did not require attendance at Anglican services. It did, however, mandate a poll tax, resented by Catholics and Quakers, for support of the Anglican church. Laws influenced by Protestant conceptions of morality also infused the criminal code and business law.

The assembly, in support of the Anglican establishment, organized vestries as quasi-governmental organizations to perform church and public business in twenty-two of the thirty parishes, and it provided new church buildings for most. Vestrymen were elected to collect church taxes and poor rates, and to pay for support of a minister and often a church school. Evincing continued resentment of Catholics, a 1715 law allowed vestrymen to remove children from a Catholic mother if their Protestant father died, so that they "be Securely Educated in the protestant religion." By the time of the Revolution, Anglicanism was well established in Maryland.[31]

The English American colonies of the seventeenth century expressed their Calvinist Christian ideology in social organization. American colonists accepted a communalistic society in which they were expected to subordinate their selfish interests both to conform to the will of God and to secure the greater good of communal welfare. Law combined with a strong respect for hierarchy, order, and Christian brotherhood to reinforce these social values. "Establishment" in colonial America constituted much more than the political unification of church and state. It is better appreciated as the societal reflection and perpetuation of Christian values shaping not only law and politics but all aspects of colonial intellectual and cultural life. Although the specific doctrinal and institutional components of this Christian establishment varied between colonies, this essential shaping of colonial American perspective did not.

2 Revolutions in Churches and Society

No one can serve two masters: for either he will hate the one and love the other, or he will be devoted to the one and despise the other. You cannot serve God and mammon.

Matthew 6:24

ECONOMIC REALITIES in seventeenth-century America supported religious teachings in giving colonial law a communitarian orientation. Colonists generally remained in or near the communities in which they were raised, fostering close relationships. Individual families could not supply all of their own needs and came to rely on a system of informal exchange with neighbors. Partly because of the rareness of currency, barter systems arose throughout the colonies through which a southern pastor might be paid in tobacco, a New England storekeeper in eggs, and a Philadelphia merchant in homemade baskets. All sections of the country retained an agricultural emphasis throughout the colonial era, and seasonal production combined with close-knit societal association to render formal systems of economic exchange superfluous. Most transactions were recorded in ledger books, without any formalization of the debt in promissory notes, bills of sale, or other forms of contract. Enforceability relied on trust and a community of interest.

Intellectual and economic factors had rendered this legal system archaic by the middle of the eighteenth century. Increasing commercial specialization and the production of market crops, especially in the mid-Atlantic and southern colonies, required a more formal legal system. Consumer demand for imported goods and luxuries similarly exceeded the practical purposes of ledger accounts. Perhaps the biggest change was just the increase in intertown trade and economic diversity that involved exchanges between strangers or distant acquaintances rather than friends and neighbors. In the early 1700s, colonies began introducing paper currency. The transformation of the economy was both reflected in and encouraged by commercial law. Judicial attention to the developing law of contracts predated its widespread business implementation in the colonies, providing a legal structure for economic adaptation. English common law had long recognized contract rights, and colonial assemblies had made debts on paper bills rather than ledger-book debt assignable in the mid–seventeenth century. Turn-of-the-century merchants relied on promissory notes and conditional bonds as the basis of trade and were willing and able to litigate to enforce these instruments. The popularity of written instruments derived from their certainty as formal admissions of liability. They could be used in single transactions, independent of long-term relationships. Court procedures increased in formality as well, as businessmen used attorneys expert in commercial law to present their cases. Lay pleading, emphasizing factual disputes before juries, was being replaced by attorney arguments of law before judges. Legislatures responded to these changes in litigation by enacting rules for the courts formalizing pleadings and procedures.[1]

As economic and cultural factors eroded colonial communities, America's Christians divided among those who attempted to integrate modern ideas into Christian cosmology and those who relied upon orthodox doctrine to refute modernist assumptions. John Locke published his *Essay Concerning Human Understanding* in 1690. Calvinist theology prior to that time premised man's reception of God's grace upon means other than the use of his own conscious thought processes. Locke challenged this whole understanding. The suggestion that man can know something without conscious awareness of it struck Locke as absurd. In a Christian context this was an empowering doctrine. If conscious thought were the only way of knowing, man could not know God by being helpless or dependent upon the Holy Spirit. Charles Morton published *The Spirit of Man* in 1693, premising man's conversion upon Locke's new thesis of human understanding. He asserted that man is a singular entity, a spirit, composed of body and soul, who comes to knowledge through both thought, the process of knowing through the soul, and sensation, the process of knowing through the body. Perception can be thought or sensation; knowledge is derived from either. In this way Morton accommodates Locke's conclusion that man must be aware of that which he knows while still allowing for a dynamic inward process of knowing through sensation.[2]

Morton's extension of Lockeian theory served as the theoretical basis for two new strains of American Christianity: one, an emotional and pietistic Christianity, and the other, rational religion. An early progenitor of rational religion, Dr. Samuel Clark, an Anglican minister in England, sought to integrate the natural philosophy of Newton's *Principia Mathematica* (1685) with Christianity. He published a series of lectures given in 1704–1705 under the title *A Discourse Concerning the Being and Attributes of God, and Obligations of Natural Religion, and the Truth and Certainty of the Christian Revelation*. In this text, he relied upon the Great Chain of Being, which ultimately requires a first cause. He concluded, "Almost everything in the world demonstrates to us the great truth; and affords undeniable arguments to prove that the world and all things herein, are the effects of an intelligent and knowing cause." Clark recognized man as a significant actor in determining his own salvation and the fate of the world. Man can exercise his own rationality to come to an awareness of God and his teachings. Clark found man's nature to be good, as are all things God created. Evil intent is a violation of nature, not a result of it, "a direct choosing to act contrary to the known reason and nature of things."[3] Within a few years, Clark's ideas would gain acceptance among a liberal and educated American clergy and further divide American society. Yet, as significant as rational religion was to become, it was initially subordinated to the emotional religion of early eighteenth-century revivals.

The preachers of the Great Awakening sought to overcome a perceived religious laxity by invoking their listeners to feel the saving grace of God within themselves.[4] In emphasizing personal feelings and actions, they implicitly accepted the sensory awareness espoused by Morton and a works-oriented Arminianism.[5] Yet, in rejecting man's reason as a basis for belief and reasserting the strict enforcement of scriptural rules, these preachers accommodated traditional Calvinism to the thoughts and attitudes of their time. They combined a human-centered emotional appeal with invocations to return to a more God-centered communal existence. These "New Light" preachers appealed both to the prevalence of new individualistic attitudes and the fears and confusions of their listeners. The breakdown of communities, the disruption of economic patterns, and the incursion of new ideas threatened many Americans but especially the poor, the less educated, and the rural. Thousands responded to the revivals as a way to find security in a world that ceased to make sense to them. Preachers became a "means of grace," exciting their listeners into frenzies that would influence their wills into conversion.[6] Despite its flirtation with Arminianism, the New Light doctrine restated man's depravity, his utter reliance on God's divine grace, and the Calvinist prescription to form Christian communities. Jonathan Edwards argued that man could hasten the coming of the millennium, the golden age of a world in God's image brought about by either the return of Christ or by human preaching, through "union." Union was a more beautiful social order of believers united in love. In this, the essence of Awakening preaching was brotherhood, seeking a return to earlier Christian communitarianism.[7]

Established churchmen reacted with alarm to the success of the itinerant New Light preachers, whom they perceived as destroying community. In their opposition to the Half-Way Covenant and other doctrinal modifications, the New Lights attacked the positions of families who had become entrenched in the churches despite the absence of "experiences of saving grace." Consider the joint statement of the religious leaders at Harvard in 1744:

> [Revivalist preachers] thrust themselves into Towns and Parishes, to the Destruction of all Peace and Order, whereby they have to the great impoverishment of the community, taken the People from their Work and Business, to attend their Lectures and Exhortations, always fraught with Enthusiasm, and other pernicious Errors. But, which is worse, and it is the Natural effect of these things, the People have been thence ready to despise their own Ministers, and their usefulness among them, in too many places, hath been almost destroyed.[8]

State governments acted to assist their allies, the established churches, in heading off the assault to their authority posed by the revivalists. For instance, in Connecticut during the 1740s, the legislature enacted a series of laws disciplining government officials, ministers, and churches that expressed an acceptance of separatism, itinerant evangelicalism, or emotional piety. Dissenting ministers were deprived of their salaries; dissenting judges and other public employees were deposed or censored for religious nonconformity. Yale was required to enforce religious conformity among students and faculty, and laws were passed defining the orthodox faction within divided parishes as the true established church, in possession of church property and government sanction, even if the orthodox members were in the minority. Persecution, however, only fortified the New Light dissenters, who, convinced they were "in the truth," accepted "social martyrdom [as] bearable and even honorable."[9] The orthodox churches ultimately could not accommodate the emotionally energized and empowered revivalists spawned in the Great Awakening. Dissenters migrated to new Baptist and Methodist churches, sapping power from the integrated systems of church and state.

The dissenting churches profited from the increasingly complex doctrinal accommodations that the established churches made to Enlightenment thought. Many Americans lost touch with the sophisticated sermons and elitist social attitudes that the traditionalists presented in established Congregational and Anglican churches. They longed for religious services that addressed their real concerns: Christian values as well as salvation. The Great Awakening challenged the age of reason, developing its enthusiastic piety from emotional aspects of Christian conversion. However, the revivals attacked the popular perceptions of new ideas more than the ideas themselves, pillorying immorality, greed, vice, and selfishness.[10] Revivalist preachers offered rural and poor Americans a simple conception of good and evil rooted in their free expression of love for God and each other. The preachers offered agrarian communitarianism in response to the complications and isolations of a modernizing society.

The revivalists sought a Christian society, and they turned to revitalized corporate communities and renewed ministerial authority as the means to confront threats posed to it by individualism and the free market.[11] The Great Awakening helped to unify evangelical Christians by emphasizing conversion and regeneration as bonds of fellowship. Evangelical Christians transcended doctrinal differences by subordinating theology to emotional conversion experiences and the quest for union. In this process of unifying people in a common cause against established authority, many historians have portrayed the Great Awakening as a prelude to democratic Revolution.[12] Common people created a powerful political body committed to religious liberty and the avoidance of sin and corruption. Certainly appeals to these themes were central to the building of revolutionary enthusiasm. However, the Revolution espoused radical individualism derived from Enlightenment liberalism more than communal democracy, while the Great Awakening was neither individualistic nor doctrinally liberal.[13]

The Great Awakening also created greater fragmentation within the colonies. While uniting evangelical Christians of various sects, it tended to isolate them as a body from both the established church people and the commercial and rationalist segments of the population. As early as the 1730s, the American market economy had largely outgrown the parameters of providentialism and communalism. Evangelicals, who sought to perpetuate the increasingly archaic model of religious and social integration, looked upon the new political economy with disdain. Perceiving moral decline in selfish industriousness and economic disparities as inconsistent with Christian society, many evangelical preachers condemned the greed and self-indulgence of their fellow colonists. Yet at least as great as this social-moral divide was the breach the evangelicals precipitated within their own churches. Within established churches, liberal exponents of rational religion united with their more traditional clerical brethren in opposition to the evangelical movement.[14] Arminianism combined with natural law to reshape the religion of established churches toward a humanistic moralism. The social radicals, the evangelicals, became the religiously orthodox; the social conservatives in the established churches became the religious liberals. By the middle of the eighteenth century, religion had divided American society and positioned itself as a vehicle for social change. The most vibrant growth in Christianity came among those sects castigating both society for its economic individualism and the established religious order for its perceived rejection of Christian doctrine.

More liberal clergy, building on Dr. Clark's ideas, moved to adapt American Protestantism to the influences of Enlightenment thought. God assumed a reduced role as part of the natural order, recognized as its creator and the designer of natural laws. The judgment of man's mind was reliable even for the acceptance of religious truth. Man could come to an understanding of God and his teachings by learning about nature and its laws.[15]

This new Christian doctrine altered adherents' views of themselves and their world. Whereas seventeenth-century Calvinists relied on a judgmental God and his moral dictates for order, liberal Christians accepted the world and themselves as moral and rational in creation. To them, freedom led to order and restraint to chaos. Religious appeals had to address man's reason and the observable laws of nature. In this context, mysticism and the supernatural demeaned both God and man.[16]

Liberal Christianity did not espouse libertarian doctrine. The laws of God and nature were to be followed, but they necessarily had to be reasonable. Christianity's moral teachings could be removed from its supernatural beliefs. John Locke early recognized that the supernatural and mystical elements of Christian doctrine mitigated its own significance in establishing a useful moral code upon which to construct a civil society. Neither faith nor grace compelled a reasonable man to moral behavior. Locke contended that Jesus himself taught that faith alone is not sufficient for salvation. In addition, God required man's obedience to social laws establishing right and wrong. Because Christianity's moral laws parallel those of reason as to the requirements of a civil life, Christianity could serve as a civil religion, providing a basis of belief for the masses, "the greatest part [of whom] cannot know, . . . [and therefore] must believe." Eighteenth-century liberals sometimes remained professedly Christian because they feared that a population freed of all religious belief would result in risks to liberty and property. In a 1749 sermon in Boston's West Church, Pastor Lemuel Briant, for example, asserted that "the perfect religion of Jesus was nothing other than a refined system of morality."[17]

Liberal Christians of the eighteenth century generally accepted God as a divine creator and many continued to believe in the Trinity and in the possibility of life after death. In these regards they differed from Deists and proponents of Christian morality void of Christian belief. However, in attitude, demeanor, and even in some beliefs they appeared closer to those unchurched rationalists than to the evangelical Christians. They opposed the evangelical emphasis on piety and the emotionalism of revivals, dismissing conversion as unnecessary. Sermons were reasoned lectures combining religious truth with man's moral duty. Rev. Noah Worcester, a Massachusetts Congregationalist, contrasted these sermons with evangelical preaching, noting Baptist pastors eschewed reason, confused scripture, and appealed to those "who possess weak judgments, fickle minds, and quick and tender passions." Leading liberal minister, Charles Chauncy of Boston, dismissed Edwards as a "visionary enthusiast . . . not to be minded in anything he says."[18]

The proliferation of religious sects and the increasing divergence of doctrinal beliefs within American Christianity during the eighteenth century weakened the position of established churches. As evangelical dissenters called for religious freedom, they furthered the division between themselves and the doctrinally liberal establishment. Their opposition to established religion arose from a desire for free religious practice and from a resentment of tax support for churches they deemed unworthy of spreading God's truth. By the eighteenth century, persecutions for dissenting religious beliefs had become quite rare and were nearly always premised upon grossly disruptive social behavior. But increased toleration did not provide religious freedom. The dissenters believed that liberty from coercion and restraint was necessary for people to pursue affectionate union. The love of God and one another must be an expression of free will. Therefore, religious establishment was an impediment to union. The very emotional responses denigrated by the liberals were also essential to union. Crying, raving, and singing may have seemed irrational and socially disruptive to some, but they helped to build community through shared experience. Evangelical preaching and the emotional communalism it fostered repudiated both liberal religious doctrine and the individualism perceived to be at its roots.[19]

Conversely, mid-century liberals usually did not question the need for a tax-supported church as an essential means of regulating morals and social behavior. Social stability depended upon a virtuous public, and a moralistic religion seemed the most expedient means of creating one. By the time of the Revolution, republicans often willingly enlisted a liberal-minded clergy in service to social needs.

Religious debates took a backseat to the issue of political sovereignty during the Revolution. Yet Revolutionary-era events profoundly influenced the role of churches in the new republican society. At this time, religiosity was probably at the lowest point in American history. A small minority of Americans bothered to attend any church services. Of church members, over 70 percent were women, a figure that underlines the relative insignificance of religion in the lives of Revolutionary-era men.[20] The clergy further adapted sermons to the changing attitudes of their parishioners. The Revolutionary generation preferred an optimistic religion of a benevolent God to the Calvinist emphasis on man's depravity. Rational religion crept into the doctrines of all established churches. God was frequently referred to and conceived of as creator; Christian religion came increasingly to be understood as a moral code; and the American people and the nation they might form took on reverential qualities to rival the divine. Even in Massachusetts, skepticism abounded. Established Boston clergymen such as Charles Chauncy and Jonathan Mayhew rejected Trinitarianism. In Virginia, the gentry generally preferred law to scripture as a source of written authority. Social values reflected the shift to legalistic individualism over Christian communitarianism as justice came to mean "giving to each his own" and law became the preferred method of resolving rights and disputes.[21]

Perhaps the greatest change in American Christianity occurred as a result of the confluence between religion and nationalism that arose amid the patriotic enthusiasm of the war years. In countless sermons, ministers rewrote the history of the Pilgrims and the Hebrews so that both told the same story. Both were depicted as chosen societies, in which political freedom and religious piety were integrated in public virtue. The Puritans quested for political and ecclesiastical liberty, and one was necessary for the other. Revolutionary-era preaching encouraged a breach with a corrupt British society impeding Christian union. Civil millennialism was both eschatological, in presupposing a coming judgment day, and political, in its acceptance of Whig ideology. The issue was whether victory would go to the forces of God or Satan. Britain's acknowledged luxury and corruption, imposition of unjust taxes, and threats of establishing an American bishopric made it possible for Americans to perceive a Satanic threat in British tyranny. Political liberty was necessary to preserve America's heritage as a chosen people, free to act virtuously in constructing a state conducive to the practice of God's will. Sermons reflected a redirection of mission into a nationalistic program. The "chosen people" remained in covenant with God but toward different ends—republican government and a productive economy.[22]

Republican revolutionaries used Christian religion as an institutional and ideological tool. Clerical calls for liberty engendered passionate antipathy for British domination while simultaneous invocations to duty and virtue provided orderly restraint within the revolutionary movement. To use religion as a means of social manipulation and control is not the same as to rely on

Cartoon, 1769—Colonists are depicted throwing the works of John Locke and John Calvin at an Anglican bishop attempting to embark in America. Enlightenment liberals and Calvinist Pietists united at the time in their antipathy to Anglican establishment in the colonies. Courtesy Presbyterian Historical Society, Presbyterian Church (USA) (Philadelphia).

religious doctrine and belief as the basis of civil society, however. Christian churches played a key but carefully restricted role in the movement toward independence. This fact was not lost on some ministers. Letters written by Samuel West, Congregational pastor in Boston, to the *Boston Independent Ledger* under the pen name "Irenaeus" during 1780 argued that religion should not be considered necessary because it cultivated the virtue required for self-government, but because "obedience to the whole moral law is a religious duty because it is the law of God." For these reasons, "Irenaeus," in a letter of April 17, supported established churches as an integral part of any legitimate government.[23]

Despite the fact that approximately one-half of the signers of the Declaration of Independence were skeptics who could not fairly be considered Christians, political leaders hesitated to admit their own agnosticism or to divorce their country from its Christian heritage.[24] Christian morality not only served the political interests of the new nation but also united disparate peoples from Maine to Georgia in a common cultural value system. The Continental Congress accorded this cultural connection due notice during the war. At the first meeting of the Congress in 1774, it passed a proposal, though not before heated debate, that the sessions be opened with a prayer. In November 1777, the Congress proclaimed the first national day of thanksgiving, setting aside December 18, 1777, for "solemn thanksgiving and prayer." Yet public pronouncements made for social and political reasons could not mask the tepid religious mood of large segments of Revolutionary America. Even liberal pastor Ezra Stiles found cause to bemoan: "It begins to be a growing idea that it is mighty indifferent . . . not only whether a man be of this or the other religious sect but whether he be of any religion at all; and that truly deists, and men of indifferentism to all religion, are the most suitable persons for civil office."[25]

In 1778 Congress considered, without action, a motion "that the sense of the house be taken, whether it is proper that Congress shall appoint any person of ecclesiastical character to any civil office under the United States." Several states that wrote Revolutionary-era constitutions did include a ban on clergy holding elected or appointed state office. Jefferson favored these constitutional proscriptions, prompting Madison to write to him: "Does not the exclusion of Ministers of the Gospel as such violate a fundamental principle of liberty by punishing a religious profession with the privatization of a civil right?"[26]

Madison's question contains the essence of the liberal republican attitude on religious freedom. It furthermore expresses the interrelatedness of the ideas of religious liberty and the separation of church and state. Reversing the colonial model, liberal republicanism sought to privatize religion as a civil right exempt from interference from the limited powers of the state. Religious belief could be separated from one's role as public citizen, but the right to vote and participate in the democratic process could not. Madison could not believe that Jefferson sought to condition this right upon belief or occupation. He reminded Jefferson that at the root of republican insistence on religious liberty was the bedrock idea that the citizens of the state should surrender as little power and freedom to the government of the state as is necessary for it to effectuate its purposes. Yet Jefferson, and elsewhere Madison as well, worried that political leaders who, consistent with their Christian beliefs, sought to evangelize or proselytize from public office could destroy republican government.[27]

In this environment, established religious institutions were on the defensive. Anglicanism suffered the most. The seat of authority for the Church of England remained in England, a reminder of English rule. Efforts by the church to establish a North American bishopric prior to the war had contributed to the growing antagonism toward the mother country. Anglicanism could not function practically without a bishop. The rules of the church required a bishop to perform confirmations and ordinations, rendering invalid all those ceremonies performed in the colonies. Doctrinal consistency, piety, and church attendance suffered in the absence of church discipline. The church could succumb to the social and political interests of a local elite, which is exactly what happened in the South. Yet the idea of an American bishop struck Americans as papism and a further English encroachment upon colonial liberties. In the North, Congregationalists had to counter the arguments of evangelical dissenters and political liberals who variously saw religious establishment as a vestige of European influence in its creation of an artificial hierarchy, a barrier to free religious expression necessary for union, or an unjust governmental intrusion upon the rights of man.

In 1774 nine of the thirteen colonies had legally established churches. De facto establishments existed in three of the others. All people within establishment colonies were taxed for the support of a church building and the salary of a clergyman. In those colonies in which law did not specifically provide for the legal toleration of dissenters, only the established church could incorporate or perform authorized civil functions such as marriage ceremonies.

To evangelicals, the Revolution was a battle for religious as well as political liberty. The corrupt system of the past had to be overthrown to provide fertile ground for the growth of a new Christian nation. In 1770 Baptist minister Isaac Backus published "A Seasonable Plea for Liberty of Conscience Against Some Late Oppressive Proceedings Particularly in the Town of Berwick." Backus was offended by seeing friends and family imprisoned and fined for refusing to pay taxes in support of a church they believed to be in error. In 1773 he refined his argument in the publication of "An Appeal to the Public for Religious Liberty Against the Oppression of the Present Day," in which he even wedded his commitment to religious liberty to an endorsement of separation of church and state (a position from which he would subsequently back away). In support of his argument Backus struggled to unite Lockeian conceptions of liberty and biblical prescriptions for religious freedom. Yet he ultimately relied on his understanding of Christianity, asserting that Christ's kingdom cannot be subordinated to or in league with government: "God has appointed two different kinds of government in the world which are different in nature and ought never to be confounded together; one of which is called civil, the other ecclesiastical government." According to McLaughlin, Backus sought separation, in 1773, in order to secure a "truly Christian state."[28]

Baptists used their support of the Revolutionary War to campaign for religious freedom in Massachusetts and Virginia. They led the vanguard of religious dissenters in calling for disestablishment. Virginia Presbyterians joined Baptists in petitioning efforts between 1776 and 1779. Yet immediate results in these two states disappointed the petitioners. Virginia postponed its action on the issue until after the war. Massachusetts responded with "window dressing." In 1779 a Baptist minister was invited to give that year's election sermon in Boston. Massachusetts could show its appreciation for the dissenters' support of the war but would not disestablish its church. John Adams was blunt and humorous: "The Baptists might as well expect a change in the solar system as to expect that the Massachusetts authorities would give up their establishment."[29]

Immediately following the Declaration of Independence, the Continental Congress urged the newly independent states to solidify their political legitimacy through the drafting of new constitutions. An additional purpose—that of redesigning society to more closely conform to republican ideals—would also be served in this process. The Revolution sought to remove any existing social structures premised on patronage and privilege. While social equality was not a goal, legal equality was. Eliminating artificial hierarchies meant eviscerating established churches of their political power. Eleven states drafted constitutions in 1776 and 1777. In Delaware and Pennsylvania, elected assemblies formed conventions to draft new constitutions. All but one of the other states merely drafted their constitutions in legislative session. None was ever submitted to the people for ratification. Only Massachusetts adhered to the social contract model "that a constitution should be proposed by a convention elected for that purpose alone, and subsequently ratified through some mechanism of popular consent." The processes used to draft the constitutions minimized debates over their most controversial provisions. The new constitutions served as fundamental laws embodying revolutionary values. These constitutions became the first means by which Revolutionary-era governments sought to disestablish colonial churches.[30]

The Revolutionary-era constitutions expressed the deep divisions then existing on issues of religion and represent a mixed legacy on the issue of disestablishment. In no instance did early constitutional language determine the ultimate outcome of the disestablishment controversy within the state. In some states disestablishment appeared to be relatively easy. A majority of the nonslave population in North Carolina in 1776 did not attend church. The established Anglican Church was very weak, and the most dynamic religious sects were the Scottish Presbyterians and German Moravians in the western mountainous areas of the state. The 1776 constitution of North Carolina disestablished the Anglican Church, banned the clergy from holding office, and prohibited state support of any religion. It provided that:

> no person, on any pretence whatsoever [shall] be compelled to attend any place of worship, contrary to his own faith or judgment, nor be obliged to pay, for the purchase of any glebe, or the building of any house of worship, or for the maintenance of any minister or ministry, contrary to what he believes right, or has voluntarily and personally engaged to perform; but all persons shall be at liberty to exercise their own mode of worship.[31]

Perhaps the most radical Revolutionary-era constitution was that written for Pennsylvania in 1776. The democratically conceived document provided for broad suffrage rights, a single popularly elected legislative body, annual elections, and even the popular election of military leaders and judges. Addressing religious freedom, Pennsylvania allowed that "No man ought or of right can be compelled to attend any religious worship, or erect or support any place of worship, or maintain any ministry, contrary to, or against, his own free will and consent."[32]

The new government created by this constitution effectively destroyed the College of Philadelphia as a Tory and Anglican institution. However, Pennsylvania also embodied the ideological conflict inherent in American culture by requiring an oath in the belief of God in order to vote.[33] Pennsylvania attempted to deprive sectarian churches and church schools of previous political and economic support but to retain a Christian ethic among the citizenry.

Further evidence of the difficulty states had in addressing conflicting goals is expressed in the 1776 constitution of Maryland. In one section of this document, Maryland provided that no person could be forced "to maintain any particular place of worship or any particular ministry." This effectively ended Episcopalian supremacy but not religious establishment, for the constitution also provided: "Yet, the legislature may, in their [sic] discretion, lay a general and equal tax, for the support of the Christian religion; leaving to each individual the power of appointing the payment of the money, collected from him, to the support of any particular place of worship or minister." When the Maryland legislature attempted to act on this authority in 1780, the bill for multiple establishment encountered an early demise.[34]

The mid-Atlantic states, in keeping with their histories of religious toleration, disestablished their churches in the drafting of their wartime constitutions. Reflecting the business orientation of these states, some constitutions focused less on rights than on limiting financial obligations. New Jersey in 1776 provided that no person would "ever be obliged to pay tithes, taxes, or any other rates, for the purpose of building or repairing any other church or churches, place or places of worship, or for the minister or ministry, contrary to what he believes to be right, or has deliberately or voluntarily engaged himself to perform." Delaware used similar language in its constitution.[35]

In New England, the religious establishment held political power throughout the constitutional era. Massachusetts, for at least two generations after the Revolution, created the political model that other New England states adopted. The constitution of Massachusetts of 1780 provided in article 2 that "It is the right as well as the Duty of all men in Society, publickly and at stated seasons to worship the SUPREME BEING, the great creator, and preserver of the Universe." Having once established this duty in law, the constitution, in article 3, provided for state support to the citizens needful of fulfilling this duty.[36]

Massachusetts required communities to create and support means of religious instruction, which was to be provided by the various Protestant Christian denominations within the state. The majority of each community dictated the locally established church to which all contributed. In addition to teaching the people of the state piety, religion, and morality so as to preserve public order and ensure happiness, community churches would promote godliness by assertion of Christian values and a communitarian ethic. If sufficient private support for these functions was not forthcoming, the government would institute public support through taxation. This constitutional scheme incorporated public and private entities, religious doctrine and civic priorities, church and state authority. The primary concern was the attainment of the social good. A pure separation of church and state or of public and private institutions was not supportive of this goal and was therefore subordinated to the greater concern. The scheme conceived of in the Massachusetts constitution preserved the old colonial model of civil society. The degree of religious freedom granted there reflected New England's perpetuation of colonial ideas limited to the tolerance of diverse Christian sects. Yet even this was too much for some who found the new constitution "overly indulgent" toward Catholics.[37]

Following the adoption of the Massachusetts constitution in 1780, several Baptists refused to pay their taxes to support the local church. Five had their cattle impounded and sold for payment of the six-dollar tax. Another man was arrested and paid his tax under duress. This individual, Elijah Balkcom of Attleborough, brought suit to challenge the tax, claiming that the tax requirement of article 3 of the state constitution violated the freedom of conscience protection provided in article 2. The social and ideological divisions that attended the issue of church-state separation were reflected in the contradictory language contained in Massachusetts's first constitution. Balkcom won at the county court in Taunton in 1782. But in 1784 a similar case of *Cutter v. Frost,* which followed the Balkcom ruling, was appealed by the parish to the superior court. On October 26, 1784, Judge Sergent upheld article 3, asserting that nobody could be exempt from the tax, but dissenters could designate that their tax dollars go to support an incorporated church of their choice. The law operated to privatize dissenting religious sects even in a state that retained an established church. Only legal societies that were incorporated could receive recognition under the law.[38]

Vermont adopted language similar to that of Massachusetts for article 3 of its bill of rights:

> That all men have a natural and unalienable right to worship Almighty God according to the dictates of their own consciences and understanding, regulated by the word of God; and that no man ought, or of right can be compelled to attend any religious worship, or erect or support any place of worship or maintain any minister contrary to the dictates of conscience; *nor can any man who professes the protestant religion, be justly deprived or abridged of any civil rights, as a citizen, on account of his religious sentiment,* or peculiar mode of religious worship, and that no authority can, or ought to be vested in, or assumed by, any power whatsoever, that shall in any case interfere with, or in any controul, the rights of conscience, in the free exercise of religious worship; nevertheless, every sect or denomination of Christians ought to observe the Sabbath, or the lord's day, and keep up, and support some sort of religious worship, which to them shall seem most agreeable to the revealed will of God.

The constitution in Vermont privileged Protestants with protection of their civil rights. Furthermore, it provided a religious test for officeholders, requiring the belief "in one God" who was the "rewarder of the good and the punisher of the wicked" and that "the scriptures of the old and new testament" of the Christian bible were "given by divine inspiration."[39]

Although the Anglican Church was not established in Georgia until 1758, the state had a history of public hostility toward dissenters. In the 1740s Jews and Moravians were persecuted to the extent that nearly all of these peoples fled the state or retreated to their own enclaves. Legislative requirements that college charters provide for Anglican presidents frustrated George Whitefield in his plans to build a college during the same time period. The constitution of Georgia in 1777 reflected the shift to secular humanism in much of Revolutionary-era America. Parishes with names such as St. Paul, St. George, Christ Church, and St. James were renamed Richmond, Burke, Chatham, and Liberty Counties respectively. The Georgia constitution, like those of Tennessee, Delaware, Kentucky, New York, and the Carolinas, prohibited clergymen of any denomination from holding office in the legislature. All persons were recognized as having "the free exercise of their religion; provided it be not repugnant to the peace and safety of the state." The only limits on religious freedom concerned secular order, not religious doctrine. Yet the constitution did allow for the possibility of a legislative enactment creating a multiple establishment. Bills for this purpose were introduced in 1782 and 1784 and quickly defeated.[40]

The Revolutionary-era constitutions evinced the difficulty that the drafters had in reconciling political liberty with a desire to preserve their Christian heritage. In many states, especially in the Northeast, the religious establishment succeeded not only in retaining its government support but also in imposing test oaths and moral teachings upon the governing process.

Even the most liberal states found that Revolutionary-era constitutions expressing religious freedom served more as declarations of war than as resolutions of an issue. While the state constitutions generally protected the rights of the people to enjoy and defend life and liberty, to acquire, possess, and protect property, to pursue happiness and safety, and to exercise one's conscience and understanding in the worship of God, in the 1780s all of these realms were nonetheless subject to state regulation.[41]

The Revolution inevitably prompted many to contemplate the type of society they desired to live in. This society reflected a growing individualism in economic as well as political pursuits. American colonists who wished to stave off the encroachment of capitalism had tenuously persisted in their reliance upon communal local markets in the North and the plantation system in the South. The churches frequently served as defenders of the values and hierarchies within these communities. By the 1770s, however, commercial self-interest had largely replaced Christian communalism in the country as a whole. The growth of liberal ideology during the Revolution championed individualism over collective obligation and social cooperation.[42] American democracy, as a system of governance, imposed its own values, prioritizing legal equality over social equity.[43] In adopting this system, republicans adopted its values as well. They had no interest in returning to a premodern form of communal society. Men as diverse as Benjamin Rush, Thomas Jefferson, Noah Webster, and David Ramsay shared an ideal of American society as a flowering of culture and science and of government committed to man's nature. The free pursuit of exploration, cosmopolitanism, and the arts would realize man's potential in fulfillment of his curiosities. Religious distinctions could serve no helpful purpose by artificially isolating some from this pursuit or robbing the society of the potential contributions of all of its members. Yet this ideal had not been won in Revolution, nor embodied by many of the states in their initial constitutions. Political freedom having been won, advocates for complete religious freedom, a separation of church and state, and the building of a secular society could turn their attentions to these goals. Years later, George Washington asserted: "In this enlightened age and in this Land of equal liberty it is our boast, that a man's religious tenets will not forfeit the protection of the right of attaining and holding the highest offices that are known in the United States." At the close of the Revolution, even Washington's relatively mild claim was prescriptive more than descriptive.[44]

3 "To Form a More Perfect Union"

The Constitutional Consideration of Religion

Believing with you, that religion is a matter which lies solely between man and his God, that he owes account to none other for his faith or his worship, that the legislative powers of government reach actions only, and not opinions, I contemplate with sovereign reverence that act of the whole American people which declared that their legislature would "make no law respecting an establishment of religion, or prohibiting free exercise thereof," thus building a wall of separation between church and state.

Thomas Jefferson to the Danbury Association, January 1, 1802

RELIGION WAS NOT A PRIMARY FOCUS of the Constitutional Convention. This fact, in and of itself, speaks volumes about the Founders' ideas for the new nation. The broad purpose of the convention was to form a government to address republican conceptions of public purposes. That religion should play almost no part in this program was an indication of the radical departure the new government would be from the past. Rather than premise society on an ethic derived from Christianity, the Founders turned to a legal ethic derived from Enlightenment conceptions of individual integrity. Liberty, not communitarianism, was to be the chief goal of good government.

Nowhere is this protection of individual liberty more evident than in article 1, section 10, of the Constitution. And nowhere is it more evident than in this section that contract law, embodying liberal ideas of individual autonomy, was to be the chief means of protecting individual liberty. The "contract clause" of the Constitution provides that "No state shall . . . pass any . . . law impairing the obligations owing to contracts"; in other words, no perceived public interest or communitarian ethic shall be deemed superior to the rights of private individuals to contract for their own betterment.

Implicitly, law was reconceived in the Constitutional Convention—from supporting communitarian ideals consistent with Christian morality to serving ideals of individual liberty consistent with Enlightenment perceptions of man's reason and rationality. A new understanding of "rights" provided the theoretical basis for a new type of law. With the Christian message therefore diminished as an ideological component of the new government, what role would be left to the churches?

Efforts to form a more perfect union during the constitutional era involved as much tearing down the past as building the new. While the innovative primary laws of the federal government and most of the state governments by 1790 could prescribe the separation of church and state, the practical needs of continuing to provide social services, particularly in education and care for the poor, required a temporary toleration of the old colonial model in which church and state worked together to serve the public good. Still, the new primary laws expressed the voice of reform that would demand, by the close of the century, that the nation's institutions conform more closely to the individualistic ideal.

The national debates over the U.S. Constitution's religious provisions were remarkably free of the contentiousness that characterized the ideological and cultural division between liberal secularists and supporters of a Christian commonwealth from the 1790s to 1819. In large part, the disestablishment battle was waged at the state, not the national, level. Yet, despite the relative absence of vituperative debate on the issue of religion during its drafting, the Constitution provided a radically new legal framework for religious institutions within American society. The new legal framework addressed two distinct but interrelated concerns: religious freedom and the separation of church and state. Religious freedom was the major issue addressed in constitutional debates. Certainly, the constitutional separation of church and state derived less from the provisions addressing religion than from the broad liberal interpretation ultimately given the primary law by the Marshall Court in its exposition of the contract clause.[1] But the basis for the Court's later action was an essential part of the new legal framework, not left for amendments to consider.

The constitutional separation of church and state cannot be understood apart from the delineation of public and private institutions. While colonial America paid little attention to this distinction in harnessing all available resources to address societal needs, the Constitution in article 1, section 10, provided for the independence of private institutions from public control. The Constitution effectively prohibited a governmental reliance upon private means to serve public ends.

This is not meant to minimize the importance of the First Amendment in the disestablishment battles. By recognizing religious belief as an individual right protected from governmental intrusion, the Bill of Rights reconceived of religion as extraneous to the governing of the society. More than protecting religious liberty, the First Amendment prohibited congressional attention to religion, specifically Christian values and morality, in forming public laws. With religion still widely understood as offering moral imperatives, the constitutional design denied the federal government a role in moral regeneration. The church itself was implicitly repositioned within the new republic. Instead of functioning primarily as a social institution to which the people owed allegiance, the church became a vehicle through which its members could formulate and express their own personal religious sentiments. Once religious belief was considered to be beyond the scope of governmental authority, churches were considered to be outside the realm of governing. From their new position on the periphery of institutionalized civil authority, the churches were free to exert moral authority and offer dissent from governmental policies. As significant as this change was, it went largely unrecognized by church leaders until the 1790s.

The first mention of religion came several weeks into the convention in Philadelphia in the summer of 1787. Benjamin Franklin proposed opening each morning session with a prayer, conducted by "one or more clergy from this city." Alexander Hamilton referred to this idea as a divisive recourse to "foreign aid." Many shared his feelings that God's help was not needed. Madison recorded the lack of enthusiasm for Franklin's proposal: "After several unsuccessful attempts for silently postponing the motion by adjourning, the adjournment was at length carried without any vote on the motion." Similarly, the Federalist Papers made few references to religion—most prominent among them the one made by Madison in "Number 10," in which he repeats a concern he voiced at the convention, identifying a "zeal for different opinions concerning religion . . . [as one of the] latent causes of faction."[2]

The constitutional debates expressed the same attitude toward religion as was expressed by the Continental Congress in its passage of the Northwest Ordinance, also in 1787. In the ordinance, Congress asserted the value of religion in service to man, providing: "Religion, morality, and knowledge, being necessary to good government and the happiness of mankind, schools and the means of education shall be encouraged." Instead of professing an acceptance of God and his teachings as absolute, the ordinance announces a tentative and conditional acceptance of religion so long as it serves congressional priorities. Elsewhere, the ordinance provided for religious freedom to all individuals "demeaning [themselves] in a peaceable and orderly way."[3]

Religious discussion, in the context of the debate over the Constitution, focused upon its ability to secure a moral populace. Omitted from nearly every passage is any reference to Christian doctrine as an embodiment of absolute truth, to the need to form the government in accordance with God's teachings, or to the desirability or inevitability of subordinating man's will to God's plan or providence. Instead, a nonsectarian moralism was described—void of supernaturalism, emotionalism, and any promise of God's intervention. It is this religion that was invoked as a guide to moral behavior, resting as much on man's own reason as upon God's dictates.

One of the major concerns of the drafters and ratifiers of the Constitution was the degree to which the citizenry embodied sufficient virtue to manage self-government.[4] Religion arose as a possible means of instilling virtue. To some degree, concerns over American virtue transcended political differences. Dr. Benjamin Rush, a liberal Christian, speaking in support of the Constitution at the Pennsylvania Ratifying Convention, contended that the morals of the people had been corrupted by the imperfections of government, and he cited the general disregard of religion and disrespect of ministers as proof of his assertion.[5] Many antifederalists also recognized the need for moral virtue, but they did not see a powerful government as a means to engender it. Charles Turner expressed the position: "Without the prevalence of Christian piety and morals the best republican Constitution can never save us from slavery and ruin." He encouraged the new government to lead by encouraging morality among the people so that future governments might be reduced, "the people more capable of being a Law to themselves."[6]

Yet some who believed religion to be not only the basis of virtue but also the reason for America's success uneasily watched the convention's progress. They expressed dismay at their fellow citizens' refusal both to accord due appreciation for God's role in their recent crusade for freedom and to find a role for him in the new government.[7] The Rev. Thomas Reese, a Presbyterian pastor in Salem, South Carolina, wrote in 1788: "It is more to my purpose to observe, that the general neglect of religion which prevails among us, is one great, if not the chief cause, why our laws are so feeble in their operation." As Americans of this perspective reviewed the proposed Constitution, creating the first Western society in several hundred years not to establish a Christian church, they wondered whether the republic could survive without a religious alliance. A New Hampshire polemicist wrote in 1788 that "civil governments can't well be supported without the assistance of religion." Certainly the drafters were aware that many ardent Christians believed that their work diminished the roles of religion and the church in the new republic.[8]

There is evidence that the drafters rejected the notion that religion could help inform a citizenry with the virtue necessary for republican self-government. James Madison confided to his friend Thomas Jefferson:

> The inefficacy of this restraint [religion] on individuals is well known. The conduct of every popular assembly, acting on oath, the strongest of religious ties, shows that individuals join without remorse in acts against which their consciences would revolt, if proposed to them separately in their closets. When indeed Religion is kindled into enthusiasm, its force like that of other passions is increased by the sympathy of the multitude. But enthusiasm is only a temporary state of religion, and whilst it lasts will hardly be seen with pleasure at the helm. Even in its coolest state, it has been much oftener a motive to oppression than a restraint from it.[9]

Where religion would fail, the law would not. For men like Madison and Jefferson, law would provide the restraint on threats to self-government, the check on parochialism and self-interest. The Constitution ensured the contest of factions through federalism, representation by a disinterested elite, and separation of powers. In the resolution of disputes, law was, in Jefferson's words, the "conclusive authority" so long as it was written "with a single eye to reason."[10]

While the question of republican virtue raised a conceptual issue regarding the place of religion in the new republic, specific constitutional provisions fostered debates more threatening to ratification. Religion arose during the ratification process as a significant constitutional concern in three contexts: the use of religious tests for federal office holding, the absence of any national religion or commitment to God, and the protection of religious liberty. In every instance, the final document endorsed individual liberty over perpetuating a community premised on Christian belief.

Article 6 of the Constitution provided that "no religious test shall ever be required as a qualification to any office or public trust under the United States." While adoption of this clause provoked no controversy in Philadelphia, a writer to the *Maryland Gazette* after the convention presaged the ensuing debate over ratification:

> The part of the system, which provides that no religious test shall ever be required as qualification to any office or public trust under the United States, was adopted by a very great majority and without much debate—however, there were some members so unfashionable as to think that a belief in the existence of a Deity and a state of future rewards and punishments would be some security for the good conduct of our rulers, and that in a Christian country it would be at least decent to hold out some distinction between the professors of Christianity and downright infidelity or paganism.[11]

These "unfashionable" people came mainly from the clergy. The Rev. Caldwell, a Presbyterian minister, addressed the North Carolina Ratifying Convention on July 30, 1788, on the danger of this provision. He interpreted the prohibition of religious testing as an invitation to "Jews, Heathens, and Pagans of every kind, to come among us." At the same convention, another speaker doubted the ability of Catholics to be true republicans when they elevated the pope and even their priests above the rank of other men. He argued for their exclusion from office on these grounds. In South Carolina, Mr. Patrick Calhoun expressed a more veiled concern that the Constitution allowed for "too great latitude" in matters of religion. Reese argued that the government did use oaths every day in its courts and that, therefore, "If oaths be thus necessary to the administration of government, religion must be too; for where there is no religion there can be no oath. Take away the belief of a deity, a providence, and a future state, and there is an end of all oaths at once."[12]

Major objections to the exclusion clause were raised at the Massachusetts Ratifying Convention. Mr. Singletary complained that the Constitution failed to require those in power to have "any religion." He argued that men had not improved—they were still wicked at heart. Singletary advocated a requirement of Protestant Christian belief that would make "Papists," "Infidels," and other unregenerate souls ineligible for office. Another speaker found the absence of a religious test "a departure from the principles of our forefathers, who came here for the preservation of their religion; and that it would admit deists, atheists, and others into the general government; and people being apt to imitate the examples of the Court, these principles would be disseminated, and of course, a corruption of morals ensue." Writing as "Agrippa" to the *Massachusetts Gazette,* James Winthrop sarcastically contrasted the drafters' commitment to central authority for the purposes of interstate harmony with their inattention to religion. "Uniformity in legislation is no more important than in religion; yet, the framers of this new Constitution did not even think it necessary that the president should believe in God." Colonel Jones told his fellow delegates at the Massachusetts Convention that governors ought to believe in God and Christ and be members in good standing in a church, because "a person could not be a good man without being a good Christian."[13]

Perceiving the test oath issue as intertwined with religious establishment, the dissenting sects in Massachusetts largely supported the Convention's draft. The Reverend Payson responded to Colonel Jones's call for religious testing for officeholders with the assertion that God alone can judge man's conscience. Government should not presume to intrude upon his dominion. Similarly, Isaac Backus observed, "Many appear to be much concerned about it, but nothing is more evident, both in reason and in the holy scriptures, than that religion is a matter between God and individuals." Backus went on to refer to religious tests as a source of "tyranny."[14]

In the North Carolina Convention, the Rev. Abbott, a Baptist itinerant preacher; combined with Mr. Spencer, a liberal judge; and Mr. Iredell, a Federalist lawyer and businessman, in contesting Caldwell's calls for a religious test. These men argued for "religious liberty" on the basis that "the divine author of our religion never wished for its support by worldly authority." In Connecticut, William Williams, a onetime theology student from Harvard who chose to enter business and public service, expressed a typical compromise position in his letter to the *American Mercury* in February 1788. He expressed his wish, as a delegate to the Federal Convention, that all reference to a religious test be omitted in lieu of a provision espousing God's "providence and the authority of his laws." Yet he saw a benefit to the nation in a constitution that does not "restrain offices to any particular sect, class or denomination of men or Christians, in the long list of diversity."[15]

In Massachusetts, the Rev. Daniel Shute, a Liberal Arminian Harvard man and Unitarian minister, provided the political conduit between the evangelical and rationalist voices of toleration. He refuted assertions of man's wickedness and expressed confidence in the judgment and moral character of the people to choose leaders wisely. He then voiced a call for toleration: "most men . . . are rigidly tenacious of their own sentiments in religion, and disposed to impose them upon others as a standard of truth—Far from limiting my charity and confidence to men of my own denomination in religion, I suppose, and believe, sir, that there are worthy characters among men of every denomination— . . . and even among those who have no other guide in the way to virtue and heaven, than the dictates of natural religion."[16]

In this integration of the test oath issue with the cause of religious liberty, dissenting sects, religious liberals, and secular humanists found common ground. As historian Sidney Mead asserted, the secular rationalists had no interest in preserving God's dominion to judge matters of conscience. They could agree with the evangelical dissenters that religion was a matter of conscience and beyond the scope of governmental authority. They also sought to secure the best men for national leadership positions regardless of religious belief. In Federalist No. 52, for example, Madison wrote that Congress's door must be "open to merit of every description . . . without regard to . . . any profession of religious faith." Religious belief was a private matter to be protected from governmental interference. Historian H. Trevor Colbourn has noted the reliance upon Trenchard and Gordon in the drafting of the new nation's constitutions. Cato's *Letters* were frequently cited in newspapers as authority. Consistent with the ideas presented in these letters, the Founders understood liberty to include "the Right of Every Man to pursue the natural reasonable and religious Dictates of his own mind; to think what he will, and act as he thinks, provided he acts not to the Prejudice of another." In Priestley's terms, it is "the right [by which a man] has to be exempt from the control of the society, or its agents; that is, the power he has of providing for his own advantage and happiness."[17]

In a letter to the *Connecticut Courant* in late 1787, "A Landholder" (Oliver Ellsworth) identified what he perceived as a fear of some "very worthy persons" that the new government was unfavorable to religion. He disputed the basis for this fear, arguing that the Constitution must be more concerned with limiting the powers of government than with prescribing beliefs for the citizenry. Conceiving of religion as a right of personal conscience rather than as the basis of all truth and justice placed it beyond the scope of government.[18]

Many of those who argued against religious tests also expressed disdain for the emotional excesses of religious enthusiasm. Again, using Mead's terms, differences in worldview between evangelical pietists and secular rationalists, despite agreement on the issue of religious testing, percolated just slightly below the surface of the debate. In gaining alliance with evangelicals of the dissenting sects, supporters of the Constitution appealed directly to the evangelicals' fears of domination by the entrenched religious oligarchy. Providing for the continuation of religious diversity promised a free market of opinion; it ensured the dissenters of their coexistence with the traditional churches in American society. The Federalists took every advantage to emphasize the relationship between diversity, toleration, and freedom of religious opinion.[19]

Ultimately, the exclusion of religious testing did not pose a significant obstacle to ratification. Similarly, the omission of any appeal to God's assistance in the new governmental venture offended some, but it did not prevent ratification. Comments on this issue during the debates serve mostly just to demonstrate the persistence of a core group of providentialist Christians who could not quite accept either a conception of God as removed from human life nor the success of the new nation without his intervention. Congregationalists, meeting in assembly in June 1788, proposed "that some suitable Testimony might be borne against the *sinful omission* in the late Federal Constitution in not looking to God for direction, and of omitting the name of God in the Constitution." In Connecticut, one delegate advocated "an explicit acknowledgment of the being of God, his perfection, and his providence" in order to secure his blessing for the American enterprise. Ministers and their adherents who continued to look for and find God's active involvement in the lives of men refocused their attention on the morality issue that seemed to have defined Christianity for many Americans. As a source of moral authority, God could continue to play a key role in civil society even if excluded from government. A frequent theme of sermons in the early republic was that "morality [was] . . . the all important link between religion and civilization." The people were empowered with the duty to bring God into American society by way of their moral behavior. Constitutional-era preaching hinted at the battle over the design of the broader civil society hidden in the debates over the civil government.[20]

The major issue concerning religion to arise during the debate on the Constitution, and the one still debated by contemporary judges and politicians, concerned the protections of religious liberty eventually codified in the First Amendment. The First Amendment was proposed during the process of ratification to address concern over the failure of the Constitution to protect the essential rights of individual citizens from the power of the state. In November 1787, James Wilson noted that the absence of a bill of rights constituted a major roadblock to ratification but admitted surprise at this development. He remembered that a bill of rights was not even discussed at the convention in Philadelphia until three days before dissolution, and he surmised that the delegates all assumed that the rights not given to the government were retained by the people. Wilson argued, in debate with John Smilie over the need for a bill of rights, that to enumerate rights of people relative to government is, in effect, to limit those rights by reversing the traditional assumption of a social contract. Instead of reserving rights to the people, those not mentioned may be presumed to be sacrificed to the government.[21] Whatever logic there may have been to Wilson's argument, it was not sufficient to quell the demands for rights protection.

The first objection Thomas Jefferson made to the draft of the nation's charter was "the omission of a bill of rights." Similar demands were heard throughout the various state conventions considering the document. In Virginia, George Mason published his "Objections to the Constitution" in an Alexandria newspaper, chief among them being: "There is no declaration of rights; and the laws of the general government being paramount to the laws and constitutions of the several states, the declarations of rights in the separate States are no security." In New York, the "Federalist Farmer" wrote: "There are certain unalienable and fundamental rights, which in forming the social compact, ought to be explicitly ascertained and fixed—a free and enlightened people, in forming this compact, will not resign all their rights to those who govern." In North Carolina, Mr. Spencer addressed his fellow delegates, asserting: "I still think that a bill of rights is necessary. This necessity arises from the nature of human societies. When individuals enter into society, they give up some rights to secure the rest. There are certain human rights that are not to be given up, and which ought in some manner to be secured."[22]

The most prominently cited right in need of protection from the state was freedom of religion. Jefferson mentioned it first in his listing of rights to be mentioned in the Bill of Rights.[23] His concern focused less on the nature of religion as such than on the right of each person to his or her own thoughts and beliefs. For liberal advocates of Enlightenment reason, religion was presumed to be a matter of personal conscience rather than a body of doctrinal belief shared by the community. The amendment expressed a desire by Americans to see themselves as freethinkers and autonomous actors whose religious attitudes were a private matter rather than as members of a Christian society who willingly sacrificed liberty and conscience to secure social conformity with God's teachings. While their Calvinist forefathers may have come to America for the freedom to practice a particular conception of the Christian religion, most Americans in the 1780s sought more broadly to secure a freedom of conscience from state authority.

Representative of many letters written in support of religious freedom during the constitutional debates is the following passage submitted by "Centinel" (Samuel Bryan), a Philadelphia merchant, to his city's *Freeman's Journal:*

> but there is no declaration, that all men have a natural and unalienable right to worship almighty God, according to the dictates of their own consciences and understanding; and that no man ought, or of right can be compelled to attend any religious worship, or erect or support any place of worship, or maintain any ministry, contrary to, or against his own free will and consent; and that no authority can or ought to be vested in, or assumed by any power whatever, that shall in any case interfere with, or in any manner controul, the right of conscience in the free exercise of religious worship.[24]

The *Virginia Gazette* published Richard Henry Lee's letter to Governor Randolph on December 6, 1787, urging Virginia not to ratify the Constitution without a bill of rights that provided in some form "that the right of conscience in matters of religion shall be secured." He premised his position not on man's duty to God, nor on his need to provide for his salvation, but on the need to legally restrain the government from encroaching upon man's basic human rights. He referred to religion obliquely in this argument, as included in a "right of conscience," understood as consistent with Blackstonian law.[25]

The debate over the need for religious freedom clearly centered on this legalistic conception of belief as a private matter of conscience beyond the scope of governmental authority. Yet, as previously noted, some historians have contended that securing religious freedom was an inevitable result of religious pluralism and not the constitutional expression of ideological commitment.[26] Still others have maintained that the First Amendment precludes only the government favoring one sect at the expense of all others, and that the Founders recognized and intended the United States to be a "Christian nation."[27] Both the issues of religious pluralism and the extent of religious freedom embracing non-Christian beliefs were raised in the constitutional debates. The record indicates that pluralism was not the reason why the First Amendment was enacted and that religious freedom was conceived as an absolute right.

To argue that the government was prohibited from intruding into matters of religion simply because religious diversity made the establishment of any single religion impossible is to frame a positive right in negative terms. The absence of a national religion did not arise by default. There never was an attempt to establish a national religion, and the First Amendment sought to ensure that whatever uniformity of religious belief there might one day be, Congress would not act on that consensus. This point, combined with a refutation of the extent of religious diversity at the time of the Constitution, is made in a letter published in New York in 1787: "It is true, we are not disposed to differ much, at present about religion; but, when we are making a constitution it is to be hoped, for ages and millions yet unborn, why not establish the free exercise of religion, as a part of the national compact. There are other essential rights, which we have justly understood to be the rights of freemen."[28]

Religious pluralism and the inadequacy of constitutional amendments to prevent legislative tyranny were raised in arguments against a bill of rights. Those opposing the bill of rights who were trained in the law and well versed in constitutional theory contended that, so long as the people are sovereign, no constitution is unalterable and no rights secure. Therefore, the best protection of rights is a multiplicity of opinion and a cultural respect for the opinions of others.[29]

These arguments effectively defeated themselves, however, for if no constitutional provisions could limit tyranny of popular expression or protect essential rights, then the major reasons for a social contract were lost. While religious pluralism was raised in the debate over freedom of religion, this assertion surfaced only in response to the call for bill of rights protection of religious freedom and not as a reason to forgo establishment. In other words, pluralism was an argument raised against the need for the First Amendment rather than, as some suggest, the reason for its enactment.

Further, there is no evidence either of the protection of religious liberty being limited to Christians or of that protection being considered apart from a separation of church and state. Delegates to the convention had expressed admiration for the Virginia State Constitution's declaration of rights well before the ratification controversy over a bill of rights. Attention had focused on the provision of religious freedom, which Madison rewrote for George Mason to clarify that the intent was not toleration but rather "the idea of religious freedom as protected by the separation of church and state."[30]

Calls for a bill of rights securing religious freedom made clear that the right derived from the nature of man, not from the religious conditions prevailing in American society. No matter how pervasive the Christian religion might be, it could not be allowed to limit one's right to freedom of conscience. The Founders intended the First Amendment to secure absolute freedom of belief. In no way was it meant to limit any citizen's options to a selection among one of various competing Christian sects. This is evident in the language used by the states in calling for a bill of rights and in the language adopted by the first Congress in drafting the amendment.

Seven states published their ratification of the Constitution with resolutions seeking the inclusion of a bill of rights. Six of the seven included specific suggestions to guarantee religious freedom. Pennsylvania expressed a need for a bill of rights, "establishing these unalienable and personal rights of men, without the full, free, and secure enjoyment of which there can be no liberty, and over which it is not necessary for a good government to have control." The first of those listed provided that "The right of conscience shall be held inviolate and neither the legislative, executive, nor judicial powers of the United States shall have authority to alter, abrogate, or infringe any part of the Constitutions of the several states which provide for the preservation of liberty in matters of religion." New Hampshire offered: "Congress shall make no laws touching religion or to infringe on the rights of conscience." North Carolina insisted on a guarantee of religious freedom without offering specific wording. New York asserted "that the people have an equal, natural, and inalienable right freely and peaceably to exercise their religion according to the dictates of conscience." Maryland suggested "That there be no national religion established by law; but that all persons be equally entitled to protection in their religious liberty." South Carolina declined to make a specific suggestion as to the need for an amendment establishing religious freedom, but Charles Pinckney, speaking on May 14, 1788, at his state's ratifying convention expressed strong sentiments consistent with the invocations of the other states. He asserted that the people's rights must be superior to governmental authority: "We have been taught here to believe that all power of right belongs to THE PEOPLE—that it flows immediately from them, and is delegated to their officers for the public good—that our rulers are the servants of the people, amenable to their will, and created for their use." He specifically sought protection for religious belief to make Americans "the first perfectly free people the world had ever seen," noting that even in Great Britain, religious freedom is not a protected civil right.[31]

The eventual joint resolution embodying the Bill of Rights provided in its preamble, as a result of concerns expressed in the ratifying conventions to prevent an abuse or overreaching by the federal government of its powers, "that further declaratory and restrictive clauses should be added." Throughout the debates in the various states, in the written proposals for amendments offered by the states, and in the promulgation of the amendments themselves, the right to absolute liberty of conscience regarding religious belief is recognized as beyond the reach of a legitimate government. This right derived from man's nature and was accorded respect in the implementation of republican political theory conceiving of a limited government in service to man. References to freedom of religion refer to it as "full," "natural," "perfect," and "inviolable" and define it further as a matter of "conscience," "reason," or "conviction." There is no record of its acceptance by default in efforts to establish a national religion, nor of its acceptance because of the practical necessity posed by the plurality of American religious sects. To assert otherwise, as noted by religious historian Leo Pfeffer forty years ago, is unfair to the Founders' commitment to "principle."[32]

The secular language of the Constitution defined the institutional framework of American society. This is exactly what the Founders intended. Madison wrote, "we are now digesting a plan which in its operation will decide forever the fate of Republican Government."[33] Some Christians openly expressed concern with that very premise, fearing that a secular constitution marginalized God and religion. Sermons and pamphlets during this era exclaimed the irreligiosity of the Constitution:

> The manners of the people, though so little attended to by our legislators, are confessed by all to be of the utmost consequence in a commonwealth. The most profligate politician can expatiate on the necessity of good morals; but we hear little of religion from our most respected statesmen. When the discussion is of politics, she [religion] is generally kicked out of doors, as having nothing to do either with morality or civil policy. The inseparable connection between this daughter of heaven and her genuine offspring, morality, is forgotten, and her influence on civil society is almost wholly overlooked.[34]

Yet such protestations were of little consequence in the republican afterglow of revolution, and those protesting found themselves marginalized dissenters to the design of the new republic. As Jack Rakove writes, "ultimately," the ratification of the Constitution addressed "the character of the nation Americans aspired to form."[35]

Despite the secular language and tone of the nation's foundational documents and the humanistic tradition from which they derived, did the American government, in practice, not remain true to its Christian heritage? Certainly a mere recitation of selected historical events can support such a conclusion. During the 1770s and early 1780s, the Continental Congress passed laws pertaining to Sunday observance, public worship, days of thanksgiving, and Christian education. In 1777 Congress authorized the importation of twenty thousand bibles. In 1782 it issued a resolution in praise of Robert Aitken for the publication of an American edition of the Bible. All of these events occurred prior to ratification of the Constitution, however. Afterward, President Washington was inaugurated in conjunction with services held in St. Paul's Chapel performed by the chaplain of Congress. Numerous times in the administrations of Washington, Adams, and Madison, the president acted on Congressional requests to issue proclamations of days of thanksgiving to God for the nation's success. And in numerous treaties with Native Americans between 1780 and the 1830s, Congress appropriated federal funds to support Christian agencies in "educating and civilizing" the Indians and in "promoting Christianity." The very idea of giving thanks to a deity for worldly success implied an acceptance of his ability to actively intervene in the course of men's lives. Among the early presidents, only George Washington seemed even remotely comfortable with this implication. Yet he not only refused to take communion but routinely walked out of church before the performance of the ritual.[36] In public communications, Washington always conditioned religious references upon the nation's need for a moral and virtuous citizenry and carefully protected religious belief as a matter of individual "conscience" that would be respected by the separation of church and state.[37] He cited "the establishment of civil and Religious liberty [as] the motive which induced me to the Field," and as president he wrote to Baptists, Quakers, Jews, and Catholics of his and his government's commitment to "liberty of conscience." He wrote further of "mankind becom[ing] more liberal" and of his "hope ever to see America among the foremost nations in examples of justice and liberality."[38] To the Hebrew congregation in Newport, Rhode Island, in 1790, he expressed with obvious pride his feeling that:

> It is now no more that toleration is spoken of as if it were the indulgence of one class of people that another enjoyed the exercise of their inherent natural rights, for, happily, the Government of the United States, which gives to bigotry no sanction, to persecution no assistance, requires only that they who live under its protection should demean themselves as good citizens in giving it on all occasions their effectual support.[39]

Perhaps most explicitly, the "Treaty of Peace and Friendship" with Tripoli signed during his administration provides in article 2 that religious differences cannot be a cause of enmity between the nations, "as the government of the United States of America is not, in any sense, founded on the Christian religion."[40]

John Adams also issued two proclamations of thanksgiving and in his first expressed his rationale for doing so. He posited that proclamations for a day of prayer invoked "a duty [among the citizens] whose natural influence is favorable to the promotion of that morality and piety without which social happiness can not exist nor the blessings of a free government be enjoyed."

Consistent with Federalist doubts regarding the peoples' virtue, Adams issued the proclamations to create a proper republican spirit in the American peo-. ple. Jefferson, however, rejected even this during his administration, insisting that any official reference to God and his blessings violated the First Amendment. Madison reverted to a legalistic deference to Congress in the issuance of three proclamations, noting in "Whereas" clauses in each that Congress requested the act of him and he would comply. Once out of office, he expressed regret even for these tepid proclamations, wishing he had followed the lead of Jefferson.[41]

Numerous treaties with Indian nations during the early republic provided funds to Christian missionaries and philanthropic societies to "educate and civilize" Native American peoples. However, rather than an indication that the Founders did not understand the First Amendment to prohibit all support of religion, this fact provides insight into contemporary attitudes regarding Christianity and the difficulty the new government had in assuming control for public functions and wresting responsibility from previous providers. Christianity was regarded as a moralizing, and hence civilizing, influence upon people. The Indians, generally perceived as "uncivilized," were deemed to benefit from the moral teachings of Christianity. Historian Bernard Sheehan has noted that the philanthropy of the early republic emanated from a "universalizing tendency" of the Enlightenment doctrine of human equality. In efforts to incorporate the Indians into mainstream American culture, steps were taken to provide them the physical, educational, economic, and cultural tools necessary for them to make the transition. Missionaries thus served a secular governmental purpose even as they pursued their private religious goals. Alexis de Tocqueville observed that the missionaries were themselves practical men, devoted as much to securing American political interests as God's interests. Secular and spiritual interests coincided for neither the first nor the last time in American history. As president, Jefferson expressed objection to the practice of converting the Indians in order to civilize them; yet even he accepted the treaty provisions as a temporary expedient. The government's use of missionaries to civilize the Indians is perhaps best seen as a final expression of an archaic system rather than as an endorsement of Christianity by the new government.[42]

The federal and state constitutions provided the legal prescription for the formation of public institutions. The early republic faced the problem of reconciling society to the dictates of primary law. Colonial societies relied upon an integrated alliance of public and private, secular and religious organizations to address social needs. These associations were challenged by constitutional provisions that protected private contracts from governmental intervention, separated church and state, and accorded legal equality to members of society expressing unpopular and even contentious opinions. The integrated corporate communities of America's past could not long survive in this legal environment.

Colonial American society had generally accepted that the harnessing of water power for mills, the creation of canals, bridges, and roads for transportation, the formation of banks and insurance companies to provide financing and security necessary for economic growth, the exploration of wilderness areas for potential settlement, all served the entire community. In the colonial era, licensed entrepreneurs, oftentimes with monopoly interests, pursued private initiatives that addressed public needs. There appeared to be no conflict in government's granting special privileges to those who were first or best at providing the socially desirable improvements in infrastructure and economic growth. The perception of corporations as quasi-public entities was reflected in the fact that legislative action, frequently premised upon a showing of public interest, created all corporate charters even into the 1790s. Similarly, churches were used to serve social needs for education, care for the poor, and keep community records.

Private goals did not mesh so easily with public desires in the early republic, however. Licensed monopolies defied modern conceptions of the free market and of legal equality. Property rights, once established in contract, according to article 1, section 10, of the Constitution, were to be superior to legislative authority, thereby rendering governmental oversight of private enterprise for the social good a legal and political nightmare. Perhaps most significant, religiously inspired public service could not be relied upon to address republican goals and the values of a liberal economy.

The issue of education arose during the constitutional convention in the context of a broader debate on whether legislative powers should be conceptually framed or specifically enumerated.[43] On August 18, 1787, a proposal to vest the legislature with additional powers was presented and referred to committee. Included therein were independent proposals: "To establish a University"; "To encourage by proper premiums and provisions, the advancement of useful knowledge and discoveries"; "To establish seminaries for the promotion of literature and the arts and sciences"; and "To establish public institutions, rewards, and immunities for the promotion of agriculture, commerce, trades, and manufactures."[44]

The proposal for a national university created the most interest among the delegates. Benjamin Rush had made a public plea for a national university in an essay published in the *American Museum* magazine in January 1787. The idea generated support for a variety of reasons. Most existing colleges in America retained into the 1790s a theological influence and an emphasis on classical studies. College presidents and faculty were almost exclusively clergymen, and attendance in church as well as classes in Christian doctrine and ethics were required at nearly all schools. Rush, Franklin, Jefferson, and many others advocated a more modern, practical, and secular curriculum, offering courses in government, history, law, medicine, agriculture, commerce, and manufacturing. A national university, centered in the nation's capital, could provide classroom instruction in these matters while offering students exposure to the processes of political leadership. Just as important, it could train America's future leaders in a civic virtue void of denominational influences. Lastly, the availability of a first-rate school for the future elite of America in America would encourage scholars to stay at home and thereby avoid the contaminating effects of European luxury and licentiousness that were the risks of education abroad.[45]

Charles Pinckney proposed vesting in Congress a right "to establish a university in which no preferences or distinctions should be allowed on account of religion." Madison seconded the motion. It came up for a vote before the convention as a whole on September 14, 1787, and was defeated by a vote of six to four. Only Governor Morris spoke against the proposal, not antagonistic to the idea of a national university but contending that the specific enumeration of a congressional power to that end was "unnecessary."[46]

There were two other reasons for the defeat of the proposal. In the First Congress on May 3, 1790, Roger Sherman reported, "A proposition to vest Congress with the power to establish a National University was made in the General Convention; but, it was negatized. It was thought sufficient that this power should be exercised by the States in their separate capacity." The second factor in the proposal's defeat was the issue of religion. If the school were to be a religious institution, of what denomination would be its affiliation? If it were to be secular, how was the teaching of virtue and morality to be accomplished?[47]

Therefore, despite general acceptance of education as a social priority, the federal government in the early republic simply did not provide for it in any substantive way. State and local governments during this period began to assume a more significant role in education. In adopting additional responsibilities for functions previously handled by the churches, state governments engendered debate over the nature of religion in the society and the roles that government, church, and private charity would play. These early secular initiatives into education, and poor relief as well, are characterized by regional differences. New England perpetuated the role of the church in these functions longer than the mid-Atlantic or the South.

The mid-Atlantic states preferred to rely on secular private charities instead of churches to provide schooling. Despite the enactment of legal directives to ensure broad-based educational opportunities for children in Pennsylvania, Delaware, and New York, state and local governments found it difficult to raise the money and create the bureaucracies necessary to fulfill their duties. Private individuals stepped in to provide the services the public was unwilling to support with its tax dollars. In Philadelphia, wealthy merchants in 1799 founded the Philadelphia Society for the Establishment and Support of Charity schools for the "gratuitous instruction of the poor."[48] In 1800 in New York City, with a population of over sixty thousand, no tuition-free schools existed. In 1805 a group of public-spirited citizens called attention to the fact that the only schools in New York City were church schools and private schools for profit. Fearing the effects an uneducated and impoverished generation of children would have upon the future of the republic, volunteers solicited funds for the creation of the first free school in New York that was open to the public. It was built and opened in 1809.[49]

Southern states found more initial success in creating public secular schools. Virginia, Maryland, and South Carolina each adopted statewide public education programs before 1805. The state-funded schools were to teach reading, writing, and arithmetic. Despite laws providing for public funding, most of the support for the schools came from private funds. Consistent with the growing secularization of southern society by this time, no mention was made, in any state, of instruction in morality or religion. Certainly religious texts, including the Bible, continued to be used in classrooms. Yet, in the South as elsewhere, the use of new texts expressing virtues in secular rather than religious terms and containing lessons void of biblical teachings gradually increased with their greater availability. While the schools were open to all, preference in admission was given to poor orphans and to children of indigent parents.[50]

Other states acted creatively in seeking to fund common schools. In 1796 Delaware created a school fund from the sale of tavern and marriage licenses and in 1817 began funding the education of the poor with one-thousand-dollar annual grants to the counties. In 1812 Maryland created a school fund from a bank tax. Kentucky in 1798 and 1808 granted land for academies. By 1828 most states had created permanent school funds, the income of which was used to supplement the local funding of schools. The funds were generated by the sale of lands, lotteries, and special taxes.[51]

In New England, state educational policies recognized the continued religious establishments. While taxes, approved at town meetings, provided the funds for public education, local instruction generally conformed to the religious and moral precepts of the town church. An emphasis on religious instruction continued even after the 1780s, when Massachusetts and Connecticut created state funds and regulatory guidelines to assist localities in educating the young of those states.[52]

Even in states that began new programs in public education, private church schools continued to flourish. Denominational academies dominated the preparatory school market in the late eighteenth and early nineteenth centuries. The growth of new Christian sects contributed to the proliferation of denominational academies. The Methodists founded the Ebenezar School in Virginia in 1785, the Bethel School in Kentucky in 1790, the Cokesbury School in South Carolina in 1793, and the Newburry County School in South Carolina in 1796.[53] In many locations these denominational academies provided the only educational opportunity. Even when state laws both required localities to provide schools and offered financial support, public schools frequently were not created. In rural areas education remained a secondary concern, as many communities even with state help could not afford the cost of public education or find suitable teachers.

The early state constitutions and legislative programs addressing education demonstrate that most states struggled with how to grant religious freedom and separate church from state while still providing for the states' educational needs. Continuing the colonial reliance on the churches to teach children eliminated the need for increasing state authority and taxes in order to meet a societal need. Constitutions were written not merely as legal documents creating political entities but also as plans for harnessing social resources to address societal concerns.

Care for the poor had traditionally been a church function in western Europe before the colonization of America. Parishes continued to perform this role in most of colonial America. New England's colonial integration of church and state actually reduced the role of its churches in poor relief as theocratic governments assumed responsibility for tending to the weak, aged, and incompetent in fulfillment of man's obligation to God. Each town in Massachusetts generally provided for its own poor. Yet when disasters struck, as in 1675 when King Philip's War created a refugee problem, the General Court assumed broader responsibilities to address public needs. Other New England colonies followed the Massachusetts model. By a law issued in 1673, Connecticut provided that "every town . . . shall maintain their [sic] own poor." In 1702 legislation outlined procedures for the duties of selectmen or overseers of the poor and also provided for taxes for the defense and care of the poor. In 1713 the state created a system of workhouses and houses of correction.[54]

By the early 1700s New England's treatment of the poor reflected changes in social perception. Enlightenment liberalism encouraged a view of man as being capable of solving his own problems. Poverty was neither a providential opportunity to practice charity nor an inevitable condition that befell those on the fringes of social productivity. As corporate communities broke down, New Englanders felt less inclined to assume the financial burden of providing for the destitute—especially newcomers to town, vagabonds, or the morally bereft. Many towns passed "warning out laws," requiring vagrants and possible dependents to leave. In 1719 Irish immigrants considered likely to require public support were not allowed to disembark from a ship in Boston harbor.[55]

As the eighteenth century unfolded, New England adopted new means of addressing the poor, building workhouses for those who could work and imposing criminal sentences upon the poor to remove them from the streets. The Revolution and the constitutional era brought little official change to this structure, as government in this region had a long history of involvement in poor relief. The most significant change was in the money spent by the state. Expenditures for poor relief dropped relative to prewar highs, and churches assumed greater costs in providing charity to the poor.[56]

Outside of New England, colonial churches had assumed sole responsibility for poor relief, a condition that was intolerable in the early republic. Each of the original southern states, during the 1780s, created a position of county overseer of the poor. Kentucky did so in 1793. These states also set tax rates to cover the expense of poor relief. The law transformed a colonial parish responsibility into a public secular concern.[57] Prior to the Revolution, church wardens within each southern parish either settled dependents in private residences, supplemented their means with church funds drawn from poor taxes, or removed the poor from their jurisdiction. The colonial governments supported the churches in these responsibilities. However, the liberal mood of postrevolutionary society reflected little concern for the welfare of the distressed. While churches evoked moral duties in support of their efforts, elected overseers had no equivalent means to combat popular indifference. In 1781 the North Carolina legislature noted that the poor were "reduced to great distress to the scandal and disgrace of society." In response, North Carolina undertook a program of building almshouses at public expense. The houses expressed society's growing intolerance of the poor, at once removing them from public interaction and compelling them to labor.[58]

The colonial model for poor relief that prevailed in the mid-Atlantic states was similar to that existing in the South. Colonial parish churches used a variety of means to address local poverty, including settlement, apprenticeships, and charitable relief payments. Colonial laws required residents within church parishes to pay taxes both to sustain the church in its mission and to support it in these civil functions. In 1773 New York attempted to control the churches in performance of these duties by appointing state overseers of the poor to supervise the church officials. The temporary partnership between church and state in this function did not last long. In 1784, for example, New York abolished the parish as a form of civic designation and repealed all laws providing public funds to religious organizations even for the performance of public service.[59]

Colonial Pennsylvania combined the Calvinist attitudes of Christian duty with the modern embrace of economic self-fulfillment. William Penn wrote to his wife, "Pity the distressed and hold out a hand of help to them; it may be your case; and as you mete to others God will mete to you again." Early Pennsylvania incorporated Christian charity into its civic program for poor relief. In 1705 the assembly provided that the county justices of the peace elect two overseers of the poor for each township, "to be employed for the relief of the poor, indigent and impotent persons, inhabiting within the said Township." One of the means townships used to care for the poor was to pay workhouses to employ and shelter them. Quakers built and operated a number of Friends almshouses for this purpose in the early 1700s. As in other colonies, Pennsylvanians expressed less toleration of poverty after the early 1700s. Recipients of poor relief were required to wear a large "P" on the right sleeve of their garments, and increased regulations restricted the influx of vagabonds or poor immigrants.[60]

During the Revolution, the Overseers of the Poor operated as a private charitable enterprise supported and led by such men as John Dickinson and Joseph Wharton. However, the Revolution took a toll on the family fortunes of the Overseers, so that in 1781 the legislature passed an act for the public support of the corporation to enable it to continue to provide its public services.

The board of the Overseers soon found the public assistance insufficient to the needs of the poor and in the 1780s repeatedly pleaded with the assembly for greater public action. Finally, in 1788 the assembly consolidated Philadelphia's major poor relief organizations into a single corporation, Guardians of the Poor of the City of Philadelphia, and provided for increased tax support.[61]

During the constitutional era, Americans reconceived of religion as a matter of personal conscience. This reconception compelled not only a tolerance of a wide range of beliefs but also the protection of religious belief from government interference. Religion, as a matter of individual conscience, was appreciated as serving individual and private needs and longings, not as addressing communal and public concerns. The protection of religious freedom in state and federal constitutions derived from this reconception of religion. Framed in this way, freedom of religion required more than mere toleration; it required the abstention of government from intrusion into personal and private matters. Churches, and religious doctrine, would have to be removed from public institutions.

In removing the churches from their colonial role in providing education and poor relief, state governments of the early republic began to impose a liberal secularism. This removal of the churches from their traditional roles, more than the language expressed in the primary laws of the nation or the states, awakened church people to the divisiveness in cultural ideals then existing in the new nation. Now aware of the threat that the laws posed to their goals of a Christian commonwealth, Christian leaders rushed to undo, or at least to clarify on more palatable terms, the constitutional provisions guaranteeing religious freedom. Religious freedom evidently led inevitably to the separation of church and state—something few Christian leaders desired. By this time, however, the primary laws of the nation and the states had been drafted, and in these laws lay the seeds of legal actions that would compel even greater separation. One war having been won, a new war was just beginning.

4

God Is as Man Makes Him

Ideology and Religion in the Early Republic

Religious organizations in America are "unrecognized by law except as voluntary associations of private citizens."

Lord Bryce, comment after a trip to the United States

THE UNITED STATES from 1789 to 1820 was divided by an ideological conflict over the values of the new nation. Many historians have noted the fragmentation of political consensus in the Federalist-Republican divide, but the ideological debate over values during this period is only minimally explained by party label. While secularists among the Jeffersonian Republicans appear to have spearheaded the liberal position, some of their opposition came from within their own party and some of their support came from Federalists, as the Marshall Court's use of the contract clause demonstrates. This debate over values, then, was ideological rather than political. It concerned the role of the church and the issue of disestablishment, but its major focus was the extent to which law and social institutions would embody a Christian communitarian ethic or an individualistic rights-oriented perspective. Those who looked to God for authority contended over a series of social issues with those who found authority in man's use of his reason. Education, crime and punishment, regulation of business and entertainment, and responsibilities for the poor all presented opportunities for each side to assert its position, and all served as battlegrounds in the ideological war for control of the new nation's values.

The prominent legal historian William Nelson has written that "although little legal change occurred during the war itself, the attempts of the revolutionary generation to explain and justify the war and its political results set loose new intellectual and social currents which ultimately transformed the legal and social structure of the new state."[1] During the early republic, the nation's laws had to be rewritten to conform to republican principles. As American society adopted a liberal version of republicanism at the turn of the century, law came to express a firm commitment to protecting individual liberty and a rejection of communitarian values.

As early as 1787 an English visitor to America, the Rev. Charles Nisbet, noted with despair the growing individualism among the people of the new nation. He commented that Americans seemed to want and to need cohesion but could not find it, given what was for him their distorted framework of values. He wrote that popular sentiment expressed "the moral duty of the people to pursue their own happiness"—that each is his "moral agent. . . [free] to dispose of himself and be his own master in all respects."[2] Many American clergymen were coming to the same realization by the close of the eighteenth century, bemoaning not only a change in people's values but, more significant, the substitution of reason for religion as a basis of those values. Their sermons and writings reflect a divergence in approaches to deal with this development. Some ministers repositioned religion in service to society as a means of securing moral behavior, while more ardent traditionalists took to their pulpits to condemn the loss of piety in the new nation.

In the early republic, contracts defined social relationships.[3] Contract law recognized the parties to a contract as equals, bound by law to perform their mutual obligations. It assumed that any potential party to a contract was reasonable, rational, and capable of making his own bargain. Community status, Christian brotherhood, and social deference became irrelevant in the enforcement of a wide range of social activities, ranging from the sale of goods and labor to marriage and military service. Moreover, contract law asserted its own system of morality. Performing one's contractual obligations, nothing more nor less, established one as trustworthy. Frequently this morality was at odds with both Christian teachings and America's communitarian heritage.

The contrasting worldviews may best be illustrated by an example. Assume that a wealthy farmer was relaxing in a 1790 tavern having a beer with other local gentlemen, when a poor drunk, a father of four young children, came into town leading his last cow. The cow was not a prime specimen, worth perhaps five dollars. Its owner wanted only to spend the afternoon with a bottle of whiskey, which cost two dollars. He asked the bar patrons if anyone would buy his cow. Receiving no offers, he encouraged interest by proposing the sale of the cow for only four dollars. Still there was no offer. Finally, the rich farmer, knowing the poor man's alcoholism and the price of a bottle of whiskey, offered two dollars for the cow. An agreement was reached, hands were shaken, the money and the cow were exchanged. In the contract law of the 1790s, the agreement would be enforceable. The bargain was acceptable for having been struck between two legal equals who owed no duty to each other besides that embodied in their contract. The poor man's alcoholism and the needs of his family would be of no concern in the enforcement of the contract. Yet the legality of the bargain does not render it acceptable under traditional conceptions of Protestant Christian morality, which proscribe taking advantage of a neighbor's weakness in order to enrich oneself while causing harm to that neighbor. Perhaps even more significant, in colonial America such a contract would most likely not have been enforced because of overriding concerns with community welfare. Equity, not contract law, would have prevailed.[4] In a colonial parish, where fair prices were set by community standards rather than by market conditions, the wealthy assumed a duty to care for the poor, and moral imperatives discouraged excessive drinking and the poor care of children. Religion served as the basis of colonial moral values and of colonial law.

Contract law derived from the basic Enlightenment truths of human equality and economic freedom. It recognized no privilege, but also no duty beyond that expressed in the contract. It preserved the free wills of individual actors to pursue their own interests unencumbered by the values or restrictions of the government, the clergy, or a social elite. During the early republic, legally free and equal citizens took control of their own lives in contracts addressing everything from marriage and home to employment. In a common-law system in which precedent created rules of law, the doctrine of contract law, instead of Christian morality or equity, applied to determine right from wrong in society. Judges replaced clergymen as social arbiters, and between 1783 and 1820 the number of attorneys increased at a rate four times that of the national population.[5]

The burgeoning growth and influence of contract law after the Revolution embodied a liberal republican ideology also expressed in the new nation's institutions. Conceiving of the new republic as a nation of laws, not of men, judges intentionally tried to render decisions that were unencumbered by social interests—including those of the clergy. Law imposed a harsh rationality untempered by sentimental appeals to sympathy or ethical duty. The communal welfare was not something to be decreed by a moral or governing elite but was rather to be pursued through, in the words of Thomas Jefferson, "each individual seeking his own good in his own way."[6] To Jefferson this was an ideal, not a deprecation of moral values. Jefferson appreciated, far more than his peers, the magnitude of law's ability to transform his society. While men like Washington and Hamilton perceived republican virtue to be the province of an educated and wealthy elite, Jefferson understood that once the law made all men equals the common man would practice republican virtue because his economic freedom depended upon the maintenance of his political freedom. The Jeffersonians who controlled the White House, the legislature, and most of the statehouses through 1828, during what is referred to as the "Era of Good Feelings," were even more rabid in preserving economic freedom than was their party's founder. Accordingly, the conception of virtue changed to reflect the egalitarianism inherent in a system of free enterprise, expanding to include a recognition of the moral value of labor. In the early republic, labor itself was deemed virtuous, with wealth and productivity the respective personal and societal rewards. In this era, government functioned primarily to preserve an environment in which individuals were free to pursue their self-interests in competition with others. This was largely a negative function, exercised chiefly by the courts as arbiters ensuring a level field of play. One irony of Jeffersonian America was that, despite the Democratic Republican party's preference for legislative over judicial lawmaking, the courts adapted social practice to liberal ideals through private law court cases.[7]

While political leaders fought their constitutional and public law battles over how much the new nation was going to reflect "republican virtue" or "democratic self-interest," the decision was largely being made in the private law forum. The importance of private law courts derived in part from the legal confusion following the Revolution. The legal historian Morton Horwitz finds that postrevolutionary America had to reconstruct the legitimacy of law on a consensual foundation. This required either legislative enactment, reliance on custom, or, as James Wilson suggested, acceptance of common-law judges as agents of a sovereign people. The judges themselves chose the third option in the absence of any other authority. Judges came to see their function as having expanded beyond the mere application of existing law to the reshaping and modifying of the law to meet the needs and wants of a growing society. Judges believed they could be more responsive than the legislatures—they had to be, for their dockets would not wait for legislative direction. Judicial authority implicitly remained checked, for if the legislature disagreed with a developing common-law doctrine it could always reverse it. Meanwhile, the growth of judicial authority created an expanded role to be played by common-law judges in directing the nation's course into the nineteenth century. In the early republic these judges applied both the body of contract law available through precedent and the doctrine upon which it rested to a wide variety of cases.[8]

The judicial assumption of greater power did not meet with universal approbation. Jefferson wrote in 1785 that, by applying their own sense of right and reason, judges had sought to render the law more certain but instead made it more uncertain.[9] Republican theory provided that under a constitutional framework judges were to follow the letter of the law as expressed by the populace through its legislature. Partially in response to these attacks, a self-conscious judiciary moved to ensure greater legitimacy by insisting on published reports of common-law precedents, relying on stricter enforcement of legal rules of procedure and thereby sharpening pleadings and limiting the role of juries, elevating the stature of a professionalizing bar, and relying on established common-law principles to instruct juries or set aside jury verdicts. In the process, law became even more ordered and rational and less vulnerable to moral or ethical influences.

From 1780 to 1820 the law changed from a body of preexisting rules to be discovered and applied by judges to an embodiment of liberal republicanism that could create social change. As legal historian Peter Hoffer notes, lawyers and judges "used legal modes of reasoning to transform the common law from a body of precedent to an abstract idea of what good law should be." Horwitz contends that the change in property laws in the early republic reflects a reconception of property rights from recognition of one's right to the peaceful enjoyment of one's own property to a social recognition of property embodying the potential for productivity and development.[10] Judges generally shared a liberal interest in economic development and could foster a prodevelopment agenda through changes in common-law doctrines. Contract-law principles were used to rewrite the laws of property, negligence, nuisance, marriage, and labor relations. In each of these doctrinal areas of law, common-law rules expressed the shared belief of the liberal judges and their business partners that moralistic concern for the quiet and the weak cannot disrupt the pursuits of the exuberant and the strong.

In applying this developing law of contracts in the early republic, common-law courts rejected the old principle that a contract was rooted in the justice or fairness of the underlying exchange. This doctrine was antagonistic to merchants because it did not always compel parties to live up to their business agreements. By the 1830s Justice Story could legitimately look back on fifty years of legal history to express the prevailing rule of contracts as the "will theory of contract law." Assuming parties to a contract to be free and equal actors, the law gave effect to the "will of the parties" as expressed in their bargain.[11]

The elimination of political controls over economic endeavor unleashed a previously unparalleled increase in commercial activity.[12] Historian Gordon Wood described this new social ideal as a "liberal, democratic, commercially advanced world of individual pursuits of happiness . . . [defined by the] promotion of entrepreneurial interests of ordinary people [in] their endless buying and selling, their bottomless passion for luxurious consumption." In a letter of April 6, 1786, a friend of Jefferson's expressed the joy Americans felt in their economic expansion, reciting but a few examples: "Population is increasing, new houses building, new lands clearing, new settlements forming, and new manufacturers establishing with a rapidity beyond conception." The *Niles Weekly Register* from December 1816 described an "Almost universal ambition to get forward." In a public address in Portland, Maine, in 1825 Charles Stewart Davis lauded the growth of individual freedom behind this economic growth, in reference to the "useful and generous strife of competition and emulation" then prevalent.[13]

Not all observers expressed similar enthusiasm for these social changes. Benjamin Rush's despair lies barely hidden between the lines when he writes:

> In walking our streets I have often been struck with the principal subjects of conversation of our citizens. Seldom have I heard a dozen words of which "Dollar," "discount," and "a good Spec" did not compose a part. . . . Not only our streets but our parlors are constantly vocal with the language of a broker's office, and even at convivial dinners, "Dollars" are a standing dish upon which all feed with rapacity and gluttony.

The substitution of a free market economy in place of paternalistic management eroded the sense of community that existed prior to the Revolution, creating for many a frustrating sense of disorientation. William Wirt derided

Dr. Benjamin Rush—Rush in many ways epitomized the tension inherent in America's acceptance of Enlightenment liberalism and its devotion to Christianity. Courtesy Presbyterian Historical Society, Presbyterian Church (USA) (Philadelphia).

his fellow Virginians for their decline in communitarian sympathies, noting that despite their great wealth they eschewed "public improvements" such as "roads and highways," and "public education."[14] A man's work, and in the case of a hero such as Washington or Jefferson even his image on an unimaginable array of trinkets and keepsakes, was converted into a commodity. Contract law created an equality of opportunity, but it imposed a depersonalizing objectivity upon all Americans.[15] Contract law also provided an ideological basis for ignoring the poor. In a land of equal opportunity, poverty could more easily be seen as a product of laziness, extravagance, wantonness, or stupidity. Further, one's social duties, once governed by proscriptive law and not prescriptive Christian morality, extended only as far as one's own inclinations required.

By the 1790s social change had become a political issue, ripe with contention over the role of religion in American society. Religious dissenters had generally aligned themselves politically with candidates opposed to religious establishment, most frequently Republicans. Jefferson's candidacy in 1800 stretched the limits of this political connection. Baptists, for instance, were generally sympathetic to Republicans, but they distanced themselves from the radical religious sentiments of Jefferson. The *Newark Gazette* professed that the major issue of the campaign was "God—and a Religious President; or . . . Jefferson—and no God!!!" The candidacy and election of Jefferson challenged assumptions about the providential inspiration of the nation's early successes and the attainability of the goal of a Christian society. Thomas Robbins, a Connecticut minister, expressed his hopes and fears to his congregation in 1800: "I do not believe that the Most High will permit a howling atheist to sit at the head of the nation." During the summer and fall of 1800, Lucius Horatio Stockton of New Jersey lectured and handed out pamphlets prophesizing the end of Christian religion in America if Jefferson were elected. The issues in the campaign of 1800 not only concerned economic growth, foreign policy, and the limits of government power to intrude upon free speech and political expression but also concernd the religious future of America.[16]

Many clergymen advocated support of Federalist candidates in 1800 in the hope that Christian doctrine could influence popular sentiment and government policies as a vital political force in the creation of a Christian commonwealth. Ministers in 1800—and in subsequent contests between Federalists and Republicans—used their influence to connect Christian goals with voting behavior. Ely advised his Connecticut congregation, "We are a Christian nation: we have a right to demand that all our rulers in their conduct shall conform to Christian morality; and if they do not, it is the duty and privilege of Christian freemen to make a new and better election." It is hard to imagine a Republican candidate of the early 1800s even referring to an elected official as a "ruler," much less requiring a religious litmus test. The goal for men like Ely remained what it had been for earlier believers— the creation of a fully Christian society.[17] The problem was how to achieve this goal in the context of a society that valued liberty of thought. To profess as one's goal the universality of Christian belief is to assert to nonbelievers that their beliefs, ideas, and values are wrong and, furthermore, need to be changed. Yet, in a society in which religion is a matter of individual conscience (that is, a concern of private minds rather than public truths), any attempts to achieve cultural purity of religious sentiment would challenge both the legal idea of religious liberty and the prevailing cultural acceptance of religion only in service to man.

The liberals in the Republican party offered an alternative humanist vision, but they recognized that speaking out against religion was not an opportunistic political move. Jefferson muted his religious comments during 1800, and Aaron Burr was counseled by his advisors to be mindful of the Presbyterian vote and to be sure to attend church periodically. Silence on religious issues should not be misinterpreted as an endorsement of a Christian influence in affairs of state among the Republican leadership. In discussing religious freedom as early as 1786 in a letter to Jefferson, Madison wrote, "I flatter myself [that] this country [has] extinguished forever the ambitious hope of making laws for the human mind."[18] More than an expression of Republican attitudes on the limited scope of government and the need to protect civil rights, Madison's statement reflects an implicit understanding of religion as subject to each man's personal understanding. Madison could argue that society and its government must move to embrace the undeniable truths of natural law, but he made no such claim regarding Christianity. To the Republican leadership, Christianity remained a theory sprung from the minds of men—not a truth delivered to them by God through the being of Jesus Christ. Law, not religious belief, served as the final arbiter for these men. When Jefferson and Madison wrote the Kentucky and Virginia Resolutions in protest of the Alien and Sedition Acts, they argued that the enactments were wrong because they violated natural rights and republican laws. It was law that had to be protected, through an independent judiciary—in Madison's words, acting as an impenetrable "bulwark provided against . . . legislative" encroachments upon the Bill of Rights. Elsewhere he warned of "the danger of silent accumulations and encroachments by Ecclesiastical Bodies [that] have not sufficiently engaged attention in the United States."[19]

Jefferson, too, refused to subordinate law or policy to Christian prescriptions for the good society. He saw law as both embodying the philosophical essence of the American Revolution and constituting the means by which American society could be reformed to reflect the values of the Revolution. Primarily, he sought through law to eradicate all vestiges of aristocracy and to eliminate all impositions on individual freedom that derived from an archaic code of Christian communitarianism. In this way he could foster the development of a republic based on individual merit and initiative.[20] One of Jefferson's chief complaints regarding the judiciary was its tendency to read Christianity into the common law, creating public policy never enacted by any legislature. Describing his vision of ideal government in his first inaugural address, Jefferson refused to consider the imposition even of Christian morals upon the governors or the governed, advocating only "a wise and frugal government which shall restrain men from injuring one another, which shall leave them otherwise free to regulate their own pursuits of industry improvement, and which shall not take from the mouth of labor the bread it has earned." Both a higher moral order and the paternalistic elite necessary to enforce it were absent from this conception.[21]

Jefferson accepted most of the Bible as myth, the trinity as fiction, and Jesus as a mere mortal—an exemplar of man's innate moral sense, and therefore exhibit "A" of the Enlightenment's conception of man as inherently benevolent as well as reasonable and rational.[22] He excised the Bible to reduce it to a treatise of moral behavior demonstrated through the words and actions of Jesus as a moral man. In this form, once void of mysticism and any promise of salvation, he felt that the text would offer a moral lesson.

During the early 1800s, in statehouses across America, Republicans fought for the total separation of church and state on grounds that "conduct alone is the subject of human laws," and religious belief is a matter of one's own conscience. When relying on man's ability to perceive truth through reason and science, religion remained unverifiable and problematic. In 1809 in the North Carolina House of Delegates, during debate on whether to require a Protestant test oath for state office holding, Jacob Henry argued: "the day, I trust, has long passed, when principles *merely speculative* were propagated by force." After 1800 all new states had to provide guarantees of religious freedom in order to join the union. The act creating the Louisiana Territory in 1804 provided for religious freedom, as did the 1819 treaty with Spain concerning ceded Florida territories. These policy initiatives under Republican presidential administrations extended religious freedom on the implicit assumption that religious beliefs could not be proved and therefore remained speculative, subjective, and well beyond the realm of rational government.[23]

The transformation of a communitarian society dependent upon Christian ethics to an individualistic society rooted in legal rights was part of the process of separating church and state. Between 1780 and 1820 the population of the United States more than tripled. Perhaps more significant, however, by 1821 the nine new states formed since ratification of the Constitution contained over 25 percent of the nation's people. Americans, in pursuit of dreams and fortunes small and large, moved west, and in the process broke up families and communities as they built farms and businesses. The new legal framework of the early republic fostered and accompanied this pace of development. American governments had granted less than one dozen charters of private incorporation in the entire colonial era. In the early republic, charters of private incorporation embodied the use of contract-law principles to enable individuals to pursue commercial goals, enriching themselves and benefiting society. Over three hundred charters were granted from the 1780s to 1800; and in the first fifteen years of the new century, governments issued nearly two thousand new corporate charters. During the 1780s states ceased to require special legislative enactments of incorporation and established bureaucratic offices to process incorporation requests. The U.S. Congress also sought to assist in the process of economic expansion, voting in 1810 to require postmasters to keep their offices (already open seven days a week) accessible to the public for extended hours. Subsequent legislation required the offices to be kept open all day.[24]

Jefferson's own efforts to revise the laws provided object lessons for Republicans serving in courtrooms and statehouses after 1800. While serving with George Wythe and Edmund Pendleton on the Committee to Revise the Laws of Virginia from 1777 to 1779, Jefferson prioritized inheritance reform. He sought to respect each individual's rights to property—a key component of his liberal republican ideology. Inheritance reform influenced how Virginians thought about themselves and their families. Most Americans of that era died intestate, without wills, and state statutes dictated the distribution of assets. Jefferson rejected adopting the principles of inheritance recently presented by Sir William Blackstone in his *Commentaries on the Laws of England*. Blackstone perceived the family as a corporate institution. English law functioned to preserve the "family's" property through recognizing a patriarchal dynasty. Mirroring the communalistic paternalism of other laws in place during the colonial period, primogeniture awarded decedents' lands to their oldest sons, establishing them as patriarchal benefactors for others in their families. Dower, a law providing a minimal share of a decedent's estate to his wife while dividing the bulk of the personal property among the children, assumed the duty of a male son to care for his mother. A further encumbrance upon the freedom of heirs was embodied in the law of entail, which allowed a testator (one who drafts a will) to restrict the uses of inherited property and to prohibit its sale or other alienation during the recipient's lifetime. Jefferson hated the impositions of dependency, duty, and restriction of progress contained in these laws. In his reform of Virginia's laws he abolished entail and primogeniture and created new inheritance rights for daughters and even illegitimate children.[25]

Other states soon followed the model presented by Jefferson's reform of inheritance laws. Yet inheritance law reform constituted only one part of the broad changes that occurred in family law during the early republic. The household was reconceived as a "collection of distinct individuals," rejecting the ideas of corporate patriarchy. Law, embodying liberal ideology, became the means of protecting individual rights. For individuals to be equal within a society, they first had to be equal within the family.[26]

Perhaps no personal legal matter better illustrates the change in values in late eighteenth-century America than does marriage. First, the decision to marry became less a concern of family economics and more a consideration of personal desire. Second, during the Revolutionary era and the early republic, laws recognized a greater liberality to granting divorces. Marriage remained a sacred union, but this understanding was tempered by protecting, in the words of a 1775 magazine article, the "reasonable liberty" of the two parties to the marriage "contract." A marriage contract, like all others, had to be a voluntary agreement between two equal parties. Michael Grossberg, in his explanation of the Jeffersonian transformation of family law, refers to Sir Henry Maine's theory of societal progress in moving from a "status" (based) society to a "contract" (based) society. He quotes Maine on this point: "the individual was 'steadily being substituted for the family as the unit of which civil laws take account.'"[27]

Republican leadership also required changes in education to better equip the young to participate in a democracy. This preparation included moral instruction, but only in the context of a practical education. The Republican party tapped into an issue that by the 1790s had gained widespread social support. One of several "Essays by a Farmer," published in the *Maryland Gazette* between February and April 1788, made the following argument:

Seminaries of useful learning, with the professorships of political and domestic economy might be established in every county, discarding the philosophy of the moon and skies, we might descend to teach our citizens what is
useful in this world—the principles of free government, illustrated by the
history of mankind—the sciences of morality, agriculture, commerce, the
management of farms and household affairs—The light would penetrate
where mental darkness now reigns.—Do these things and in very few years,
the people instead of abusing, would wade up to their knees in blood to defend their governments.[28]

The change in the public's conception of morality, embracing civic virtue
over religious piety, was accompanied by other secular emphases that also
were reflected in society's educational goals. Benjamin Rush encouraged
education as a means not only of "amass[ing] wealth" but also of fostering patriotism: "Above all he must love life and endeavor to acquire as
many of its conveniences as possible by industry and economy, but he
must be taught that this life 'is not his own' when the safety of the country requires it."[29]

Writing in 1790 Noah Webster criticized the old academic attention to
"dead languages" and stressed both the interest and social utility of
teaching history, commerce, geography, ethics, and government. Webster
recognized that the students were merchants, mechanics, and farmers of
tomorrow: "It is an object of vast magnitude that systems of education
should be adopted and pursued which may not only diffuse a knowledge
of the sciences but may implant in the minds of the American youth the
principles of virtue and of liberty and inspire them with just and liberal
ideas of government and with an inviolable attachment to their own
country." One year later, Robert Coram concurred in Webster's sentiments, when he wrote:

No modes of faith, systems of manners, or foreign or dead languages should be
taught in those schools. As none of them are necessary to obtain a knowledge
of the obligations of society, the government is not bound to instruct the citizens in any thing of the kind.—No medals or premiums of any kind should be
given under the mistaken notion of exciting emulation. Like titles of nobility,
they are not productive of a single good effect but of many very bad ones: . . .
In republican governments the praises of good men, and not medals, should be
esteemed the proper reward of merit.

People had to be prepared to assume productive societal roles. Education
prepared the young for those roles. Coram argued that the social contract's
protection of private property was premised on the assumption that every
person in the society would have an opportunity to earn a living. He then
concluded that:

> As it is by the knowledge of some art or science that man is to provide for subsistence in civil society. . . . These means of acquiring knowledge . . . should be as inherent qualities in the nature of the government, that is, the education of the children should be provided for in the constitution of every state. Education, then, ought to be secured by government to every class of citizens, to every child in the state. . . . Education should not be left to the caprice or negligence of parents.[30]

Not surprisingly, several church groups bemoaned the deemphasis of religion and community in American society. Sermons noted the sacrifice of enduring happiness within God's kingdom for the temporal pleasures of selfish pursuit. The Associated Presbytery of Pennsylvania felt compelled to issue a solemn warning to Americans. In it these churchmen decried the abundance of "infidels" and cautioned that those who "ascribe a freedom of will to fallen man" risk the eternal damnation of their souls for the momentary pleasure of earthly satisfaction.[31]

Alexis de Tocqueville observed that "while the law allows the American people to do everything, there are things which religion prevents them from imagining and forbids them to dare." The growth in extramarital sex, consumption of alcohol, and usurious business practices in the early republic gives some indication of just how little most Americans felt religion hindered their pursuits. Historian Richard Godbeer refers to a "Sexual Revolution" in America during the late eighteenth century. From the Revolution until the 1820s, between one-third to one-half of all first births were products of premarital or extramarital sex. Drinking also increased in the early republic as taverns came to epitomize the egalitarianism of the postrevolutionary era. Gentleman and ruffian, employer and employee drank together in public denizens and private parlors. In 1810 the United States produced over 22 million gallons of liquor in fifteen thousand distilleries, nearly all of which was consumed domestically by a mere 7 million Americans. This amounts to three gallons of liquor (not including beer and wine) for every man, woman, and child in the country. Those who bemoaned the loss of community in America were not looking in the bars. Holidays, especially the Fourth of July, were celebrated less as days of reverence and thanksgiving than as opportunities for all forms of sensual gratification.[32]

Godbeer notes that the growing awareness of individual rights, including a perceived "right to privacy," fostered new social attitudes that considered a neighbor's sexual behavior, drinking, and church attendance none of anyone else's business. He rightly identifies and examines two components of this social movement: the decline of "the prerogatives of patriarchal absolutism," as a means of elite control of a community's moral behavior, and the growth of a sophisticated or cosmopolitan ideal of "genteel libertinism" that justified the pursuit of personal satisfaction among comfortable men and women in the postrevolutionary era. Both components are compatible with revolutionary ideas of liberating the individual from artificial restraints, be they economic, political, or social in focus. Godbeer describes "young people" in the aftermath of the Revolution, who "took full advantage of the increasingly permissive atmosphere, experimenting sexually not only within the context of courtship, but also as they dallied in more casual and transitory liaisons." For a time, neither men nor women incurred censure or loss of stature for such actions.[33]

Various church groups condemned this behavior as a decline in American morality, but their censure did not stop with sex and alcohol. Despite the prohibition of "laws respecting religion" in the U.S. Constitution and in those of several states, ministers of different denominations united in calls for a return to legislation derived from Christian morality. Isaac Backus, Timothy Dwight, Lyman Beecher, and Jedidiah Morse all decried theater, profanity, card playing, gambling, and drunkenness and encouraged legislation to prohibit them. They found little support for subordinating commercial interests and personal liberties to evangelical notions of morality. At the same time, some private social organizations provoked fear and distrust from outsiders. Evangelical ministers viewed with suspicion any private clubs that were closed to the community at large, wondering what sinister plans might be afoot. In the 1790s Backus launched an attack on Freemasons as "worshippers of Diana [more] than lowly Jesus." Baptist churches in New England responded by making masonry a cause for excommunication. Ministers also attacked the popularity of reading novels, especially Gothic romances, as promoting immorality. In their minds the romances emphasized sexual passion and reading was itself an individualistic selfish activity—a wasteful unproductive use of time that could be used in service to God or man. The fact that most of these books were written and read by women was seen as further evidence of societal decay and corruption. This clerical reaction to certain reading expressed as well as any issue of the day the depth of division between Enlightenment liberals and those who, in the early republic, still looked to God for authority.[34]

To some extent, the contrasting attitudes toward women in the debate over romantic novels indicate another source of friction between the contesting parties. Liberal reforms in the laws regarding marriage, inheritance, property ownership, and sexual activities provide evidence of an increased recognition of women's rights in the early republic. Yet few if any Jeffersonians could ever be confused for a women's liberationist. That said, advances for women in business, education, and sexual freedom seemed to parallel the decline in religious influences in government and society. From Warrentown, North Carolina, in the early 1800s, after the disestablishment of the Anglican Church, Rachel Mordecai could write to her friend in England that, despite being a Jewish female, all the opportunities she sought were open to her. Her father operated a successful female academy in their hometown. Many ministers saw the decline in their own authority as more than coincidental with the simultaneous rise of women's social participation. One preacher condemned the practice of dissenting clergy who allowed "women to pray in public and permit[ted] every ignorant man to preach that chose." The Anglican church recognized no real role for women in worship service or society outside the home until much later in the nineteenth century.[35]

Cultural division is further evident in the reaction to liberal reform of criminal laws. Colonial governments had accepted biblical pronouncements as prescriptions for punishment. The Book of Deuteronomy sanctioned the use of up to forty stripes, and through the Revolution nearly all colonial courts frequently assessed thirty-nine strokes of the whip. In addition, biblical support for the death penalty was used to defend its use for a variety of public offenses. In the late eighteenth century, corporal punishments were reduced and moved indoors and the death penalty was eliminated for all crimes except murder. During the 1790s Benjamin Rush wrote that the death penalty was "irrational" and "anti-republican"; republics "appreciate human life . . . they consider human sacrifices . . . offensive."[36] Further, the social contract idea—that governmental authority consisted only of that which the people gave it—rendered the death penalty an absurdity. No people could vest the government with a right they themselves did not have—the right to kill.

Yet criminal reform provoked a reaction from many clergymen. In their opposition to reform, providentialists expressed the conception of government as an instrument of God rather than as man's construction. Attempts to rationalize government were characterized as man's usurpation of God's instrument. In "A Sermon Preached at the Execution of Abid Converse" in 1788, the Rev. Aaron Bascom legitimized the event that his hearers were to witness: "the counsel of heaven determined that such a prodigy of vice should no longer infest society." The minister at Scots Presbyterian Church in Philadelphia, the Rev. Robert Annan, attempted to discredit Rush, a complex Universalist, who despite his desires for a virtuous community endorsed most of the liberal Republican programs. During their debate over the death penalty, Annan referred to Rush as a "Socinian skeptic" and a "Deist." Annan told his listeners that Rush "wanted to eliminate God from governing the world."[37]

Executions in early America through the eighteenth century approximated religious ceremonies. Clergy offered penitence, afterward assuring the crowd that the condemned man would merit salvation through his atonement for his sins while on earth. The people were reminded of ultimate justice at the "judgement day" and encouraged to be obedient to God and society. Ministers linked civil laws to religious truths and civil disobedience to sin. In the process, they elevated the importance both of religion and of the clergy. A New York Presbyterian minister insisted that, as the Old Testament recognized the death penalty, its abolition would be "most offensive to Jehovah." Another owned a bookmark embroidered with a depiction of a hanging.[38]

Criminal law during the early republic was being transformed by liberal doctrine. No longer intended for the purgation of sin but rather for atonement for social transgressions, punishment was redesigned to fit the crime. This change reflected a reconception of crime as being a violation of man's laws punishable by reasonable instruments of his own government. God was not a part of this form of law enforcement, and neither was the clergy. Liberal reform of the criminal laws substituted man's law and his rationality for God's law and clerical interpretations. Like changes in education and poor relief, reform of criminal laws constituted a vital aspect of the process of disestablishment. As did the other two issues, criminal reform divided the American clergy, as many liberal Christians supported humanitarian changes in the law. Objections emanated from those who sought man's continued subordination to the will of God and to themselves as expositors of that will. Implicit in this division is the conflict over social ideals—whether the United States would be a Christian society living in accordance with God's moral prescriptions or a realm of relative liberty in which each individual determined his or her own priorities and sought to fulfill them.

During the 1790s few if any Americans recognized the Constitution, or changes in legislative or common law, as having resolved this issue. Furthermore, most of the states still supported established churches. So, while conservative clergymen had reason for concern, they were by no means defeated. Nonetheless, changes in American society had already repositioned the churches. William White, an Episcopal minister in Philadelphia, wrote of postrevolutionary America that "all denominations of Christians are on a level, and no church is farther known to the public, than as a voluntary association of individuals, for a lawful and useful purpose." Churches adapted to the changing social and legal environment of the 1790s by reforming themselves as corporations. Many congregations frustrated denominational attempts to impose uniform doctrines by incorporating as separate legal bodies—an independence that was generally recognized by the courts. Perhaps most significant was that many established and dissenting sects began to resemble each other in membership, message, and social function.[39]

The relative homogenization of mainstream religion in the early republic derived from ministerial attempts to gain or retain church membership by adapting their religious messages to popular sentiments. This does not reflect any tepidity of commitment among the clergy or the laity. Christian doctrines and messages have changed repeatedly and continue to do so, without diminishing either the religion's central message or its adherents' commitments to it. Yet the extent and the rapidity of changes in the early republic indicate a noteworthy receptivity to adaptation to prevailing social values that prior generations of pastors preferred to censor.

In response to the secular concerns of the population, the absence of doctrinal control by the denominations, the need for competitive marketing in order to appeal to voluntary members, and the pervasiveness of the Enlightenment humanist worldview, the doctrinal message conveyed in many churches in the early republic took on an entirely new array of defining characteristics. Many religious historians have noted that, in large part, God's word was sublimated to man's purposes and a "lowest common denominator" form of Christianity served as what has been called the "civil religion" or the "religion of the republic."[40] This integration of Christian morality with republican self-government is far different than the integration of church and state. In this theology, Christian moral teachings were used in conjunction with nationalistic sentiments and Enlightenment ideas of human agency to create a system of shared belief among Americans.

Yet this apparent commonality in belief was chimeral. For Christian communitarians, morality derived from the Bible as the word of God. Timothy Dwight, for example, asserted that "Morality . . . is merely a branch of Religion; and where there is not religion, there is not morality."[41] Conversely, for liberal secularists, morality derived from the recognition of the rights of others, best protected by the developing contract law. Both groups could accept the golden role—an admonition to treat others as you yourself would like to be treated. Accordingly, both groups could share the same moral code, but not the same beliefs. Historians who have noted agreement on this moral element have been inclined to minimize the extent of the ideological conflict it masked.

Law in the early republic came to enforce a moral code consistent with liberal ideology while it left religious belief a matter of personal conscience. The biblical pronouncement "Thou shalt not steal" was transformed by American law into a protection of the natural right of people to private property and the legitimate exercise of governmental authority to protect citizens in that right.[42] The "religion of the republic," as essentially a doctrine of moral behavior, retained a role in encouraging virtue among the citizenry. But this constituted a very unusual religion—weak in theological doctrine, doubtful even of its imperative of the supernatural and spiritual realm, yet stubbornly resolute in a devotion to biblical teachings concerning the moral behavior of its chosen people. The religion of the republic contributed to the peace and stability of society, but not to the greater glory of God.

This pragmatic use of Christian morality implicitly placed God in service to man, reversing the traditional order of religious deference. Expressed another way, the moralistic Christianity of the early republic, rooted essentially in each man's conscience, "ignore[d] the fact that religion throughout its history has been more than conscience." Religion, as a social instrument for the encouragement of virtue, was void of its profession of absolute truth and hope of salvation. Paul Tillich put it bluntly: "Can religion be used as a tool for something else? And the answer, of course . . . no. If religion is the state of being ultimately concerned, it cannot be the tool for something else. The ultimate cannot be the tool for something non-ultimate." Yet that was precisely what the religion of the republic was. De Tocqueville appreciated how this nationalistic and moralistic version of Christianity united Americans in a common belief system: "All the sects in the United States belong to the great unity of Christendom, and Christian morality is everywhere the same— . . . I do not know if all Americans have faith in their religion—for who can read the secrets of the heart?—but, I am sure that they think it necessary to the maintenance of republican institutions."[43]

Countless preachers during the early republic intermixed religion and nationalism in conditioning the success of the American republic upon its maintenance of Christian virtues. In the process, these members of the clergy implicitly subordinated faith to the role of tool to be used for a greater good. For example, even traditionalist John Reed, a Presbyterian minister in Boston, argued that history showed how man's devotion to God resulted in improved social manners and morals. Certainly preachers were put on the defensive during this time period—church membership and attendance were declining, and religious doctrine seemed at odds with so many of the new ideas and patterns of behavior that permeated society. It is not surprising that ministers looked for ways to make their messages more relevant to their listeners and to capitalize on prevailing sentiments and concerns to keep and attract members.[44]

To some extent, Americans during this time seemed genuinely confused as to how to separate their reverence for God from their reverence for national ideals. Church buildings were frequently used for civic celebrations and voting. In part, this use derived from colonial times when church and state were integrated. Yet the church also served as a place to renew respect, commitment, and obedience. These sentiments were felt and expressed for the nation and its leaders in buildings built for the worship of God. In Salem, Massachusetts, in 1810 the women of the town decorated the Congregational church in red, white, and blue to celebrate the Fourth of July. Over the pulpit they laid a gold laurel wreath inscribed with the names of all four American presidents. No one objected to using the church to "worship" America's national heroes—this despite its transparent "sacrilege" or "blasphemy," in blatantly violating God's commandment to put no others before him. Throughout the United States, people visited and beheld possessions of the Founders on display in churches as "national relics and icons"—Washington's sword, Franklin's cane, and a battle flag used in the War for Independence.[45]

Many clergy and politicians sounded alike in tone, if not in substance. In a Fourth of July oration, the Rev. Cyprian Strong compared George Washington to Moses: "In the case of the Hebrews, God qualified and raised up Moses, as the leader of his people. In like manner, God raised up a Washington to guide the American Israel out of the captivity of tyranny into the promised land of liberty and peace." Strong placed God in the midst of the Revolution in an attempt to understate the role of any man, even Washington. Conversely, on July 4, 1808, in Lexington, Kentucky, William Barry evoked a religious quality to the winning of political liberty without any attribution of American success to divine intervention. Rather, Barry spoke of liberty as being worthy of worship: "This day is consecrated to freedom. Millions of our countrymen now assemble at the Temple of Liberty, and perform their worship at her shrine; and so long as her genius presides over and controuls the destinies of the Republic, this Anniversary will be distinguished with peculiar joy and grandeur."[46]

Several religious corporations expressed their roles in service to the state as means of attracting members. In 1819 the Presbyterian General Assembly urged its ministers "to impress upon the minds of their hearers the all-important truth, that the religion of Jesus Christ, in its vital power and practical influence is the best friend of civil society, as well as essential to the eternal well-being of man." In another annual "Narrative of the State of Religion," the Presbyterian Church asserted that "the presence of this Church is the best safeguard of nations, and its growth and stability the surest pledge of their prosperity and strength." The Rev. David Tappan from Massachusetts told his congregation that Christian piety and morality "invariably lead to national honor and prosperity . . . [while] every species of irreligion and vice contributes, either directly or remotely, to disgrace, enfeeble, and destroy a community." Even some ardent supporters of establishment felt the need to appeal to listeners through revisionist history. The Rev. Daniel Sanders of Medford, Massachusetts, told his listeners: "The genius of Columbus was illumined, soul fortified, and his little vessel guided by an agency evidently not his own." It is very likely he believed this; it is nearly certain he used this assertion before his congregation because it provoked nationalistic as well as religious enthusiasm.[47]

In combining religious messages with nationalistic sentiment, many clergymen continued to perceive America as a Christian nation and to believe it shared their vision of a world won over to Christ. No matter what means these ministers used to attract and keep adherents, their ultimate goal remained the same: "a Christian civilization preparing the way for God's kingdom."[48] Frequently preachers phrased their advocacy for the universal adoption of Christian norms in language compatible with prevailing ideas on religious freedom, but interjections of man's piety, deference to God, or impotence in the face of God's providence evince religious understandings and goals at odds with people who envisioned free and strong Americans building a new nation by independently pursuing their private dreams.[49]

Political affiliation was not always a good indication of someone's position in this ideological debate. Republican Samuel McClintock—pastor of the Greenland, New Hampshire, Congregational Church, and considered a radical among some of his Congregational peers—continued to accept a world of providence, in which God controlled through the exercise of natural laws: "in the common method of his government over the nations of the earth, God brings to pass his designs by means and instruments, and as it were, conceals himself in his immediate operations, behind the scene of nature."[50] Preachers of McClintock's inclinations expressed a willingness to work within an Enlightenment ideological framework and a societal system in which religion was a voluntary pursuit. Accommodation, however, did not mean surrender of the hope of the universal triumph of Christianity.

Evangelical preachers who struggled with the prevailing societal commitments to worldly success continued to remind their listeners of the social problems engendered by individualistic and commercialistic behavior of

Americans. Many of these clergymen believed that their positions compelled them to speak out against irreligion. However, even in these messages, preachers appealed to commonly held values and attitudes. Social reform became a vehicle by which shared values and a concern for national improvement could be used to engender new religious enthusiasm. Public sentiment, rooted in Christian morality, could substitute for civic endorsement of Christian doctrine. During a temperance rally, Charles Grandison Finney expressed his willingness to use public pressure rather than the police power of the state to achieve Christian aims: "And the multitudes will never yield until the friends of God and man can form a public sentiment so strong as to crush the character of every man who will not give it [alcohol] up." Similarly, Lyman Beecher perceived voluntary religious societies as "a sort of disciplined moral militia to act upon every emergency and repel every encroachment upon the liberties and morals of the State." Yet, in this attention to social rather than doctrinal concerns, some contemporaries could see an acceptance of the religion of the republic as the new form of American Christianity. As Colin Wells, biographer of Timothy Dwight, has recently noted: "the tendency of the clergymen like Beecher to focus on temperance or the protection of the Sabbath would appear [to some] as a dwindling of the Second Great Awakening into a mere preservation of middle-class morality and outward signs of piety."[51]

If, by law, the church could not be integrated into the governing institutions of the state, then, according to these preachers, it would stand apart from and superior to the state—a kind of moral watchdog drawing its power from the religious truth exercised through a corps of believers. A writer to the *Connecticut Courant* in 1803 argued that "civil government is subservient to the great interests of religion."[52] For these crusaders, the protection of religious liberty did not mean a tolerance of irreligion and immorality.

Many of these clergymen wanted to continue to use their positions as moral leaders to influence social policy. They forced Americans to see that government could not remain neutral. Their desires to build a Christian community divided them from liberal secularists and provoked public debate on the role of religion. Ideological conflict over national values accompanied arguments over support for the church. Isaac Backus could favor disestablishment of particular churches but not a religiously impartial government: "every soul ought to feel a necessity always to obey the revealed will of God . . . ; and that in each community, necessity ought to be laid upon every member to submit to the government of it or to be excluded therefrom."[53] Bela Bates Edwards asserted: "Perfect liberty does not imply that the government of the country is not a Christian government. Most, if not all, of our constitutions of government proceed on the basis of the truth of the Christian religion." Likewise a writer to a Connecticut newspaper in 1801 contended that Presbyterians and Congregationalists had only fought in the Revolution on the assumption that someday "Calvinism . . . would be omnipotent in the United States." Jesse Appleton, Congregational President of Bowdoin College, argued that the essential tenets of Christianity ought to govern all earthly pursuits:

> Though civil society is a very interesting state of human existence, there is another, which in point of importance and duration, is infinitely more so. In less than a century, we ourselves, our families, and connexions, together with the present population of our country, and the world, shall, with enlarged capacities for enjoyment or suffering, be transferred to another state. As to the existence and duration of this state, Christianity is the only religion on earth, which gives us authentic and satisfactory instruction.[54]

Some clerical leaders asserted that a Christian commonwealth could never exist without government assistance, and they openly campaigned for national establishment. In 1806 the Rev. Samuel Brown Wylie wrote a treatise in which he argued that the gospel ministry and civil magistracy are not two distinct governments but, rather, two branches of one government. By divorcing government from Christianity, America had rendered the civil magistracy unable to enforce moral laws. The prevailing licentiousness, selfishness, and greed were results of this ungodly government. Timothy Dwight, president of Yale, wrote to President John Adams expressing his disappointment in the Constitution's failure to mention God and asking him to use his influence to establish a national religion.[55]

Less significant people than Dwight wrote to the nation's leaders encouraging them to use their influence to make the United States a more Christian nation. The Rev. Jaspar Adams, president of the Episcopal College of Charleston, sent a pamphlet he had written, entitled "The Relations of Christianity to Civil Government in the United States," to President James Madison and Chief Justice John Marshall. In it he contended that "the people of the United States have retained the Christian religion as the foundation of their civil, legal, and political institutions." Marshall responded by distinguishing for Adams the people of a society from the civil government of that society. Madison found that Adams's writing reflected the "excessive excitement" of the times. "Reason will gradually regain its ascendancy," he wrote, "the tendency to a usurpation on one side or the other or to a corrupting coalition or alliance between them, will be best guarded against by an entire abstinence of the government from interference in any way whatsoever, beyond the necessity of preserving public order, and protecting each sect against trespass on its legal rights by others."[56]

The idea of a government remaining neutral over values coincided with the use of contract law as a means of restructuring society. Contract law accords the individuals to any bargain the right to assert their own goals, values, and priorities. The law enforces the bargain, not the values contained in it. Yet implicitly, contract law endorses individualism over communitarianism by its refusal to impose a communitarian ethic upon contracting parties.

The differences between Christian communitarians and liberal secularists erupted in conflict over education, business expansion, and the imposition of legal restraints on private enjoyments. The conflict over the teaching of the young was a battle over the vision of American society itself. Jeffersonian Republicans sought to teach practical knowledge and a humanistic morality fitting the young for business, politics, and citizenship. Their opponents objected to the loss of deference to God, the threat to social order, and the degradation of public morals that such a humanistic curriculum promised. It is precisely these variant views of American society that precipitated the campus eruptions of the early republic (see chapter 7).

Increasingly after 1790, as education became the means to instill not only moral virtue but also business competence, it was removed first from the control of the parents and then from that of the church.[57] In the late eighteenth century there was growing sentiment that public education was a fundamental duty of government and that the opportunity to receive a free education was a basic right of citizenship. Joel Barlow, a Jeffersonian Republican from Connecticut, asserted that a societal recognition of individual rights implied the existence of civic duties. While a religious man of the 1600s may have conceived of those duties as providing for the poor and ministering to the fallen, a Republican in 1800 was more likely to conceive of his duties to require striving to improve himself financially, which would benefit the nation's growth, and working to be an informed voter, which would protect the nation's future. The state had to prepare the citizenry to assume those duties. Education was not "merely family concern; . . . [but] a civil and even a political concern." In 1793 the American Philosophical Society printed Nicholas Collins's "An Essay on the inquiries in Natural Philosophy which are most beneficial to the United States of America." For Collins, science and enlightened learning were set as antagonistic to the teaching of Christian doctrine. Collins referred to Christianity as "that gloomy superstition disseminated by ignorant illiberal preachers" and anticipated a future when "the phantom of darkness will be dispelled by the rays of science and the bright charms of rising civilization." An editorial in the *Connecticut Courant* of July 4, 1791, called for government funding of universal education: "If the basis of a good constitution of body is laid in infancy, how much more requisite is it that the foundation of virtue should be laid by an early education. Learning, like liberty, should be the natural inheritance of our children. This can be the case to a competent degree, by ordaining that schools and instructors shall be appointed sufficient to instruct all and paid out of the treasury of the corporation."[58]

Implicit in the government's encouragement of economic and geographic expansion and secular education was a rejection of Christian goals for America. Secular policies rejected Sabbath-day protection, corporate communities of believers, and the Bible as the source of ultimate truth. Changes in both civil and criminal laws had removed many sanctions rooted in Christian doctrine and ethics. Despite reformers' calls for reimposing restrictions on

the sale of alcohol, curbing business hours, and criminalizing immoral behavior, states and localities largely averted such "blue laws" until the Jacksonian era. By the early 1800s not only had America's founding documents
and public institutions rejected the formerly prevalent practice of acceding
to biblical truths, but national policies had taken on a decidedly contentious
and secular tone as well.

In response, Christian reformers organized themselves using the same
methods and forms used by their ideological opponents.[59] Religious bodies,
as private corporations, drafted petitions to Congress seeking to have their
views represented. The General Assembly of the Presbyterian Church asked
Congress to prohibit Sunday mail service, and the Congregationalists and
Baptists filed a joint petition requesting Congress to regulate the sale of
Bibles, so that none would be sold "without its being carefully inspected and
certified to be free from error." Other groups incorporated to distribute
Bibles, publish periodicals and journals, and serve as vehicles of social reform. In September 1810, one of these new publications, *The Religious Instructor,* editorialized "On the Religious Education of Children": "True religion consists in choosing the will of God in preference to his own. His
authority is absolute. It should silence all our perverse reasonings and obtain
from us an implicit obedience. And as a parent to his child in God's stead,
he ought to require from the child an entire submission to his authority."[60]
Some publications depicted the nation engaged in an ideological civil war.
An 1811 essay offered:

> In our own country, notwithstanding the revivals of religion, in different
> places, it may be said that the great body of the people are not religious; and
> our Lord has testified that they who are not for him are against him. The lead-
> ing part in several of the states, are thought to be of this sort. With respect to
> many of them, they make no profession of religion, but slight its obligations,
> and seem to feel a degree of gratification and triumph, when religious customs
> are set aside.[61]

Religiously conceived voluntary associations reflected the concern, and
even hostility, felt by some Christians toward the mainstream culture. The
founders of the American Tract Society in 1814, committed to publishing
pamphlets and books expressing Christian doctrine and morals, conceived
of secularists as "the enemy" and expressed their contest with the "satanic
press" in terms of war: "there is in this direction an invasion of the private
virtue and public morals of the nation, more insidious, but not less formidable, than the approach of a foreign army, with all the demoralizing influence
of war." The extent of social division—and the degree of religious difference
it contained—is further evident in the hostility directed toward Freemasonry, with its embrace not only of liberal republicanism but also of rational
religion and secular millenialism. A letter to a Connecticut newspaper expressed the opinion that liberalism had gone too far:

I am a friend to true liberty of a good conscience, but we hear of some having an evil conscience. What is liberty of conscience but a freedom from sin and error; and what is liberty of error but a prison for conscience. Suppose our present Congress in their [sic] present session pass a declarative resolve granting universal toleration to all opinions and free liberty to Familists, Libertines, Erastians, Anti-trinitarians, Anabaptists, Antinomians, Arians, Sabellians, Montanists, Arminians, Socinians, Deists, Mortalians, Gnosticks, Fatalists, Atheists, Universalists, Romanists, Sandemonists, Seekers, Shakers, &c., &c. In a word, room for Hell above ground. What can be expected but that such heretical errors will turn Christ's Academy into the Devil's University.[62]

Similar disgust, prompting a call for separate church schools, was voiced within newly incorporated church bodies during annual meetings. The Reverend Alexander, speaking to the General Assembly of the Presbyterian Church in 1808, condemned the new initiatives in secular education and called for churches to construct their own schools or seminaries: "If you would have a well-disciplined army you must begin by appointing good officers. The great extension of the physical sciences and the taste and fashion of the age, have given such a shape and direction to the academic discourse, that, I confess, it appears to me little adapted to introduce a youth to the study of sacred scriptures." Baptists were encouraged to support the new charitable corporation, the Baptist Education Fund, and to raise money for new colleges in Rhode Island and Massachusetts.[63]

The growth of Sunday Schools after 1800 reflects one approach taken by some churches to counteract the rise of secular influences. Advocates of church-based Sunday Schools offered various reasons in support of their programs. Church classes provided an alternative "to spend[ing] the day in comparative idleness" or "the ordinary employments and amusements of the week." As all children "possess[ed] the same sinful nature," it was necessary "to take advantage of [their] susceptibility and imbue them with the principles of religion." An opponent of such programs conversely argued that religious children were always afraid and morbid, "lost to all sense of pleasure and given over to gloom and melancholy."[64]

The ferocity of ideological debate spawned fears of antidemocratic plots. In awareness of the political effects of Christian publications and political sermonizing, some supporters of Jeffersonian Republicans became convinced of a plan to organize Christians as a voting bloc to undo disestablishment in those jurisdictions in which it had succeeded. A new generation of pamphleteers addressed this threat, led by Robert Owen's *New Harmony Gazette* and Francis Wright and George Houston's Free Press Association of New York.

Conversely, others saw the onslaught of the revolution in law resetting values in business, education, and community morals as an inescapable threat that had to be defeated instead of avoided. Timothy Dwight called "modern liberality . . . no other than mere indifference to truth and error, virtue and vice." Castigating the prevalent use of judges and contracts to serve where ministers and oaths once did, he declared: "You must take your side . . . will you make marriage the mockery of the register's office? Will you enthrone a Goddess of Reason before the table of Christ?" Nathaniel Emmons, one of the leaders of the New Divinity movement shared Dwight's belief that ministers had been too much marginalized for the good of society. "Politicians and moralists may read fine lectures upon the public and private virtues," he wrote in 1803, "yet, their best speculations upon these subjects are totally destitute of the force and obligations of religious discourses."[65]

Some preachers found state laws prohibiting clergymen from holding office—commonly enacted after 1790 by states that had disestablished their churches—as particularly offensive. It was as if the government, having once privatized the churches, sought further to deny religious messages from even reaching the legislative floor. Jeremy Belknap observed: "A monopolizing spirit in some politicians which would exclude clergymen from all attention to matters of state and government; and which would prohibit us from bringing political subjects into the pulpit, and even threaten us with the loss of our livings if we move at all in the political sphere . . . I consider politics as intimately concerned with morality, and both with religion." In a great understatement, the Rev. John Eliot of Boston proffered that "as an order of men, the ministers are not respected in this country as they once were." An indication of just how little some members of the public valued the clergy is evident in Elis Smith's oration in Gray, Maine, on July 4, 1810, in which he said of ministers supported by tax dollars: "The fact is, other men find employment, as they are useful, and were the clergy a useful set of men, there would be no need of a law to oblige people to buy them." In this quotation we see the influence of free-enterprise ideas and contract-law theory on the values of people living in the early republic. Value implies a productivity that can be measured in the amount another is willing to pay for one's labor. By this standard, the clergy had very little social standing.[66]

It soon became apparent to many church leaders that they and the church did not hold the same positions in America that they once had because America itself had changed. Churches, after the Revolution, redesigned themselves to be better positioned to recruit members and to hold property. Doctrines were refined, ministers' roles were changed, and changes were made in the ways churches organized and held property. In many ways, American religion and America's churches would be far different in 1820 than they were in 1790.

America's churches were anything but united in fighting the changes brought about by independence. Various denominations offered doctrines amended by popular understandings of man and his reason in order to attract members. Traditional Calvinism came under attack from Unitarians who rejected the divinity of Christ, from Universalists who scorned the existence of hell and damnation, from Methodists who repudiated the idea of

perseverance of saints (that is, the idea of election without need of moral behavior), and from various Arminian sects that rejected sovereign grace or
election entirely. Just as the law's adoption of liberal ideology influenced the
restructuring of family relationships respecting individual roles and duties,
so theological recognition of individual consciences restructured religious
conceptions of familial functioning. Baptist minister John Leland applied
the postrevolution liberal atomistic view of children to religious teachings,
instructing his parishioners that children have independent consciences by
which they must voluntarily come to God. Religion was a personal matter
that could not be any more imposed by parents than by the state. Each person, as an autonomous decision maker, had to be true to his or her own conscience. Such religious teachings had profound importance in a society re-
casting its forms of social organization, and they unintentionally reinforced
the breakdown of corporate communities. As the views of mankind
changed, so too did ideas of God. Jared Sparks, Unitarian minister, reasoned
that the nature of God must reflect mankind's sense of justice: "Should we
not detest a human magistrate, who would be . . . unreasonable, vindictive,
and cruel? . . . how can we love that in God, which is so abhorrent to every
principle of our nature in men."[67]

Sparks's message is that for God to be acceptable to Americans in 1800,
he must embody their values. While several Christian churches adapted
their messages to the value-oriented "religion of the republic," others
sought a return to a less secular brand of Christianity. The Second Awakening, beginning in the 1790s and persisting for over thirty years,
evinced a desire among Christians to adapt their faith in recognition of
Enlightenment truths without embracing the social embodiments of Enlightenment thought.

Despite the contributions of the Second Awakening and the proliferation
of denominational alternatives, church attendance declined in America's
cities at the turn of the century. Salem minister William Bentley asserted
that "All the churches in Boston have not so many male church members as
one church a half a century ago did contain."[68] Whatever growth Christianity experienced in the early republic came from rural areas.

After the Revolution, Christianity in America prospered primarily within
sects attracting the poor and the alienated. Baptists, Methodists, and other
minority churches gained vigor by appealing to those who could not understand the social dynamics of the market economy and bemoaned the loss of
their corporate communities. These churches offered an alternative moral
doctrine to adherents to make them feel comfortable with themselves—
elevating the humble people by attributing evil to the worldliness of the
rich, the proud, and the learned. The growth of these denominations is evident in the change of Americans' religious affiliations. The percentage of
church members among the American people doubled in the fifty years since
its low in 1776; the old established Congregational, Anglican, and Presbyterian
Churches all declined during this era.[69] New denominations came increasingly

to be vehicles to express dissent with prevailing beliefs and behaviors. Frequently referred to as evangelical for their emphasis on reform through preaching, they took dead aim at the prevailing liberal culture of 1800 America.

Methodism sought a revolution in morals through an acceptance of God's love and forgiveness, preaching that Christ died for the sins of all humans, and mankind was free to live a moral life of commitment to God. Methodists eschewed drinking and popular forms of entertainment and advocated the moral purgation of American society. Tapping into the nationalism of the early nineteenth century, Methodists frequently conjoined man's moral and patriotic duties. In the words of one preacher, Americans, as "free citizens of Zion . . . [should] prize those liberties . . . purchased with the blood of Christ." Freedom, liberty, and recent Revolution intertwined with Jesus' sacrifices on Calvary. Methodists urged a unification of American Christians unhindered by sectarian difference. Methodist ministers invoked popular images of moral duty to attack social decay. They used a hopeful promise of love and redemption and an uncomplicated theological doctrine conducive to Christian unity to spur the growth of Methodism in the early 1800s.[70]

Over time, differences in policy between Baptists and Jeffersonians limited the formers' embrace of the Republican party despite a shared commitment to disestablishment. Baptist doctrine accepted the providence of God and man's innate sinfulness. Baptist ministers told their followers that untimely deaths, sufferings, and natural disasters were punishments for sinful behavior.[71] Despite their early support of disestablishment, Baptists encouraged their legislatures to enact laws that were consistent with biblical prescription. When these efforts failed, they returned to earlier visions of small Christian communities and rejected the liberal values inherent in the nation's law. Refuting the liberal contract ideal in business, they imposed penalties upon members for price gouging and sharp dealing. Rejecting the idea of marriage as a contract between equals, wives were punished for disobedience to their husbands. To enforce these rules and preserve their communities from the liberal effects of secular laws, the Baptist Church discouraged access to the courts, prescribing that "Brother ought not to go to Law with Brother but all matters of a legal nature between Brethren ought to be settled in the Church." Well into the 1800s these churches continued to rely upon expressions of equity more common to the colonial era. They refused to enforce the repayment of debts in depreciated paper money while the nation's courts upheld the contract terms on face value.[72]

As communities became more diverse in their beliefs and lifestyles, many congregants openly wondered to what extent the support of religious freedom must come at the expense of integrity of belief. The Baptist Church struggled in 1813 with repeated questions concerning "holding fellowship with Churches retaining as members men who are Free-Masons."[73] Further repudiating the religious tolerance that seemed to accompany their endorsement of disestablishment, Baptists evinced scorn for Shakers and other radical sects. Elder Valentine Rathbun of Pittsfield, Massachusetts, invoked the use of government authority in the form of grand juries to prosecute those who held "erroneous opinions" and to discover their "blasphemies, adulteries, fornications, breaches of Sabbath, and other breaches of law which they may have been guilty of." Isaac Backus, at the Baptist vanguard for disestablishment, himself condemned Shakers as preaching "heresy" and wrote that "No government can be maintained in civil states without appeals to God to avenge injustice, perjury, and unfaithfulness."[74]

Onetime "dissenting sects" and strong advocates of religious toleration and disestablishment, Methodists and Baptists took positions during the 1800s advocating government intervention in prescribing morals and proscribing heretical beliefs. Their leaders and ministers espoused a Christian communitarianism evocative of the colonial era and discredited the liberal values of contemporary society. Yet they were far from extremists. Some especially devout evangelical groups refused even to marginally integrate their religious beliefs and practices with prevailing cultural ideas and behaviors. Radical sects such as the Shakers, the Oneida community, and some groups of Baptists formed their own communal societies as expressions of dissent against pervasive practices. Envisioning themselves as successors to a long line of Christians who set out to create Godly societies, they returned to earlier American practices of strict church discipline and societal homogeneity. The brethren of the Tennessee River Baptist Church, in 1810, asserted an absolute authority "to act in church order on all things that may come before them," and they undertook to intervene in family and business disputes. Recalling a prior age of communal values, members were disciplined for such offenses as "fraud," "usury," "sharp [business] practices," and poor use of "leisure" time. Evangelical communities taught that common social amusements were nothing less than "sinful frivolities that set men and women on the path to hell."[75] Sunday in most of rural America, from Ohio, Illinois, and Indiana south to Alabama, Kentucky, and Mississippi, may have been another day in the fields or perhaps a time for friends to gather to drink, play games, fight, and eat until satiated. In more urban areas, Sunday involved doing business as usual, with full mail service and few shop closings. These exclusionist evangelical societies tolerated neither.

An essential component of many evangelical groups was the enculturation of "self-abasement," "humility," and "awe and trembling" before the Lord. One providentialist mother reminded her children that their lives were "vile and sinful" and that they would suffer "doom," "utter darkness," and "torments eternal" in Hell's fire unless they found salvation in Jesus. She taught them to pray: "I am a lost undone creature by nature and I have added and made myself more vile by practice." In advocating self-denial above self-assertion, these people repudiated the humanist premises of the ongoing republican experiment. They rejected the reliance upon human curiosity and the pursuit of happiness to drive the American people to grow and prosper.[76]

In some extremist positions, the evangelicals gave voice to the essential conflict between religion and science as means of knowing. Frequently, groups recognized God's speaking to them in ways that transcended differences in language and culture. They believed that preaching communicated a spirit beyond the meanings of the words used, fostering conversion by religious alchemy, void of reason and rationality. Some extremists even took pride in the fact that their contemporaries "denounced [them] as fools" and regarded them as strange or hostile people. They rejected a reliance on thought and science for discovering truth, preferring the use of faith in God and his written word. Francis Wayland, Baptist minister, responded rhetorically to Enlightenment philosophers: "On what [must] our hopes for eternity rest, our hopes for pardon and salvation and everlasting life, but on the truths of the gospel."[77]

Far from constituting a united people, Americans of the early republic were divided in their beliefs and lifestyles and maintained very disparate goals for their country. Enlightenment ideas had rendered traditional Christian beliefs problematic for portions of the well educated in society. A gentleman at the turn of the century described the large number of "nothingarians" among his peers, understood as those "who were either totally indifferent or actively hostile to religion of any kind in any form."[78]

Even the established Congregational churches of New England underwent change in the early republic. The leaders of the Second Awakening sought to reinvigorate Christianity with new ideas and hoped to bring people back into the faith. Some devastated New England clergy turned to the once deplored method of revivals to regain the allegiance of the people. The Second Awakening would use the means utilized by the evangelists—"preaching plain gospel truths"—to convey an old Calvinist message. It is likely the Awakening would not have succeeded at all, and certainly not to the extent that it did, had not the French Revolution served as an example for Awakening preachers of the inevitable social excesses to be derived from Enlightenment philosophy. The French Revolution provided a foreign manifestation of a domestic evil, allowing preachers to condemn immorality and infidelity abroad rather than at home. Americans could still save themselves from the fate that had befallen the French.

In an age of human empowerment in politics, law, social lifestyle, and economics, large numbers of people eschewed a doctrine that considered man not only innately sinful but also powerless to effectuate his own salvation. American Christianity changed in recognition of this fact. Yet, while adaptations were being made, many of the Second Awakening preachers perceived themselves as returning to an older Calvinist tradition. The divide of the early eighteenth century between Old Lights and New Lights gave way to a new controversy between adherents of Old Divinity and New Divinity theologies.

The Second Awakening involved clergy in attempts to build upon Edwards's ideas in order to reconcile Calvinist doctrine with Enlightenment reason. Its goals were not evangelical zeal so much as spiritual seriousness and moral reform. Timothy Dwight, named president of Yale in 1795, combined Jonathan Edwards's recognition of man's duty to God with the influences of the Scottish Enlightenment addressing man's moral agency. To Dwight, man's decision to follow God could be explained as a product of his moral inclination to "do good" as much as of concern for the future of his eternal soul, "for no rational mind which thoroughly understood the implications of infidelity and Christianity could choose the former." Dwight understood religion, government, and civil society to be intertwined in a battle of good versus evil—a crusade against "irreligion, immorality, and government by the rabble." Dwight's teachings at Yale gave root to the growth of the New Divinity school, which attempted to use sophisticated rational arguments in support of traditional Calvinist doctrine.[79]

At first, the New Divinity movement was a response from within the Congregational Church to the internal threat posed by the Unitarians. Unitarianism represented the Congregationalist response to the Enlightenment, embodying a New England expression of Deism. The early Unitarians held an absolute belief in God but denied the deity of Jesus. They also maintained a universalist faith, believing that from God's omnipotence one could reasonably conclude that all people on earth must be equally redeemable. Whereas the evangelicals asserted man's depravity or ruined state, Unitarians believed men chose to sin "by a voluntary violation of a known duty in obedience to either of the appetites or passions." God, as a just and moral entity, condemns only those who are culpable. The growth of Deism and Unitarianism prompted Jefferson to write that "I trust that there is not a young man now living in the United States who will not die a Unitarian." Orthodox Calvinists had to respond to this threat from within as well as the growing secular humanism confronting the church from society at large.[80]

The conflict within Christianity during this time is a microcosm of a larger ideological conflict occurring simultaneously within American society. Debate focused on the nature of man, the extent of his free will, and his ability to use it for productive purposes. In addition, conflicting images of man produced differing conceptions of God. For example, Unitarian minister William Channing contended that a belief in a degraded human nature "tends to discourage the weak, to give excuses to the bad, to feed the vanity of the fanatical, and to offer shelter to the bad feelings of the malignant."[81]

In his emphasis upon the adverse social effects of a certain belief, Channing presupposed that man was able to choose to believe what he will of man's nature. Nathaniel William Taylor, Dwight's student at Yale, and others of the New Haven school of theology disputed that man had this freedom. The nature of man was determined by God and realized after his commission of sin in the Garden of Eden. Revealed truth did not lose its legitimacy because of its implications for social behavior or even for salvation. To Taylor, Unitarianism elevated man over God by using man's reason to postulate God's intent.[82]

None of these theological debates occurred within a social or legal vacuum. Ironically, contract law would be used to resolve conflicts over religious doctrine and church authority, providing stark evidence of its increasing importance in American society. Differences within New England Congregationalism led to the need to clarify the new legal status of churches. The suits addressing church status in New England mirrored similar developments in the mid-Atlantic (see chapter 5). In an early case in Falmouth, Maine, a Universalist minister of an unincorporated church sued the parish (the county) for a portion of the funds that had been collected in religious assessment taxes. The court followed an earlier ruling, from 1785, holding that a religious society had to be incorporated under the laws of the state to receive a portion of the tax dollars.[83] The laws of incorporation derive from contract-law principles. As the Marshall Court would explain, incorporation serves as a contract with investors or donors, securing for them a commitment to use their funds in specified ways. In Boston, at about the same time, Unitarians came to control all but one of that city's old colonial churches as well as the Harvard faculty. Some old-line Boston churches schismed or split, with the more traditional Congregationalists generally leaving their old churches to form new ones. Outside of Boston, in the community of Dedham, a majority of the congregation accepted a new Unitarian minister, prompting the orthodox members to leave. They sued for the right to the name "First Congregational Church," the church records, and church assets. In his decision, Justice Parker of the Massachusetts Supreme Court held that "A church cannot subsist but in connection with some *corporate* parish or religious society." Absent incorporation, a church had no "legal qualities" or status to hold property. The dissenting Orthodox Congregationalists lost their battle to retain their church based on a legal deficiency—lack of corporate status.[84] Throughout New England between 1800 and 1820, Orthodox descendants of the Puritans seceded from their churches, and in doing so they lost the history and property attached to those churches.

Churches in the early republic had no special legal status, even in New England, to distinguish them from other corporate entities. They were subject to the harshness of legal doctrines that treated all members of a society as equals and compelled them to secure their interests through contracts and incorporation. Whatever diminished public role the church might retain—for encouraging virtue or morality, or for addressing the needs of society through education or poor relief—did not confer upon it a privileged status above the laws of the state. Churchmen had to realize that their churches, much like their personal beliefs, were legally recognized as private concerns. Even in states with established churches, the law worked to treat the churches as private voluntary organizations. This raised the specter of an eventual conflict between public policy and law in those states that continued to fund and otherwise support their churches. The vitriolic debates in the early republic over the values of the new nation provided intellectual context for the political and legal battles of the era that would ultimately fulfill the implicit constitutional mandate to separate church and state.

5 | Revolutionary-Era Disestablishment
The Case of New York State

Moderate affections for proper objects you are allowed. . . . By such means you will fill your places in society . . . ; at the same time you will enjoy the best thing in human life, the friendly feelings of the heart.

The Rev. James Fordyce, "Sermons to Young Women"

STATES THAT DISESTABLISHED THEIR CHURCHES during the Revolution acted with an urgency spawned in the enthusiasm of the war for independence. Established Episcopalian or Anglican churches were especially vulnerable during this time as exemplars of English government and aristocratic privilege. The mid-Atlantic states relied on the developing corporate law to effectuate the separation of church and state during the Revolution.

Corporate law in the colonies provided a means for the legislatures to achieve social goals. If roads, bridges, or mills were needed, a colonial legislature would receive requests from individuals offering to operate a road, bridge, or mill as a business. The legislature would grant a corporate charter, frequently providing some monopolistic privileges, to the chosen individual or individuals. Corporate charters were grants of power to individuals allowing them to address public needs and to reap financial benefits commensurate with the needs they addressed. During the colonial era, colonies granted rights to incorporate only to those churches that were recognized under laws establishing religion. This limited grant of rights to incorporate persisted, in some cases, after the Revolution and prevented churches of dissenters from receiving and holding property. Churches were granted charters only as institutions serving the public interest—a role that dissenting churches did not fulfill.

Conversely, in the early republic, corporate charters were issued by administrative agencies to allow private individuals to pursue personal goals of business growth. The charter served as a form of contract-law protection for the investors in the enterprise. The changing nature and use of the corporate form was expressed early in the mid-Atlantic colonies, specifically in cases involving churches.

The roots of the transformation of corporate law can be seen in an early case over church property in Rhode Island. In 1676 John Clarke, a pillar of the First Baptist Church in Newport, died and left a large bequest to the church to be held in trust for the relief of the poor, especially those among them who feared God. The English Law of Charitable Uses from 1601 prohibited bequests to any church other than the Church of England. Rhode Island's charter required that the colony's laws not be repugnant to the laws of England. But what the English did not know would not hurt them—and all the colonies frequently engaged in activities that, if advertised in England, might well have formed the basis of charter revocation. Rhode Island permitted the trust to be operated by the First Baptist Church.

In the early 1700s, however, a trustee affiliated with the church used trust land for his own benefit—a misdeed brought to the attention of the city government. The council proceeded to attempt to seize the property. The conflict reached the Rhode Island General Assembly, which produced the colony's first law on charitable trusts. The assembly gave trustees unprecedented discretion to use trust funds in various ways broadly consistent with the purposes of the trust. Atypical of colonial law, and suggestive of changes later in the century, the Rhode Island law conceived of the trustee as owing nothing to the public—his only duty being to the trust.

Trust law and corporate law constitute different substantive areas—the legal doctrines of one not necessarily being applicable to another. Yet in the first half of the eighteenth century the idea of using a legally created entity (whether a trust or a corporation), which was protected by the same legislature that created it, to serve purely private purposes was a radical reconceptualization of law. Once the Rhode Island Assembly expressed its position on the independence of trusts from public oversight, it was not a great leap to envision similar freedoms for corporations.[1]

While the decision prefigured a time in which churches would serve private, not public, goals, the assembly could not have predicted the results of its decision. Various denominations took advantage of Rhode Island's absence of religious establishment by incorporating to address a wide range of church goals. The first to do this was the Anglican Trinity Church in Newport, but others soon followed. Given the protection of law to address private goals free from public scrutiny, incorporated churches in Rhode Island broadened the range of their activities. Baptists founded what would become Brown University. Congregationalists started intercolonial mutual aid societies, and Anglicans established missionary organizations. The Rhode Island model accommodated the religious diversity and entrepreneurial enthusiasm that characterized the colonies just south of the rogue colony and offered them a means of achieving their social goals.

After the Revolution, the mid-Atlantic states utilized corporate law to restructure their communities. Pennsylvania's laws on religious corporations demonstrate the changing attitudes toward churches and the transformation in the tenets underlying law from the colonial era to the early republic. In 1712, and again in 1715 after the Crown rejected its initial proposal, the Pennsylvania Assembly provided a statutory guarantee of the right for any religious society to receive, hold, and spend gifts to be used for churches, cemeteries, hospitals, schools, and poorhouses. In the petition accompanying the 1715 act to England, the assembly noted the colony's need to support providers of social services. Given a communitarian ethic and a prevailing Christian worldview, the colonial assembly sought to harness private energies managed by churches to address public needs.

In 1791 Pennsylvania passed a law that allowed the attorney general, rather than the legislature, to grant charters to "religious, literary, and charitable societies." The statute provided that no religious society could have more than five hundred dollars' annual income. When various churches objected to the State Commission on Corporations regarding this cap, the commission held that the cap was "the utmost extent to which religious corporations could be permitted to draw away the property of our citizens from the general purposes of society."[2] In the early republic, churches were redefined, under law, as private organizations serving private and not public goals. Rather than perceiving churches as helping society address its concerns, the commission clearly recognized them, in the 1790s, as impediments to social progress as public institutions might more rationally conceive of it.

Pennsylvania had a progressive history of incorporating churches and charitable organizations even in the colonial era. Henry Muhlenberg, an influential Lutheran minister from the Halle Academy in Prussia, sought to protect his church's property from what he perceived as a semihostile government in the middle 1700s. The Halle school conceived of property rights in negative terms—that is, as means of protecting one's own from plunder, not as an obligation of stewardship. He drafted a constitution for his church that defined specific pastoral and vestry authority and provided powers to the lay members of the church to elect officers and even veto recommended courses of action. The charter of incorporation issued to his church provided property protection to a largely democratic private entity that sought to take advantage of Pennsylvania's relatively liberal protection of religious freedom. Its purposes were private, not public, and it sought protection from the government rather than its help. Muhlenberg's church in the 1750s looked a lot like churches elsewhere would look in the 1800s. By that same time, Pennsylvanians had formed various civic organizations that utilized the corporate form—schools, libraries, fire companies, and mutual aid societies. As the colony came to recognize private concerns as the purpose of private corporations, it became further entrenched in a legal realm that protected individual rights rather than shared responsibilities as the basis of community.[3]

New York, too, had a longer history with liberal forms of corporate law than many of the other colonies. This derives from its emphasis on commerce since its formation as a colony. From its inception as the Dutch colony of New Amsterdam, New York witnessed a perpetual tension between economic and religious interests. New York faced these conflicting interests in contests over religious diversity in the seventeenth century, public support for the church as a civil institution in the eighteenth century, and the ultimate deemphasis of Christian teachings within civil law, education, and public policy at the close of the eighteenth century and the beginning of the next. Liberal ideas influencing the development of contract law after the Revolution resolved these battles in reconceiving of the church as a private entity.

In New York, legal disestablishment was effectuated early, being written into the Revolutionary-era constitution without significant debate. This early legal resolution of the issue could occur in New York because of the absence of a dominant sect or denomination. In this environment, dissenting churches could unite in common cause to effectuate change more easily than in states with strong establishments. New York reflects the social diversity and political moderation of mid-Atlantic American culture during the Revolutionary era. Yet, even here, constitutional prescription did not ensure social change, as New Yorkers fought over social values for nearly fifty years. In New York, this fight was waged in the context of economic expansion. In its rapid economic growth in the postwar period, New York came to epitomize the republican "era of good feelings." Business interests polarized issues of regulation and morality—and forced a confrontation over individual liberties. New York's resolution of these ideological, social, and cultural tensions in the process of disestablishment constitute its own unique response to issues confronting the entire nation in the early republic.

The Dutch West India Company founded New Netherlands in 1624, constructed its first Indian trading post at Albany in 1626, and immediately established the Dutch Reformed Church and endorsed its strict Calvinist doctrine. Settlers were required to pay tithes to support ministers, their churches, and their social programs, including religious education and monetary relief for the poor. Church officials reported to the director general of the colony who oversaw the performance of these programs. From the outset, however, the trading company viewed the church with suspicion. The traders themselves evinced little enthusiasm for building a Calvinist community, preferring the drinking, fornication, brawling, and moneymaking offered in the wilderness. The company sought to expand its economic base in New Amsterdam and saw religious toleration and the offer of material rewards as the best means of pursuing its ends. In 1638 the Dutch West India Company asserted that "every man shall be free to live up to his own in peace and decorum," the earliest pronouncement of religious toleration in the colonies. However, in response to political pressure in Holland, the company revoked its pledge of toleration and agreed to a new charter in 1640, which provided that "no other religion shall be publicly admitted . . . except the Reformed, as it is at present preached and practiced by public authority in the United Netherlands; and for this purpose the Company shall provide and maintain good and suitable preachers, schoolmasters, and comforters of the sick."[4]

Despite this formal pronouncement, the Dutch West India Company encouraged the influx of English dissenters from the north and the religious diversity they brought. In 1663 Governor Pieter Stuyvesant was told to "shut your eyes, at least not force peoples' consciences, but allow every one to have his own belief, as long as he behaves legally, gives no offense to his neighbors and does not oppose the government." Nevertheless, during this period, the Dutch Reformed Church in the colony succeeded in compelling the local government to persecute Quakers, to refuse the disembarkation of a Lutheran minister, and to attempt to drive a group of Jewish immigrants from the colony until stopped from doing so by company officials.[5]

The Dutch Calvinists, like their English counterparts, tried to subordinate all communal activities to their conceptions of Christian ethics. Brewing, baking, meat production, and woodworking were subject to wage and price controls. Furthermore, private behaviors were governed by an overriding concern for the communal welfare.[6] Yet economic interests and religious divisions frustrated Stuyvesant in his attempts to control the community up until the time that the English took over.

In 1664 Charles II of England presumed to grant the land composing New Netherlands to his brother James, duke of York. Shortly thereafter, four English warships anchored offshore and demanded and received the Dutch surrender. The ethnic diversity of the colony, including not only Dutch and English settlers but also immigrants from Germany, Sweden, and Africa as well as an integrated Native American population, combined with James's desire to found a Catholic refuge to continue the relative toleration afforded under Dutch rule.

The English took over a colony in name only; it was really a collection of disparate colonial units. Commercial Manhattan, Puritan Long Island, and Dutch Reformed settlements on the Hudson constituted distinct and independent colonial ventures, each with somewhat different legal systems. The first twenty-five years of English rule is a story of proprietary interests trying to unify recalcitrant communities under one legal and social system. As was to be expected, religion would play a role in this attempt. In 1665 the duke's laws provided that any church of the Protestant religion could become an established church. Each township was required to publicly support a Protestant church and minister: "Every inhabitant [being forced to] contribute to all charges both in Church and State."[7] The Dutch believed this law to give them equal status with members of the Church of England. The latter doubted this and resented the confusion in the law that fostered this belief. Further adding to the confusion, Catholics were not able to benefit from any legal establishment in pursuit of their own religious practices, but they were free to practice their faith free of persecution. This changed in 1683, when the New York Assembly reasserted the government's commitment to protect freedom of conscience to all who "professe faith in God by Jesus Christ" so long as in their practice of their faith they do not threaten the public peace or welfare. New York's multiple establishment law widened to embrace Catholicism.[8]

The law not only required the colonists to support a church and its minister but also "all parochial affairs," including poor relief and the protection of public morality. Confusion seemed to predominate, as different religious, ethnic, and community groups held different perspectives of the extent of establishment in New York. A series of royal governors after 1675 attempted to impose an Anglican establishment and were largely frustrated by recalcitrant colonial legislatures. The differences of opinion over the nature of the colony's religious tolerance resulted in disruptions of public peace on several occasions and reflected hostility to any state religion.[9]

Sensitivity to matters of religion was probably heightened in New York because of the relative diversity of its population and the relative liberality of its laws. Political events in Europe combined in the late 1680s to light a powder keg of religious and social resentment in New York. In 1685 the one-time Catholic duke of York became king of England; the same year Louis XIV revoked the Edict of Nantes, which had tolerated the presence of Protestant Huguenots in France. James II immediately created the Dominion of New England, incorporating the colonies of New York, New Jersey, and Pennsylvania with those of New England. The mistrusted Sir Edmund Andros was named governor of this dominion, prompting fears throughout not only New York but all of the northern colonies concerning political integrity and the maintenance of existing religious structures.

When William and Mary replaced James upon the throne in the Glorious Revolution of 1688, a group of successful merchants claimed that the unpopular provincial government was illegitimate. Led by Jacob Leisler, a member of the Dutch Reformed Church who was liked by most Protestant groups in New York, these businessmen refused to pay taxes until a new government from the new king and queen had been established and the customs collector, a Catholic, had been removed from office. When the existing provincial government refused to proclaim the ascendancy of the new monarchs, a mob drove government officials from office and closed the courts and customhouse. Leisler was named interim lieutenant governor. He organized a new government and formed a militia from among his Protestant supporters, reopened the government buildings, and undertook to hold the colony until further direction came from William and Mary.

Leisler's supporters expressed in pamphlets that they had lived in "great dread—[that the deposed King James was plotting] to Damn the English nation to Papery and Slavery," and saw themselves as protectors of both the Protestant religion and the rights and liberties of Englishmen. Resentment of Leisler's low social status combined with religion to create problems between Leisler's laborers, businessmen, and craftsmen and the landed grandees that had profited under Stuart rule. By 1690 these grandees had written to the Crown that New York was being governed by a rabble. Certainly, confusion seemed to reign, as elections proliferated to fill every conceivable office and frequently resulted in violence between factions. King William sent Colonel Henry Slaughter to New York to restore order and rid the colony of Leisler and his followers. He arrived in 1691, arrested and executed Leisler, an early martyr in the colonies' movement toward democracy. Slaughter held elections for a new common council and assembly and secured enactment of the Judiciary Act of 1691. The law created a Supreme Court of Judicature, which was to follow English statutory and common law (not Dutch), and sheriffs and justices of the peace needed to promote a moral Christian community through enforcement of civil and criminal laws.[10]

This attempt at building a Christian community, if not a religious establishment, was followed in 1693 by the passage of the First Ministry Act, which called for church wardens and vestrymen to be elected by the public. The vestrymen raised taxes to pay the salaries of "good and sufficient Protestant ministers." The wardens enforced church discipline and community morality.[11] The institutional beginnings for an Anglican establishment were well under way by 1702, when Lord Cornbury arrived as the new governor.

Cornbury was himself a zealous Anglican churchman. From the moment of his arrival in the colony, he worked with the Society for the Propagation of the Gospel, an Anglican missionary group based in England, to bring Anglican clergy to New York. During his tenure, Trinity Church was founded in New York City and numerous other pastorates were created throughout the colony. A great influx of English settlers to New York between 1690 and 1730 hastened the development of the Anglican Church and its influence in the assembly. In 1705 Cornbury succeeded in enacting a second Ministry Act requiring each town to support an Anglican church. The law further outlawed Catholicism and preaching without a state license and provided for roles for the Anglican Church and its doctrine in educating the colony's young people. In 1708 the general assembly passed "An Act for Suppressing Immorality" aimed at punishing drinking, amusements, and fornication.[12]

Yet, generally, it was difficult for religion to capture the interest of New Yorkers. Formation of new churches lagged far behind the increase in population. Churches in the state tried to fulfill their traditional responsibilities of poor relief and education, but interest in these social functions barely exceeded popular interest in religious doctrine. Churches frequently had to select schoolmasters from outside their membership to teach in church-funded schools. Rather than encouraging the growth of religion, establishment tended to contribute to its decline. New Yorkers resented the involvement of Anglican churches in civic responsibilities as well as the obligation to pay for them. Presbyterians in Rye were forced to close their church between 1705 and 1720 because they could not contribute both the necessary support of their own minister and the taxes required for maintaining an Anglican priest.[13]

In 1713 John Sharpe, chaplain of the king's army in New York, remarked that, "there is hardly anything which is more wanted in this country [N.Y.] than learning, there being no place I know of in America where it is less encouraged or regarded." The weakness of Anglican-sponsored education in New York persisted despite a program introduced in 1709 by the Society for the Propagation of the Gospel to settle a number of schoolmasters among "the children of the planters" in the colonies, "to instruct them in reading, writing, and the principles of the Christian religion as taught and professed in the Church of England." As late as 1762 Anglican schools outnumbered Dutch, French, and Hebrew schools only by a two-to-one margin.[14]

The very existence of an Anglican establishment encouraged dissenters to engage in acts of rebellion ranging from civil disobedience to violent protest. In 1707 Frances Makemie and John Hampton, Presbyterian ministers in New York City, were arrested for preaching without a license from Lord Cornbury. In court they claimed that the 1705 Ministry Act violated their "Liberty from an Act of Parliament made the First year of the Reign of King William and Queen Mary which gave us Liberty" of religious conscience. In opposition, Cornbury argued successfully that the law the preachers referred to applied only in England and not in the American plantations. In 1710 in Jamaica, Long Island, town residents seized the church and ministry constructed as a Presbyterian pastorate but converted to serve the Anglican Church after 1705. They drove the Anglican minister out of town and subsequently brought suit in provincial court for title to the church's property. The court found in favor of the townspeople, at once both calling the legitimacy of the Anglican establishment into question and encouraging subsequent rebellions against local Anglican churches.[15] These disputes of the early eighteenth century questioned the legitimacy of New York's Anglican establishment on grounds that it violated people's rights as Englishmen, denied property rights, and imposed an elite minority's religious opinion upon the consciences of the majority. Enactment of the second Ministry Act in 1705 did not convince New Yorkers of the existence of a religious establishment in their colony.

New York experienced tremendous social change in the first half of the eighteenth century, much of which prefigured changes in other sections of America. Law became professionalized as formally trained "barristers" replaced self-taught lawyers, established a bar association, and relied heavily on English legal precedent. Of course, increases in trade and commerce influenced the professionalization of law. These same forces resulted in a huge increase in taverns and inns, dram shops, coffee houses, and breweries. Especially noteworthy is the prominent role played by women in New York businesses. Women commonly owned not only retail stores catering to domestic needs but also taverns and manufacturing businesses. This comparatively early commercial involvement of women may have derived from Dutch influences. Under Dutch law, women suffered far fewer of the restrictions on economic and political behavior than did English women. New Yorkers also developed a taste for luxury goods that people in other parts of the country would not match until after the Revolution. Fantastic markets, by the standards of the time, grew up along the East River to purvey goods imported from Europe and Asia.[16]

Amid this commercial expansion, religion made little headway. Despite indifference, growing resentment, and the occasional acts of rebellion, the Anglican minority persisted in its programs. In fact, between 1702 and 1774, the Anglican church made its most concerted efforts to reform New York into a Christian community. Its efforts provoked more animosity than religiosity. Whether because of Anglican repression or a general irreligiosity, not even the Great Awakening stirred New Yorkers to piety. Thousands of people,

Francis Makemie was tried in New York in 1707 for preaching without a license. Makemie contended that God had called him to preach, a calling that no government on earth could regulate. Henry A. Ogden illustration courtesy Presbyterian Historical Society, Presbyterian Church (USA) (Philadelphia).

nearly all of them very poor, came to hear George Whitefield during his visits in 1739 and 1740; yet, except for a slight growth in followers of the Baptist sect, the effects were short-lived. In 1744 a visitor to the state found "not a grain of enthusiasm" anywhere she traveled. Yet, during this same time period, prosecutions for preaching without a license increased, Jewish residents were denied the right to vote, and new Anglican schoolteachers were settled in the schools.[17]

The Anglican administration also sought to instill a greater degree of Christian communitarianism through legislation restricting commerce. In 1731 as part of the royal charter that created the City of New York, the administration expressed its program as necessary for "a collective civic good." Many of the economic restrictions contained in the new law were merely restatements of earlier code provisions dating back to the time of Dutch rule. Regulations set wages and restricted price increases; fixed the weight, quality, and composition of all commodities deemed "essential"; and established supervision for people pursuing a plethora of business endeavors—among them, bakers, butchers and tavern owners, chimney sweeps and grave diggers. The charter also provided for the creation of new monopolies to build and repair docks, wharves, and streets. The intention behind the laws was to provide necessary goods and services to all people of the community, even the poor. However, the effects of these regulations, by eliminating competition, were to limit the opportunities for growth of those in the middle class while enriching a few propertied monopolists.[18]

New Colonial laws also followed a familiar pattern of imposing duties on those in positions of relative prominence to take actions to resolve societal concerns. One such law attempted to control mischief caused by apprentices and young indentured servants. Despite their youth these boys and girls, oftentimes ill-clad and hungry, roamed the city streets and taverns at night, engaging in gambling, fighting, unlicensed selling of goods, and prostitution. To address these concerns, New York City imposed eight o'clock curfews on apprentices and juvenile servants, created night schools to give them alternative activities, and gave their masters additional authority to punish them while holding the masters responsible for failure to control their charges. These reactions evince once again a patriarchal attitude reflected in law—the community and the master were to step in to control people deemed unable to control themselves. These controls not surprisingly sparked unrest among the servants. In 1734 young maidservants, mostly girls in their early teens, organized in protest against their susceptibility to frequent harsh beatings from their mistresses' husbands who attempted to keep them indoors at night.[19]

Throughout the first half of the eighteenth century, New York dealt with an increase in poverty by imposing increases in the poor tax, in one period tripling it in fifteen years, and boarding the poor with wealthy families. Still, most of the poor were assisted by local churches. The provision of educational and poor relief services, though a priority of the Anglican Church, re-

mained a matter of town-by-town initiative. New Yorkers exhibited little enthusiasm for public programs that taxed or otherwise limited their freedoms
in order to support the poor. In 1707 church wardens were ordered by the
Common Council to require recipients of aid to wear a red badge, with the
hope that embarrassment might encourage them to leave the city or at least
avoid seeking aid. During the early 1700s an almshouse was created to house
vagrants and the poor out of town, and new whipping posts and pillories
were constructed to punish those who persisted in roaming the city streets.[20]
New Yorkers chafed at laws that attempted to conform behavior to Christian
concepts of social duty and communal brotherhood and that were common
in other colonies.

Still, reaction to Anglican initiatives remained somewhat muted until two
new concerns surfaced in the 1750s that galvanized dissent against the established church. These uprisings are distinguishable from earlier revolts in that
they subordinated a concern for religious freedom to the perceived threat posed
by a state religion to other civil rights. As New Yorkers entered the latter half of
the century, they were less inclined to fix their rights in English law.

The first concern arose from fears of an Anglican bishop being placed in
New York. At midcentury, Anglicans constituted less than one-tenth of the
colony's population. Nevertheless, the establishment of the Anglican
Church in New York made that colony a prime candidate for a North American bishopric seat. Beginning in the 1750s, concern in New York escalated
over the threat to liberties perceived to result from such a move. A request to
the secretary of the Society for the Propagation of the Gospel by the Anglican clergy in New York for assistance in procuring a bishop prompted vigorous objection. In the 1760s the New York City Society of Dissenters organized to thwart what it contended was a plot to subject the colonies to
further imperial control. The society argued that opposition to a bishop
arose not from any disaffection toward any man on account of his religion,
but from concerns over religious and civil liberty.[21] Fear of the installation of
a bishop and its meaning for New Yorkers united various groups of dissenters
and unchurched people in the decade preceding the Revolution.

The roots of the second concern were planted in 1746, when the state assembly created a board of directors to pursue the creation of a college for
New York, to be funded through a public lottery. In 1751 a board of trustees
was created to make the school a reality. Seven of the ten board members
were Anglicans. Early proposals described the school's purpose as advancing
learning through a college in which the Church of England would hold a
preferential position. Trinity Church donated land in Manhattan for the site
of a new college, conditioning the gift on the school's use of the Anglican
liturgy and the appointment of an Anglican college president. In taking the
initial action to create the school, the board noted the appropriateness of
aligning it with the Anglican Church, for it enjoyed a constitutional preference within the province. Three non-Anglican attorneys, William Smith Jr.,
John Morin Scott, and William Livingston, reacted with outrage to the idea

of the assembly sanctioning an Anglican school for New York. In 1752–1753 they organized and published *The Independent Reflector,* a periodical devoted to dispensing a libertarian ideology, to express opposition to the new school plan. Smith, Livingston, and Scott denied the establishment of Anglicanism as the exclusive religion in New York, arguing that even the despised Ministry Act of 1705 recognized the people's freedom to choose their own ministers. They went further, in advocating that any college created by the people of the province ought to be a secular institution offering a "liberal education," in which the study of "Divinity be no part of the public exercises of the college." Learning was, to them, independent of religious doctrine and should be regarded as such by the legislature: "Should the college be founded upon an Act of the Assembly, the Legislature would have it in their [sic] Power, to inspect the conduct of its Governours, to divest those of Authority who abuse it, and to appoint in their stead, Friends to the Cause of Learning and the General welfare of the Province." They called any proposed Anglican school a "Nursery of Bigotry and superstition—An engine of persecution, slavery, and oppression—A fountain . . . [of] infectious streams . . . [that will] poison all of our enjoyments."[22]

The attacks upon the proposal prompted Anglican responses from both sides of the Atlantic. In one especially telling retort, the Anglicans asserted that "inequality, hierarchy, monarchy, patriarchy, obedience to authority, and an established church . . . were the true principles of social organization."[23] With the exception of "obedience to authority," which was significantly redefined, each of these "principles" would be attacked and largely or completely removed from American society during the Revolution and the social reorganizations of early republic. Yet, in the 1750s, this argument garnered support even from some New Yorkers.

In 1754 a charter for King's College was issued and the new school opened in the vestry room of Trinity Church. Still, conflict over public funding of the school continued until 1756. In that year the assembly agreed to give half the lottery money to the school and to use the other half to build a jail and a hospital in which to quarantine victims of contagious diseases. Many New Yorkers regarded the new school as an intrusion of the church into their city and resented the use of any public funds for its support.[24]

The events of the 1750s and 1760s clarified the tenuous position of the Anglican Church in New York and further encouraged dissenters in their desires to topple the establishment. The continuation of the Anglican establishment became a major issue in the assembly elections of 1769. A variety of religious dissenters, including Presbyterians, Dutch Reformed, Lutherans, Quakers, and unchurched, formed a party behind William Livingston, one of the former publishers of *The Independent Reflector.* They promised to repeal the laws of establishment. The DeLancey party, composed primarily of Anglicans and wealthy Dutch, defeated the insurgents only by dividing the dissenting sects among themselves, converting the debate from the merits of establishment to the potential domination of New York's government by a sect that, unlike the Anglicans, might claim majority status. Apparently, if there is one thing colonial New Yorkers feared more than rule by a minority it was rule by a more powerful majority. Despite the DeLancey party victory at the polls, the new assembly responded to the issues expressed during the campaign by attempting to reduce religious privileges. The legislature used law to attempt to place all churches on an equal footing. All Protestant sects were permitted to incorporate, and dissenters could petition for exemptions from church taxes in the four counties where they remained. Even these modest assembly initiatives were rejected by the governor and the Provincial Council.[25]

In 1766 the First Protestant Church chose to ignore the governor and petition for incorporation directly to the Crown. Its petition was denied on the grounds that "the King had a duty to uphold the exclusive rights of the Church of England." In May of that year, over eighty clergymen and deacons from dissenting churches throughout the colonies met in New York, decried the authority of Parliament over the practice of their religion, and voiced continued opposition to the imposition of a bishop upon America.[26]

On the eve of Revolution less than one in ten New Yorkers attended an Anglican church. People of Dutch heritage formed the majorities of the populations in numerous New York towns. Only one-half of state residents were of English descent. However, before dissenters could disestablish the state church, they had to overcome their own fear and dislike of each other. As was the pattern in other colonies, Baptists and Presbyterians led the movement for disestablishment. Lutherans, Quakers, and Moravians were slow to follow. The Methodists in New York tended to support their former brethren of the Church of England. Revolutionary fervor helped the dissenters, as antagonism toward English rule could very easily be expressed in antipathy for the Anglican Church. Evangelical preachers challenged the authority of the religious establishment and of Parliament in sermons that integrated religious and political freedom with the means of finding Jesus' truth. Hostility to Anglicans prompted New Yorkers in the four counties in which the church was established to close the doors to the churches and drive the preachers from their homes. The mob violence used against Anglicans during the war in New York was matched only in sporadic other instances, such as in the riots over the imposition of price controls as a means of rationing. By 1775 Anglican clergymen Charles Inglis, Thomas Chandler, and Myles Cooper had become convinced that calls for religious freedom would be used to destroy Anglicanism as a symbol of English rule.[27]

It was not only the Anglican Church that was under attack. Advocates for disestablishment resented the idea of any religious body controlling education, the economy, and private relations as extensions of a duty to preserve the public's morality. The Revolution sought to secure the liberty of free men to pursue their individual interests without unreasonable restraint. Here, as elsewhere, individual freedom meant in part economic freedom, but perhaps nowhere in the colonies were the interests for economic freedom greater than in New York. Resentment increased in the early 1770s as taxes rose to support the ever-growing number of poor and to punish an increasing number of criminals. To many New Yorkers, the taxes imposed by their own assembly, run by Anglicans, were as abhorrent as Parliament's taxes. The loyalist attitudes of several of the leading Anglican ministers further alienated New Yorkers. Revs. Chandler, Inglis, Vardill, and Cooper, president of King's College, all presented wealth, rank, distinction, and membership in the Anglican Church as prerequisites for governing. By the spring of 1776 the government of New York was in a shambles, and in June Governor DeLancey fled New York City. In recognition of the absence of the old regime New Yorkers raised rents, prices, and wage demands; stayed out late in taverns; and took advantage of the hundreds of new prostitutes plying their trade night and day. New Yorkers experienced economic and social freedom before political freedom had even been declared, much less won.[28]

Following the advice of the Continental Congress for each new state to draft its own constitution, the old Provincial Congress of New York convened on August 2, 1776, as delegates to the Convention of the Representatives of New York. Religious freedom was addressed in the opening pronouncement of a "day of fasting, humiliation, and prayer to Almighty God [for] his divine assistance in the organization and establishment of a form of government for the security and perpetuation of the civil and religious rights and liberties of mankind." The representatives appointed a committee of fourteen members to prepare a draft constitution ("plan of government"). This committee rejected a proposal for a multiple establishment raised by Presbyterian minister John Rodgers. Instead, the members proposed language providing that all people be free to exercise their own religious beliefs. This provision, expressed in article 38, came before the representatives as a body in early 1777. John Jay spoke for those in attendance who feared the participation of Catholics in the republic so long as they professed belief in and devotion to the pope as God's agent on earth. Jay suspected that Catholics' allegiance to a foreign ruler limited their commitment to the republican principles of the new government. He suggested limiting religious freedom to practices not "inconsistent with the safety of the civil society." When this suggestion failed to garner sufficient support, he proposed that all Catholics be required to take an oath of allegiance to New York and its laws as superior to the orders of the Pope. This too failed, but the representatives adopted the oath as necessary for all new immigrants, thereby limiting the likely immigration of new Catholics into the state without limiting the religious practices or beliefs of current residents.[29]

Several clergymen participating in the Convention supported the idea of religious freedom only so long as it did not imply that government would shun religion. J. H. Livingston, pastor of the Dutch Reformed Church in Albany, argued that the state must "promote religion in general" as well as "defend it from all persecution." Others led a movement for religious tests upon officeholders; one Presbyterian clergyman contended it was a generally acknowledged fact that Protestants made the best governors. This movement, like that led by Jay, failed to convince the liberal representatives to put religious restrictions upon civil rights. In its new constitution of 1777, at article 38, New York State provided:

> Whereas we are required by the benevolent principles of rational liberty, not only to expel civil tyranny, but also to guard against the spiritual oppression and intolerance, wherewith the bigotry & ambition of weak & wicked priests & princes have scourged mankind: This Convention doth further, in the name & by the authority of the good people of this State, ORDAIN, DETERMINE, & DECLARE, that the free exercise and enjoyment of religious profession and worship, without discrimination or preference, shall forever hereafter be allowed within this State to all mankind. Provided that the liberty of conscience hereby granted, shall not be so construed, as to excuse acts of licentiousness, or justify practices inconsistent with the peace or safety of the State.[30]

Little attention was paid to the drafting of the constitution by the people of New York. Most New Yorkers concerned themselves primarily with the war and their own sustenance. The convention representatives met secretly in various cities in order to escape discovery by the British. The press did not even know the nature of their debates nor the pace of progress on their task.[31]

Convention representatives expressed a desire to accomplish not only the task of legal disestablishment but also to repudiate the establishment of the past years, which they regarded more a de facto than a de jure establishment. To make this clear the convention published a statement: "That all such parts of the said common law, and all such of the said statutes and acts aforesaid, or parts thereof, as may be construed to establish or maintain any particular denomination of Christians or their ministers . . . be and they hereby are, abrogated and rejected."[32]

Refusing to acknowledge that a state religion had ever been established, the representatives nonetheless rescinded all laws that could be inaccurately construed as establishing a religion. Elsewhere in the constitution, ministers of any religious faith were banned from holding state office. As unequivocal as the convention representatives were in separating religion from their new government, the early legislature of the state proceeded to attempt to further clarify and strengthen the constitutional provisions. In 1779 the legislature even passed a law sentencing Trinity Church minister Charles Inglis and his wife to death.[33] A subsequent proposal to seize the property of the church was comparatively mild.

However, it was neither the primary law of the state nor subsequent legislative enactments that provided the design for disestablishment in New York. Instead, it was a judicial decision that relied on contract-law principles. The court used a law derived from liberal republican ideology to protect property from public action. Near the end of the war, a legislative committee chaired by Assemblyman Yates recommended confiscation of church property. Trinity Church had received its land in a letter from Queen Anne in 1714, which made a grant "to the Rector and inhabitants of the City of New York in commission of the Church of England, as by law established." As there was no longer any church "by law established," the land must, the committee reasoned, be held by the people. The committee report came before the legislature in 1784. Meanwhile, Trinity Church objected to the proposed confiscation and consulted church members Alexander Hamilton and Robert Troup for legal advice.[34]

Hamilton had just argued on behalf of the defendant in the case of *Elizabeth Rutgers v. Joshua Waddington*, decided on August 27, 1784, by Judge James Duane in New York City. This case addressed the government's possession and redistribution of private property in quite a different context from that of Trinity Church. The plaintiff, Elizabeth Rutgers, owned a brew house prior to the outbreak of war. On September 10, 1776, the British army conquered New York City. The commander in chief of the king's army took possession of the brew house. On September 28, 1778, he gave a license to the Waddingtons to operate the business for the benefit of the British soldiers. The Waddingtons ran the business until May 17, 1783. However, during only one stretch of time during this period was there a verifiable contract. The court found a written contract supported by evidence of consideration in the form of rent to exist between Mr. Joshua Waddington and the commander in chief only between April 30, 1780, and March 17, 1783.[35]

On March 17, 1783, the New York legislature enacted a law to provide compensation to landowners dispossessed of property "by reason of the invasion of the enemy" during the war. Mrs. Rutgers sued on the basis of that statute for compensation for her business losses and for the return of her property. In a significant assertion of the importance of common law, the court considered the legitimacy of the statute by its conformity to common law, and it held that "restitution of the fruit, or in other words, the rents and issues of houses and lands, which have been bona fide, collected by or under the authority of the British Commander, while he held possession of the city, cannot, according to the law of nations, be required." Judge Duane, mayor of the city and acting as chief judge of the Mayor's Court, held that the legislature could not act to deprive the defendant, Hamilton's client Joshua Waddington, of his rights under contract. The court limited the statute to apply only when the party enriched by the British army's possession of property was not the beneficiary of a lawful contract. In the case before it, Mrs. Rutgers was awarded compensation only for the period before April 30, 1780, and after March 17, 1783.

Hamilton used the judicial reasoning from the *Waddington* case to counsel Trinity Church. Hamilton's victory in this case constituted a legal recognition of the common law of contracts as embodying certain republican ideals that not even a state legislature could contravene. More specifically, contracts made with the Crown or its agent were valid, even when made during war when the king's authority was denied by the colonists in the midst of revolution. In this legal context, Trinity's contract with the Crown from 1714 must certainly be sustainable. Confronted with this reasoning, the legislature opted not to pursue the committee's recommendation to confiscate the property of Trinity Church. Here the developing laws of private property, enforced through contracts, were given early expression to redefine the roles of churches in American society. The legislature implicitly recognized the church not as a public entity but as a private business. The common law, used as a check on legislative action, limited the confiscation of church lands as an unlawful exercise of government power encroaching on private enterprise. As law professor Elizabeth Mensch asserts, "republicanism required not legislative confiscation of Trinity's property [to eviscerate all remnants of privilege] but rather reconfirmation of her holdings." The law, newly imbued with the ideology of the Revolution, determined this result. The court recognized private property rights as protected against state action. The legislature had to recognize that after disestablishment, the church stood as a private corporation, its rights protected by the same law that protected the rights of all citizens.[36]

The decision in this case set the course for future legislative action. After the judicial recognition of contract rights as superior to legislative enactment, the legislature had little choice but to limit its disestablishment initiatives to comply with the prevailing contract-law doctrine. Unable to attack church property, the legislature at least forced the churches to reorganize along more liberal republican terms. In late 1784 the New York State legislature passed four laws asserting a new legal status for churches in the state. Each was enacted with near unanimous support and excited almost no attention in newspapers, sermons, or other forums of civic debate.[37] The Trinity Church Act "abrogated, abolished, annulled, repealed, and made void" the old charter of the Church created by the Crown, the Ministry Act of 1693, and all subsequent and other laws relating to the Anglican establishment or Trinity Church, the leading Anglican body in New York. The legislature found provisions of the 1697 charter "inconsistent with the spirit and letter of the Constitution of the State."[38] The purpose of these acts was to eliminate the legal monopoly that had been held by the Anglicans by being the only churches able to incorporate. Under the new law, all sects could incorporate, and therefore hold property. The new law further repudiated any "pretentious claims . . . that the Episcopalian churches were [ever] established," an assertion that contributed to "the great vexation and disquiet of the good people of this state."[39] In the Church Incorporation Act, the legislature recited that under British rule and the presumed Anglican establishment "many charitable and well disposed persons have been prevented from contributing to the support of religion for want of proper persons authorized by law [that is, corporations] to take charge of their pious donations." Accordingly, the law created a system of general incorporation for all religious bodies to follow. Trinity Church, and other churches in the state, chartered their institutions using this new corporate model.[40]

As elsewhere in the new republic, the articulation of the legal model for religious institutions in New York did not resolve the ideological debate over the values and beliefs that would prevail in the society. That debate continued; its ultimate resolution, however, would now have to be reached in the context of a new legal design for social institutions. Churches were recreated as private institutions, protected by rights of incorporation. The legislature of New York, unable to interfere with private contract rights, would have to find new means of addressing public needs. By separating public and private institutions, the legislature implicitly separated state and church as well. Legal doctrine determined the form of church-state separation in New York, but legislative liberals committed to removing religion from government showed how use of the form could serve liberal principles.

The legislature also acted on the concern expressed by John Jay during the drafting of the constitution. It provided that all elected officials and appointees swear that they "renounce and adjure all allegiances and subjections" to any foreign official "in all matters ecclesiastical as well as civil."[41] A Catholic who was bound by his religious beliefs to live in accordance with the pope's directives could not take this oath.

King's College had been closed during the Revolution. In 1784 a group of moderates acting under the influence of New York City Mayor Duane petitioned the legislature to issue a new charter to the school recognizing "that Liberality and that civil and religious freedom" won the war. The legislature went much further. Composed of representatives hoping to secure the principles of the Revolution, it created a new University of the State of New York, in which several campuses were united under a governing board of regents. The new university was to reflect the liberal attitudes of the state, being open to all residents and offering them a practical education to prepare them for business or political careers. The legislature also provided that, as a public institution, the school would no longer reflect religious sentiments. The original regents of the university included church delegates, but government officials and elected county representatives comprised the majority of the board. In 1787 the state legislature eliminated all clerical representation among the regents, banned chapel, and eliminated a religious requirement for the university president and test oaths for the faculty. It provided that "no professor shall be in anywise whatsoever accounted ineligible, for or by any reason of any religious tenet or tenets, that he may or shall profess, or be compelled by any bye law or otherwise to take any religious test oath whatsoever."[42]

Alexander Hamilton perceived the changes in New York State's institutions as paralleling those in the marketplace. Whether the issue was religion, education, or commerce, Hamilton sought to increase accessibility. In this, he acted surprisingly like his eventual antagonist, Thomas Jefferson. Their later disagreement must be seen as existing over means more than goals. When Hamilton wrote that "all monopolies, exclusions, and discriminations of traffick, are pernicious and absurd," he very well could have been writing on behalf of the man from Virginia.[43]

In both the substance and tone of the legislative enactments of the 1780s, the New York legislature evinced a hostility to the Anglican/Episcopalian Church and the use of state authority in furtherance of religious goals. However, the legislation is drafted in positive terms, granting all church bodies the right to incorporate. The common-law rights to contract were specifically recognized as belonging to churches. These enactments presented state policy as a secular matter, unencumbered by the influences of the churches and their doctrines. Conforming to the liberal property law concepts, churches were removed from their roles as public institutions and repositioned within civil society. But implementing this policy was not easy. New Yorkers encountered a reaction from religious leaders who felt marginalized by the new state government. In addition, New Yorkers found it difficult to remove the churches from past roles without accepting a significant diminution in public services.

Reaction to the secular constitution among New York's Christians began even during the war years. The Dutch Reformed General Body, responding to the liberality of the new constitution and its potential contribution to a further decline in Christian piety, sent a letter to Governor Clinton in 1780, reminding him of the government's duty to suppress the "spirit of licentiousness [which has contributed] to the perversion of the good order of society and the discouragement and depression of holy religion." Ministers in all sects expressed despair at the increase of earthly concerns, moneymaking, infidelity, and moral laxity during the war years. In 1777 the Rev. Ichabod Lewis asked to be relieved of his duties in his White Plains pastorate due to the "melancholy and broken state" of his congregation.[44]

While the clergy bemoaned the lack of religious piety in the war years, however, its problems only increased after independence had been won. Some of the dissenters who had earlier advocated disestablishment now lamented the effects of a true separation of church and state. All churches found it difficult to operate in an environment where there could be no tax for church buildings or ministers' salaries. The new law permitting incorporation forced a new structure upon the churches, treating them as private businesses rather than public partners, and making them totally dependent on donations and volunteers. The Anglicans confronted the postwar era with the need to rebuild physically and spiritually. Many of their churches had been destroyed in war riots, and many of their ministers and Tory constituents had fled to England. Now they faced the prospects of community antagonism and the lack of tax support.

Perhaps even more disturbing to the clergy of the traditional churches was the continued growth of irreligiosity. People, empowered by the liberty to pursue their economic and political desires, focused their energies on worldly pursuits. Most New Yorkers, unencumbered by Christian invocations to charity and admonitions of greed, accepted the pursuit of self-interest and moneymaking as a reflection of their new legal equality and not a cause for shame. One enterprising lawyer wrote: "The circumstances of no taxes, no military, no ranks, remove every sensation of restraint. Each individual feels himself rising in his fortunes; and the nation rising with the concentration of all this elasticity, rejoices in its growing greatness." Some members of the clergy, distressed by the greed and social striving they witnessed, condemned contemporary society and advocated a return to Christian communitarianism. One minister offered this panageic to Christian society on July 4, 1799: "Whenever religion spreads an universal influence through society, there is nothing out of place; there is no crowding for the highest seats. It teaches one to think others better than himself, and to wait unambitious, till he is bidden to go up higher."[45]

Both men and women in New York in the 1790s benefited from the liberal commercial environment to create new businesses. Consistent with their active roles in business even before the Revolution, women in New York established restaurants, bakeries, confectioneries, seamstress shops, and coffee houses as well as other craft-oriented endeavors derived from their domestic duties. In addition, women in the early 1800s began to travel more by themselves, to take employment outside of the home or their own business, and to be the preferred hires for some professional positions such as teachers. This change in women's social status offended those who desired that they remain in more traditional roles. In her work *Women of the Republic,* Linda Kerber notes that many books and pamphlets began circulating at this time proposing models for female propriety and domestic life.[46] Churches sponsored many of these works. In addition, ministers addressed this issue from the pulpit. Typical of many sermons contrasting men's and women's natures and suitabilities for business, one preacher found a woman's "circumstances peculiarly advantageous for the exercises of devotion and for the presentation of virtue," unlike those of a man who must engage in "the bustle of life" and the "ferment of business." Women were taught by the church to limit their appetites, control their desires, and subordinate themselves to men, in recognition of "your softness, weakness, timidity, and tender reliance upon man; your helpless condition in yourselves and his superior strength for labor." While the liberal ideas spurring commercial growth encouraged women to pursue new opportunities, clerical predilections for biblical definitions of rules and duties, community integrity, and the retention of social hierarchy restrained many women from these pursuits. In this way too, liberals and traditional Christians divided in New York over the shape of the new society and the values it would reflect.[47]

In the process of repudiating predominate lifestyles, many traditionalists isolated themselves from their society. Further alienating some clergy was their reaction to the growth of Deism, Unitarianism, and a number of radical sects originating after the war that seemed to traditional churchmen as the worst form of blasphemies—contributing both to the moral decline of their society and the weakening of the churches themselves. The Presbyterian Synod expressed disgust with the ministers of those "corrupt forms of religion" who express "unsound principles" and "horrible errors."[48]

As such churchmen perceived their neighbors' values to edge ever further from those espoused by traditional churches, they moved to isolate themselves from the sinfulness around them. Corporate churches operated as communal enclaves of Christianity within a threatening realm of rampant individuality. Church discipline extended to address an increasing array of parishioner conduct, no longer limited to church attendance and doctrinal compliance but including "neighborliness" and "quarrelsomeness." Reminiscent of an attitude of their colonial forbears, church members subordinated their own wills to the authority of the communal whole. In a sermon of 1784, the Rev. Abraham Beach of Trinity Church in New York exhorted his parishioners to stand against the secular society that threatened them: "Let us build our hopes of future prosperity on the firm basis of Religion and Virtue—against a Superstructure raised on this Foundation, the Storms of adversity may beat in vain."[49] To contrast the shallowness of human pursuits with the depth of Christian piety, another minister reminded his listeners that the rewards of a Christian life were not limited to worldly glories:

> [Christ's] Kingdom is different from the kingdom of this world. The benefits and penalties of these are temporal but of that spiritual. The benefits of Christ's Church or Kingdom are remission of sins; grace to assist our infirmities; a victory over the world, the flesh and the devil; and the reward of eternal happiness in the kingdom of glory. The penalties also are purely spiritual—exclusion from the society of the faithful—the loss of divine favour;—and without repentance, eternal misery.[50]

As New York society generally adapted to the liberality of the new laws, some of its members persisted in a spiritual Christian worldview focused on the kingdom of God. They stand in sharp historical contrast to those who perceived the world around them as a realm of endless opportunity in which to satisfy their very real and immediate desires.

During the Revolution, some New York communities began taking steps to limit the roles of churches in providing public services. Colonial parish churches in New York had used the same means as those in other regions to address local poverty. Church wardens, acting with the authority of the colonial government, settled the poor with wealthier families able to provide for them, assigned wayward youth to masters to serve as apprentices, and distributed charitable relief payments to those temporarily impoverished by ill luck or poor decision making. Yet increasing problems in the areas of poverty, crime, and vagrancy prompted concern from New Yorkers about how well the churches were performing their functions. In 1773 New York attempted to control the churches in performance of these duties by appointing state overseers of the poor to supervise the church officials. This temporary partnership between church and state did not last long.[51]

After the war New York acted to remove the churches from positions of public responsibility, oftentimes creating greater social problems. In 1784 New York State abolished the parish as any form of civic designation. All laws providing for public payments to religion or the church in performance of societal duties were repealed. New laws reflected liberal republican ideals of limited government, self-sufficiency, and the separation of church and state. Poor relief was redefined, consistent with Jeffersonian ideology, as a private or family obligation, only secondarily to be addressed by the state. A 1784 statute recognized relatives (to the degree of relatedness of grandparent-grandchild but not uncle-niece) who were able to support their kin as legally responsible to do so. If an impoverished individual came to the attention of the state, the justice of the peace for the county in which he was found could assess his relatives the cost of his temporary support. State law prescribed further secularization in addressing this social concern. Each town, city, or district was to elect overseers of the poor who worked under the direction of the justices of the peace. The overseers had authority to make rules and regulations for poor relief. They proceeded to sell contracts of labor for the poor to people who desired and were able to afford servants rather than to assign the poor to people of means. They also began to compel able-bodied poor to work, or they removed them from town and raised money for the administration of these duties. Each of these functions depended upon writs or orders from the court. The overseers determined the appropriate tax rate to be charged the local citizenry and forwarded it to the county supervisors for approval.[52]

Between 1790 and 1820 New York City completed the first stage in its development into the business and finance capital of the world. Men whose family names would become icons of wealth for two centuries such as Astor, Dodge, Phyfe, and Hepplewhite came to the fore. The population doubled between 1800 and 1820, owing to employment in the shipping industry, early wage-based industries, and small businesses catering to a new class of luxury consumers. The latest, sometimes daring, fashions, fine furniture, porcelain, and jewelry were all imported and found ready buyers. In the fifteen years between 1792 and 1807, the value of imports through New York City increased from 1.4 to 7.6 million dollars. New York became the nation's leading port by 1800.[53]

The rapid commercial growth of New York left many poor people in its wake. In general, New Yorkers attributed poverty to faults in character among the poor and acted to remove and reform them. In 1788 the New York legislature created almshouses and recognized a social obligation to provide medical attention to the sick among the poor. Sending the most desperate among the poor to almshouses provided the removal of the poor from public view and the opportunity for rehabilitation. In 1803 Mayor Livingston of New York City proposed creation of a municipal workshop to house the poor and harness their productivity. Reflecting similar concerns, state-sponsored medical care was premised on returning poor sick people to work while reducing the risk of social contagion. An increasing numbers of those who could not be productive, such as the mentally ill and women with small children, were simply dropped off at almshouses, resulting in overcrowding. As social duty became a function of legal obligation rather than Christian benevolence, New Yorkers' patience with the unfortunate declined.

Local governments organized in the 1790s created public offices responsible for highways, poor relief, record keeping, property protection, and tax collection. Two decades earlier New York's churches had administered the poor relief programs and worked with local officials to maintain records and collect taxes. The new government programs accomplished little in stemming the increase of poverty. An aversion to taxes and an intolerance of the poor themselves combined to render public programs inadequate to address local needs. The state relied upon private organizations to fill the void. It is not surprising that many of these private groups evinced attitudes similar to those of the legislators. The New York Society for Prevention of Pauperism announced its ideal in 1821: "No man who is temperate, frugal, and willing to work need suffer or become a pauper for want of employment."[54]

In 1806 the New York Orphan Asylum was founded by a group of wealthy women concerned with the growing number of homeless children in New York City. Their private solicitation for money proved disappointing, and in 1808 they petitioned the legislature for funds. The New York Assembly created a lottery to support an orphanage administered by the private charitable organization.[55]

Many private associations were composed at least in part of Christian members. Early nineteenth-century Christianity, while not yet adopting the social gospel, recognized adherents' duties to express benevolence toward their fellow men, requiring efforts to make them moral and to reform their manners, habits, and beliefs. The Rev. Nathaniel Emmons of Franklin, Massachusetts, reminded his congregation in 1809 that a failure to act to prevent the sin or degradation of others would "incur the highest displeasure of the final judge." In this spirit, a group of wealthy New Yorkers formed the New York Humane Society in that same year to preserve the "purity of public morals" and lectured the poor on the evils of sin while providing them with free soup and bread.[56] In reaction to their diminished political role, churches themselves actually pulled back from providing social services. The minutes of Trinity Church in New York City during the 1780s and 1790s contain repeated resolutions that the money collected in church services be "applied by the Rector for the use of the poor of the congregation" rather than the poor of the neighborhood or the city at large.[57]

As difficult as it proved to be to provide for the poor after removing the churches from their former role, it proved even more difficult to sustain schooling without church involvement. Prior to the 1790s religious instruction had dominated education in New York.[58] Creation of a republican government brought with it a new recognition of societal dependence upon an educated citizenry holding republican values. Governor Clinton's first address to the New York legislature in 1783 encouraged the creation of a state university system with the authority to charter academies. In 1787 the board of regents of the newly created university received a committee report that encouraged the board to initiate a public school system: "the erecting of public schools for teaching reading, writing and arithmetic is an object of very great importance, which ought not to be left to the discretion of private men, but be promoted by public authority."[59]

The board acted upon this recommendation in 1787, 1793, and 1794 without avail, until in 1795 the legislature agreed to raise fifty thousand dollars in annual tax revenues to distribute to localities to maintain public schools. By 1798, 1,352 schools received state funds under the act, and 59,660 children were being taught in them. Yet in 1800 the bill was allowed to lapse without renewal.[60] In New York City that year, with a population of over sixty thousand, no tuition-free schools existed.

In the early 1800s groups of private citizens sponsored various educational efforts addressing the plight of New York's children. Many of these efforts incorporated religious instruction. Resentment of the religious influences in education prompted a liberal response. In 1812 the legislature again established a common school fund, making money available to all existing schools, whether or not affiliated with a church. "An Act for the establishment of Public Schools" created school districts and organized administrative bureaucracies, established teaching standards and state inspections, required districts to assess parents a portion of the cost of education unless the parents were unable to pay, and conditioned a school's receipt of funds upon its acceptance of these terms.[61]

By the early 1820s the Free School Society, a liberal and nonsectarian body, had become active in providing education to New York City's children. When the Bethel Baptist Church group in New York City received state funds in 1822 to construct a new school, the society objected. The grant constituted a break from previous policy and prompted a reconsideration of the meanings of earlier laws. In a petition to the state legislature, the Free School Society argued that the use of public funds to support denominational education violated "the sacred principle of our Constitution, that church and state shall not be united." Not content with petitioning the legislature, the society initiated a public campaign to prevent state aid to denominational schools. A state commission to consider the formation of public schools resulted from these efforts. In 1825 the commission recommended creating a common school system. Its report cited only secular goals of education being essential to the preservation of the republic. Even more indicative of a new liberal emphasis on education, the commission endorsed several new teaching methods recently adopted in parts of Europe and recommended consideration of Lancastrian textbooks and use of Rousseau's *Emile* concerning the duties and roles of a teacher.[62] This movement culminated in an amendment to the state constitution in 1825: "The proceeds of certain public lands belonging to the State, together with the Fund denominated 'The Common School Fund' (supported by tax dollars), shall be, and remain a perpetual Fund, the interest of which shall be inviolably appropriated to the support of common schools throughout the State." Governor DeWitt Clinton, in 1826, explained a significant change in educational policy derived from this new law:

> An important change has taken place in the free schools of New York. By an arrangement between the corporation of that city and the trustees of the free school society, those establishments are to be converted into public schools, to admit the children of the rich as well as of the poor, and by this annihilation of factitious distinctions, there will be a strong incentive for the display of talents, and a felicitous accommodation to the genius of republican government.[63]

In 1828 and 1829 the legislature increased the state school tax "to be applied exclusively to the purposes of the common schools."[64]

Yet, in 1831, the Roman Catholic Benevolent Society submitted a request to the trustees of the School Fund for support of a new Catholic school in New York City. Following the 1825 legislation, the Free School Society changed its name to the Public School Society, reflecting its new affiliation with the New York public schools. Responding to the request of the Catholic Church, the trustees of the Public School Society minced no words in clarifying their understanding of the new republican educational system. They contended that the creation of the fund was a final victory "of liberal principles in education over sectarian views," and that by law "all churches and religious Societies [were] deprived of participation."[65] The trustees objected to the Catholic "corporation select[ing] the orphans to be admitted into this asylum" and then providing them with religious instruction. Granting the corporation's request represented "a virtual abandonment of those 'cardinal principles' which were established in 1825" and ran "contrary to the fundamental principles of liberty and equal rights—to the Constitution of the State—and to a recent act of the Legislature."[66] Acknowledging "the humane and laudable purposes of [the corporation in] assisting and relieving the poor, and of protecting and educating orphan children," the society trustees nonetheless professed that law and republican principles mandated religious charity schools "ought, in the opinion of this Board, to be supported by voluntary donations and not by compulsory levies."[67]

The actions of the New York legislature and the political action groups sponsoring public education in the second and third decades of the nineteenth century illustrated broader social changes. Once willing to subordinate the ideological commitment to separating church and state to the pragmatic needs of poor relief and education, New Yorkers moved—increasingly after the Revolution, and then even more after 1800—to take public institutional control over the servicing of public needs. The Republican governments of the "era of good feelings" were not willing to allow private corporations to determine public policy. Part of the reason for this refusal was the increasing ideological divide between rationalist liberals and a reinvigorated group of Christian minority activists.

Renewal of Christian activism began during the 1780s and 1790s among New York's traditional Christian churches. The clergy of the Episcopal, Presbyterian, and Dutch Reformed churches became impatient with the state's inattention to the problems of declining morality. Refusing either to accept or to comprehend the intent and significance of the disestablishment provisions in New York's constitution or the state's subsequent legislation, they advocated governmental action to infuse the people with a new appreciation of Christian duty. In its convention in 1785 the Episcopal Church resolved to encourage the state to observe both the Fourth of July and the first Tuesday in November as "days of Thanksgiving to Almighty God," converting what they perceived as occasions for secular revelry into opportunities to remember and give thanks for God's blessings. Implicitly, the convention rejected a growing national consensus that America's independence and growth were due to human endeavor more than God's will. In 1796 the Washington Presbytery of the Associated Reformed Church petitioned the legislature for strengthening the Sabbath laws. They were cautioned by their New York City brethren:

> At present Infidelity is the fashion and infidels are men of consequence. Too many of them fill places of public responsibility; the Holy Sabbath reckons implacable enemies among Judges, Legislators, interpreters of the law and executive officers. The probability, therefore, in our own judgment is that if the law for the suppression of immoralities on the Sabbath should be now submitted to revision, instead of being improved, it would be abolished altogether.

The petition was withdrawn. Two years later William Linn, Dutch Reformed pastor in New York City, encouraged the "universal spread and influence" of Christian virtue as indispensable to "national prosperity and happiness."[68]

Yet his was only one more lonely voice, ineffectual against the growing secularism of American culture. No new laws were enacted in New York during the 1780s and 1790s to strengthen Christian values and communitarian ideals. Even the few laws from the colonial era that remained, such as those on blasphemy, were generally ignored as anachronisms of an earlier age. The mood of the people regarding religious prescription was remarkably cool. Charles Nisbet remarked in 1797 that religion had been nearly extinguished "by the Equality and Indifference of Religious Opinions that is established by our Political Constitutions." He found only two strong "churches" remaining—"Anythingarians, who hold all religions equally good, and the Nothingarians who abhor all religions equally."[69]

By the turn of the century, most churchmen began to recognize the infeasibility of returning to an earlier church-state relationship. The dissenting clergy in the Presbyterian and Dutch Reformed churches never imagined that disestablishment would result in the total separation of church and state and the marginalization of Christian doctrine by a secular society. Yet, twenty years after the Revolution-era constitution, that was precisely what they encountered. They responded by utilizing the only alternative left. The new laws favored private initiative over collective public action. Incorporation served as the new means by which groups of individuals could work together, protected by law, to pursue goals beyond the reach of each of the members of the group acting singly. It proved successful in building bridges, mills, and factories; perhaps it could be utilized by the churches as a vehicle of opposition to state policy.

In the late 1790s Christian churches began to overcome past sectarian differences in recognition of common concerns. Representatives of the Dutch Reformed, Presbyterian, and Associated Reformed churches began meeting in periodic conventions. By 1801 the Dutch Reformed and Presbyterian churches in New York and Pennsylvania reached a plan of union with the New England Congregationalists. The primary purpose of these alliances was to pool the financial powers of the participants in cooperative efforts in publishing, missionary outreach, and expression of social and political dissent. In 1798, for example, the Presbyterian Synod of New York and New Jersey encouraged the formation of voluntary action groups to suppress vice and immorality when civil magistrates failed to do so. Churches took the initiative in promoting Christian visions of moral reform and social justice through vigilante societies.[70]

Jefferson's campaign for the presidency combined with the beginnings of the Second Awakening to create among New York's churches the urgency of war. Some traditional churches retreated from their earlier flirtations with liberal religion and restated their commitments to belief in the trinity, original sin, and the scriptural integrity of the Bible as the one true Word of God.[71] In Rochester, Presbyterians asserted their impotence before a God who "foreordained whatsoever comes to pass." The Episcopal Church instructed its seminary students to read the works of Lesley and Leland, noted Deists, so as to be better able to refute the heresies they would likely encounter. In 1803 Presbyterian minister Alexander McLeod instructed his New York City congregation: "Civil society, under whatever form of visible government, cannot be managed, as it respects the system of created being, by a more suitable character than the Messiah." Upstate in Salem, the Rev. Alexander Proudfit reminded his listeners:

> Whatever be your calling in life, endeavor to prosecute its duties, whether personal or social, with a humble dependence on God for success and an upright concern for his glory. Thus we are commanded in scripture "to be in the fear of the Lord all the day long; to acknowledge him in all our ways that our steps may be directed by him; and whether we eat or drink or whatsoever we do, to do all to the glory of God.[72]

In New York, as elsewhere during the Second Awakening, several providentialist ministers repeatedly asserted the futility of human initiative given the all-powerful controlling influence of the living God. On the occasion of George Washington's death, one speaker contrasted the symbol of America's greatness to the true deity: "Washington was but the instrument of a benignant God. He sickens, he dies, that we may learn not to trust in men nor to make flesh our arm. But though Washington is dead, Jehovah lives."[73]

Inevitably, in a democratic republic in which the churches were coming to see themselves as private entities, exercising the rights and liberties available to them under law, the clergy would begin using the pulpit to invoke Christian-oriented social policy. As the New York Methodist Church affirmed at its general conference in 1808, Christians longed for "the universal spread of Scriptural truth and holiness over the inhabitable globe."[74] The Christian utopian dream of a society united in Christ was unsheathed during the early 1800s as a sword to combat secular humanism. When the people controlled their own political destinies, voting became a means of pursuing this Christian ideal. The Rev. John Mason preached that "the principles of the gospel are to regulate [people's] political as well as their other conduct." He scoffed at the idea that "religion has nothing to do with politics!" asking rhetorically, "Where did you learn this maxim?" To the contrary, he offered, "the Bible is full of directions for your behavior as citizens," citing in example Col. 3:17: "And whatsoever ye do in word or deed, to do all in the name of the Lord Jesus."[75] Other New York ministers expressed similar sentiments to their congregations, representing civil government as a "subsidiary" to God's grand design of preparing saints for the future and "the civil magistrate as God's officer."[76]

Jefferson's candidacy provoked such fear in these New York ministers that they openly campaigned against him in their sermons. Some of the reaction to Jefferson stemmed from his own limited statements on Christianity. Jefferson wrote: "The legitimate powers of government extend to such acts only as are injurious to others. But it does me no injury for my neighbors to say there are twenty gods or no god. It neither picks my pockets, nor breaks my leg."[77] This philosophy of government premised the separation of church and state on a more fundamental concern than the state's preference of one sect over another. Clerical leaders confronted the realization that the rationalist understanding of disestablishment implied the inability of the government to acknowledge even the most basic Christian tenets as true or relevant to the nation's course. Moral judgments and encouragements were certainly outside the scope of law and government. To a New York clergy already struggling to accept the effects of disestablishment in that state, Jefferson's candidacy threatened the perpetuation of the Christian dream for American society. Responding to Jefferson's statement, Mason wrote: "This is nothing less than representing civil society as founded in Atheism. For there can be no religion without God. And if it does me or my neighbor no injury, to subvert the very foundation of religion, by denying the being of God, then religion is not one of the constituent principles of society, and consequently society is perfect without it."[78]

Nearly buried beneath the religious language of the ministers involved in the New York debate is the derivative issue of what worldview would dominate in the construction of American society. Jefferson advocated a public abstention on matters of religion. Many clergymen correctly interpreted this position as effectively atheistic. Public abstention amounted to the denial of a single religious truth; and once a government rejects the idea of one religious truth, it is rendered unable to act upon any religious doctrine in constructing the laws, values, and policy aims of that society. But the idea that any God could himself, or herself or itself, be relativistic is absurd—how can any true living God accept all suggestions of his, her, or its own existence as merely speculative or one of many unprovable theories? If God could not accept religious relativism, how could America? The advocacy of religious relativism is logically inconsistent with the acceptance of any true, living God. Accordingly, the ministers insisted that when a government assumed such a position, it rejected the existence of God as well as God's role in governing.

The libertarianism of Jeffersonian republicanism restricted the freedom of each individual of the society only when his or her actions impaired the equal right to freedom enjoyed by a fellow citizen. People were subordinated to no greater truth than the respect for each other's civil rights. This rationalistic, humanistic, and eventually legalistic approach denied not only the relevance of Christian teachings such as the Ten Commandments, but also the authority of any governmental institution to impose them, as irrational and tyrannical restrictions, upon a free people. Christian commonwealths, in which individuals subordinated themselves and their interests to a government acting in accordance with God's laws, were inconceivable in a Jeffersonian republican construct. The realization of this, after twenty-three years of adjustment to disestablishment in their own state, further frustrated New York's conservative Christians.

In an attempt to overcome the problems they confronted, many sought to undo the laws that created those problems, refusing to accept disestablishment as a proscription of all government activity in support of the one true religion. As the Rev. Alexander McLeod stated, if Christianity is a true religion, it is the magistrate's "duty to remove every exertion for the removal of [its] introduction. Coercion, indeed may never be used in order to make his subjects religious; but it may be used in order to suppress immorality, profaneness, and blasphemy; and in order to remove the monuments of idolatry from the land."[79] The political appeals of New York's ministers during this time came very close to appeals to revoke the disestablishment laws and impose a Christian religion upon the people of the state.

New York's clergy united in pushing for the passage of new laws that might reinvigorate the Christian commonwealth by proscribing immoral and selfish behavior. Earlier calls for blue laws, restrictions on female labor, and a reinvigoration of crimes against morality had failed. Yet in the first few decades of the nineteenth century, the conflict in worldviews manifested itself in debates over economic freedom. Most of the sharpest critiques of

American society in the early republic came from both evangelical and traditional clergymen bemoaning the licentiousness, acquisitiveness, and greed of people in their society and pushing for the restriction of economic freedoms as a means of curbing people's insatiable appetites.[80]

By the early nineteenth century, Jeffersonian liberals had come to see personal freedom as embodied by individual involvement in the free market, and economic justice as the product of that involvement.[81] In this ideological framework the market acted as the sole regulator of prices, and public interest was tied to the interests of consumers. Free labor meant the ability to sell one's labor without restriction. Advocates of communitarianism argued that the resultant increase in poverty, misery, and inequality since the Revolution only confirmed the need for communities premised on Christian duty and the moral imperative of concern for each other's welfare. Christian doctrine provided not only a basis for rejecting the individualism of American society but also a responsibility to overcome perceived unfair consequences of a purely rational economic system.[82] These arguments ran headlong into the prevalent free labor ideology of the early republic protected by contract law.

A legal contest embodying this ideological conflict arose in New York in 1809. In this trial, laborers were prosecuted on the common-law doctrine of criminal conspiracy in interfering with contracts. Journeymen cordwainers, acting in concert, refused to work for any employer who offered wage rates below their demands. They further refused to work alongside any cordwainers who accepted lower pay, putting pressure on them to join their society. This action limited the rights of unorganized cordwainers to set the rates for their own labor, in other words, to reach their own contractual bargains. It further imposed what were then perceived as unnatural labor prices upon the cost of goods in the marketplace. The court found that the conspirators attempted to limit the economic freedoms of the unorganized cordwainers and the employers. The prosecution called the action the "most tyrannical violations of private right."[83]

The common law in New York squarely supported the free market. The journeymen cordwainers were looking to the model of the past, concerted action rooted in equity and communitarian values, rather than to the present. As collective labor action was increasingly seen as a product of an alternative value system, so too was the traditional role of the clergy in addressing matters of morality increasingly seen as a threat to the burgeoning system of liberal values. Church leaders' support for moral reform of New York society provoked condemnation by fearful business leaders. Ideological conflict precipitated social tension. When Elder Josiah Bissell, of the Third Presbyterian Church in Rochester, led a boycott of merchants in that town who did business on Sunday, the affected businessmen responded in the press to what they called a violation of the rights of individual conscience threatening the "free spirit of our [republican] institutions." When various pastors brought petitions before the legislature encouraging the passage of state laws prohibiting labor and commerce to be conducted on the Sabbath, businessmen responded with pamphlets and periodicals alerting New York-ers to the threat of religious control of civil law and institutions. During the second and third decades of the nineteenth century, a number of innovative periodicals entered these debates on the side of liberal ideas and market growth. Frances Wright moved the *New Harmony Gazette* to New York and re-named it the *Free Enquirer*. Robert Dale Owen, a critic of organized religion as well as an advocate of private business interests, began publishing the *Daily Sentinel*. The harsh tone of these periodicals tied church-led reforms of busi-ness practices to a denial of civil liberties and a corruption of republican in-stitutions. George H. Evans, writing in the *Working Man's Advocate,* de-nounced the "Church and State Party," consisting of anti-Masonic churchmen, as "the most dangerous Secret Society that ever existed in this Republic."[84] In 1792 Joel Barlow, one of the "Connecticut Wits" to serve in the Jefferson and Madison administrations, published his *Advice to the Privi-leged Orders*. He initially intended the piece for a European audience that had not separated church and state, but he subsequently found its message meaningful in his home country. Barlow supposed that mankind would never accept the irrationality of an elite group of people controlling its fel-low citizens. Accordingly, he saw religion as the means by which churchmen overcame man's reason and moral sense to justify their privileged position:

> Recourse must therefore be had to mysteries and invisibilities; an engine must be forged out of the religion of human nature and erected on its credulity, to play upon and extinguish the light of reason which was placed in the mind as a caution to the one and a kind companion to the other. This engine, in all ages of the world, has been the church.[85]

Judges and legislators used the power of law to protect private actions from Christian attacks. Separation of church and state, occurring simultane-ously with the rise of liberalism, resulted in the diminution of doctrinal Christian influences in public policy. The religion of the republic became an expositor of a social morality, essentially derived from Christian doctrine but independent of its spiritual bases, which supported a social brotherhood premised more on equal rights and personal freedoms than Christian love and communitarianism. Even Deists and agnostics could attribute some so-cial benefit to the roles played by churches espousing such doctrines. In a late New York blasphemy case, *The People of New York v. Ruggles,* Chancellor Kent condemned Ruggles's misbehavior. Yet in private the chancellor re-ferred to Christianity as "a barbaric superstition."[86] The blasphemy now en-forced by the civil government punished social disruption more than disre-spect of the deity.

This distinction was not lost on the New York clergy. The full impact of the Constitution's secular prescriptions provoked a reaction from those who were silent during its drafting. The Rev. John Mason now saw the failure to mention God in the nation's charter as a "neglect" of the providential power "who gave us our national existence and saved us from anarchy and internal war." Calls for a return to a greater social and political recognition of a spiritual Christianity expressed clerical concerns with the secular values of political institutions and the concomitant loss of Christian communities. The Rev. John Henry Hobart of New York City's Trinity Church sought a revitalization of society by its reintegration of God's will and the teachings of Christ into its political processes:

> They seldom bring into view the divine institution of the Christian Church, and the divine origin of its powers . . . the duty of submission is made to rest not on its claims to a divine origin, but on the motives of mere expediency; and hence the exercise of its discipline is not regarded as a duty demanded by the authority of its divine Head, and the purity of its sacred character, but as dictated merely by those considerations of policy which influence secular associations, and as left entirely to human discretion.

The Rev. Benjamin Moore, bishop of the Episcopal Church in New York, went even further in a charge given before his Episcopal brethren, calling the present state of religion in America "far different from the determination of God himself . . . which was a dispensation of divine wisdom, [in which] religious and civil institutions were intimately blended together."[87]

In 1832 the clergy revived a long campaign for legislative appointment of chaplains in government and military institutions in the state of New York. After years of fighting the incursion of religion into political processes and policies, a committee of legislators reporting on the proposal unloosed unusually vitriolic reaction in its published report:

> there is an evil spirit abroad, seeking to infuse its baleful influence among the people, to obtain a dominant power in the civil government, through which to manage all the political concerns of the nation, and thus to establish ecclesiastical dominion on the ruins of our free republican institutions. . . . But it is not true that Christianity as such is the law of the land. The Constitution is the supreme law of the land; by virtue of which the mosque, the synagogue, the Christian church, and all other churches and religions are placed on equal grounds.[88]

During the 1820s New York business and population grew at a fast pace in large part due to the construction of the Erie Canal. Western New York had experienced the revivals of the Second Awakening in 1812–1813 and again in 1816–1817. Prior to that time religion in the region had generally conformed to a minimalist Christian doctrine. Churches maintained only titular affiliation with denominations, held services void of creeds or doctrinal recitations, and focused energies upon educating the children in their towns. Despite their adoption of doctrinal blandness and a civic orientation intended to appeal to large audiences, however, western churches attracted far less than half of their townspeople to join or attend. The effect of the revivals was to divide the new evangelicals from the traditional churches of the region. Spurred by the revivals, evangelicals became a significant force in social reform in western New York.[89]

Evangelicals may generally feel themselves to have little in common with the less pietistic communities in which they live. This was especially true in western New York between 1813 and 1825. Laborers on the canal distinguished themselves from upstate farmers in their ethnic backgrounds, language, drinking, and social practices. As the traditional churches had been unable to change New York society into a more Christian commonwealth, the evangelical churches would sacrifice broad reform for pietistic example. In this way, the evangelicals of upstate New York were reminiscent of the Puritans of the early seventeenth century. In 1814 the Baptist Association of New York even called upon its churches to serve "like a city on a hill" within their communities. Earlier, the association's circular letter instructed members that "Christians are to distinguish themselves from the rest of the world by their sobriety, regard to religion, and shunning even the appearance of evil."[90] Even traditional churches, overtaken by the evangelical movement of the Second Awakening, began to separate themselves from the broader society in setting a Christian example. Churches came to constitute an alternative community to which Christians could escape. The Virgil Congregational Church Covenant expressed fear of "worldly contamination" and required members to "renounce the service of the devil, slavery of sin, and the love of the world." All evangelical churches in the region prohibited their members from recourse to the civil courts to resolve disputes, providing an internal juridical option. They also all published rules governing members' behaviors. The Cortland Congregational Church proscribed the following behaviors on the Sabbath: traveling, visiting, recreational walking, worldly conversation, reading of newspapers or nonreligious books, and any preparation of or attention to food or dress that could have been performed earlier.[91]

In response to the evangelical movement and its alternative vision, church membership nearly tripled by 1830. Initially, traditional churches expressed fierce opposition. Methodist circuit ministers were described by one churchman as "uneducated" and "unauthorized" by God.[92] Yet the Second Awakening contributed mightily to the growth of many Christian churches and helped to refocus fellowship outreach programs. The attempts by New York's turn-of-the-century religious leaders to redesign society by legislative initiative proved futile. Lacking the political power to institute reform, churches looked inward for moral influence. The failures of the clergy to contribute to the laws of the state regarding business practices convinced them of the need to play a new role in the republican society. New Yorkers still listened to the churches as shapers of public morality, even if not as contributors to public policy. The evangelical examples of moral leadership, rather than divorcing Christians from their communities, provided them with moral authority to contribute to the civil dialogue. The roles of religion and the churches increased in New York and in the nation in the era of reform after 1830. Once churches became external to the governing process, they could become important leaders of social criticism.

In New York after the Revolution the state's churches had to adopt—and then adjust to operating within—a corporate form. Once they succeeded in doing so, they gained more power and influence than they ever held under laws of Anglican establishment. New York's governments, state and local, also had to adjust to the privatization of the churches. During the process of disestablishment, governments only slowly assumed responsibility for societal tasks previously performed by the churches. As both churches and governments in New York tried to find their ways under a new system of laws, ideologues professing a Christian communitarianism or a liberal rationalism continued to fight for victory in the larger battle over the values of American society.

6

Southern Republicanism and Constitutional-Era Disestablishment

The Case of South Carolina

I am now persuaded [that] the utmost any clerical establishment in America can afford is a bare maintenance from year to year.

D. L. Bowen to Thomas Waites, April 19, 1813, on the condition of the Episcopal Church in South Carolina

IN NEW YORK THOSE WHO SOUGHT to perpetuate a Christian commonwealth encountered the overwhelming power of liberalism in laws that freed the people of that state from social duties predicated upon religious belief, morality, or Christian obligation. In South Carolina people of similar sentiments were supported in their opposition to liberal reform by a planter elite that sought to use the church as a means of preserving a culture premised on hierarchy and social deference. Liberalism threatened not only the position of the church in southern society but also the anachronistic business and social relationships that characterized the region.

Much of the recent study of the growth of liberal contract-law principles in the early republic has concentrated on northern states. In *Juries and Judges versus the Law,* however, F. Thornton Miller argued that the South resented and fought the imposition of contract law as potentially destructive of its premodern economy. Contract law gave power to the courts to overcome provincial considerations in asserting human equality and property rights, implicitly including the right to sell one's own labor. Similarly, Timothy Huebner, in *The Southern Judicial Tradition,* notes that "the principle of community interest informed southern judicial thinking about law and the economy." For example, as late as the early 1800s in Virginia, Judge Spencer Roane stated that a corporation has no reason to exist if its purpose was "merely private or selfish, if it is detrimental to, or not promotive of the public good."[1]

The battle for disestablishment in South Carolina reflected that state's opposition to the intrusion of "foreign" law and liberal ideals. The church in South Carolina came to prominence by assuming an unusual role in social control, and it survived an initial Revolutionary-era battle of constitutional disestablishment to maintain a position of social prominence. Despite the influence of distinctly southern factors, the case of South Carolina's disestablishment supports Mead's thesis. The dissenting clergymen who fought for their rights to incorporate and grow their congregations in the first phase of South Carolina's disestablishment opposed the provision of complete religious freedom twelve years later. More important, the battle over disestablishment in South Carolina reflects the same tension between communal Christianity and individual liberties that existed in other states. South Carolina's Baptist, Methodist, and Presbyterian dissenters sought a Christian commonwealth, not a libertarian secular republic. However, their religious beliefs did not permit the construction of this commonwealth along racial lines. In advocating a racial equality before God and a need to abolish slavery, these sects challenged more than just Anglican establishment. Evangelical conceptions of the social good proved to be inconsistent with South Carolina's planters' interests. As dissenting sects grew and gained political power, they posed a threat to an increasingly paranoid planter elite. Complete disestablishment was won only by overcoming the low-country elite's fear of liberalism by positioning religion as an even greater threat to slavery.

Although no court decision expressed the legal basis for disestablishment in South Carolina as happened in New York and would happen in New Hampshire, the use of law to separate public and private spheres was a necessary precondition to disestablishment in this state. Disestablishment once more followed and conformed to the legal separation of public and private spheres. In the case of South Carolina, this legal separation arose in the drafting of the state's primary law to more clearly adhere to the principles of republicanism. The distinctive diminution of all public institutions that could threaten the private rights of the southern gentry was expressed in South Carolina's Constitution of 1790. The church was transformed into a private institution when its power as a public institution became too threatening.

Circumstances combined to make South Carolina a somewhat religiously diverse community from the start. The proprietors of the colony, needing laborers, encouraged immigration through a policy of limited religious toleration. Scottish covenanters came in droves following the fall of Cromwell's commonwealth and the Restoration of Charles II. The revocation of the Edict of Nantes in 1685 initiated a diaspora of French Protestants, the Huguenots. In addition, some second- and third-generation New Englanders began to seek greener pastures in the late 1600s as a result of changes in Puritan religious doctrine and their desires for land. Sugar planters from the West Indies moved to the Carolinas to escape the islands. Each of these various Protestant groups correctly perceived Carolina as offering a religious refuge and an economic opportunity.[2]

Despite the religious diversity of the settlers coming to South Carolina after 1680, political and economic power remained with an Anglican elite.

Huguenots worshiping in the wilderness—Following the revocation of the Edict of Nantes, French Protestants known as Huguenots emigrated from France to more religiously tolerant environs in Europe and America. Many came to South Carolina in the early 1700s. Courtesy Presbyterian Historical Society, Presbyterian Church (USA) (Philadelphia).

Members of this elite viewed the influx of foreigners and dissenters as a greater risk to social order than to their own tepid religious sentiments. They tightened religious prescriptions in order to control the new settlers. The Carolinas operated with separate governments even before formal division of the colonies in the second decade of the eighteenth century. In December 1691 the South Carolina Parliament passed "An Act for the Better Observance of the Lord's Day, commonly called Sunday." This law prohibited the "profane practices" of idleness, disorderliness, drinking, shooting, gaming, and other "vicious exercises, pastimes, and meetings."[3] The North Carolina Assembly established the Anglican Church in 1701. The South Carolina Assembly, despite a minority of Anglicans within the colony, followed suit in 1704. At the same time, the Anglican members of the assembly voted 12–11 to enact legislation excluding non-Anglicans from the government.

The dissenters appealed to the Lords Proprietors objecting to the changes in religious policy. They found a supporter in Daniel Dafoe, member of the

House of Lords. Dafoe helped the dissenters by writing pamphlets supporting religious toleration in the colonies. In response, the House of Lords requested the Crown to "deliver the said Province from the Arbitrary Oppres-
sions under which it now lies." The Lords' action was premised both on an
appreciation of the sort of religious toleration that had been engendered
during the Glorious Revolution of 1688 and on the deleterious effects of religious prejudice upon colonial profits. In response to the Lords' action, the
assembly repealed its act only to pass a new church act in 1706. The Lords
allowed this law to stand.[4]

Southern Anglicanism reflected the educated cosmopolitanism of southern planter society in the eighteenth century. The newly established church
emphasized social conformity, civic order, and a rational Arminian doctrine.
It embodied social conservatism with religious liberalism. Dissenters responded to the establishment of the Anglican Church by moving inland
away from the controls of the strong Anglican parishes. The inland areas,
also known as the piedmont in contrast to the lowland south, were less suitable for growing commercial crops. The geographic separation of Anglicans
and dissenters reinforced the economic and social positions between these
groups. Legislation in the early 1700s further exacerbated these differences.
The Church Act of 1706 denied dissenters the right to vote. And in 1716 the
legislature created "parishes," corresponding to Anglican church territories,
as the basic form of local government. The parishes assumed responsibility
for record keeping, poor relief, and more sporadically, education. In 1722
one quarter of all tax revenues in the state went to the Anglican Church.[5]

These actions, too, prompted responses from religious dissenters. A group
of Huguenots objected to the Board of Trade in London over the colonial assembly's use of the parish church as the seat of municipal government. Although the Board of Trade sided with the dissenters, it was powerless to create an alternative civic government. As a result the parish church retained its
de facto status as a governmental institution throughout the colonial era.[6]

Ironically, despite the secular nature of its founding and the minority status of its established church, Anglicanism in South Carolina became one of
the strongest of the colonial establishments. Anglican establishment resulted
from the elite's desire for a strong church as a vehicle for maintaining social
order. The Church Act of 1706 establishing the church provided the Anglicans with considerable political powers over their fellow citizens. It provided
that the Anglican church of each parish was to serve as the courthouse of
that parish and the place of posting for all proclamations and public notices.
The church was given the responsibility of all parish record keeping, including records of baptisms, births, marriages, deaths, burials, and tax collections. The church administered the poor relief efforts for each parish, including tax collection and distribution of alms. The church also established
apprenticeships for destitute orphans, assigning impoverished children to
work for wealthy church patrons. Church officers served as public officials in
positions as vestryman, rector, churchwarden, sexton, clerk, and register. As

the rector saw to the "spiritual welfare" of the parish, the vestrymen addressed the "promotion of the good laws of the Province and the easy dispatch of Parish business." All public officials were required to take an oath, pledging "to conform to the religious worship in this Province, according to the Church of England." Low-country planters assumed nearly all of the positions of authority within the church and used it as an institution to solidify their economic and political dominance of South Carolina society.[7]

In South Carolina, as in New England, the established church confirmed the social status of its members, influenced the content of civil laws, and served as a fundamental institution for the preservation of social order. St. Philips Church, one of the two leading Anglican churches in Charleston, operated an ecclesiastical court well into the mid–eighteenth century. The court functioned to enforce breaches of civic order, levying fines for Sabbath breaking, swearing, and other disrespectful activities. All people within the parish, Anglican or not, were subject to the church court's jurisdiction.[8] Even in civil courts, Christian morality influenced the law. Colonial magistrates in South Carolina, as easily as those in New England, invoked religious concerns as a basis for their decisions. In 1703, magistrate Nicholas Trott castigated two illicit lovers for plotting the murder of the woman's husband by discussing at length the "sin" of their crimes and their violation of God's laws as well as man's.[9]

Yet, unlike New England, the church in South Carolina perceived its duties of social control as paramount to its responsibilities to foster Christian communitarianism. Certainly, these concerns oftentimes coincided, but in the South the latter was clearly subordinated to the former. The emphasis upon preserving social order detracted from the role of the church in attending to other social needs. St. Philips did start Charleston's first hospital, but only in response to the urgent medical needs presented by the smallpox epidemic in 1738. The church existed for nearly fifty years before starting a school, and then it catered more to the local elites than to the poor.[10] Education in colonial South Carolina reflected the peculiar local attitudes about status. Wealthy individuals sent their sons to boarding schools in Europe or the northern colonies and seemed unconcerned with providing education to the broader public. As one historian writes, the South Carolina elites believed "the business of the lower classes was to serve rather than to think."[11] Education remained a matter of ecclesiastical concern but held a low priority within the churches. Church-sponsored schools served as means of promoting community and instilling values in other colonies. The disregard of education by South Carolina's Anglicans evinces their greater attention to social control.

To some degree, the failure of the Anglican Church to build schools and hospitals is consistent with the colony's general laxity in creating infrastructure. Colonial laws in South Carolina proscribed the same types of "immoralities" as those of other colonies. However, enforcement of these laws suffered as the southernmost colony lacked not only the ecclesiastical but also the judicial and administrative infrastructures that, by the early 1700s, had come to exist even in Virginia and Maryland. As a consequence, in parts of the colony, informal or serial "marriages," really temporarily monogamous cohabiting relationships, were as common as ecclesiastical marriages. This state of affairs angered and frustrated members of the clergy. The Rev. Charles Woodson, an Anglican itinerant, condemned the rampant "concubinage" that existed in the colony and threatened prosecution of "whoever did not attend to be legally married." Another Anglican minister, Gideon Johnston, complained of the "polygamy and incestuous marriages" that were "often countenanced" in his own parish. Pastor Francis Le Jau encouraged greater public posting both of laws prohibiting sexual relations outside of marriage and of the penalties that could be imposed for the violation of these laws. Some communities embraced the call for greater policing of public morals, as reflected in Craven County's 1749 petition for land to support a ministry in order "to suppress the vice and immorality now greatly prevailing in those parts of this province." Just three years later, the good people of a settlement on the Peddee River petitioned for a county court to control vice, including people "cohabiting with their neighbors' wives" and others "living in a most lascivious manner while the petitioners have no way or means to suppress them." As Godbeer notes, many in South Carolina during the 1700s still "expected the government to take responsibility for moral reform by establishing and sustaining religious as well as judicial institutions."[12]

South Carolina's religious establishment differed from that of New York. The rise of a business culture in eighteenth-century New York fostered a liberal idealism at odds with Christian communitarianism. The established Anglican Church in New York represented British control and the subordination of individual rights and interests and, therefore, appeared threatening to the dynamic business interests and social concerns of the colony. In South Carolina economic growth resulted from traditional agrarian pursuits rooted in community interdependence. Liberal ideology, with its assertions of human equality, threatened the paternalistic deference that sustained South Carolina's agrarian community far more than did the church. While New Yorkers, even by the mid-1700s, had come to perceive the Anglican Church as an archaic vestige of meritless privilege, South Carolinians concurrently perceived it as a vital aspect of social order. Disestablishment, therefore, would have to be driven not by those who sought greater freedoms to pursue business goals but rather by those dissenters who chafed at the burden posed by the established church to their practice of religion.

For the first half of the eighteenth century, dissent remained minimal, as advocates of religious establishment stressed the need of religion for social stability and cohesion, implicitly relying upon the Anglican Church as an institution uniting white people against the threat posed by the majority of the colony's residents being kept as slaves. Dissenters quieted their opposition to an established church and saw value in unity. Most of the Huguenot churches affiliated with the Anglicans in 1706. Even then, Anglicans constituted a minority of the population throughout the century. In 1710, 42.5 percent of the six thousand white people in South Carolina were Anglicans. The Presbyterians, mostly Scottish immigrants, had greater numbers but lacked the economic and political power to wrest religious freedom from the Anglicans. The differences in religious doctrine that precipitated antagonism in the North were minimized in deference to social concerns in the South. In 1729 South Carolina's Congregationalists and Presbyterians, united in a joint synod, accepted the "Adopting Act," professing that all Calvinist sects shared "in all the essential and necessary articles, good forms of sound words and systems of Christian doctrine."[13]

As the black population of South Carolina increased in the eighteenth century, ever greater importance was attached to social order. By 1720, 65 percent of the residents of South Carolina were African immigrants or their descendants. Slaves adapted their mode of worship to the Christian message they received in their new home, emphasizing the magic and mysticism common to both Christianity and their native African religions. Their religious practices, especially the emotional singing and dancing in which they engaged, frightened many of the slaveholders. Some of the same practices, when expressed by whites as part of the Great Awakening, were seen as threats to the social as well as the religious order. These fears were heightened when George Whitefield's visit was followed by the 1739 Stono Slave Rebellion. Religion, once a tool for the preservation of order was now understood as being used by some to foment disorder. Letters to the *Charleston Gazette* expressed desires of leading South Carolinians to prohibit Whitefield and other emotional preachers from speaking in their state because of their abilities to provoke rebellion. The Rev. Alexander Garden, an Anglican minister, castigated Whitefield for his "crude Enthusiastic Notions" and their disquieting effects upon society.[14]

The Great Awakening emboldened dissenting preachers to seek social reforms and presented the first challenge to South Carolina's Anglican establishment. In the 1720s New Light Presbyterian minister Gilbert Tennant, influenced by Theodore Frelinghuysen, preached an emotional and pietistic message from his New Jersey pulpit. Young Oliver Hart and Tennant's son, William, heard and were inspired by this message. In 1752 Hart came to South Carolina as pastor of the First Baptist Church of Charleston. William Tennant became the minister of the Circular Church, an ecumenical congregation housed a little way down Meeting Street from Hart's church. Together, they would lead a crusade to disestablish the Anglican Church.[15]

By the 1750s Charleston had blossomed into a burgeoning trade center, a thriving port, and the hub of the affluent planters' social scene. Beautiful mansions housed the wives and children of the colony's richest planters. They spent much of the year in Charleston to escape the loneliness, insect infestation, and diseases of lowland plantation life. Their parties, balls, and entertainments were without peer in the colonies, rivaling those of the European capitals in the same era.

Oliver Hart notes that "Revival" came to Charleston in his Baptist church in 1754. The revival of which he speaks expressed a doctrine that modified the old Calvinist tenets through an acknowledgment of human potential. Hart conceived of Jesus Christ as a mediator between two natures, "divine and human." Jesus provided the means by which "fallen, stupid Men" might worship the deity. Jesus also provided a human example of moral behavior toward which all people might reasonably strive. In encouraging his listeners to pursue personal improvement, Hart's preaching implicitly attacked the rigid social hierarchy of Charleston society. His Baptist church, like Tennant's Circular Church, welcomed all comers, developing an early ecumenical forum for religious discussion and social leveling.[16]

By the 1770s Tennant and Hart had come to assume prominent positions in South Carolina's movement toward political revolution. Hart served on Charleston's Council of Safety from 1775 onward, and Tennant sat in the Provincial Congress. Tennant also preached sermons and wrote letters to the *South Carolina Gazette and Country Journal* encouraging revolution against those who endeavored to keep Americans, in his words, in "the most abject slavery." Tennant made clear that a key aspect of this "slavery" was the denial of religious liberty to dissenting sects and the mandatory support of a minority church.[17] Both men were, in part, motivated to support revolution as a means of disestablishing the Anglican Church. This need to win religious liberty legitimized recourse to revolution to secure political independence.[18]

Tories constituted at least one-fifth of the South Carolina population at the time of the Revolution. After the British captured Charleston in 1780, the community's divisions came into sharper focus as economic interests often diverged from political sentiments. This internal conflict prompted republican leaders to clarify the historical and ideological bases of their devotion to the Revolution. In the process, men who had been prominent members of the Carolina "aristocracy" confronted their understandings of political equality and the government's duty to protect civil rights. David Ramsay's oration in July 1778 was an attempt to reconcile economic inequality with political equality: "Republics are favourable to truth, sincerity, frugality, industry, and simplicity of manners. Equality, the life and soul of the commonwealth, cuts off all pretensions to preferment but those which arise from extraordinary merit." But, while certain members of the South Carolina elite may have legitimized disparities in wealth on the basis of greater effort and talent, they found it a harder proposition to defend the privileged status enjoyed by the Anglican Church. As in New York, antagonism to anything British fostered attacks on the established church. Henry Purcell, an Anglican minister who published a pamphlet entitled "Strictures on the Love of Power in the Prelacy" had to be placed under bond to preserve the peace.[19]

South Carolina moved to form its own independent government even before the Declaration of Independence resounded from Philadelphia. In March 1776, the new State of South Carolina (the second of the former colonies to take this action) issued its first constitution in conjunction with

Circular Church, Charleston, SC—The Circular Church served as the Rev. William Tennant's church during South Carolina's initial drive toward disestablishment. The radical evangelical and ecumenical nature of the church is reflected in its unusual circular shape and its imposing brick facade. Photograph courtesy of Gissendanner Photography.

its own declaration of independence. The intent of the document was to establish a provisional government to address the war. Suppression of Tory sympathizers and the defense of the state were the chief concerns. The colonial commons was transformed into the House of Representatives. This body elected the upper chamber of the legislative council from among its own members. The bicameral legislature then jointly elected the president of the state.[20]

The new government was less than democratic. Not only did it retain its closed and aristocratic cast, but civil rights, including the issue of religious freedom, were unaddressed. Oliver Hart had written to Henry Laurens of his hopes for religious reform, days before the drafting of the constitution: "We hope to see liberty sit regent on the throne and flourish more than ever under the administration of such worthy patriots." His hopes were dashed when he saw the new plan of government. That spring, the dissenting clergy gathered under the direction of William Tennant to plan for "securing an equality in religious privileges." Tennant was chosen to present the group's work, a petition for disestablishment, before the general assembly: a task he performed on September 11, 1776.[21]

His comments before the assembly reflected the priorities of dissenting ministers. The petition specifically objected to the establishment of one "particular denomination of Protestants in distinction from and preference to all other denominations." The ministers referred to the prejudicial treatment of one sect fomenting discord and a dangerous discontent within society. In closing, the petition called for a guarantee:

> That there never shall be any establishment of any one religious denomination or sect of Protestant Christians in this state by way of preference to another; that no Protestant inhabitant of this state by law be denied the enjoyment of any civil right merely on account of his religious principles, but that all Protestants demeaning themselves peaceably under the government established by the Constitution shall enjoy free and equal civil and religious privileges.

If these provisions of the dissenters' petition were not adequately clear, Tennant's own comments left no room for confusion. He cited the inability of dissenting clergy "to marry their own people" and the unfair competition between the Anglicans, for whom "the law builds superb churches" and those denominations who must "build their own." Perhaps the most significant problem, he felt, was that the law allowed only one church to incorporate; it alone could hold property, sue in the court system, and collect alms and bequests.[22] Tennant made certain the assembly understood that the dissenters did not wish the state's legislators to abstain from addressing religion, but only to stop favoring one sect over another: "The state may do any thing for the support of religion without partiality to particular societies or imposition upon the rights of private judgment." Tennant championed the authority of the assembly to punish vice and encourage virtue.[23]

By late 1776 South Carolina reformulated its governmental structure. Practicalities of political administration may have sparked the desire for a new constitution, but civil rights and the disestablishment of the Anglican Church garnered more enthusiasm. Christopher Gadsden and Charles Cotesworth Pinckney supported Tennant and Hart in calling for disestablishment in the fall of 1776.[24]

Tennant again went before the assembly on January 11, 1777, to advocate disestablishing the Anglican Church. He limited his appeal to the need to put all Protestant Christian churches on an equal legal footing. Shortly thereafter, Oliver Hart expressed confidence that the dissenters' desires would be realized if they "will be careful to attend the next session of the Assembly." That spring the assembly adopted the dissenters' petition of January 11, allowing any church to incorporate if (1) it expressed belief in one eternal God, heaven, and hell; (2) it worshiped God publicly; (3) the God it worshiped was that of the true Christian religion; (4) it professed the Old and New Testaments to be divinely inspired, that is, the "word of God"; and (5) it acknowledged that whatever man's other commitments to God, he was under a lawful duty to bear witness to the truth, that is, to swear oaths pursuant to American legal requirements.[25] The assembly's action gave Protestant Christian churches, except Quakers, equality under the law. Non-Christians remained unable to incorporate their religious institutions.

Disestablishment of the Anglican Church did not occur until the new constitution, adopted in March 1778, expanded upon the assembly's earlier action. In the new constitution South Carolina declared that "The Christian Protestant religion [is] the established religion of this State." Further, "no person shall, by law, be obliged to pay towards the maintenance and support of a religious worship that he does not freely join in, or has not voluntarily engaged to support." Yet all voters and officeholders were required to swear to their belief in "God, heaven, and hell" as understood in Protestant Christian doctrine. Individual Episcopal congregations needed to reform themselves by incorporating as private independent bodies. For years afterward, they lacked a central organization, a bishop, and a diocese. Yet, once the anti-British feelings of the war years passed, Episcopal churches resumed significant roles in South Carolina society. The law may have made all churches equals, but Episcopalian members rendered their denomination socially superior.[26]

The Constitution of 1778 was not much more democratic than the earlier one. It retained high qualifications for voting and office holding, limiting both "rights" to long-standing citizens with large amounts of property. Representation in the assembly favored the low country over the piedmont. Christopher Gadsden critically charged the new constitution with preserving "as high a tincture of aristocracy as possible."[27] And, while the new document recognized due process protection and liberty of the press, religious freedom was limited to Protestant Christians.

This limited freedom constituted success for William Tennant, Oliver Hart, and the other dissenting clergy. They never advocated or sought religious freedom as a matter of individual conscience. They only desired their own versions of Christianity to be legally recognized as viable alternatives within the state. The establishment of Protestant Christianity gave them everything they wanted—the legal right to perform Christian services, hold property, and proselytize within a political environment committed to enforcing Protestant Christian values and morals. On March 19, 1778, Oliver Hart wrote in his diary: "This Day the New Constitution of the State of South Carolina was signed . . . by which our Privileges civil and religious are secured to us upon the most liberal and permanent Foundation." On March 24 he wrote his brother Joseph in Pennsylvania to inform him of Tennant's death. Hart had preached the funeral sermon, and he confided to his brother his satisfaction in his friend's ability to see his project through to completion: "religion is set free here."[28] Neither Tennant nor Hart expressed any disappointment at the failure of the 1778 constitution to recognize complete religious liberty.

Prior to the Revolution only four corporations had been founded in South Carolina. The 1778 constitution encouraged all organizations of fifteen or more people to "incorporate. . . . and give themselves a name or denomination by which they shall be called and known under law." Only incorporated entities were able to hold and receive property; and not just churches, but voluntary associations and business organizations of all varieties had to incorporate to pursue their own goals under protection of law. Philanthropic societies and private schools founded in South Carolina after the war were predominantly secular, reflecting the postwar decline of Anglicanism and the enthusiasm with which postwar South Carolinians pursued business and secular goals. Yet this profusion of new entrepreneurial endeavors did not reduce the role of parish churches in South Carolina. The 1778 constitution did not attempt to divorce churches from their public roles; it merely recognized all Protestant sects as capable, under law, of performing them.[29]

Episcopal churches in South Carolina during the early republic willingly adapted to prevailing social norms instead of attempting to guide social mores. As in other parts of the country, religion and morality were seen by many to be essential to the economic and political success of the new nation. South Carolina's traditional clergymen comfortably positioned churches in service to the state. A strong providential current in South Carolina's churches appeared to subordinate the success of the Revolutionary ideals to God's will.[30] The real message, repeated over and over, was that society's need for a church rested on that church's ability to secure worldly success for its adherents. The Rev. Samuel Stanhope Smith, in a sermon titled "Religion as Necessary to National Prosperity," asserted as a "certain and invariable" rule "that the prevalence of virtuous manners among our people, and their respect to the institutions of religion, is usually connected with national prosperity."[31]

In their business dealings as well as in the scope of their social programs, South Carolina's traditionalist churches reflected their participation in and acceptance of the ideals of their society. Southern churches not only frequently condoned slavery, but they often held slaves themselves. An example of slave trading engaged in by the Claremont Episcopal Church expressed that church's acceptance of the peculiar institution. It also shows the growing use of contract law rather than principles of fairness or equity to resolve financial disputes in the South—even those involving the sale of human beings. In the early spring of 1825 the Claremont Episcopal Church contracted to buy two slaves at a cost of twelve hundred dollars. Between the date of purchase and the date of delivery, the value of the slaves increased to fourteen hundred dollars. The seller demanded an extra two hundred dollars from the church. In a letter of May 15, 1825, the church asserted its intention to determine the price of the slaves "by the contract price and not by the amount they might fetch on the open market." In a subsequent letter, the church denied the authority of an arbitrator to determine the slaves' value. It supposed that the contract alone determined the value of the commodity being sold. An arbitrator had no power "to make a new contract and to set any other valuation on the negroes than the market price would warrant at the time of sale of them."[32] In this dispute, the church operated like any private corporation in asserting contract law as determinative, and equity irrelevant, in the transaction of a salable commodity. The sense of community endorsed by the church was that of a collection of individuals united by a system of interlocking duties created by law.

Yet despite this acceptance of contract law South Carolina's Episcopal churches reinforced a type of Christian communitarianism that was different from that expressed in the North. Historians Eugene Genovese and Elizabeth Fox-Genovese have observed that the southern clergy subordinated political consensus to its "primary concern—saving souls . . . [which] meant building Christian communities." Traditional Protestant messages of deference and respect took on new meanings in South Carolina's society governed by a planter elite instead of a religious oligarchy. By the Revolution, southern Protestantism in Virginia and the Carolinas embraced a Newtonian context for religious belief, postulating that God acted through natural law.[33] Social hierarchies also expressed this natural law in their recognition of a natural aristocracy. Traditional churches recognized this social hierarchy and paid deference to elites. Planters assumed almost feudalistic obligations for social justice within their communities, which explains why South Carolina's churches did not encourage or participate in social outreach programs as much as did their brethren in the North. Education and, to a lesser degree, poor relief would have implicated the churches in a form of social leveling or social reform that threatened not only the secular elite but also the churches' status in southern society. Consequently, the Episcopal churches of South Carolina, though legally responsible for providing traditional services, made few efforts to educate, feed, or clothe the poor. During the decade after the Revolution, the churches and local governments remained under the control of a planter elite. Much as in the early colonial society, churches and public governance remained integrated; however, in the early republic, South Carolina's Episcopal churches clearly served a subordinate role in service to the elite.

Following the lead of the traditional churches, the reformed Calvinist churches of the low country temporarily retained a communitarian emphasis expressed in paternalistic terms that could rationalize hierarchy, social deference, and even slavery. By the 1780s, however, a new voice emanated from backcountry preachers or social outsiders who castigated the churches for failing in their duties. Low-country churches may have maintained social position by avoiding moral prescription and endorsing economic hierarchy, but backcountry evangelical churches played much greater roles in their devotees' personal lives. The growth of the Baptist Church in the piedmont led to its control of functions previously assigned to the Anglicans. After enactment of the Constitution of 1778 the Baptist Church, or any other previously dissenting sect, could assume public responsibility for education, poor relief, and record keeping. Each could function as an "established church" within its community under South Carolina's Protestant Christian establishment. In addition to poor relief and education, Baptist churches interceded in family disputes, business dealings, and intracommunity disagreements. In all these dealings, the evangelical churches substituted Christian values for legal rationality. The Rev. Frederick Dalcho encouraged the proliferation of church schools, noting: "Our youth are in much less danger of remaining ignorant of Virgil, and of Homer, than of Jesus Christ and his Apostles." He further admonished the clergy who teach morality but not faith, producing a parishioner who "is a moral, but not a Christian man. He is a disciple of this world but not a follower of the Saviour. He may be a scholar of Socrates or Epictetus, but not of Jesus Christ. His home and his happiness are here and not in heaven." In this criticism of the more traditional low-country churches, evangelical clergymen encouraged a more proactive form of Christian worship. In the process, they threatened the low-country elite and the Anglicans who were more liberal in doctrine.[34]

The greatest threat to the low-country elite came from the newly recognized churches' criticism of slavery. Backcountry evangelicals had spoken out against slavery since the Great Awakening. In an "Open Letter to the Inhabitants of Maryland, Virginia, North and South Carolina concerning the treatment of their Negroes," published in 1740, George Whitefield called for the end of the institution and the "proper care of [the African's] souls." He even went so far as to conceive of a massive slave insurrection, noting: "should such a thing be permitted by providence, all good men must acknowledge that the judgment would be just."[35] Other evangelicals took up Whitefield's argument throughout the 1750s and began not only preaching but writing letters to the press in opposition to slavery. While the war had distracted these preachers from their attacks during the crucial years in which the Protestant Christian establishment was created, in the 1780s they and their successors returned to the battle with a vengeance. South Carolina's planters began to fear the influences of evangelical Christian sentiments upon their social system.

By the 1780s the backcountry population had grown sufficiently to worry the tidewater elite. South Carolina's delegation to the Constitutional Convention in Philadelphia in 1787 still reflected the low-country dominance of South Carolina politics. But the very idea of a constitutional convention provoked a challenge to the state's existing primary law from the "yahoos" from the West. This pejorative term used by the low-country planters referred to both the evangelical Baptists and Methodists in the piedmont and the increasing number of people who would later be referred to as Jeffersonian Republicans found in that region. Despite the tidewater elite's proclivity to put these two groups together, members of each frequently held very different goals.

Liberal exponents of Jeffersonian concepts of democracy began to question the restrictive nature of their own state constitution. Proposals for a constitutional convention started to appear in the press by the mid-1780s. In an editorial from September 7, 1786, the *Gazette of the State of South Carolina* argued that, though the war was won, "the American Revolution is just begun [as] the whole government must be made to conform to democratic principles." Many of the state's liberals found it especially discomforting that the Constitution of 1778 had been adopted by legislative action without convention. They tried in 1784, 1785, and 1787 to create a constitutional convention so as to have a document superior to the legislature and not subject to amendment through its proceedings alone. During these years the House of Representatives actually passed bills to form a convention to create a constitution in greater conformity with "pure republican principles," but each time the Senate fought off the attack. Calls for a new state constitution focused primarily on republican theory and the need to protect civil rights. Republican concepts of political equality and freedom of conscience required a reconceptualization of South Carolina's social institutions.[36]

By 1787 complete religious freedom, requiring the abolition of the Protestant Christian establishment of 1778, had become a rallying point for the liberals. Unlike the disestablishment campaign of 1778, this crusade was carried by those who premised their position on both the need of the government to recognize natural rights and the perception of religion as a matter of personal conscience. In this debate the liberals expressed significant distaste for all organized religion. At the climax of the debate, the *City Gazette* of Charleston published a letter from an American living in Paris: "France is indeed upon the eve of complete freedom; a new era is evidently approaching; political liberty in Europe must copy the example of America and will certainly be followed by a great and general change in many religious tenets of the present day, as soon as the empire of reason shall have established itself a little further over the minds of men." This writer found political freedom best expressed by those philosophers who sought to challenge religious beliefs that kept men subordinate not only to a god but inevitably also to other men. These philosophers, "by drawing a distinct line of separation between spiritual and temporal concerns, have paved the way for universal peace, harmony, and good will among men."[37]

The contest in South Carolina pitted reason against revelation, liberty against piety, and legal equality against legal privilege. Evangelical clergymen recognized a need to clarify for their parishioners on which side of the battle line they were to stand. They chose to bind themselves to other Christians in opposing liberal reform. Methodist Bishop George Foster Pierce scorned those who rejected God's truth for one of man's own devise: "This specious, insinuating infidelity is distilling its poison under the patronage of science, education, and knowledge." The Rev. Thomas Reese wrote that God has "favored us" but "if we abuse the gifts of Providence, turn our liberty into licentiousness, and provoke the vengeance of Heaven by our daring impiety, and shocking immoralities, what can we expect, but that a righteous God will give us up to the fatal consequences of our own vices, and inflict upon us a punishment which we justly deserve." More liberal pastors found it more difficult to openly support a continued establishment. The Rev. Richard Furman, Oliver Hart's successor at the Charleston Baptist Church, remained silent on the disestablishment issue but advocated defeat of a companion provision that would prevent ministers from serving in state office.[38]

Incongruence between Christian doctrine and slavery alerted South Carolinians to the political risks inherent in any form of religious establishment. The last thing the southern planters wanted was their own churchmen encouraging the limitation or abolition of slavery as being inconsistent with the teachings of Jesus. While most of the low-country ministers avoided any connection between slavery and un-Christian behavior, Baptist and Methodist itinerants drew the connection in the most uncompromising terms. Both sects had made significant inroads into the tidewater region and were protected as members of the Protestant Christian establishment and as incorporated institutions. Convinced of the rightness of their message and secure in their commitment to proselytize, bolder preachers such as the Revs. Francis Asbury and Thomas Cook aggressively denounced slavery before low-country audiences. This activity provoked great intolerance among the planters and a reconsideration of what was meant by religious freedom within a Christian establishment. One gentleman, arguing under a pen name in the *City Gazette* of March 20, 1789, advocated that Asbury and Cook, by then well-known itinerant preachers, not be allowed to speak in Charleston.[39] Each was a leading Methodist minister, however, and the law protected ministers of all Protestant Christian seats.

As the campaign for complete disestablishment gained momentum, many of the same evangelical preachers who condemned slavery expressed the need for religion to play a prominent role in state governance. They referred to the need not only to preserve one true faith but also to preserve the influence of Christian teachings upon society. This influence had now become a source of fear to a planter elite that had already confronted hostility to slavery at the national Constitutional Convention. Alarmed at the possibility of being attacked by a group of preachers whom they supported through the legal establishment of Protestantism, these planters opted not to fight disestablishment. The planter elite from the low country aligned with the political liberals from the piedmont to limit the influence of Christian teachings upon South Carolina society.

In 1789 the legislature succumbed to calls for a new constitution. In February a Senate committee was to meet with a delegation from the House of Representatives "to consider whether a convention of the people should not be called to consider and amend the Constitution of this State." In April the legislature decided to form the convention; the delegates would be elected in a special election in October.[40]

Having won the fight for a convention, the two component groups of the new alliance began mobilizing forces to secure favorable provisions within the new primary law. The greatest concerns of the low-country planters were to relocate the capital back to Charleston and to preserve the representational imbalance, through the apportionment of seats, that gave them a disproportionately large legislative voice. The preservation of a Christian establishment, once a priority, now contained too many risks. The liberals were willing to sacrifice short-term political power for broader democratic provisions in the constitution. They desired the elimination of primogeniture laws, a relaxation of voting and office-holding requirements, and an expansion of civil rights, including a complete separation of church and state. Each group was able to gain its primary goals in forming an alliance against the churchmen who favored a continued Protestant establishment. Together, they relied upon the ideals of republican ideology—equality, self-determination, and liberty as the basis for a new legal code. By providing a legal recognition of "civil rights," these groups could preserve their mutual and independent interests.

The conceptual integration of disestablishment with a general expansion of civil rights was described in a series of letters to the *City Gazette* written by "The Reflector." In his first letter, he argued that the upcoming convention had the purpose "of correcting defects" in the existing constitution. The primary law of the state was to recognize that "freemen are all equal," regardless of their religious beliefs: "We expect the new constitution to be framed upon the principles of equal liberty and we charge you to guard our natural rights from invasion with the most jealous care . . . [and to] secure . . . [our] religious liberties." In a subsequent letter, the author expanded upon the concept of equal liberty, arguing that current constitutional tests of wealth and belief as prerequisites to voting rendered full enjoyment of the rights of citizenship conditional and treated equals as unequals. The prescription of any religion should not be made upon any free man.[41]

The language used by "The Reflector" reinforces historian Edmund Morgan's assertion that republican liberties in the South were understood as assertions of equality among white free men and did not include black slaves.[42] There can be no mistaking the Reflector's use of "freemen" in instances in which writers in nonslave states would use "men" or even "people." The argument raised by the liberals in South Carolina in 1790 was that no free white man should be subject to the opinions or beliefs of another free white man—his equal. In acceptance of this argument, low-country elites and backcountry yahoos overcame class and regional distinctions to rewrite the state's primary law as an implicit protection of the interests and thoughts of white men.

This does not explain, however, the extra steps taken by the convention to ostracize the Christian churches. The 1790 constitution abolished parishes (substituting counties), created a new state court system with exclusive jurisdiction over all legal matters in the state, provided for complete liberty of religious belief, and denied all clergymen the opportunity to hold state office. The reorientation of religion into the private sphere reflected a growing acceptance of liberal ideals, the increasingly secular nature of South Carolina society, and the fear of Christian condemnation of slavery.[43] Evangelical extremism had threatened the planters' relationship with their tidewater churches. Equality, at least for white men, had come to appear less problematic than the potential of truly Christian communities.

Disestablishment in South Carolina, as in all other states, involved much more than a change in the primary law or a revocation of the requirement that citizens support the churches. It involved the removal of the churches from their roles in public governance. In this change can be seen the importance of ideological debate to the disestablishment issue and the radical nature of the process. Liberal republican values came to replace Christian ethics in public institutions. Prior to 1790 churches in South Carolina had served as the public instruments of poor relief, record keeping, and to a lesser degree education. After the adoption of the new constitution, government or private citizens would have to assume these responsibilities. Wasting no time in implementing social change, the legislature of the state first addressed the issue of assisting the poor in 1791, passing a statute that provided for the election of county commissioners of the poor as public employees, to assume the duties previously held by parish church wardens. These officials determined their counties' needs and set tax levies to respond to them. After 1800 the commissioners could force able-bodied recipients of poor relief to perform labor for the state in return for their benefits. Subsequent legislation allowed road commissioners to direct any state beneficiary to work on constructing and maintaining the state's highways.[44]

From the perspective of the liberal ideology largely adopted by the Jeffersonian Republicans, it was irrational for the public to pay able-bodied people to do nothing. In South Carolina, as in New York, the secularization of poor relief initiatives was attended by a rationalization of services, through which public assistance served public needs. The individual recipient was no longer an object of charity who provided a means of expressing Christian love and duty. Rather, he was a potential contributor to the growth and progress of a new nation who must be encouraged to pull his own weight.[45]

However, South Carolina's early provisions for public-sector assumption of social responsibilities reflect a continued attachment to the old colonial system that respected paternalism, deference, and an integration of public and private resources. County commissioners of the poor continued to bind poor orphans to planters or businessmen as servants or apprentices until 1795. When the state undertook the Santee Canal project, connecting the Santee and Cooper rivers and making the port of Charleston accessible to the middle of the state, it gave a private company the monopolistic right to operate the canal for profit in compensation for undertaking its construction. Communities continued to rely upon private individuals and groups to provide education through tuition-driven schools and academies. South Carolina refused to completely embrace republican liberalism. In the South, notions of social status and attendant social duty mitigated acceptance of prevailing ideas of equality.

The public programs started by South Carolina in the 1790s addressed pressing social problems. The state's emphasis on removing beggars, deviants, and criminals reflects both the elite's continued interests in social control and the republican interest in designing new institutions conforming to republican ideals. In 1794 the state created an Orphan House to shelter unemployable children, and in 1795 it created its first penitentiary. Appointees to public boards administered both facilities and relied exclusively on state funding. The creation of new public institutions arose from a recognition that delegating responsibility to private entities entailed a loss of public control. As elsewhere, this concern arose in South Carolina primarily over the provision of education. Although the Jeffersonians generally abhorred the growth of government to address social needs, the one exception they recognized was education. The perpetuation of the republic depended upon an educated citizenry, and the state was required to recognize and perform its duties to secure its future. In 1797 Richard Beresford, a staunch Jeffersonian, published a pamphlet entitled "Aristocracy, the Bane of Liberty—Learning the Antidote," in which he urged his fellow citizens of South Carolina to support general or universal education. He contended that the state's "aristocracy" sought to retain power by keeping the mass of people ignorant. Beresford's pamphlet spawned a letter-writing campaign to the state's newspapers asking for public funding of "liberal and practical" education. These letters noted that republicanism required a citizenry able to support itself economically, independent of any community or institutional support. Republican education fostered an awareness of liberal political doctrine, building an appreciation of man's innate civil rights and the duty of government to protect them. Church schools could not be entrusted to meet these goals. The *Gazette* helped in this campaign in an editorial that noted the number of advertisements in the paper for lottery tickets sold by neighboring states to help fund their schools. The paper asked if South Carolinians wanted to continue to support other states' educational programs rather than their own and to contribute to the drain of talent from their state.[46]

In 1801 Governor Grayton proposed establishing a state college, which opened in Columbia four years later. However, it was 1811 before the Republican legislature could muster sufficient support to pass the first public education law in South Carolina. The legislation created at least one school in each of the state's forty-four election districts to teach "any white resident free of charge." But the state failed to fulfill the law's promise. Insufficient funds were raised even to pay the commissioners of education, much less to staff and maintain the schools.[47]

The public school movement succeeded primarily in generating a response from the churches. Threatened by the idea of public schools teaching "liberal and practical" knowledge, they responded by starting schools of their own. Various churches opened Sunday Schools in the second decade of the nineteenth century. The Episcopal Church founded an educational organization in the summer of 1810 and thereafter adopted a uniform text written by the Rev. Frederick Dalcho titled "The Evidence from Prophecy for the Truth of Christianity and the Divinity of Christ In a Course of Catechetical Instruction." The intent of the text was to teach that the Bible is absolute truth—a record of prophecy and fulfillment of Jesus as the Son of God. Dalcho preached that man was depraved by nature and that the combination of parental indulgence and secular education would encourage "children soon [to] betray their proneness to vanity and sin." The Presbyterian Synod of 1808 directed its member churches to establish grammar schools, a program only marginally successful even in the heavily Scottish Presbyterian piedmont area. The Second Awakening in South Carolina resulted in the founding of numerous Christian outreach and educational societies, representing Baptists, Presbyterians, and Episcopalians. All of these efforts were attempts to combat the threat of secular education, and in the words of the Charter of the Columbia, South Carolina, Theological Seminary, to finally extinguish "the twilight of unenlightened reason." In a twist on the word describing the intellectual age in which the seminary was founded, its supporters asserted that "enlightenment" came from and with religion. In all of these efforts, South Carolina churches utilized the corporate form to protect their funds and their message in a sometimes hostile environment.[48]

In South Carolina, as in the other states, the achievement of disestablishment required clarifying distinct public and private domains. This is a legal, not a theological, matter. Yet it was a debate over values, influenced by theology and republican idealism, that precipitated the establishment crisis.

The 1778 Constitution allowed all Protestant churches to incorporate as private entities yet permitted them to act as public institutions funded through taxes and serving public needs. Once churches began to threaten principles, values, and beliefs dear to South Carolinians, they had to be marginalized. To effectuate this, South Carolina recognized the social significance of the legal distinction between public and private realms. South Carolinians embraced the idea that churches should be private entities so that they could not create social policy. Without public funding these churches struggled, and private charity performed many of the societal functions previously handled by the churches. A system of private charity reinforced the status of the planter elite up to the time of the Civil War.

7 The *Dartmouth College* Case

New Hampshire's Disestablishment Crisis

Makes Law for the Nation

In casting your eyes, my fathers and brethren, over our highly favored New England, you discover many regions now dark and desolate, where once existed flourishing churches . . . ah, my brethren no doubt the religion of the heart first declined; a declension in religious practice followed; discipline was neglected; the preciousness of truth ceased to be felt; the time soon came when men could not endure sound doctrine; the ministry itself, too, in some instances, instead of struggling against the growing degeneracy, threw itself into the current and helped to augment its force: and so piety and truth decayed together, till the light of both went out.—Let the churches which survive look upon this melancholy spectacle and take warning.

The Rev. Francis Brown, president of Dartmouth College, Sermon, June 3, 1818

PRIOR TO THE CIVIL WAR, court decisions based on a shared legal ideology more than on federal legislation created a republic unified by law. During this time period, the Supreme Court rarely acted to subordinate state policy to national values. In only a few cases was this accomplished to the extent it was in the *Dartmouth College* case. Arising out of the disestablishment controversy in New Hampshire, this decision sounded the death knell for New England establishment and confirmed the supremacy of liberal contract-law doctrine in all of the United States. Focusing on the contract clause of the Constitution, the Supreme Court recognized distinct private and public institutions and protected the former from interference by the latter. The old question of religious or church involvement in serving the public good, particularly in public education, was at the core of the *Dartmouth* case.

New Hampshire throughout the seventeenth and most of the eighteenth centuries constituted New England's frontier. Typical of the frontier, it served as a haven for dissenters, yet it never lost its character as a Puritan oligarchy. King James made New Hampshire a royal colony in 1679, and he named Portsmouth merchant John Cutt as president. The king instructed Cutt that "liberty of conscience shall be allowed unto all protestants; yet such especially as shall be conformable to ye rites of ye church of England shall be particularly countenanced and encouraged." In 1680 the first provincial assembly restricted suffrage to "English Protestants" having an estate of at least twenty pounds. Despite this titular adherence to Anglican supremacy, Congregationalism remained the predominate sectarian preference of the inhabitants of the colony.

Colonial New Hampshire adopted the New England model of multiple establishment, by which each town determined the type of Protestant Christian church that would be supported with its tax revenues. In 1693, following the Glorious Revolution and its imprimatur of limited religious tolerance, the legislature passed "An Act for Maintenance and Supply of the Ministry within the Province," which encouraged each town to select and contract with a minister for its religious needs provided that, in doing so, no town "interfere[d] with their Majesties' grace and favour in allowing their Subjects liberty of contience." The Act further granted dissenters, who supported churches recognized by the legislature, the opportunity to "constantly attend the publick worship of God on the Lord's day according to their own p'rsuasion" and to be exempt "from paying towards the Support of the Ministry of the Town."[1] A certificate system was implemented, by which dissenters could show their financial support of and regular attendance at a recognized alternative church. Yet, despite its pretense to toleration, the assembly was slow to accord recognition to dissenting sects. Prior to 1770 nearly every town settled a Congregational minister, though New Hampshire Congregationalism did encompass a wide range of beliefs and practices, not limited to New Lights, Old Lights, and perfectionists.[2] Individuals seeking exemptions had to obtain a certificate from their own churches and then petition their towns for relief, a process attenuated with considerable risk of ostracization.

The established churches of every town received tax money, levied at town meetings, for the support of their ministries; the establishment, maintenance, and staffing of schools; aid to the poor; and administrative needs.[3] Throughout the 1700s town meetings served as the primary expressions of the political interests of New Hampshire residents, and the churches served as the primary means of harmonizing public sentiment.

However, by the 1760s a very few dissenters, agitating for greater religious freedom, began to question the New Hampshire laws establishing religion. In 1764 Baptists in Newton petitioned for recognition of their sect and exemption from local taxes in support of the Congregational Church. The town refused the petition and seized Baptist property for overdue taxes. This action alienated not only the Baptists but also local Quakers, who, though recognized by the legislature as exempt, sympathized with their fellow dissenters. In 1769 these groups combined to control the town meeting and passed a law exempting the Baptists from a duty to support the Newton Congregational Church. The state legislature voided this action and agreed to "set off [the Baptists] entirely from said Town," in effect forcing them to support themselves. This they were unable to do, and their church dissolved by 1771.[4] Yet, by the time of the Revolution, the fragmentation of New England Congregationalism—represented by the growth of the Baptists and protean Unitarians—weakened the Congregational establishment in New Hampshire.

In August 1776, following the flight of Royal Governor Wentworth and the directive from the Continental Congress to establish a state government, the assembly undertook to draft a constitution. In January 1777 it published its plan of government, a bare outline of rules governing elections and the meetings of the legislature. It provided no judicial or executive branches and no bill of rights. Recognizing the need for a more extensive primary law, a convention for drafting a new constitution was held in June 1778; its product, released a year later, was rejected by the voters. Another convention was called in June 1781, and its proposal was accepted in 1784.[5]

The 1784 New Hampshire constitution provides striking evidence of the ideological tension within New England at that time between liberal republican ideals and popular desires to retain or reconstruct traditional Christian communities. The constitution expressed a commitment to protect individual freedoms, including the "Right of Conscience," generally construed as encompassing religious freedom. Yet this right was subsequently explained, and limited, in a more specific recognition of each person's freedom to worship "God" without attack or molestation, so long as that worship did not disturb the public peace. Moreover, the constitution later provided that the security of society depended upon the inculcation of "morality and piety, rightly grounded on evangelical principles." To promote this morality and piety, each town was to support a church and a public teacher of the Protestant Christian religion. Determination of which Protestant sect or denomination would be publicly supported was to be made on a town-by-town basis.[6] Despite constitutional language limiting the duties of dissenters to support the established church, the New Hampshire practice of recognizing very few exemptions continued. In an 1803 opinion of the New Hampshire Supreme Court, Judge Jeremiah Smith found Episcopalians, Presbyterians, Quakers, and Baptists exempt, but not "atheists, deists, revilers, and contemners of religion and persons of no [Christian] religion at all."[7]

The established churches, nearly always Congregationalist, continued to provide vital public services. Legislation of February 8, 1791, effectively restating earlier law, directed all New Hampshire towns to raise "such sum or sums of money as they shall judge necessary for the settlement, maintenance, and support of the ministry, schools, meetings houses . . . to be assessed on the polls and estates" of residents.[8]

Very few people objected to the constitutional religious establishment of New Hampshire prior to 1800. Yet rare early objections hinted at the controversies to come. Under the pseudonym "Impartialist," young William

Plumer wrote to the *New Hampshire Gazette* in February 1782, advocating rejection of any constitution that protected only the religious freedom of Christians or contained religious test oaths for office holding. Public opinion was so opposed to Plumer's views at the time that the *Gazette* charged him three dollars to publish his unpopular essay. In 1791, during another constitutional convention, Plumer offered an amendment that would have allowed all dissenters, regardless of belief or affiliation with a legally recognized denomination, to abstain from supporting a church. The amendment failed in a popular election by a vote of 3,993–994. Plumer also sought to strike the constitutional test oath requiring officeholders to be of the "Protestant religion." This proposal failed even to come out of committee.[9] Even the Baptists and other dissenters objected to Plumer's proposals as radical and likely to undermine the Christian tenets of the society.

New Hampshire's religious establishment after the Revolution expressed the desire of its residents to create a form of government that recognized the supremacy of the Christian God and enforced Christian morality. The worldview influencing this form of government conceived of man's liberties as restrained by God's laws and Jesus' teachings. In New England, religious freedom did not imply a rejection of Christianity as truth, but only the recognition of the need for each person to find this truth in his or her own way. This is why the laws of the state could grant limited freedom—through both the ability to establish their churches as town churches and to be exempt from support of an alternative church—to many Protestants but not to Jews, Catholics, Deists, or nonbelievers. In the eyes of New Hampshire's voters in the 1780s and 1790s, these dissidents were not only blind to the need to see to their own salvation but also threatened the moral fiber necessary to the peace and security of the community. They would be made to support the community church and be held to obey laws premised on Christian teachings.

Following the legal format instituted in the early republic, viability as a dissenting institution depended upon incorporation. Dissenting sects had to be recognized by the courts or the legislature for their members to be exempt from supporting the established church. Presbyterians were legally recognized in 1803, Baptists in 1804, Unitarian/Universalists in 1805, and Methodists in 1807, as established Christianity broadened to embrace their moral teachings despite their doctrinal differences.

New Hampshire's recognition of dissenting churches as private legal entities indicates how the values of the early republic were influencing New England society and yet were modified by local ideas and practices. The Congregational Church remained a "public institution," despite its private status, because of its public role. When dissenting churches served the public by addressing broadly accepted Christian values, they too were accorded legal recognition as "public institutions." For a brief period of time in America, a church could be both a private corporation and a public institution. New Englanders saw no inconsistency in guaranteeing people's rights to believe what they would, as a private matter, while simultaneously preventing their lawful organization into a religious body that offered an alternative to prevailing values. Religion as a body of values and a basis of morality remained a public concern. Rather than serving to separate private and public institutions, state laws in New England functioned to integrate them. Private entities were incorporated under state law only when they served public interests—a perpetuation of the colonial scheme that conceived of private pursuits regulated and licensed by the state to serve public needs. For example, Judge Smith's 1803 decision in *Muzzy v. Wilkins* recognized the integrity of the Presbyterians as a legal sect only through an analysis of their public function. A variety of Protestant denominations were "equally good for the purposes of civil society because they all inculcate the principles of benevolence, philanthropy, and the moral virtues." He added, "Society has a right to judge what will promote the good of society and to provide for it at the expense of the whole," and that "Public instruction in religion and morality . . . is in every purpose a civil not a spiritual institution."[10] Even in accepting the corporate form for its churches, New England subordinated the developing contract-law model to its own conceptions of social organization. It refused to separate church and state just as it refused to divorce private rights from social needs.

Disestablishment came to New England only after the Supreme Court, in the *Dartmouth College* decision of 1819, found New England's integration of public and private institutions violative of the U.S. Constitution. The case resulting in this judgment arose from legislative attempts to restructure Dartmouth College. This case must be understood both in the context of the national conflict over the ideological foundation for society and its reflection in higher education and in the rise of Jeffersonian republicanism in New Hampshire.

The attempt of the state legislature to take control of Dartmouth College was not unusual. During the early republic, traditional Christian and liberal worldviews contested with one another on college campuses throughout the new nation, frequently precipitating campus unrest and even violence. The conflict over the teaching of the young was a battle over the vision of American society itself. Republicans sought to teach practical knowledge and a liberal morality, fitting the young for business, politics, and citizenship. Their opponents objected to the loss of deference to God, the threat to social order, and the degradation of public morals that such a liberal curriculum promised. The contrasting views of the type of morality that should be taught in the schools prompted extensive debate as early as the 1770s and 1780s, even reaching Congress and the Constitutional Convention.[11]

Higher education in the early republic continued to rely on the old colonial model. States relied upon and supported private—usually religiously oriented— colleges to serve their educational needs. Each state granted a charter to one or two institutions to fulfill its needs for higher education. Taxes, land grants, and other privileges assisted the colleges in the performance of their duties. But by the late eighteenth century, the goals of the parties to these various agreements were no longer compatible. In several situations this required a separation of the church-affiliated schools and the state in pursuit of different agendas.

An early instance of campus tension occurred during the Revolution in what was then the nation's capital. The College of Philadelphia was the only colonial college to be chartered without any religious affiliations; however, it soon came to reflect the interests of the Anglican Church, a pillar of mid-eighteenth-century Philadelphia society. During the Revolution, radicals dominated Pennsylvania politics and pushed for sweeping change in their society. One of their targets was the college. On September 9, 1779, President Reed, the highest executive of the state, assailed the trustees of the college for failing to seek "the aid of government for an establishment consistent with the Revolution, and conformable to the great changes of policy and government." The assembly promptly added its voice, asserting that the Anglican trustees were "dangerous and disaffected men" who had "troubled the peace of society, shaken the government, and often caused tumult, sedition, and bloodshed." Most significant was that they had "narrowed the foundation of the said institution," forgetting the founding purpose of the school, which was to educate the young men of the state in a nonsectarian manner. "[T]he original and fundamental principle of the College, by which it was bound to afford perfect equality of privileges to all religious denominations, had not been fully maintained." The assembly voided the old charters and reformed the school as the University of Pennsylvania.[12]

In 1789, after the Revolutionary fervor had dissipated, the original charters were reinstated and the assembly admitted that the actions of 1779 had been an unlawful deprivation of private rights by legislative action. Yet there was no returning to the prewar structure. The college was left without state funding and faced the prospects of competing with a state university. Public demand for a state university reflected desires for a broad-based secular institution rather than a denominational seminary. On September 30, 1791, unable to stand on its own, the College of Philadelphia merged into the University of Pennsylvania under the control of a joint board of trustees, of which the governor of the state served as president.[13]

Some of the same forces that restructured the College of Philadelphia during the Revolutionary War also affected King's College in New York. As one observer noted, "republican sentiments during the war could hardly tolerate the maintenance of a college named 'Kings,' the charter of which provided for the Archbishop of Canterbury to sit on its Board of Trustees."[14] The school closed until hostilities ceased. In May 1784 the New York legislature created a public corporation, the University of the State of New York, renamed King's College as Columbia College, and made it the first division of the university.

In the 1800s the tenuous relationship between the state legislature and the Episcopal Church became exceedingly strained. The Episcopalian hierarchy, due to changes in curriculum and the philosophical environment of the university, no longer deemed it a safe place to train ministers. The state resented the Episcopalian influence in the first college in its university system. In 1817 the general convention of the Episcopal Church saved both parties further embarrassment by severing its ties to Columbia and establishing its own General Theological Seminary. In that same decade Union Academy, a Congregational seminary, required creed affirmations of all trustees, teachers, and students to prevent Arminian infiltrations.[15]

Virginia was no more radical than some other states in what it did in the era of the Revolution; it merely appears that way in historical context because Thomas Jefferson was behind many of the state's actions and framed them in the most uncompromising ideological verbiage. In 1776 Jefferson's plans to transform the character of the College of William and Mary came before the State Assembly. He argued that the school failed to meet the social needs of the state and proposed to transform it into a state university free of religious influences, governed by a board responsible to the legislature. Jefferson proposed dropping divinity from the curriculum and enlarging the scope of study so as to be helpful in the training of social leaders. He planned to include in the curriculum Indian culture and language, modern languages, history, law, botany, chemistry, astronomy, mathematics, moral philosophy, natural philosophy, natural history, medicine, and ancient languages. The plan gained little support and instead alienated both the Anglican authorities in Virginia and strict secularists who did not wish even a titular Anglican school as Virginia's state college. The proposal failed in the assembly. However, in 1779 Jefferson, as governor, implemented part of his plan. He asserted that the state must act in order to ensure that "by liberal education" the young be prepared to serve as guardians "of the rights and liberties of their fellow citizens." The college, as previously constituted, could not meet the state's purposes. The board of the college was changed, divinity was eliminated, and five of Jefferson's proposed subjects were added to the curriculum with new faculty members brought in to teach them. In his autobiography, Jefferson acknowledged that he sought at that time both to remove the Anglican influence from the school and to turn the private college into a state university.[16] It is interesting that he encountered the most opposition from those Virginians who belonged to minority religious sects and who feared that Jefferson could gain state control of the school but could not rid it of its Anglican essence. They most feared an alliance between the state and the Anglican Church.

Jefferson's changes to William and Mary served as a preview of what he would do at the University of Virginia. Jurgen Herbst writes that "The [U]niversity [of Virginia] was to be, in effect, a secular church, independent of the state's denominations and churches, and a zealous guardian of republican political philosophy."[17] The school was founded by legislative action on January 25, 1819. For the next six years Jefferson, while on the Board of Visitors, devoted a considerable amount of his energies to designing the academic village, recruiting faculty, and raising contributions. The University of Virginia instituted lectures in place of recitation, selected free election of classes rather than a fixed curriculum, emphasized the teachings of science, government, law, and philosophy, and aspired to create a scholarly environment in which students and faculty lived and studied together in colleges. Jefferson's vision largely comported with the Enlightenment ideas of the secular intellectual quest, and his design raised no small amount of antagonism among Virginia's Anglican establishment. The opening of the university of 1825 reflected not only the dedicated efforts of Jefferson. It also represented acceptance of his secular plan for higher education in Virginia at that time.[18]

Presbyterians established the College of New Jersey in Princeton in 1746 as a New Light seminary dedicated to educating clergy sympathetic to revivalist preaching. Evangelical concerns were raised during the presidential tenure of John Witherspoon. A Presbyterian who stressed moral philosophy instead of doctrinaire Calvinism, Witherspoon reflected the Scottish Common Sense School of thought and his own emphasis on human agency in courses addressing science and natural-law philosophy. Under his direction Princeton broadened its educational scope—to the extent that clerical students composed only 21 percent of the graduating classes of 1776–1783, and only 13 percent between 1784 and Witherspoon's death in 1794. Witherspoon brought financial stability and academic prestige to Princeton, and the Presbyterian trustees could hardly remove him from office. Upon the death of its president, the college turned to a less scholarly and charismatic man, Samuel Stanhope Smith, to redirect its mission to educating evangelical clergy.

The concerns of the Presbyterian clergy over Princeton only escalated after 1800. In 1806 Henry Kollock, the last theology professor left at the school, resigned because of the lack of students interested in taking courses in his subject. Clerical attempts to impose greater discipline led to riots in 1807 and to the suspension of 125 out of 200 Princeton students. The Jeffersonian Republicans captured New Jersey's legislature after 1800 and promised more liberal changes in return for state funding. Finally, in 1809 the Reverend Alexander proposed to the Presbyterian General Assembly that the church abandon Princeton to the state and found an alternative seminary along the lines of Andover in Massachusetts. In 1811 the Presbyterian General Assembly adopted a plan for a Presbyterian seminary to teach students church history and the original languages of the Bible, while also being attentive to "the principle arguments and writings relative to what has been called the deistical controversy," so that they would be prepared to support the Westminster Confession "by a ready, pertinent, and abundant quotation of Scripture texts for that purpose." The pedagogy at Princeton stood in marked contrast to the Presbyterian General Assembly's expression of its educational goals: "To form men for the Gospel ministry, who shall truly believe, and cordially love, and therefore endeavor to propagate and defend, in all its genuineness, simplicity, and fullness, that system of religious belief and practice which is set forth in the Confession of Faith, Catechisms, and Plan of Government and Discipline of the Presbyterian Church." The new theological seminary opened in Princeton in August 1812. Princeton University agreed not to hire a professor of theology so long as the seminary remained in the town.[19]

The riots at Princeton were hardly uncharacteristic of the times. In 1802 students at Williams College, at William and Mary, and at Yale protested the impositions of outdated discipline. Religious faculty members at each school blamed the insurrections upon the influence of too much freethinking and the lack of community standards of moral behavior.[20] Clergy and religious faculty everywhere had to address the conflict between state support and private educational goals.

Yale College was a religious institution that accommodated change in order to preserve its favored position in the state. Public dissatisfaction with Yale—a Congregational institution at its creation but Presbyterian after the Saybrook Platform in 1705—developed early, during the tenure of college president Thomas Clap (1740–1766). Clap was a combative opponent of the New Light doctrine and was equally adamant in asserting that Yale was a product of a religious society. According to Clap, the school's purpose was to train sectarian ministers, not to teach liberal arts to future secular leaders. Students and the Connecticut legislature voiced disapproval of Clap's pedagogy, referring to the charter, which established the school as a place "wherein youth may be instructed in the arts and sciences who through the blessings of Almighty God may be fitted for public employments in both church and civil service." Critics claimed that Clap fulfilled only a part of this responsibility, the part concerning service to the church. The school's Congregational trustees accepted Clap's resignation in 1766, thereby momentarily avoiding state control.[21]

Then in 1777 the Connecticut Assembly proposed to assume responsibility over curriculum and faculty appointments. The trustees of Yale responded by naming Ezra Stiles as president. A New England liberal, Stiles encouraged academic freedom and sought to develop a superior college to serve broad cultural interests. He proposed to build a university that would both serve the economic and leadership needs of the state and encourage republican citizenship. For instance, Stiles asserted the need for a law curriculum, not to train lawyers but to form citizens by providing "the discipline and education . . . in that knowledge which may qualify them to become useful members of society." He gained legislative support for his program. Stiles sought a broad constituency, recognizing that in order to survive colleges needed multiple sources of financing. Despite his own Congregationalist background he encouraged discussion of religious and political issues in a tolerant and supportive environment. For years his suggested issue for senior debates was "Whether Civilians ought to be joined with Ecclesiastics in the Corporation of Yale College."[22]

Timothy Dwight, president of Yale University from 1795 to 1817, led religious revivals on the Yale campus that spawned similar events on campuses throughout the country. Dwight was among the most outspoken of ministers against the intellectual, economic, and social effects of liberalism. Courtesy Presbyterian Historical Society, Presbyterian Church (USA) (Philadelphia).

Although Stiles's tenure helped the church retain control of Yale through the critical years of revolution, tensions remained. The Congregational and Presbyterian churches themselves divided among Unitarians and orthodox Calvinists. Fifty years of relative religious decline following the Great Awakening came to an end in a new wave of revivals in the 1790s, as conservative churchmen sought to save both their churches and their society from the ravages of infidelity. Yale was torn apart both by intramural debate within the church and by those in society who advocated a strictly secular educational model. Beginning in 1783 a series of letters published in the *Connecticut Courant and Intelligencer* under the name Parnassus called for citizen control of the Yale corporation board and the elimination of theology from the curriculum. In 1792 in response to increasing calls for a more republican institution in its state, the Connecticut Assembly conditioned that year's monetary grant to Yale upon the corporation's consent to the addition of eight secular members to the corporate board, consisting of the governor and seven members of his council. Yale accepted.[23]

However, the secular trend at Yale was soon to be reversed. Timothy Dwight became president in 1795. He deplored the degenerate state of the campus, at which the church seemed an extraneous building and the students read Thomas Paine and evinced knowledge of French philosophy by referring to each other as "Voltaire," "Rousseau" or "D'Alembert." Dwight epitomized the Second Awakening figure who recognized the need to combat the infidelity of Enlightenment reason with the assertion of Calvinist scholasticism. He led a series of campus revivals to rescue Yale for the church, beginning with a momentous event in 1802 at which fully one-third of the students experienced conversion.[24]

Loved by the students, Dwight was despised by Connecticut Republicans. He became a symbol of "political congregationalism" to Connecticut Republicans who feared a religious hierarchy. These Republicans united with Anglicans, Methodists, and religious freethinkers in 1816 to form the Toleration Party, which succeeded in disestablishing the Congregational Church in Connecticut in 1818. The more than twenty-year battle over disestablishment provides evidence of the degree to which different groups of Americans conceived of contrasting images of their society. Dwight contended that the teaching of Enlightenment philosophy was part of a sinister plan to exterminate Christianity and destroy society from within by promoting vice and discouraging virtue. He presented the public with two alternatives, Christianity and infidelity, with Jefferson and his Republican ilk clearly joining Voltaire, Rousseau, and the other agents of Satan in the infidel's camp. The republican liberals were just as adamant and defamatory in their condemnations of Dwight.[25]

Massachusetts made Harvard its state university in its 1780 constitution. The school's charter was essentially rewritten. It created a new body, the Board of Overseers, to govern the university. The board consisted of the governor, political leaders, the university president, and Congregational ministers. Massachusetts funded the school, albeit sporadically, throughout the remainder of eighteenth century. Yet state affiliation did not create immunity to the political and religious controversies that afflicted other colleges at the turn of the century.[26]

Boston's social elite in the early 1800s constituted an odd mixture of political conservatism and religious liberalism, a unique group of Federalist Unitarians. The leading families composing this social elite also dominated Harvard and sought to protect it from both orthodox Calvinism and Republican liberalism. The divide within the church was the more easily addressed. In response to the appointment of Henry Ware, a Unitarian, to the Hollis Chair of Divinity at Harvard, Trinitarians gave up on the old school and founded Andover Seminary in 1808. The liberal Republicans were not so easily discouraged. In 1810 a tenuous Federalist majority in the Massachusetts legislature attempted to safeguard Harvard from political control by limiting the Board of Overseers to fifteen ministers and fifteen laypersons and by making it self-perpetuating. Yet in 1812, following Republican victory in statewide elections, the Senate rewrote the law to return elected officials to the board. Finally, in 1814, following another Federalist election victory, the legislature recognized the futility of continual political battles over the school. It returned to the 1810 model granting Harvard its independence but also appropriated new dollars to Bowdoin College and Williams College. (At this time, Massachusetts residents in the outlying areas of the state, including the area that would become Maine in 1820, desired their own schools.) This action was both a surrender of control over Harvard to Boston's elite (a victory for the Federalists) and the recognition of a need for alternative schools in which republican sentiments might find a more comfortable home.[27]

Pluralism in the choice of education did not assuage the liberal Massachusetts press. In 1819, the year of the *Dartmouth* decision, editorials called for the state to take public control of the centerpiece of its system for public education. Harvard continued to be seen as a home of elitism and religious fervor, both of which threatened American self-government. Editorials of the time pointedly made this connection, calling Harvard "a body made up of the priesthood and of lawyers . . . who are anxious to teach our children what to think, and how to vote, and when to act."[28]

Created by charter in 1789, the University of North Carolina opened in 1795 as a product of a postrevolution republican enthusiasm, albeit of a distinctive southern Federalist variety. The school's embrace of Enlightenment humanism expressed itself in faculty appointments and course offerings that reflected heterogeneous political and religious opinions. In North Carolina during the tempestuous early 1800s, conservatives unable to overcome the Republican control of the government responded by funding new private schools teaching their own religious orthodoxies to compete with the program of the state university.[29]

Similarly, in Vermont, two colleges reflected contrasting views of society. The state university in Burlington, founded in 1800, professed "to leave to every man a full and perfect liberty to follow the dictates of his own conscience" as to religious matters. While the legislature had the institutional authority to speak for the people of the state, many Vermont inhabitants refused to accept its pronouncements and actions as the final words on education. Middlebury College, founded by orthodox Presbyterians and Congregationalists, presented an alternative to the school in Burlington, which they perceived as "anti-Christian, dangerous to the morals of students and conducive only to clamor, confusion, and chaos."[30]

In 1799 Kentucky rechartered previously "private" Transylvania University as the cornerstone of its state university system. Yet changing the charter proved easier than changing the educational environment of the Presbyterian school. In 1801 Presbyterian professor James Welch was accused of harassing students who expressed "republican or deistic sentiments." The legislatively created board of trustees forced him to resign; but the incident evinced conflicting visions of the role of education in Kentucky. Then in 1815 Presbyterian clergyman and university principal James Blythe presented a sermon castigating the nation's republican leadership as "heathens" and asserting that the principle of separation of church and state had been "rocked in the cradle of French atheism." The legislature formed a committee to investigate the school and found the board of trustees' partisanship "an ulcer cancerous in its nature" and inconsistent with the state's commitment to republicanism. The trustees attempted appeasement by accepting Blythe's resignation and electing Horace Holley in his place. Holley, a Unitarian described as having adopted "some sentiments formerly entertained by the celebrated orator Priestley," was hardly a man in the school's historical Calvinist mold. Nevertheless, the legislature was not satisfied. On February 3, 1818, the governor signed an "act further to regulate the Transylvania University," replacing the trustees with political appointees serving two-year terms.[31]

People in Kentucky who did not share the legislature's perspective on higher education were limited in their options. Private college charters approved by the Kentucky legislature between 1792 and 1820 contained provisions prohibiting the "inculcation of religious doctrines peculiar to any one sect of Christians" and banned the use of the Bible in class, as well as courses in church history. Moreover, each charter allowed the state to "repeal, alter, or amend" it at any time if the school acted in a manner inconsistent with legislative goals.[32]

The Georgia legislature designed a system of education much like that of New York. The "University of Georgia" consisted of preparatory schools and Franklin College at Athens and incorporated state-supported and wholly private schools under its umbrella. As in other states between 1801 and 1820, orthodox Christians and Jeffersonian Republicans wrestled for control of the university. In Georgia the Presbyterians, constituting a plurality, gained political control with support of other orthodox denominations. The university functioned as a Presbyterian school system through the 1820s. In Maryland, in a similar situation, orthodox Christians retained sufficient political voice to prevent the legislature from imposing any limitations on religious preference established by schools chartered in that state.[33]

Prior to 1819, then, and throughout the United States, those who looked to God for social authority contested with liberal republicans for control of the schools. The battle over education was really a battle over the values of the society. In the process of this struggle, a new societal design began to emerge.

Several conclusions can be drawn regarding higher education in this period. First, the republican enthusiasm of the Revolutionary era, transformed into liberalism by the Jefferson Republicans, persisted into the nineteenth century to influence the form of civil institutions, including colleges and universities under state control. These influences included the demand for religious tolerance, secular curricula, and the teaching of virtue derived from republican ideals. Second, the proliferation of competing denominations and the reaction to Enlightenment humanism expressed through the Second Awakening embodied an alternative vision of society that contested with the dominant secular model. Third, the advocates of liberalism and Christian moralism both largely ignored distinctions between "public" and "private" in attempting to impose their ideal vision of civil society. The colonial model of shared public and private responsibility for serving educational needs consequently persisted in form but not in substance. Civil society continued its reliance on the combined efforts of private and public forces to provide education, but the resultant institutions were not products of community consensus as much as the results of an unresolved political and ideological contest. Fourth, the constitutional guarantees of the protection of contract, freedom of religion, and the implicit separation of church and state remained muddled as various state legislatures pursued political agendas that violated protected rights. Perhaps most important is that state legislatures consistently repudiated school and university charters in order to redesign educational institutions to serve political ends. Some religious bodies retained a modicum of control over their schools by accepting legislative direction in curricula and faculty appointments. Others relinquished established schools to the state and resolved to form competing schools under their control. Prior to New Hampshire's attempt to take control of Dartmouth College, few used the courts to attempt to enforce their rights as private corporations. State court decisions affecting the College of Washington (1797), Davidson Academy (1803), and Columbia (1807) presented a challenge to the status quo that was not fully appreciated until the Supreme Court ruling in 1819.

The early history of Dartmouth College reflects the colonial model of an integrated church and state addressing social needs with little concern for public and private distinctions. In 1740 Dr. Eleazar Wheelock, minister of the Second Congregational Church in Lebanon, Connecticut, embraced the New Light doctrine born in the Great Awakening. Three years later his more traditional parishioners asked him to leave the pulpit as part of their plans for "regulating abuses and correcting disorders in ecclesiastical affairs." Deprived of his pastorate Dr. Wheelock turned to teaching as a means of supporting himself while continuing to deliver his religious message. In 1754 he began Moors' Indian Charity School to educate the Native Americans in the message of Christ. Dr. Wheelock initially funded his school through contributions from local subscribers and missionary societies, but in 1765 he succeeded in raising substantial funds from wealthy Englishmen who were convinced of the merit of his endeavors. The chief investor in this enterprise was the earl of Dartmouth who, like other significant subscribers, was promised a trusteeship in the corporate body once corporate status was obtained. The influx of cash enabled Wheelock to address grander aspirations. Tiring in his attempts to educate the Indians, he conceived of starting a college for the training of ministers. Various colonies competed to be the home of his well-funded new school. New Hampshire offered both free land and a charter allowing the trustees considerable freedom in managing the school's affairs, and it won the contest over the school's location.[34]

As Wheelock had raised the funds for the school on the premise of educating Indians, titular adherence to that goal needed to be retained. Indeed, it was noted in the granting of the school's charter that the state was enticed to grant land to Wheelock for an Indian school, "considering that without the least impediment to the said design, the same school may be enlarged and improved to promote learning among the English, and be a means to supply a great number of churches and congregations, which are likely soon to be formed in the country, with a learned and orthodox ministry."[35] But practice, not language, proved the best indicator of Wheelock's intentions, as only eleven Indians graduated from the college before 1800.

Wheelock successfully chartered his educational operation in the name of The Trustees of Dartmouth College in 1769. He worked through the Royal Governor of the Province of New Hampshire to obtain the charter from the British Crown. The charter confirmed the major donors as trustees and gave them the sole authority to name their successors. The future of the college was secured in perpetuity, with the charter being a grant "for us, our heirs and successors forever . . . that there shall be in the said Dartmouth College, from henceforth and forever, a body politic, consisting of trustees of said Dartmouth College."[36]

The charter specifically provided that the trustees could manage the college as a lawful business operation. Eleazar Wheelock was named president and was given the authority to name his successor with concurrence by the trustees. The trustees held sole authority to elect all subsequent presidents, and to remove or appoint any officer, teacher, or employee of the school. Lastly, the charter asserted that the Trustees of Dartmouth College existed as an independent corporation, not requiring any further "grant, license, or confirmation," in order to maintain its independence in the future.[37]

In the years during and immediately after the war, New Hampshire paid little attention to the small college in the mountains. Wheelock died in 1779 and was succeeded by his son John, the first lay college president in America. New Hampshire began to increase its support of the school during the late 1780s, partly in response to efforts from Vermont to induce Dartmouth to move to that state. Dartmouth received a land grant from New Hampshire of forty-two thousand acres in 1789, another land grant in 1807, and sporadic monetary grants in the 1790s.[38] The only college in New Hampshire—created as a private, religiously inspired, educational corporation—received both state aid and private funds in support of its purpose. Moreover, Dartmouth appealed to the state legislature for support of its mission to serve the state's educational needs, as did other "private" schools during this era, and it willingly made concessions in curriculum in return.

Conflict came to Dartmouth in the first decade of the new century. Throughout the 1780s and 1790s state legislatures imposed secular curricula and the teaching of republican conceptions of virtue upon denominationally controlled institutions. By the early 1800s the religious counterrevolution reasserted demands for greater Christian piety in American society. Dartmouth came under attack for its religious laxity.

Undergraduate religious societies began forming on New England college campuses in the 1790s. The 1802 revival at Yale spawned increased religious energy at many of these schools. But it is incorrect to perceive this movement just as a battle for souls. The real issues were societal, not personal, as evangelical Americans expressed reactionary displeasure at the secular humanism that had taken over governmental and educational institutions. Some imagined the infiltration of American colleges by a conspiracy of European freethinkers influenced by French philosophers and committed to deism and anarchy. The revivals were necessary countermeasures to save young Americans from infidelity and corruption.[39] Campus evangelicals attacked not only the curricula and political values spawned by Enlightenment humanism but also the carnival atmosphere of college communities. Student drinking, moral decline, and rowdiness, combined with irreverence for God to make campuses ill-suited to their purpose of training young men for responsible positions in church and in society.

By 1804 a sufficient number of Dartmouth's trustees had aligned themselves with the orthodox resurgence to appoint Roswell Shurtleff as professor of divinity. The young professor also assumed the duties of pastor in Hanover's Congregational Church. In both positions he worked to move the community to a more vital recognition of God's place in people's lives. President John Wheelock opposed Shurtleff's professorial appointment and further resented his assumption of pastoral duties at the local church (from which he had ousted Wheelock's close friend, John Smith). While Wheelock shared the New Light religious perspective of his father, differences in religion only partially account for the president's objections to Shurtleff. Wheelock had become a leading figure in New England society and felt threatened by the intrusion of anyone challenging his authority on his campus. Differences in doctrine between the Congregationalist components involved in the schism contributed no more to the break than did conflicting ideas on the social role of religion. As Steven Novak noted in his article on the Dartmouth controversy: "What divided the two sides was this difference of mood—a sense of alarm at the dangers facing the country as well as a great faith in the meliorate power of religion."[40]

Shurtleff wasted little time in addressing the religious apathy on campus, leading a revival in the winter of 1805–1806. The revival succeeded in increasing the religious commitments among the students, many of whom began attending Shurtleff's worship sessions in town rather than those in the campus chapel. These students' new commitment to orthodoxy expressed itself in petitions for temperance and the banishment of "treating"—ritualized drinking parties accompanying major campus events. In 1809 the trustees accepted the demands of the religious faction. In response, students objecting to increased restrictions rioted, becoming drunk, burning outhouses, vandalizing more orthodox students' rooms, firing guns into the night air, and spreading garbage over the campus environs of their suspected enemies.[41]

During these years of Republican ascendancy and the rise of a liberal commercial society, many New Englanders struggled to preserve their traditional conception of republican liberties limited by civic duties and Christian morality. Speaking on the Fourth of July, 1806, in Concord, New

Hampshire, Daniel Webster (who later played a key role in the *Dartmouth* case) proclaimed: "The altar of our freedom should be placed near the altar of our religion. Thus shall the Almighty Power who protects his own worship, protect also our liberties."[42]

Such conservative New Englanders exercised significant control over Dartmouth College. Wheelock's influence over faculty appointments and campus policies continued to decline through 1809 as four new orthodox trustees joined the board—one of whom, Charles Marsh, founded the Society for the Promotion of Temperance. Piqued at his diminishing influence, Wheelock refused to punish the rioters and blamed the religious faction for engendering the unrest. He further went on the attack, accusing the trustees of a conspiracy to turn Dartmouth into a "sectarian school." Pamphlets supporting the president lamented the campus culture, which seemingly required faculty and students to wear "their badge of orthodoxy." In response, Shurtleff and his supporters referred to the president as a "liberal" who would convert the college into "a seminary of Socinianism."[43]

The debate at the college spilled over into the larger political arena. Congregational clergy throughout New Hampshire asked for prayers for the college as a "nursery of piety," which they hoped would not revert to its heathenish state. Newspapers took sides in editorials, addressing the issue at the college as representative of competing views of American society. The Republican editor of the *New Hampshire Patriot and State Gazette,* noting both his state's and the nation's acceptance of the Republican platform, condemned the changes at Dartmouth and encouraged "the future governance of Dartmouth College" as "a means of perpetuating the republican majority in the state."[44]

William Plumer, by the second decade of the nineteenth century, had matured into a political leader, but he retained an ardent liberal distrust of organized religion. A Jeffersonian Republican, he won the governor's office in 1812, lost it in 1813, but won every year between 1814 and 1817. He made the incompatibility of republican ideals and established religion the bedrock of his campaigns. Yet he was hesitant to articulate his deepest concerns in a public forum, fearing repercussions to his political aspirations. By 1813 he had become convinced that the leaders of the Second Awakening, Dwight, Beecher, Taylor, and Shurtleff among them, were fomenting a reactionary plot to overturn the Revolution. Under the pseudonym "A Layman," he wrote to the *New Hampshire Patriot,* accusing the clergy of attempting "to traduce and vilify the [republican] government, to counteract and enfeeble its measures, [in pursuit of its] publicly avowed . . . object [of] a religious establishment."[45]

By this time the question of maintaining religious establishments was being hotly debated throughout New England. Each state was very aware of the arguments made in neighboring jurisdictions. The expanded scope of the debate allowed for reference to national goals and prevailing cultural attitudes. In another letter to the *Patriot* in 1813, "A Layman" wrote:

Our Constitution has established perfect liberty to every man not only to worship God according to the dictates of his own conscience but the right of paying or not paying for the support of religious teachers as he may judge proper. This perfect law of liberty alarmed you [the Congregational clergy] . . . it left you dependent on your own merits and the good will of the people for subsistence. To relieve yourselves from this state of uncertain dependence many of you have been anxious to obtain a religious establishment. . . . In Massachusetts some of you have publicly avowed the object. The *Panoplist* of July, 1812, contends for the establishment of a permanent tribunal with power to ordain and depose ministers as they should judge proper—in fact establish articles of faith and practice.[46]

As the only college in the state, Dartmouth served both as an incubator of ideas furthering the debate and as a lightning rod for attacks by those who sought to use the school as an instrument in the broader ideological and political contest. Republican interests focused on the trustees of the college as dangerous ideologues inhibiting the state's progress. The *Patriot* published a number of letters and editorials excoriating these men for their illiberal attitudes. On September 15, 1815, Isaac Hill, the paper's editor, criticized the trustees for "their insidious attacks upon religious liberty" that "shock public feeling and call loudly for public reprehension." On September 26, he wrote: "These men stand at the head of a sectarian combination which intends to overrule, bear down, and crush all denominations of moral liberal principles." On October 10, 1815, "Junius" wrote, "Lift the curtain and you will behold a monster, horrid to the sight, grasping in his right hand the Crown and Mitre—his left hand pointing to the Inquisition—trampling under foot Religious Freedom—and on his forehead labelled UNION OF CHURCH AND STATE." One month later, an unsigned letter presented the argument that it was not the Calvinist trustees who were persecuted so much as their enemies, whom they consider to be simply "in error."[47]

In 1815 President Wheelock asked the New Hampshire legislature to investigate the college. The trustees responded on August 26, 1815, by removing him from office and replacing him with the Rev. Francis Brown, a Congregationalist minister. Brown saw his role as a missionary, asserting that "the visible church" is the vehicle for "conversion in every heathen land, and for the gradual and permanent propagation of Christian knowledge."[48]

That same year Justice Smith, in the *Moore v. Poole* decision, upheld a Congregational minister's right to be free from taxes, which provoked further outcry from dissenters of all types. This decision served as a basis for a renewal of the alliance between unchurched rationalists and Baptists and Methodists. A letter to the *Patriot* after the decision argued that it was proof of a Federalist-Congregationalist plot to establish "a law-religion."[49]

Many New Hampshire residents feared that an "aristocracy of the standing orthodox order" might transform Dartmouth into another Andover, which required religious oath taking, or that it was following the leads of Williams College and the University of Vermont in dismissing liberal presidents (Dr. Daniel Sanders in 1814 from Vermont and Dr. Ebenezer Fitch in 1815 from Williams). One letter from "A Baptist" to the *Patriot* dated February 27, 1816, accused the Congregationalists of hurling President Wheelock from office "to make room for one who had given full proof of his attachment to the orthodox Hierarchy."[50]

In the gubernatorial campaign of 1816, Republican candidate William Plumer made the Dartmouth College debate a central issue and called for legislative reform of the charter. Plumer decried the seminarian aspects of American higher education, finding the teaching of dead languages inconsistent "to the pursuits and business of this life" and the ecclesiastical emphasis of many schools "hostile to our republican system." Referring specifically to Dartmouth, he said, "When the government of our college apply [*sic*] to the people or the legislature for aid, they [*sic*] represent the college as a *public institution*." He promised, if elected, to have the legislature take control of Dartmouth and institute reform, emphasizing a curriculum useful in daily life, religious freedom, and open availability to rich and poor alike.[51]

In March 1816 New Hampshire voters elected Republican William Plumer as governor by a twenty-three-hundred-vote plurality and sent a Republican majority to the legislature. The Republican campaign depicted evangelical revivals and the funding of missions and philanthropies as attempts to convert the people to an unrepublican way of life. Plumer's early actions reflect this emphasis. He repealed the Judiciary Act of 1813, thus removing Justice Smith from office. A bill ending religious taxation was narrowly defeated by the Senate. The most significant of the first acts of the new administration was a bill restructuring Dartmouth College. In Plumer's "Message to the legislature," in which he advocated reform of Dartmouth, he referred to the college's self-sustaining board of trustees, able to operate on its own majority unchecked by popular will, as a remnant of the Crown's authority and as "hostile to the spirit and genius of free government."[52] The legislation, passed in 1816, was not unusual. Earlier New York, Kentucky, Massachusetts, and Pennsylvania had turned private colleges into state universities, modernizing and secularizing the curricula and asserting legislative control in the governance of the schools. Yet in each of these instances, the school trustees acceded to the legislative initiative; in New Hampshire the legislation served as a declaration of war.

Three different legislative actions addressing Dartmouth were enacted in 1816. Of these, the first is the most important. On June 27, 1816, the New Hampshire legislature passed an act entitled "An act to amend the charter, and enlarge and improve the corporation of Dartmouth College." In this statute, the legislature premised its action upon state interest:

Whereas knowledge and learning generally diffused through a community, are essential to the preservation of a free government, and extending the opportunities and advantages of education is highly conducive to promote this end and by the constitution it is made the duty of the legislators and magistrates to cherish the interests of literature, and the sciences, and all seminaries established for their advancement—and as the college of the state may, in the opinion of the legislature, be rendered more extensively useful.[53]

The legislature then proceeded to change the corporation's name to the Trustees of Dartmouth University, simultaneously effectuating the same change in the name of the school. The distinction between a college and a university at this time was more significant than subsequent usage of those terms may indicate. The term *university* implied a school devoted to a modern curriculum designed to prepare students for diverse roles in business, government, and the secular needs of the state. The term *college* usually referred to a cloistered academic community intended to train ministers. The name change to Dartmouth University implied substantial changes in the school's goals and methods.

The statute also increased the number of trustees by nine, from twelve to twenty-one, and named the governor as the source of all new trustees and of future replacements. Even more significant was that the act created a board of overseers, appointed by the governor to govern the university, to undertake most of the responsibilities formerly held by the trustees. The board was authorized to approve or negate any action of the trustees to appoint and remove the president and officers of the university, to set their salaries, to establish professorships, to create new buildings, and to approve all faculty appointments.[54]

In a significant change from the earlier charter, the legislature expanded the practice of religious freedom at the university. The 1769 charter prohibited discrimination against any person "of any religious denomination." Atheists, agnostics, Jews, and other non-Christians were not protected within this provision, since none of them was part of a "denomination." The 1816 legislation provided that "Sect. 8. Be it further enacted, that perfect freedom of religious opinion shall be enjoyed by all the officers and students of the university; and no officer or student shall be deprived of any honors, privileges, or benefits of the institution, on account of his religious creed or belief." By this provision, "perfect freedom of religious opinion" was accorded all officers and students, but not faculty. The legislation appears uncertain on the extent to which non-Christian faculty would be accepted at the reconstituted Dartmouth, providing only that new professorships in the theological colleges within the university could be endowed and filled by men of "any sect of the Protestant Christian religion." On the basis of specific mention constituting an exception to the general rule, faculty members in the other colleges presumably were not similarly restricted.[55]

The trustees of the college met to respond to the legislation and on August 28, 1816, issued a resolution "refusing to accept or act under" the statute. The college trustees also removed William H. Woodward from his position as secretary and treasurer of the 1769 corporation. Woodward was a Republican supporter of Wheelock, and he had taken possession of the corporation's records, account books, and seal. On December 18, 1816, New Hampshire's legislature enacted another law allowing the nine newly appointed trustees to act as quorum, thereby circumventing the refusal of the college trustees to participate in the business of the new corporation. A third act, the act of December 26, 1816, provided for five-hundred-dollar fines for each offense for anyone presuming to act as a trustee or officer of the college except as provided by law. The new university trustees reinstated Woodward in their initial meeting on February 4, 1817. Subsequently, on February 8, 1817, the college trustees sued him to recover the items in his possession, and to raise the issue of the legitimacy of the legislative action.[56] The case proceeded through the court system and reached the Supreme Court in 1819. By this time, Daniel Webster and the recently unseated Justice Jeremiah Smith represented the college. Argument began on March 10, 1819, before a packed courtroom. Webster's stirring oration on behalf of the college is often cited as the most famous in the history of oral argument before the Supreme Court. Following three days of argument, Chief Justice Marshall announced that the Court would postpone its decision in order to reach a consensus.[57]

This delay allowed both sides to campaign on behalf of their positions. While the attorneys had focused attention on political processes and contract rights, other interested parties reaffirmed the issue before the Supreme Court in broad ideological terms. In June, President Brown argued that the churches of Christ "must be instrumental in illuminating the world." Referring to Dartmouth and its trustees, he insisted that "they must be careful to select for officers, and especially for publick teachers, men who are sound in the faith and are competent to instruct others and to defend the truth." Brown outlined the philosophical divide confronting the Court, New Hampshire, and the country:

> That the labours of the philosopher were so impotent, and the preaching of the apostle attended with such energy is not strange. The mind of Plato, after all his attainments, was involved in spiritual darkness. Paul, on the other hand, was irradiated with a light from heaven, strong and clear; and the same divine spirit, who at first imparted it to his own mind, accompanied it, as it was conveyed from him to his fellow man. . . . If instead of placing Paul in contrast with Plato alone, I had supposed all the philosophers of Greece and Rome arrayed on one side against this single apostle, the general result would have been the same.[58]

Conversely, the Jeffersonians depicted the struggle as one between the ideas of the past and those of the future. Freedom of thought and belief, as well as action, was necessary for social growth and human progress: "We appeal also to your interests and the interests of the whole American family: to foster, promote, protect, and encourage every description of domestic industry, as inseparably connected with, or having a powerful influence on, our rights, liberties, and independence and our immediate happiness and prosperity."[59]

The case of *Trustees of Dartmouth College v. Woodward* is often credited with "creating" the legal right of corporations to be free from state government control, thereby enabling private enterprises to pursue charitable and business goals.[60] Yet the law of contracts, on which the protection of corporations was premised, was rooted in both domestic and English precedent prior to 1819 and was clearly expressed in the Constitution. Furthermore, the private-public distinction, which served as the essential rationale for treating the college as an eleemosynary corporation, similar to a corporate enterprise for private profit, was a fundamental derivative of basic social-contract political theory. The distinction recognized the state as a social creation that could not be entrusted with any more than the minimal delegation of authority necessary for it to protect private individual liberties. Rather than creating law in *Dartmouth*, the Supreme Court articulated and clarified, in the form of governing doctrinal rules, principles of social governance and economic endeavor that had prevailed in more diffuse form for decades. Once expressed as the supreme law of the land, these ideological and legal principles could then govern the design of American civil society.

The contract clause of the U.S. Constitution (article 1, section 10), reads in part: "No state shall . . . pass any bill of attainder, ex post facto law, or law impairing the obligation owing to contracts," as they are superior to public interests asserted by state legislatures that might be used to contravene those private contract considerations. In 1810 the Supreme Court addressed the contract clause for the first time in *Fletcher v. Peck*.[61] In this decision, the Court upheld a sale of land by Georgia despite the subsequent enactment of legislation by that state's legislature repudiating the sale. The question of the legality of the sale arose because of the discovery of political corruption affecting it. It is interesting that, in separate writings prepared for different purposes prior to the lawsuit, both Thomas Jefferson and Alexander Hamilton had found the sale of the land to be lawful.[62] Finding that the sale was a valid contract and asserting that the legislature could not throw aside all "rules of property," Chief Justice Marshall rejected the argument "that a legislature may, by its own act, divest the vested estate of any man whatever for reasons which shall, by itself, be deemed sufficient." Invoking article 1, section 10, Marshall wrote that the U.S. Constitution protected contracts and did not distinguish between those among individuals and those to which the state was a party. "When, then, a law is in its nature a contract, where absolute rights have vested under that contract, a repeal of the law cannot divest those rights." Marshall's biographer, Albert Beveridge, contended that "after his opinions in *Fletcher v. Peck* and in *New Jersey v. Wilson*, nobody could have expected from John Marshall any other action than the one he took in the *Dartmouth College* case."[63]

Yet as significant as the *Peck* decision was, an even better case for contextualizing the *Dartmouth* case is Justice Story's decision of 1815 in *Terrett v. Taylor*. This case provides an appreciation for the *Dartmouth College* decision's implicit acceptance of churches and religious institutions as private organizations, distinct from the public realm despite their dedication to public service. Story specifically refers to churches as private "voluntary associations," which are required to assume the corporate form to secure their pursuit of private ends from public interference.[64]

In 1784 Virginia disestablished the Episcopalian Church, repealing all laws providing for public support of the church, incorporating the church, and vesting the new Protestant Episcopal corporation with the church's property. Subsequent legislation required all religious societies in the state to appoint trustees to hold and manage their property. However, in 1801 the Virginia legislature asserted its right to all lands held by the Episcopal Church, because it perceived those lands to derive from that church's earlier status. As that status was now deemed irreconcilable with republican government, the legislature attached the lands and directed the overseers of the poor to appropriate the proceeds from the sale of the lands to further the overseers' public duties. The trustees brought an action for an injunction preventing the overseers of the poor from selling the church's property.[65]

The case reached the Supreme Court in 1814. The following February, Justice Story delivered the opinion of the Court. Story recited the history and rationale of Virginia's disestablishment legislation before finding that the Protestant Episcopal corporation was in fact a "voluntary association," and that

> while . . . the legislature might exempt the citizens from a compulsive attendance and payment of taxes in support of any particular sect, it is not perceived that either public or constitutional principles required the abolition of all religious corporations . . . . The revolution might justly take away the public patronage, the exclusive cure of souls, and the compulsive taxation for the support of the church. Beyond these we are not prepared to admit the justice or authority of the exercise of legislation.

In other words, Story said that Virginia could divorce the Episcopalian Church from its prior role as a public institution and recognize it as one of many private voluntary associations utilizing the corporate form to serve its private needs, but the state could not then divest the church, as a private corporation, of its property. The fact that the church had gained its property through pre-disestablishment state support did not eviscerate the property rights it held. Story's decision confirmed the correctness of the actions and reasoning of the New York legislature in not attaching the property of Trinity Church. He relied on republican ideology, which he expressed as legal principle, to reach his decision, upholding "a great and fundamental principle of a republican government, the right of the citizens to the full enjoyment of their property legally acquired." In a passage that previews the issue of the *Dartmouth* case, Story writes:

> But that the legislature can repeal statutes creating private corporations, or confirming to them property already acquired under the faith of previous laws, and by such repeal can vest the property of such corporations exclusively in the state, or dispose of the same to such purposes as they may please, without the consent or default of the corporators, we are not prepared to admit; and we think ourselves standing upon the principles of natural justice, upon the fundamental laws of every free government, upon the spirit and the letter of the constitution of the United States, and upon the decisions of most respectable judicial tribunals, in resisting such a doctrine.[66]

The *Dartmouth College* case presented an opportunity for the Supreme Court to confirm its protection of contract rights, but the Court had already done this. Alternatively, the Court may have seen a duty to determine whether a corporate charter, which is a governmental creation, was entitled to less protection from that government than other contracts. Yet this issue was also largely resolved in *Fletcher v. Peck,* as the contract in question in that case, though not a charter, was a legislative creation. The principal importance of the *Dartmouth College* case was not the pronouncement of the rule of law determining the case but, rather, the reasoning articulated by the Court. This reasoning expressed the Court's perception of distinct realms of public and private action, and the role of the courts in the protection of private action from public action. In the factual context of the case, "private" connoted a religious endeavor as much as an economic one. The *Dartmouth* case gave the Court a chance to expand upon the law expressed by Story in *Terrett v. Taylor.* The college was not a church but was a religiously affiliated organization addressing public needs through a private agenda.

Calling attention to the untenable aspects of this relationship, the Court's decision recognized the implicit constitutional separation of church and state, confirming the status of churches in America as private voluntary institutions able to pursue their own visions of society. Early in his opinion, Marshall redefined the central issue in the case in terms of a public-private distinction:

> If the act of incorporation be a grant of political power, if it create a civil institution to be employed in the administration of the government, or if the funds of the college be public property, or if the state of New Hampshire, as a government, be alone interested in its transactions, the subject is one in which the legislature of the state may act according to its own judgment, unrestrained by any limitation of its power imposed by the constitution of the United States . . . . But if this be a private eleemosynary institution, endowed with a capacity to

take property for objects unconnected with government, whose funds are be-
stowed by individuals on the faith of the charter; if the donors have stipulated
for the future disposition and management of those funds in the manner prescribed by themselves, there may be more difficulty in the case, although neither the persons who have made these stipulations nor those for whose benefit
they are made should be parties to the cause.

Resolving this issue, Marshall found that private property "both real and
personal which had been contributed for the benefit of the college, was conveyed to and vested in, the corporate body." Further, he found that this
property was used to manage the college, consistent with the intentions and
parameters expressed in the corporation's charter. Reaching a tentative conclusion, based solely on the nature of the corporation's property, Marshall
contended: "It is then, an eleemosynary, and as far as respects its funds, a
private corporation."[67]

However, the state of New Hampshire, the defendant in error in the proceedings, through attorney John Holmes argued that a corporation's purpose—
in this instance, the support of the government's interest in education—
was more determinative of the corporation's nature than the source of its
funds. Holmes asserted:

> The education of youth, and the encouragement of arts and sciences, is one
> of the most important objects of civil government. By our constitutions, it is
> left exclusively to the states . . . the constitution of the state admonishes the
> legislature of the duty of encouraging science and literature, and thus seems
> to suppose its power of control over the scientific and literary institutions of
> the state. The legislature had therefore, a right to modify this trust, the origi-
> nal object of which was the education of the Indian and English youth of
> the province.

Marshall, therefore, could not rest upon his finding that "as far as respects its funds." Dartmouth was a private corporation. Recognizing
Holmes's argument, he asked of Dartmouth: "Do its objects stamp on it a
different character?" In answer, he responded, "No." Marshall defined
public institutions not by the purposes they address, but as being part of
the "civil government." In perhaps the most crucial passage of the decision, Marshall wrote:

> Are the trustees and professors public officers, invested with any portion of po-
> litical power, partaking in any degree in the administration of civil government,
> and performing duties which flow from the sovereign authority? That educa-
> tion is an object of national concern, and a proper subject of legislation, all ad-
> mit. That there may be an institution founded by government and placed en-
> tirely under its immediate control, the officers of which would be public
> officers, amenable exclusively to government, none will deny. But is Dartmouth

College such an institution? Is education altogether in the hands of government? Does every teacher of youth become a public officer, and do donations for the purpose of education necessarily become public property, so far that the will of the legislature, not the will of the donor, becomes the law of the donation?[68]

Responding to those questions, Marshall found that "the fact that they [the college teachers] were employed in the education of youth could not have converted them into public officers, concerned in the administration of public duties, or have given the legislature a right to interfere in the management of the [corporation's] funds." Nor did the act of incorporation subject a corporation to perpetual control by the state. Incorporation allowed the new entity, as "an artificial being," "the mere creation of law," to attain "immortality" and "individuality," "properties by which a perpetual succession of many persons are considered as the same and may act as a single individual." Marshall asserted: "But this being does not share in the civil government of the country, unless that be the purpose for which it was created. Its immortality no more confers on it political power, or a political character, than immortality would confer such power or character on a natural person. *It is no more a state instrument than a natural person exercising the same powers would be.*"[69]

The fact that Dartmouth College was once perceived by the state to be an organ of public service did not, Marshall said, create a presumption that the donors to the college intended to serve the legislature's determination of the interests of the people of New Hampshire. To the contrary, the only reasonable conclusion was that they intended their gifts to address the interests and purposes of the college as determined by the trustees consistent with the charter. To protect the property interests of the donors, as well as of the corporation, the charter could not be subject to revision or manipulation by the state. Marshall writes: "The corporation is the assignee of their [the donors'] rights, stands in their place, and distributes their bounty, as they would themselves have distributed it, had they been immortal."[70] The corporation, then, formed the means by which the donors addressed their goals, and it was not a tool of the state legislature to be used to serve state interests. Incorporation allowed many individuals to come together to exert greater influence as a group than they ever could separately; and to do so perpetually, without restrictions from government that would be equally as unlawful were they asserted against individuals. In overturning the legislative action restructuring the college, Marshall asserted that legislative perceptions of the public good could not overcome the rights of individuals expressed in contracts.

The preceding legal argument constituted a sufficient basis for the Court, pursuant to article 1, section 10, of the U.S. Constitution, to void the action of the New Hampshire legislature. However, Marshall's opinion went further and in the process clarified the status of charitable institutions in the early republic. Language in the *Dartmouth* decision prefigured the Court's subsequent decision in *Philadelphia Baptist Association v. Hart's Executors* later the same year.[71] In the *Dartmouth College* decision, Marshall wrote, "Charitable, or public spirited individuals, desirous of making permanent appropriations for charitable or other useful purposes, find it impossible to effect their design securely, and certainly, without an incorporation act."[72] In this passage, Marshall articulated the basis for the doctrine that unincorporated charitable institutions are too vague to receive bequests of decedents, as their intentions cannot be given definite assurance of fulfillment without a corporate charter and an organization that establishes parameters for the future use of funds. In this way Marshall not only distinguished private charitable corporations from state governmental offices and agencies but also required a legal formalization of those charities in order for them to be legally secure in the pursuit of their purposes.

After the *Dartmouth College* decision, government could not rely upon private philanthropic associations to address public perceptions of societal needs. The public-private distinction required states to define their priorities more carefully. No longer could states delegate to private concerns the responsibility for educating young people, caring for the poor, or creating roadways, because states could no longer exercise control over how these private concerns fulfilled their duties. To continue to rely on private concerns after 1819 risked creating educational, welfare, or infrastructure systems significantly at odds with legislative perceptions of the public interest. Justice Story, in his concurring opinion, provided the states with one option to use in an effort to preserve the old system of state reliance on private action to serve public needs. Recognizing charters as contracts, Story wrote: "If the legislature mean to claim such an authority [to control the course of private corporations by legislative enactment], it must be reserved in the grant."[73] Seldom, in future years, would any corporation submit to such a provision in its charter. Instead, states needed to determine those priorities and concerns that could not be entrusted to private attention, and to establish governmental funds and offices for them. Accordingly, those social needs deemed less sensitive or important were left to charitable organizations to address as they saw fit.

In the process, civil society was redefined, separating governmental institutions from private charitable corporations. Religiously affiliated private associations pursuing their own goals remained viable on the institutional periphery of society. Marshall's language in the *Dartmouth College* decision expressed a major change in attitude from an earlier era: "These eleemosynary institutions do not fill the place which would otherwise be occupied by government, but that which would otherwise remain vacant."[74] In recognizing the private agendas of these associations and granting them legal protection, the Court perpetuated the debate over the values, goals, and purposes of American society.

The Supreme Court decision in the *Dartmouth College* case did not make new law. It relied on constitutional language, judicial precedent, and generally accepted political theory to articulate a new doctrinal rule. As law, then, this rule functioned as social authority, able to condemn and prescribe future behaviors of states and individuals.

In the early 1800s Dartmouth College confronted the same religious and political factionalism that faced American society as a whole. Two articles from the last thirty years address these issues. In 1974 Stephen Novak asserted that Dartmouth, like other colleges at the time, was "torn apart by the Protestant counterrevolution sweeping through America." Novak saw the Court's decision as a victory for evangelical Christians. In 1983 Eldon Johnson focused attention on the early republic's political debate over education. Johnson saw Marshall's decision as a Federalist victory in that state-sponsored liberal education was set back. For a while after 1819 the states lacked the funds to create new colleges to compete with existing institutions. Nonetheless, Johnson notes that, following 1819 there was a proliferation of denominational schools competing largely with each other. The real significance of the decision goes beyond either Novak's or Johnson's arguments.[75]

A case decided in the same year as the *Dartmouth College* case, *Trustees of the Philadelphia Baptist Association v. Hart's Executors,* gave Marshall an opportunity to elaborate upon the meaning and significance of his earlier pronouncement. In 1790 Virginian Silas Hart drafted his will, leaving "what shall remain of my military certificates at the time of my decease" to the Baptist Association in Philadelphia for educating youths desiring to enter the Baptist ministry. Hart died in 1795. During the intervening years (specifically in 1792), Virginia enacted a new legal code, in the process repealing all English statutes that had governed in colonial days and in the immediate aftermath of the Revolution. During this entire period the Baptist Association had existed only informally as a group of citizens united by common social and religious sentiment. In 1797 the group incorporated under the laws of Pennsylvania as Trustees of the Philadelphia Baptist Association.

The case came to the Supreme Court on the issue of whether the testator's intent could be given legal effect. Marshall found that Hart's intentions were obvious—he wanted to leave a large portion of his estate to the Philadelphia Baptist Association. However, Marshall also articulated the general rule of law that "a vague legacy, the object of which is indefinite cannot be established in a court of equity." In other words, a court could not create a legal entity in order to enable it to receive a bequest consistent with a testator's intent. As the Baptist Association was not incorporated at the time of the bequest, no legal effect could be given to the provision of the will and the money reverted back to the statutory heirs. Marshall concluded that a testator intends an association to receive funds, not the individuals who compose it. Without incorporation, under which the trustees were legally committed to serve enunciated purposes, the funds left to an association had no assurance of being used for any specific end. The Court could only recognize and enforce legal commitments, not vague sympathies. It could not turn over money to individuals unnamed in the will simply because they were part of an association. Membership in associations is transitory. In the case of Hart's bequest, Marshall asked whether the petitioners would seek to have all Baptist Association members of 1792 receive funds or all of those in 1795.[76]

The plaintiffs argued that Hart's bequest would be given effect under English law pursuant to the Elizabethan Statute of Charitable Uses. The "cy pres doctrine" allowed courts "to redirect or adjust a charity whose original purpose could no longer be fulfilled." Courts could thereby preserve the bequest and satisfy the intent of the donor as much as possible. Following English law, colonial assemblies attempted to remove obstacles to charitable activities and courts tried to give effect to donors' benevolent intentions, even when confusedly expressed.[77] Justice Story, in his concurring opinion, gave the most thorough response of the Court to this argument. Under English law, he found that charitable testaments were given legal privilege—"no such testament was void for uncertainty as to persons or objects." But this doctrine depended upon statutory, not common, law through the Elizabethan Statute of Charitable Uses. As the Virginia legislature repealed all English statutes, the Court could not rely upon the doctrine. It could not enforce a law that did not exist in Virginia.[78]

Subsequent confusion over the decision's ruling regarding the origins of the cy pres doctrine has made it difficult for some legal historians to recognize the importance of the *Hart* decision. Some historians' proclivity to see law only as an expression of social and political policy further limits their appreciation of this case. For example, Howard Miller found an inconsistency between the *Dartmouth College* and *Hart* decisions. Quoting Marshall's opinion in the former case, Miller wrote that "government 'must be disposed rather to encourage than to discountenance' educational philanthropies."[79] As *Hart* is understood by Miller to inhibit philanthropies, he saw the decisions as irreconcilable. Miller understood Marshall to have been using law as a tool to express or formulate social policy.[80] In fact, the *Dartmouth College* decision was not only consistent with the *Hart* decision but complementary to it, when the focus is not public policy, but law. Both decisions asserted the rights of eleemosynary corporations, as legal entities, to receive grants or bequests and to use them for private purposes. Both decisions also, however, rested corporate functional independence upon a legal action, the act of incorporation. In both cases it was the law that bestows and recognizes rights, not the public purposes of association. The fact that Dartmouth College pursued education as its corporate goal did not alter its legal existence or its legal rights. Neither did the fact that the Baptist Association served a public interest render its legal status different from that of other informal associations.

In both cases, Marshall and Story applied law not as a tool to shape public policy but rather as a semi-autonomous doctrine derived from republican ideology that governed man in his social pursuits. In this context the decisions reinforce each other in articulating the legal doctrine of

the early republic. Public and private spheres were to be separated in order to protect both from each other. The electorate, through majority
vote, would determine the public course of action. Yet associations,
churches, or philanthropies as private entities were free to pursue their
own visions for American civil society. The means by which protection
was to be afforded was through the enforcement of contracts. But in order for contracts to be enforced in law, they had to meet legal requirements. Certainty as to the parties and their intentions was required by
law to give contracts effect.[81]

The inclination to see legal decisions as pronouncements of social policy
understood through their adjudication of disputes has prompted several
commentators to assert that the *Hart* decision was overturned by the *Girard's
Will Case* in 1844.[82] It was not. Different facts produced a different decision
through application of the same rules of law. The production of a different
decision did not overturn the earlier legal rule. In fact, the *Hart* doctrine
continued to be relied upon for its assertion that a charitable entity must
have legal certainty, as provided through incorporation, in order to receive
bequests. In 1830, in *Inglis v. Trustees of the Sailor's Snug Harbor*, Justice
Thompson explained the ruling of the *Hart* case: "The bequest there was 'to
the Baptist Association that, for ordinary, meets at Philadelphia.' This association not being incorporated, was considered incapable of taking the trust of
a society."[83] In *Vidal v. Philadelphia (Girard's Will Case)*, the Court again cited
the *Hart* ruling with approval while distinguishing the facts of the case from
the 1819 decision. Mr. Girard's will bequeathed money to found a school
near Philadelphia to educate "poor white male orphans." He further provided in his will that "I enjoin and require that no ecclesiastic, missionary; or minister of any Sect whatsoever, ever hold office or exercise any
station or duty whatever in the said college; nor shall any such person
ever be admitted for any purpose, or as a visitor, within the premises appropriated to the purposes of the said college."[84] The issues presented by
the will were whether the City of Philadelphia could receive the funds
and whether the purposes for which Girard intended to found the school
contravened the law of Pennsylvania by discriminating against potential
teachers or administrators affiliated with a religious institution. Justice
Story ruled that the City of Philadelphia could receive the bequest as a
civic corporation able to take and hold real and personal property. Reasserting the rule of law from *Fletcher* and *Dartmouth College,* Story found
that a corporation may receive and use property just as a private person
may. Story merely distinguishes the *Hart* case, for in that instance no lawful corporation existed; in this instance, one did. From 1819 to 1844
there was no change in the legal doctrine. Story also noted that Virginia
had repealed the Elizabethan Statute of Charitable Uses whereas Pennsylvania had not, which therefore granted the Court greater discretion in
fashioning relief. However, it was unnecessary even to address this latter
point, the issue of corporate status being determinative of the result.

As to the second issue, Story concluded that despite Girard's proscriptions on religious teachers, his intent could be given legal effect: "And in America, it has been thought, in the absence of any express legal prohibitions, that the donor might select the studies as well as the classes of persons who were to receive his bounty without being compellable to make religious instruction a necessary part of those studies."[85]

Legal historians have interpreted this sequence of Supreme Court decisions as a change in disposition toward favoring charitable institutions. Looking mainly at the cases from *Hart* to *Vidal,* they have missed the important and consistent role that law played in separating and defining public and private spheres while establishing laws for the protection of the latter. The *Dartmouth* case as well as Story's opinion in *Terrett v. Taylor* are essential parts of this legal sequence. Law did not change; rather, society changed to conform to earlier legal pronouncements. This social change was mandated by the Court's decision in the *Dartmouth College* case. No longer could government rely upon private corporations to serve governmental purposes. Instead, private institutions reflected the private concerns of their benefactors. Contract law served as the means of protecting those concerns.

In the process of separating public and private spheres, the Supreme Court asserted what many Americans had contended for decades—that the Constitution separted church and state. Social policy, political ideology, even contemplated prescription of religion, were all subordinated to contract law. Hereafter, all churches legally would be equal private institutions regardless of differences in doctrine and degrees of support. After the *Dartmouth College* decision, New England's religious establishment could never be the same. Later in 1819 New Hampshire's Toleration Act ended the system of tax-supported religion in that state.[86]

The *Dartmouth College* case presents two tremendous ironies. First, although the Jeffersonians lost the case they won the point they had hoped to make in revising American society. Republican legislatures had been taking over private schools in order to minimize their teaching of religious values and doctrines and to use the schools instead to foster liberal secular sentiments and to impart practical knowledge. While the Supreme Court prevented Republican legislatures from doing this, it also called attention to the general infeasability and inappropriateness of any state using a private school for public purposes. In delineating private and public spheres, the Court effectively cut off state support for private religious educational institutions and encouraged the founding of state schools addressing a secular curriculum. This was the Jeffersonians' goal all along, with no better model existing than that of the University of Virginia. Second, in the *Dartmouth* decision and other contract clause cases, the Marshall Court endorsed the Jeffersonian Republican preferences for a society of free and independent economic actors contributing to the social good by pursuing their own private goods. The Federalist Supreme Court helped to overturn the paternalism of governments that saw themselves better able to manage society through legislation than individuals could through their private business and social dealings. In this way, the Court hastened the transformation of American culture from the integrated communitarianism of the colonial era to the individualism of the early nineteenth century. This was hardly the platform of the Federalist party or the personal preference of many of the Federalist judges. Law, based on republican ideology, not personal interest, determined the rulings of the Court.

More narrowly, the *Dartmouth College* decision of 1819, by preventing state control over private educational corporations, clearly separated public from parochial education. Yet only a few states deemed it worthwhile to found, construct, and fund their own schools—Indiana in 1820, Alabama in 1831, and Delaware in 1833. To the degree that other states continued to rely on private institutions to meet educational needs, they did so with an explicit understanding of the limits they had in shaping the education provided by these schools. The unacceptability of these terms to state legislatures stranded many private schools. In need of money, the existing colleges turned to a traditional source of financing—religious institutions. The multiplicity of sects or denominations in the early nineteenth century, each seeking to build its membership, used colleges not only to train clergy but to be competitive vehicles for each sect's distinct religious message. Lefferts Loetscher, longtime faculty member at Princeton Theological Seminary and historian of education in the early 1800s, says of these denominational colleges:

> [They] offered the traditional classes and mathematics, and sometimes included interesting examples of the current progress of the natural sciences, but all were taught more descriptively than critically. Thus [their] graduates were ready to receive eagerly and uncritically the elaborate scholastic theology—or at least its conclusions—which confirmed their world view and promised the necessary degree of stability to the social structures which they headed.[87]

The decades following the *Dartmouth College* case witnessed an "unprecedented increase in the number of private colleges," as denominations founded new schools as well as took over existing ones. The development of contract law in the early republic has been credited with, in Willard Hurst's terms, a release of energy, contributing to the dynamic expansion of American commercial, industrial, and economic growth. Historian Jurgen Herbst has added that the securing of contract rights for private schools spurred the competitive environment in which various denominations presented their visions of American civil society free from state interference.[88]

The history of Bowdoin College in Maine provides an excellent case study of the effect of the *Dartmouth College* decision. One historian of Bowdoin, Ernst Christian Helmreich, wrote that the college "was founded in an age of religious indifference," not so much "as a school or seminary or theological institution but . . . as a college devoted [at least in large part] to the useful arts and sciences."[89] While Bowdoin's founding and early curriculum do reflect republican sentiments regarding the desirability of practical education, the date of its founding in 1794 is less indicative of an age of "religious indifference" than of religious debate and transformation. Bowdoin reflected both the republican enthusiasm of the postrevolutionary era and the humanistic influences upon religion in America expressed in Deism and Unitarianism. The Massachusetts legislature created the school in part to offer a religious and political alternative to Harvard and in part to appease voters in its northernmost district. Another historian of the school, Charles Calhoun, noted that the founding of Bowdoin in Maine was a product of a desire for Maine statehood by the elite of that district and a desire of the people of Massachusetts to stabilize the virtues of republicanism among the youth of the state. He reported that the college was conceived to "honor the republican ideology of the . . . nation's founders." Bowdoin was founded without any denominational attachment. The first minister of the school's chapel, the Rev. Samuel Deane, was himself a humanistic figure of the Enlightenment, a member of the American Academy of Arts and Sciences, described as both a "proto-Unitarian" and "undemanding in his theology."[90]

The school's first president, Joseph McKean, confirmed the school's dedication to republicanism. In his inaugural speech, McKean stated that Bowdoin was "founded and endowed for the common good, and not for the private advantage of those who resort to [it] for education." In a new nation dependent upon the initiatives of learned men, students gained an education to fulfill societal needs and were to "qualify [themselves] for usefulness" and "exert [themselves] for the public good."[91] To men like McKean and Deane, religious instruction encouraged the virtue necessary for republican self-government but was merely a means to an end.

The religious counterrevolution, or Second Awakening, came to Bowdoin in the first decade of the nineteenth century. The Rev. Jesse Appleton, an evangelical Congregationalist, succeeded President McKean in 1807 and introduced a series of revivals and a less tolerant religious environment. In response, the Baptists, with help from the Methodists and other dissenting sects, chartered an alternative school in 1813, which opened its doors in 1817 as the Maine Literary and Theological Institution. This school, eventually to become Colby College, sought state support by advertising its more tolerant religious attitudes. One of its founders, Senator William King, complained of the now pietistic Bowdoin: "It is conducted upon too narrow principles to live; and will die a natural death."[92] The Republican press joined in attacking Bowdoin. In October 1817 the *Eastern Argus* reported that the New Hampshire legislature had freed Dartmouth from "the thralldom of oppressive hierarchy and aristocracy" in taking control of the newly organized Dartmouth University. It called for similar changes at Bowdoin or the legislative support of competing institutions.[93]

The brewing controversy over Bowdoin arose concurrently with Maine's statehood. The Federalists, in control of the Massachusetts legislature, attempted to secure Bowdoin's independent Congregational and Federalist nature from encroachments on its power by a Maine government likely to be controlled by Republicans. In the Act of Separation finalized on June 19, 1819, the Massachusetts legislature provided that "the President, Trustees and Overseers of the college shall have, hold, and enjoy their powers and privileges in all respects; so that the same shall not be subject to be altered, limited, annulled or restricted, except by judicial process according to law."[94] The legislature further provided that any changes to the act required the agreement of both state legislatures. Maine seemingly agreed to give Massachusetts a continuing voice in the governance of the new state.

In October 1819 the citizens of Maine sent delegates to Portland to draft a state constitution. Extensive debate concerned state funding of higher education. By this time the Supreme Court had issued its decision in *Dartmouth College,* and the ruling took center stage in the debate. Both sides acknowledged the importance of education "in a free government, resting on the virtue and intelligence of the people," and the need for institutions of higher learning to bring together the "poor and the wealthy" to benefit from a useful education and "learn the great principles of equality and subordination, and that merit alone is the passport to preferment."[95] The issue, after the *Dartmouth College* decision, was how these educational goals were to be served. In the words of one speaker advocating state control: "can all this be done while the management of our literary institutions is exclusively in the hands of [private] individuals, whose views may be adverse to the best interests of the government and over whose conduct the state shall have no controlling power?" Opponents argued that schools "have prospered when the state had nothing to do with their government . . . [and] if abuses should arise, the Judiciary is the proper tribunal to correct them."[96]

The advocates for state control prevailed. The discussion then proceeded to what form the state control might take. The approved proviso at "Article VIII, Literature," read as follows:

> *Provided.* That no donation, grant or endowment, shall at any time be made by the Legislature to any Literary Institution now established, unless at the time of making such endowment, *the Governor and Council shall have the power of revising and negativing the doings of the trustees and Government of such Institution, in the selection of its officers and the management of its funds.*

Mr. Shepley, of Saco, moved to amend the proviso by striking the wording italicized above and substituting even stronger language that required legislative control of all recipients of state education funds. He argued, "I wish the legislature to have the power to see the funds properly applied."[97] Supporters of Shepley's amendment were frightened by the *Dartmouth College* case; unless the state took firm control of the entities receiving state funds, the people of the state would have no control over how these entities addressed social needs. According to one speaker: "By the highest judicial tribunal in our country it is decided that these literary institutions are independent of the government of the State in which they are situated and which has founded and endowed them and unless this convention engrafts into the constitution a provision to the contrary, it will be of binding force here." This speaker also noted that while the citizens of New Hampshire failed to restrain the "arrogance . . . of the Trustees of their only college . . . their discussion of principles has excited a spirit of inquiry throughout the nation, which will not be extinguished . . . till salutary reformations take place in our literary institutions." Another speaker asked: "Ought there to be a literary institution in a state not subject to the control of the laws, nor subservient to the government that protects it."[98]

Despite the prevalent sentiment to condition state support of Bowdoin upon state control, the Act of Separation concerned the delegates. One admitted to being "mortified at the provision . . . imposing shackles on us. . . . Are we too ignorant even to be made sensible of the importance of knowledge? And does Massachusetts therefore undertake to prescribe for us?"[99] The seeming unreasonableness of the restriction in the Act of Separation, especially in the aftermath of the *Dartmouth College* case, resulted in agreement to simply ignore it.

The Shepley amendment passed 151–18, providing that Bowdoin could not receive state funds unless the Maine legislature had previously been given authority to "alter, limit, or restrain the powers vested" in the corporation. In this action, Maine sought to respond to the *Dartmouth College* case by protecting its citizenry from unrepublican agents who might use state funds to corrupt the youth of the state. As the emotional closing argument of Mr. Holmes indicated, the perceived threat to unrepublican education came primarily from religious sects and the political parties they might foment:

> The gentleman from Fryeburg has alluded to the doctrine established by a late decision of the Supreme Court of the United States. It goes to set up a literary institution, beyond the reach or control of the laws of a State. Let gentlemen be warned by this dangerous result. Let them never tolerate any power but that of the United States, within their jurisdiction, that shall be above their control. *The time may come when creeds may be established, sects created, and parties built up, dangerous and destructive to the safety of the State and the liberties of the people.* Corporations may exist with power to fill their vacancies and perpetuate their existence. Against such evils we ought now to erect an effectual barrier. I hope the motion will prevail.[100]

The immediate religious environment at Bowdoin, shaped by President Appleton, already represented a danger in the minds of many Maine citizens. Appleton was replaced in 1819 by William Allen, the man who had headed "the short-lived Dartmouth University." Allen believed in fostering a collegiate environment cultivating arts and sciences in service to the state. He argued that college and state shared an "essential unity of . . . interests." After the constitutional provision conditioned state funds upon legislative influence over the school, Allen led the movement for the college to surrender its exclusive right to modify its charter. By 1820 the Boards of the College voted to accept legislative restructuring and petitioned the state for the continuation of the three-thousand-dollar annual grant raised from the bank tax "and for such other donations as the legislature, in their [*sic*] wisdom, may be disposed to make." The legislature responded by extending the annuity payments through 1831.[101]

In 1821 the legislature exercised its new authority, increasing the number of trustees and overseers and giving the governor the right to appoint the new members of these boards. President Allen created four new chairs in mathematics, modern languages, natural sciences, and moral philosophy. However, the relationship between Allen and the legislature began to decline in the late 1820s, and in 1831 the legislature passed a new law requiring a two-thirds majority of both Bowdoin's boards to reelect the president. Allen's reelection bid failed in September 1831, and he was removed from office.

He sued the college, through its treasurer Mr. McKean, for "salary and fees" due to him, claiming that the legislature acted unlawfully in revising Bowdoin's charter. He relied on the *Dartmouth College* case and the Act of Separation. The case was brought in federal court under the diversity doctrine and, in a bit of irony, came before Justice Story traveling on his northeastern circuit in May 1833.[102] Justice Story framed the issue in the case similarly to the issue in the *Dartmouth College* case fourteen years earlier: "Is it the erection of a private corporation for objects of a public nature, like other institutions for the general administration of charity? Or is it, in the strict sense of law, a public corporation, solely for public purposes, and controllable at will by the legislative power, which erected it, or which has succeeded to the like authority?"[103]

Framing the issue in this way, Justice Story had clear precedent in the *Dartmouth College* decision. The interests of the founder, the state of Massachusetts, were secured in contract and not abrogated by the creation of the new state of Maine. The legislature of Maine was bound by the charter of the school as originally conceived by Massachusetts. Only the boards of the college could change its charter rights. The changes made in 1820, Justice Story found, were inconsistent with the Act of Separation and were therefore contrary to the expressed interests of the founder, which the trustees were bound to represent. The restructuring of Bowdoin was, accordingly, not lawful. Not only did Allen win his suit, but Bowdoin was freed from legislative control and recognized as a private eleemosynary corporation.[104]

Following the *Allen v. McKean* decision, the state of Maine refused to provide further support to Bowdoin College. Needing money in 1846, the trustees and overseers of Bowdoin drafted a declaration in support of their request for funds from the Congregational Church. The declaration provided that, despite a lack of religious identification in the charter, "yet, from its foundation [Bowdoin] has been, and still is, one of the orthodox Congregational Denomination." Furthermore, the boards and faculty were composed so that "such instruction be given by officers of that religious faith."[105] Bowdoin College, founded as a fountainhead of liberal education, by the 1840s had become the last bastion of orthodox Calvinism in New England. In the 1840s New England's colleges epitomized denominational pluralism and interdenominational competition. Waterville (Colby) was a Baptist school, the Episcopalians had Trinity College, Yale was the home of liberal Congregationalists, the Unitarians controlled Harvard, and the Orthodox Congregationalists assumed control of Bowdoin.[106]

Churches were not the only founders of private schools in the aftermath of the *Dartmouth College* case. New York University provides one of many examples demonstrating how private individuals in the 1820s and 1830s took advantage of corporate laws to begin institutions devoted to their purposes. Desiring a school that, unlike Columbia, would serve the interests of an aspirant middle class, John Delafield and Myndert Van Schaick raised over one hundred thousand dollars from New York merchants, tradesmen, lawyers, and bankers who purchased stock at twenty-five dollars per share during 1830. Albert Gallatin, former member of the Jefferson administration, was elected the school's first president. Gallatin espoused an English language curriculum, making it possible to earn a college degree suiting one for life in business or politics without ever reading one word of Latin or Greek. Moreover, the school allowed members of the community to enroll in classes even though they sought no degree. The goal of the founders was to improve the educational standing of New York's middle class by making history, philosophy, literature, business and commerce, engineering, architecture, art, astronomy, and foreign language accessible. No church funds were solicited or pledged, and the state's involvement was limited to granting the act of incorporation on April 21, 1831.[107]

While the *Dartmouth College* case privatized religion, it also secularized and expanded the public realm. The Supreme Court decision verified and encouraged the efforts of state governments, in states that had long ago disestablished their churches, to assume responsibility for what were now clearly public, as in governmental, functions. Religion was truly separated from government as governmental institutions grew to replace churches in providing necessary social services.

The public model of higher education expressed the American republic's adoption of an Enlightenment secularism that embodied its own form of religion. This "religion of the republic,"[108] reduced Christian doctrine to its lowest common denominator, essentially a code of moral behavior expressed in the golden rule, and positioned God as a benevolent but uninvolved creator of natural laws. Consistent with this system of belief, schools taught practical knowledge, framed moral teachings in the language of civic virtue, and tolerated a wide range of religious expressions. Most "private" schools, founded and supported by denominations, expressed alternative understandings of God and espoused different prescriptions for education and the form of American society. The major importance of the *Dartmouth College* case is not simply the delineation of private and public realms but the perpetuation of the alternative visions of American society made possible by the legal recognition of public and private spheres. The decision, then, fostered the American reliance upon philanthropy noted by Alexis de Tocqueville just over a decade later. By protecting the legal right of Americans to pursue different visions of American society through memberships in smaller communities, what de Tocqueville found as a uniquely American form of political expression was given life.[109]

The *Dartmouth College* case, by demanding formal legal structures for religious and philanthropic organizations, encouraged American culture to move from the colonial model, in which community involvement in everything from barn raisings and quilting bees to the public militia, church, and school reflected informal personal relationships, toward a society premised on contract and formal institutional structures. Robert Gross has noted how the growth of formal and impersonal philanthropic associations weakened individual duties to care for neighbors and exercise one's charitable impulse in community affairs: "People now had an excuse to turn away beggars from their door[s]." They could simply let the charities care for them; "and if those institutions wouldn't aid them, then the unfortunates could be dismissed as unworthy."[110]

The courts' impositions of the legal requirement of formal corporate status restructured the way civil society was organized. By incorporating, voluntary associations became free from government interference. Contract law provided for their continued existence and functional role in American society. However, it also compelled the restructuring of social relationships in accordance with a liberal ideology, which prioritized individual freedoms over community values. Therefore, although Plumer, a Jeffersonian Republican, lost the *Dartmouth* case, the long-term effects of the case constituted a victory for the Jeffersonians.

Law, as an expression of liberal republican ideology, determined the design of American civil society. The Constitution, in the contract clause and elsewhere, required government to respect and protect private property. In order to do so, a thick black line had to be drawn between public and private spheres. Distinguishing public and private spheres became the means by which the disestablishment of religion could be effected, not only separating church and state but imposing a new system of values in place of the old Christian communitarianism. Law never could resolve the substantive debate between liberals and conservative Christians as to what values would permeate the society—that is surely a political matter. But law could and did determine the institutional structure in which the debate could continue. Religion, as a matter of private belief vested in private organizations devoted to its dissemination, was removed from any role in public governance, but it remained a vital contributor to American values.

Conclusion

IN ADDRESSING THE FORM rather than the substance of the early republic's debates over the nature of man and the truth of religious doctrine, American law preserved a realm in which those debates could continue. Certainly, those debates in the early twenty-first century are as heated and polarizing as at almost any time since those nascent days of the republic. The early history of church-state separation in the United States is a story of ideas rather than of interests, a story of law as an arbiter in the debate protecting private parties on both sides from cultural subordination of their arguments by a too-powerful public government.

Earlier generations of historians, since the time of Henry Adams, have identified cyclical periodizations in America's past.[1] Anne Norton has asserted that cultural vacillations between individualism and a strict conformity to community norms can be explained by Americans' inheritance of conflicting ideologies derived from the Reformation and the Enlightenment.[2] In this context, law preserves both components of America's cultural identity, perpetuating whatever vitality might derive from ideological conflict and the reconsideration of cultural ideals, beliefs, and values.

It has recently been reasserted, this time by a distinguished scholar and professor of law, that the separation of church and state was not contemplated by the drafters of the Constitution.[3] This study refutes that assertion. While the Constitution did not directly separate church and state, it did provide the ideological and legal structure that made separation not only possible but inevitable.

Throughout the new United States, the process of disestablishment involved a series of steps. In the introduction of this study, two conceptual steps were referred to: the design of primary laws eliminating public support for religion and the removal, by the states, of churches from their old roles of public service. It is now possible to summarize the ideological and legal developments that composed these two conceptual steps. First, liberal republican ideology, perceiving religious liberty as a natural right, served as the basis for the reconceiving of religion as a private matter of conscience protected from governmental interference by the primary laws of the nation and the states. Second, this ideology also compelled constitutional recognition of the private right to contract, as an expression of equality and freedom of independent action, as superior to the public interest as expressed through legislative enactments. Third, the development of contract/corporate law in the early republic provided the basis for distinguishing the private and public realms delineated in the constitutional protection of the aforementioned rights. Fourth, the church, as a private corporation composed of members sharing similar religious beliefs, was found to be an inappropriate institution to assume roles in governance and the shaping of public policy. This final step, taken in a series of court and legislative actions, separated church and state and fulfilled the constitutional mandate implicitly captured in the prohibition upon religious tests and the protection of private beliefs and contracts from public interference. The process of disestablishment took nearly fifty years. The final disestablishment of religion in Massachusetts in 1833 can be seen as the culmination of the Revolution begun in 1775. Law, as an expression of liberal ideology, provided the means of social change consistent with revolutionary ideals.

Ironically, even as the forces for separation of church and state were winning their final victory in 1833, they were losing much of their power among Americans. By the Jacksonian era, Enlightenment liberalism was on the decline. Evangelical Christianity would resurface as a force in determining American social policy with the prominence of the social gospel movement. Adapting to their new positions as private voluntary associations, able to attack prevailing social attitudes and public initiatives from protected positions within civil society, churches and religiously inspired groups constituting the "Benevolent Empire" influenced the Victorian-era reconsideration of much of the liberal agenda. A plethora of state and national laws intended to improve morality and rebuild a communitarian ethic redesigned America from the 1830s into the 1890s. In this and in subsequent resurgences of American Christian communitarianism can be seen the ultimate power of law as an arbiter in American society. Law, while prohibiting private organizations from assuming roles in public governance, nonetheless protects their rights to proselytize, lobby, and campaign for changes in the broader society, consistent with their own organizational beliefs and goals. The decision over the viability of religious truth and the nature of man is resolved by American law only to the extent that it preserves a civil context for debate.

Notes

Introduction

1. Peter Gay, *The Rise of Modern Paganism,* vol. 1 of *The Enlightenment: An Interpretation* (New York: Random House, 1966). See also Henry F. May, *The Enlightenment in America* (New York: Oxford University Press, 1976).

2. Please understand that I use "man" as well as the pronouns "he," "his," and "him" throughout the text to refer to both male and female members of the human race.

3. Alexis de Tocqueville, *Democracy in America* (1838; New York: Penguin Books, 1984), 47; Ann Norton, *Alternative Americas: A Reading of Antebellum Political Culture* (Chicago: University of Chicago Press, 1986); May, *Enlightenment in America,* xii–xiv; John Thomas, *Alternative America: Henry George, Edward Bellamy, Henry Demarest Lloyd and the Adversary Tradition* (Cambridge: Belknap Press of Harvard University Press, 1983).

4. Sidney E. Mead, *The Lively Experiment: The Shaping of Christianity in America* (New York: Harper and Row, 1963), 38. The use of the terms *pietism* and *pietists* will generally be avoided in this text so as not to cause confusion. Recent scholarship has defined pietism as a religious phenomenon limited to continental Europe between 1670 and 1730. Mead and many of his contemporaries were far less restrictive in their usage. See F. Ernest Stoeffler, ed., *Continental Pietism and Early American Christianity* (Grand Rapids, MI: Eerdmans, 1976); Paul P. Kuenning, *The Rise and Fall of American Lutheran Pietism: The Rejection of an Activist Heritage* (Macon, GA: Mercer University Press, 1988); Lefferts A. Loetscher, *Facing the Enlightenment and Pietism: Archibald Alexander and the Founding of Princeton Theological Seminary* (Westport, CT: Greenwood Press, 1983); Milton J. Coalter Jr., *Gilbert Tennant, Son of Thunder: A Case Study of Continental Pietism's Impact on the First Great Awakening in the Middle Colonies* (Westport, CT: Greenwood Press, 1986).

5. Sidney E. Mead, *The Nation with the Soul of a Church* (New York: Harper and Row, 1975), vi–vii.

6. Sidney E. Mead, *The Old Religion in the Brave New World: Reflections on the Relation between Christendom and the Republic* (Berkeley and Los Angeles: University of California Press, 1977), 2.

7. William Warren Sweet, *The Story of Religion in America* (New York: Harper and Bros., 1950); Anson Phelps Stokes and Leo Pfeffer, *Church and State in the United States* (New York: Harper and Row, 1964); Thomas Hanley, *The American Revolution and Religion* (New York: Catholic University of America Press, 1971); Milton Klein, "New York in the American Colonies: A New Look," *New York History* 53 (April 1972): 132–56. More recently John Noonan argues that diversity combined with a new Christian doctrine largely void of absolutism in order to make disestablishment possible. He asserts that James Madison's preference for pluralism as a vital check on institutional authority

served as the conceptual basis of the constitutional compromise on religion—law accommodated belief. In effectuating compromise Madison was influenced by the teachings of Witherspoon and retained his mentor's Christian rationalism. John T. Noonan Jr., *The Lustre of Our Country: The American Experience of Religious Freedom* (Berkeley and Los Angeles: University of California Press, 1998). However, see Edwin Scott Gaustad, "A Disestablishment Society: Origins of the First Amendment," *Journal of Church and State* 11.3 (1969): 409–25, which combines the traditional interpretation with a recognition that ideological differences over the nature of man prompted reevaluation of the establishment model.

8. Martin E. Marty, *Righteous Empire: The Protestant Experience in America,* in the Two Centuries of American Life series, ed. Harold Hyman and Leonard Levy (New York: Dial Press, 1970), 37. Marty contends that real innovation occurred not in the early republic's legal disestablishment of the churches but in the seventeenth century when colonies formed without established churches in Rhode Island, Delaware, and Pennsylvania (ibid., 39). See also Louis Hartz, *The Liberal Tradition in America* (New York: Harcourt Brace Jovanovich, 1991). In asserting that religious diversity was minimal, I concur with Richard B. Bernstein, in *Are We to Be a Nation? The Making of the Constitution* (Cambridge: Harvard University Press, 1987), who asserts that "most Americans [at the time of the Constitution] shared the common heritage of Protestant Christianity" (9–10).

9. Jefferson's famous language is from his letter to the Danbury Association, January 1, 1802, in *The Writings of Thomas Jefferson,* ed. Albert Ellery Bergh (Washington, DC: Thomas Jefferson Memorial Association, 1903), 16:281. Edward S. Corwin, in "The Supreme Court as National School Board," *Law and Contemporary Problems* 14 (Winter 1949), writes, "what the establishment of religion clause of the First Amendment does, and all that it does, is to forbid Congress to give any religious faith, sect, or denomination preferred status" (10).

10. William G. McLoughlin, *New England Dissent, 1630–1883,* 2 vols. (Cambridge: Harvard University Press, 1971), and *Isaac Backus and the American Pietistic Tradition,* in the Library of American Biography series, ed. Oscar Handlin (Boston: Little, Brown, 1967).

11. Christopher F. Mooney, *Public Virtue: Law and the Social Character of Religion* (Notre Dame: University of Notre Dame Press, 1986); Richard John Neuhaus, *The Naked Public Square: Religion and Democracy in America* (Grand Rapids, MI: Eerdmans, 1984); Robert L. Cord, *Separation of Church and State: Historical Fact and Current Fiction* (New York: Lambeth Press, 1982); Glenn T. Miller, *Religious Liberty in America: History and Prospects* (Philadelphia: Westminster Press, 1976); John Witte Jr., "The Essential Rights and Liberties of Religion in the American Constitutional Experiment," in *Notre Dame Law Review* 71 (1996): 371–445; Michael W. McConnell, "The Origins and Historical Understanding of Free Exercise of Religion," *Harvard Law Review* 103 (1990):1409–517. Their works have produced a historical refutation that has not been rooted in the history of disestablishment. See Isaac Kramnick and R. Lawrence Moore, *The Godless Constitution: The Case against Religious Correctness* (New York: W. W. Norton, 1996); Leonard W. Levy, *Blasphemy: Verbal Offense against the Sacred, from Moses to Salman Rushdie* (New York: A. A. Knopf, 1993); Leonard W. Levy, *Constitutional Opinions: Aspects of the Bill of Rights* (New York: Oxford University Press, 1986).

12. Philip Hamburger, *Separation of Church and State* (Cambridge: Harvard University Press, 2002). For a detailed critique of this work, see author's review published on H-Net, March 2003.

13. David Paul Nord, "Systematic Benevolence: Religious Publishing and the Marketplace in Early Nineteenth-Century America," in *Communication and Change in American Religious History*, ed. Leonard I. Sweet (Grand Rapids, MI: Eerdmans, 1993), 243.

14. The Rev. Timothy Dwight, "A Discourse on Some Events of the Last Century," in H. Shelton Smith, Robert J. Handy, and Lefferts A. Loetscher, eds., *American Christianity: An Historical Interpretation with Representative Documents* (New York: Scribner, 1963), 1:534, 538. See also Peter S. Field, *The Crisis of the Standing Order: Clerical Intellectuals and Cultural Authority in Massachusetts, 1780–1833* (Amherst: University of Massachusetts Press, 1998): 1, 51–57.

15. Robert E. Shalhope, *Toward a Republican Synthesis: The Emergence of an Understanding of Republicanism in American Historiography*, in *William and Mary Quarterly*, 3rd ser., no. 29 (1972), 49. Shalhope asserts that republicanism dominated the political consciousness of the American people during the revolutionary era.

16. Gordon S. Wood, *The Radicalism of the American Revolution* (New York: A. A. Knopf, 1992), 169 (quotation), 174–75, 179–81.

17. Ibid., 169–82, 189–225. See also Lawrence J. Friedman, *Inventors of the Promised Land* (New York: A. A. Knopf, 1975).

18. See, generally, Gordon S. Wood, *The Creation of the American Republic, 1776–1787* (New York: W. W. Norton, 1969).

19. Gordon S. Wood, "Interests and Disinterestedness in the Making of the Constitution," in *Beyond Confederation: Origins of the Constitution and America's National Identity*, ed. Richard Beeman et al. (Chapel Hill: University of North Carolina Press, 1987), 102.

20. See Joyce Appleby, *Capitalism and a New Social Order: The Republican Vision of the 1790s* (New York: New York University Press, 1984), and *Liberalism and Republicanism in the Historical Imagination* (Cambridge: Harvard University Press, 1992).

21. Lawrence M. Friedman, *A History of American Law* (New York: Simon and Schuster, 1973); Kermit L. Hall, *The Magic Mirror: Law in American History* (New York: Oxford University Press, 1989); Morton J. Horwitz, *The Transformation of American Law, 1780–1860* (Cambridge: Harvard University Press, 1977); James Willard Hurst, *Law and the Conditions of Freedom in the Nineteenth-Century United States* (Madison: University of Wisconsin Press, 1956). See also Michael Grossberg, *Governing the Hearth: Law and the Family in Nineteenth-Century America* (Chapel Hill: University of North Carolina Press, 1985); R. Kent Newmyer, *Supreme Court Justice Joseph Story: Statesman of the Old Republic* (Chapel Hill: University of North Carolina Press, 1985); Christopher Tomlins, *Law, Labor, and Ideology in the Early American Republic* (New York: Cambridge University Press, 1993); Mark Tushnet, *The American Law of Slavery, 1810–1860: Considerations of Humanity and Interest* (Princeton, NJ: Princeton University Press, 1981); Edmund S. Morgan, "The American Revolution Considered as an Intellectual Movement," in *Paths of American Thought*, ed. Arthur M. Schlesinger Jr. and Morton White (Boston: Houghton Mifflin, 1963), 11–33.

22. Christianity in America has been redefined, sustained, and reprioritized in a series of revivalist periods known as awakenings. In the Great Awakening of the first half of the eighteenth century, strict Calvinist doctrine was modified to take account of the individualistic impulses of the Enlightenment and incipient capitalism. The result was a form of religion that identified emotional conversion as man's means of receiving grace. This movement spawned the growth of many dissenting sects, such as Methodists and Baptists. It also gave birth to a division within the Congregational Church between "old lights" and "new lights," the latter accepting an emotional component to

religious belief and practice that empowered the believer in securing his or her own salvation. From 1790 through the 1820s America experienced a Second Awakening, largely in response to the perceived irreligiosity of American culture and the humanistic impulses dividing the churches themselves, such as Deism and Unitarianism.

23. Christopher Tomlins has noted the importance of this public-private division during the early republic. Tomlins, *Law, Labor, and Ideology.*

24. Perhaps most noteworthy are the following: Bernard Bailyn, *The Ideological Origins of the American Revolution* (Cambridge: Harvard University Press, 1967); Appleby, *Capitalism and a New Social Order* and *Liberalism and Republicanism;* Wood, *Creation* and *Radicalism;* Lance Banning, *The Jeffersonian Persuasion: Evolution of a Party Ideology* (Ithaca: Cornell University Press, 1978); Drew McCoy, *The Elusive Republic: Political Economy in Jeffersonian America* (New York: W. W. Norton, 1982); Pauline Maier, *American Scripture: Making the Declaration of Independence* (New York: A. A. Knopf, 1997); Jack N. Rakove, *Original Meanings: Politics and Ideas in the Making of the Constitution* (New York: Random House, 1997).

25. G. Edward White, *The Marshall Court and Cultural Change, 1815–1835,* vols. 3 and 4 of the History of the Supreme Court of the United States series, ed. Paul A. Freund and Stanley N. Katz (New York: Macmillan, 1988), 3–4:50; Appleby, *Capitalism and a New Social Order.*

26. Gordon Wood commented recently that the next consideration in the development of this historiography needs to be the role of religious debate in the ideological contest of the early republic. Untitled lecture presented at Indiana University, Bloomington, Fall 1995.

27. Edward White, *Marshall Court,* 61.

28. Tomlins, *Law, Labor, and Ideology;* Grossberg, *Governing the Hearth.*

29. The major works of these instrumentalists are Hurst, *Conditions of Freedom;* Horwitz, *Transformation;* Hall, *Magic Mirror;* Friedman, *History of American Law.*

30. Two excellent essays address the weaknesses of the instrumentalist school: Christopher Tomlins, "A Mirror Cracked? The Rule of Law in American History," in *William and Mary Law Review* 32.2 (Winter 1991): 353–97, and Michael Grossberg, "Legal History and Social Science: Friedman's History of American Law, the Second Time Around," in *Law and Social Inquiry* 13 (1988): 359. Works explaining the relative autonomy of law include Grossberg, *Governing the Hearth;* Tomlins, *Law, Labor, and Ideology;* Tushnet, *American Law of Slavery.* Holly Brewer asserts there is a close interconnection between political ideas and laws. See Holly Brewer, "Beyond Education: Republican Revision of the Laws Regarding Children," *Thomas Jefferson and the Education of a Citizen,* ed. James Gilreath (Washington, DC: Library of Congress, 1999), 48–62, also Holly Brewer, *Constructing Consent: The Legal Status of Children and American Revolutionary Ideology* (Chapel Hill: University of North Carolina Press, 2000), which explores how republican ideology influenced the development of law in the early republic. On the same issue, see Mark D. McGarvie, "In Perfect Accordance with His Character: Thomas Jefferson, Slavery, and the Law," *Indiana Magazine of History* 95.2 (June 1999): 142–77.

31. The term "discourse" as a description of law's functional role has been used by Christopher Tomlins in *Law, Labor, and Ideology.*

32. Edward White, *Marshall Court,* 6–7. William E. Nelson, "The Eighteenth-Century Background of John Marshall's Constitutional Jurisprudence," *Michigan Law Review* 76 (1978): 893–960.

33. Michael Zuckerman, "Holy Wars, Civil Wars: Religion and Economics in Nineteenth-Century America," *Prospects* 16 (1991): 205–40. This essay contains a fine

review of the earlier historiography. See also D. G. Hart, "The Failure of American Religious History," *Journal of the Historical Society* 1.1 (Spring 2000): 1–32. Levy, *Constitutional Opinions,* 4 (quotation).

34. Reinhold Niebuhr, "A Note on Pluralism," in *Religion in America,* ed. John Cogley (New York: Meridian Books, 1958), 42–51; May, *Enlightenment in America;* Michael Kammen, *People of Paradox: An Inquiry Concerning the Origins of American Civilization* (New York: Random House, 1972); Field, *Standing Order.* It is interesting, however, that Field nonetheless sees the "Dedham case," *Baker v. Fales* 16 Mass. 487 (1821), as the critical event in the movement to disestablishment in Massachusetts. He perceives the decision as emanating from social forces, however, rather than from ideological ones.

35. Thomas Jefferson, *Notes on the State of Virginia,* Query 17 in *The Portable Thomas Jefferson,* ed. Merrill D. Peterson (New York: Penguin Books, 1975), 209; Johann D. Shoepf, *Travels in the Confederation, 1783–1784,* trans. and ed. Alfred J. Morrison (Philadelphia: W. J. Campbell, 1911).

36. Thomas E. Buckley, *Church and State in Revolutionary Virginia, 1776–1787* (Charlottesville: University Press of Virginia, 1977), 181–82; Rakove, *Original Meanings,* 311–12; Leo Pfeffer, "The Case for Separation," in Cogley, *Religion in America,* 66; Fred J. Hood, "Revolution and Religious Liberty: The Conservation of the Theocratic Concept in Virginia," *Church History* 40.2 (1971): 170–81.

37. Quotes from McLoughlin, *Isaac Backus,* xii (Jefferson), 149 (Backus).

38. A representative sampling of current works addressing disestablishment in Virginia includes George M. Marsden, *Religion and American Culture* (San Diego: Harcourt Brace Jovanovich, 1990); Buckley, *Church and State;* Rhys Isaac, *The Transformation of Virginia, 1740–1790* (Chapel Hill: University of North Carolina Press, 1982); James Madison, *James Madison on Religious Liberty,* ed. Robert S. Alley (Buffalo, NY: Prometheus Books, 1985); Thomas E. Buckley, "After Disestablishment: Thomas Jefferson's Wall of Separation in Antebellum Virginia," *Journal of Southern History* 61.3 (August 1995): 445–80; A. Glenn Crothers, "'One Undivided Current': Politics, Society and the Religious Settlement in Virginia," *Southern Historian* 14 (1993): 5–17; Daniel L. Dreisbach, "Thomas Jefferson and Bills Number 82–86 of the Revision of the Laws of Virginia, 1776–1786: New Light on the Jefferson Model of Church-State Relations," *North Carolina Law Review* 159 (November 1990): 69.

39. Petitions quoted in Buckley, *Church and State,* 181–82; law quoted in Stokes and Pfeffer, *Church and State,* 71.

40. *Boston Recorder,* 16 September 1820, 151.

41. *Baker v. Fales,* 16 Mass. 487 (1821), known as the Dedham case.

42. A representative sampling of current works addressing disestablishment in Massachusetts includes Mary Kupiec Clayton, "Who Were the Evangelicals? Conservative and Liberal Identity in the Unitarian Controversy in Boston, 1804–1833," *Journal of Social History* 31.1 (1997): 86–107; John D. Cushing, "Notes on Disestablishment in Massachusetts, 1780–1833," *William and Mary Quarterly,* 3rd ser., 26.2 (1969): 169–90; Marty, *Righteous Empire.*

43. An argument to the contrary is presented in Philip Greven, *The Protestant Temperament: Patterns of Child Rearing, Religious Experience, and the Self in Early America* (New York: A. A. Knopf, 1977).

44. *Walz v. Tax Commission,* 397 U.S. 664, 670 (1970).

45. Pfeffer, "Case for Separation," 78. In adjusting to society's new conception of churches as private corporations, after the 1820s they turned to social reform, or the "social gospel" as it has been called. Francis Wayland, a Baptist minister in 1838,

said of voluntary associations: "They are frequently supposed to be the great moral means, by which the regeneration of the world is to be effected" (Robert S. Handy, *A Christian America: Protestant Hopes and Historical Realities* [New York: Oxford University Press, 1971], 46). Specifically, evangelicals pursued temperance, prison reform, abolition, and Christian education. In this effort, Christian leaders expressed a continuing desire for Christian communities and social harmony. For further reading, see Lori Ginzberg, *Women and the Work of Benevolence: Morality, Politics, and Class in the Nineteenth-Century United States* (New Haven: Yale University Press, 1990); Charles I. Foster, *An Errand of Mercy: The Evangelical United Front, 1790–1837* (Chapel Hill: University of North Carolina Press, 1960); Clifford S. Griffin, *Their Brothers' Keepers: Moral Stewardship in the U.S., 1800–1865* (New Brunswick, NJ: Rutgers University Press, 1960); Paul Boyer, *Urban Masses and Moral Order in America, 1820–1920* (Cambridge: Harvard University Press, 1978); Gregory H. Singleton, "Protestant Voluntary Organizations: The Shaping of Victorian America," *American Quarterly* 27 (1975): 549–60.

46. See *Gitlow v. New York,* 268 U.S. 652 (1925); *Near v. Minnesota,* 283 U.S. 697 (1931); *DeJonge v. Oregon,* 299 U.S. 353 (1937); *Cantwell v. Connecticut,* 310 U.S. 296 (1940); *Marsh v. Alabama,* 326 U.S. 501 (1946). For a report on the Kansas action, see "Evolution Struggle Shifts to Kansas School Districts," *New York Times,* August 25, 1999. Bob Riley quoted from "Alabama Rejects $1.2 Billion Tax Increase," *USA Today,* September 10, 2003, A1.

1—Toleration versus Freedom

1. Quoted by Robert A. Gross, "Giving in America: From Charity to Philanthropy," in Lawrence J. Friedman and Mark D. McGarvie, *Charity, Philanthropy, and Civility in American History* (New York: Cambridge University Press, 2003), 32.

2. The Rev. Nathaniel Ward, "The Simple Cobbler of Aggawam in America," in Timothy L. Hall, *Separating Church and State: Roger Williams and Religious Liberty* (Urbana-Champaign: University of Illinois Press, 1998), 53.

3. McLoughlin, *Isaac Backus,* 7. The extent to which Calvinist thought influenced all versions of American Christianity, even Catholicism, is noted in Amanda Porterfield, "Protestant Missionaries: Pioneers of American Philanthropy," in Friedman and McGarvie, *Charity, Philanthropy, Civility,* 54–55. Lawrence M. Friedman asserts that "Massachusetts law was not common law at all; it was a new-fangled system of law, based on the Bible" (*History of American Law,* 35). But also see Stephen Innes, *Creating the Commonwealth: The Economic Culture of Puritan New England* (New York: W. W. Norton, 1995).

4. Zuckerman, "Holy Wars," 212, citing Stephen Foster, *Their Solitary Way: The Puritan Social Ethic in the First Century of Settlement in New England* (New Haven: Yale University Press, 1971). See also Mooney, *Public Virtue,* 10–11.

5. Brewer, "Beyond Education," 49.

6. See Mark McGarvie and Elizabeth Mensch, "Law and Religion in Colonial America," in *Cambridge History of American Law,* ed. Michael Grossberg and Christopher Tomlins (forthcoming, 2005). See also Gross, "Giving in America," 33.

7. Edmund S. Morgan, "The Labor Problem at Jamestown, 1607–1618," in *Shaping Southern Society: The Colonial Experience,* ed. Timothy H. Breen (New York: Oxford University Press, 1976), 17–31, 19.

8. Many historians develop the religious and social differences between New England and Virginia and the attendant emphasis Virginians placed on profit and in-

dividual pursuit. Among the best is the aforementioned work by Timothy Breen, *Puritans and Adventurers: Change and Persistence in Early America* (New York: Oxford University Press, 1980). Virginia's early laws and pronouncements on religious fidelity and values may appear analogous to those of New England, but the post-Reformation Christianity of the Virginians lacked the fervor of New England Puritanism. The dispersion of Virginia's colonists across larger territories limited the development of towns and the enforcement of law and community standards. Jon Butler finds that by the 1650s, despite the maintenance of laws reinforcing Christian morality and worship, Virginians were largely bereft of Christianity. Jon Butler, *Awash in a Sea of Faith: Christianizing the American People* (Cambridge: Harvard University Press, 1990), 38–39. Rhys Isaac adds that, although Virginians remained familiar with Judeo-Christian cosmology into the eighteenth century, religious practices such as church attendance, family prayer, and adherence to moral proscriptions declined nearly to extinction. Churchgoing retained significance primarily as a social event, at which the gentry expressed its civic dominance and responsibility. Isaac, *Transformation of Virginia*, 68, 120.

9. Joe M. Henderson, *Fighting Poverty in the U.S.: Past, Present and Future Roles of the Church and the State* (Ph.D. dissertation, Doctor of Ministry, School of Theology at Claremont, CA, 1984), 55.

10. Richard W. Pointer, *Protestant Pluralism and the New York Experience: A Study of Eighteenth-Century Religious Diversity* (Indianapolis: Indiana University Press, 1988), 137; Lawrence M. Friedman, *Crime and Punishment in American History* (New York: HarperCollins, 1993), 23–26, 32–37. See also Edwin Powers, *Crime and Punishment in Early Massachusetts, 1620–1692: A Documentary History* (Boston: Beacon Press, 1966).

11. Handy, *Christian America*, 121 (quotation); Mead, *Old Religion*, 2.

12. Leonard W. Levy, *The Establishment Clause: Religion and the First Amendment* (New York: Macmillan, 1986); 4–5.

13. In accommodation of the new charter granted in 1691, Massachusetts provided in its laws of 1692 that each town was to appoint "an able, learned, orthodox minister or ministers" and was to be responsible for the cost of his salary, the church, and its support. Dissenters continued to petition to England that their religious freedom was being denied. In 1727 Massachusetts responded by creating exemptions to church tax obligations. The law required a dissenter to obtain a document from his minister, certifying that he attended a dissenting church within five miles of his home and objected to the established religion as a matter of conscience. Exemption thus merely redirected the dissenting taxpayer's funds to a preferred church. Not all churches were recognized by the legislature as qualifying for exemption, only some Protestant churches qualified, and furthermore, some dissenters had no access to their chosen sect within five miles of their homes. Of course, atheists and agnostics could take no advantage of this law.

14. Perhaps the best summary of the development of religious pluralism in the American colonies can be found in Sydney E. Ahlstrom, *A Religious History of the American People* (Yale University Press, 1972).

15. Sweet, *Story of Religion;* Stokes and Pfeffer, *Church and State;* Marty, *Righteous Empire;* Charles P. Hanson, *Necessary Virtue: The Pragmatic Origins of Religious Liberty in New England* (Charlottesville: University Press of Virginia, 1998).

16. Levy, *Blasphemy*, 238–66 (esp. 264–65, 265 [quotations], 265–66); Miller, *Religious Liberty*, 46.

17. Bruce H. Mann, *Neighbors and Strangers: Law and Community in Early Connecticut* (Chapel Hill: University of North Carolina Press, 1987), 5–6 (business laws); Hurst, *Conditions of Freedom*, 37–39 (eastern seaboard).

18. J. R. T. Hughes, *Social Control in the Colonial Economy* (Charlottesville: University Press of Virginia, 1976), 126–27; Gary Nash, *The Urban Crucible: The Northern Seaports and the Origin of the American Revolution* (Cambridge: Harvard University Press, 1979).

19. Hughes, *Social Control*, 133 (rewards); William E. Nelson, *Americanization of the Common Law: The Impact of Legal Change on Massachusetts Society, 1760–1830* (Athens: University of Georgia Press, 1994), 47; Paul R. Lucas, *Valley of Discord: Church and Society along the Connecticut River, 1636–1725* (Hanover, NH: University Press of New England, 1876), 6 (clergy).

20. Edmund S. Morgan, *The Puritan Dilemma: The Story of John Winthrop*, the Library of American Biography series, ed. Oscar Handlin (Boston: Little, Brown, 1958), 67. Laws concerning the market were often predicated upon moral imperatives of equity or fairness. The Bible served as the source of these concepts, as shown by the 1658 revision to New Hampshire's legal code reciting that man's law must conform "to the ancient platform of god's laws . . . [and to principles of] moral equity." Richard B. Morris, "The Judeo-Christian Foundation of the American Political System," in Robert S. Alley, ed., *James Madison on Religious Liberty* (Buffalo, NY: Prometheus Books, 1985), 109–14, 112.

21. Nelson, *Americanization*, 36–38.

22. David Thomas Konig, *Law and Society in Puritan Massachusetts: Essex County, 1629–1692* (Chapel Hill: University of North Carolina Press, 1979), 104; Friedman, *History of American Law*, 45.

23. Marvin K. Singleton, "Colonial Virginia as the First Amendment Matrix: Henry, Madison, and the Assessment Establishment," in Alley, *Madison on Religious Liberty*, 157–72, 158.

24. Ahlstrom, *Religious History*, 188–92. By the Act of 1639, the General Court of Massachusetts determined that responsibility for the poor rested with each town or community. *Charters and General Laws of the Colony and Province of Massachusetts Bay* (Boston, 1814), 173. Other New England colonies subsequently fashioned similar laws. Regarding the role of the church in poor relief in New England, see Walter I. Trattner, *From Poor Law to Welfare State: A History of Social Welfare in America* (New York: Macmillan, 1989), 16; and Robert W. Kelso, *The History of Public Poor Relief in Massachusetts, 1620–1920* (Mont Clair, NJ: Patterson Smith, 1969), 35–41; Roy M. Brown, *Public Poor Relief in North Carolina* (New York: Arno Press, 1976), 10–25; Edward Warren Capen, *The Historical Development of the Poor Law of Connecticut* (privately published Ph.D. dissertation, Columbia University, New York, 1905), 22, 41–44, 59–63.

25. Robert Beverley, *The History and Present State of Virginia* (Chapel Hill: University of North Carolina Press, 1947), 255–60 (255).

26. Arthur Evans, "Mulberry Trees Can Provide Scientific, Historical Lessons," *Richmond-Times Dispatch*, March 13, 2003, 138.

27. Ahlstrom, *Religious History*, 171; Levy, *Blasphemy*, 258.

28. The history of religious establishment in Rhode Island is drawn from a chapter to be published in a forthcoming book, McGarvie and Mensch, "Law and Religion." The sources used in writing this chapter include Sydney V. James, *Colonial Rhode Island: A History* (New York: Scribners and Sons, 1975), *John Clarke and His Legacies: Religion and the Law in Colonial Rhode Island, 1638–1750*, ed. Theodore Dwight Bozeman (University Park: Pennsylvania State University Press, 1999), and *The Colonial Metamorphosis in Rhode Island: A Study of Institutions in Change* (Hanover: University Press of New England, 2000); Gertrude S. Kimball, *Providence in Colonial Times* (Boston: Houghton Mifflin, 1912); Donald Skaggs, *Roger Williams' Dream for America*

(New York: P. Lang, 1933); Hall, *Separating Church and State;* Edwin S. Gaustad, *Liberty of Conscience: Roger Williams in America* (Grand Rapids, MI: Eerdmans, 1991).

29. Penn quoted in Gaustad, *Liberty of Conscience,* 195. See also Stephen M. Feldman, *Please Don't Wish Me a Merry Christmas* (New York: New York University Press, 1997), 137.

30. Barry Levy, *Quakers and the American Family: British Settlement in the Delaware Valley* (New York: Oxford University Press, 1988); Frederick Tolles, *Meeting House and Counting House: The Quaker Merchants of Colonial Philadelphia, 1682–1763* (Chapel Hill: University of North Carolina Press, 1948); Dietmar Rothermund, *The Layman's Progress: Religious and Political Experience in Colonial Pennsylvania, 1740–1770* (Philadelphia: University of Pennsylvania Press, 1961); Stephanie G. Wolf, *Urban Village: Population, Community, and Family Structure in Germantown, Pennsylvania* (Princeton, NJ: Princeton University Press, 1976); Aaron Spencer Fogleman, *Hopeful Journeys: German Immigration, Settlement, and Political Culture in Colonial America, 1717–1775* (Philadelphia: University of Pennsylvania Press, 1996); Michael Zuckerman, ed., *Friends and Neighbors: Group Life in America's First Plural Society* (Philadelphia: Temple University Press, 1982); A. G. Roeber, *Palatines, Liberty, and Property: German Lutherans and Colonial British America* (Baltimore: Johns Hopkins University Press, 1993). Several authors have described Pennsylvania and the mid-Atlantic states in contrast to New England as developing an early emphasis on individualism and a market economy due to heterogeneous populations and a devaluation of religion. Gary Nash, "Social Development," in *Colonial British America: Essays in the New History of the Early Modern Era,* ed. Jack P. Greene and J. R. Pole (Baltimore: Johns Hopkins University Press, 1984), 233–61, esp. 238–39; James T. Lemon, *The Best Poor Man's Country: A Geographical Study of Southeastern Pennsylvania* (Baltimore: Johns Hopkins University Press, 1972).

31. The history of religious establishment in Maryland is drawn from a chapter to be published in a forthcoming book, McGarvie and Mensch, "Law and Religion." The sources used in writing that chapter include Stephen Botein, *Early American Law and Society* (New York: A. A. Knopf, 1983); Gregory A. Wood, *The French Presence in Maryland, 1524–1800* (Baltimore: Gateway Press, 1978); Lois Green Carr and David Jordan, *Maryland's Revolution of Government, 1689–1692* (Ithaca: Cornell University Press, 1974); Ahlstrom, *Religious History;* Michael Graham, "Meetinghouse and Chapel: Religion and Community in 17th-Century Maryland," in *Colonial Chesapeake Society,* ed. Lois Green Carr, Philip D. Morgan, and Jean B. Russo (Chapel Hill: University of North Carolina Press, 1988), 242–74; Alice E. Mathews, "The Religious Experience of Southern Women," in *Women and Religion in America,* 3 vols, ed. Rosemary Ruether and Rosemary Skinner Keller (San Francisco: Harper and Row, 1981), 2:193–232; Joseph H. Smith, "The Foundations of Law in Maryland, 1634–1715," in *Selected Essays: Law and Authority in Colonial America,* ed. George Athan Billias (Barre, MA: Barre Publishers, 1965), 92–115; John D. Krugler, "Lord Baltimore, Roman Catholics, and Toleration: Religious Policy in Maryland during the Early Catholic Years, 1634–1649," *Catholic Historical Review* 65.1 (1979): 49–75; Tricia T. Pyne, "A Plea for Maryland Catholics Reconsidered," *Maryland Historical Magazine* 92.2 (Summer 1997): 163–81; Beatriz Betancourt Hardy, "Roman Catholics, not Papists: Catholic Identity in Maryland, 1689–1776," *Maryland Historical Magazine* 92.2 (Summer 1997): 139–61; Elizabeth A. Kessel, "A Mighty Fortress Is Our God: German Religious and Educational Organizations on the Maryland Frontier, 1734–1800," *Maryland Historical Magazine* 77.4 (Winter 1982): 370–87; John D. Krugler, "Sir George Calvert's Resignation as Secretary of State and the Founding of Maryland," *Maryland Historical Magazine* 63.3 (1973): 239–54.

2—Revolutions in Churches and Society

1. Mann, *Neighbors and Strangers*, 2–22, 27–70.

2. James Hoopes, *Consciousness in New England: From Puritanism and Ideas to Psychoanalysis and Semiotic* (Baltimore: Johns Hopkins University Press, 1989), 11–13, 26–41, 52–60. See also Kerry S. Walters, *The American Deists: Voices of Reason and Dissent in the Early Republic* (Lawrence: University of Kansas Press, 1992).

3. Dr. Samuel Clark quoted in Ralph Ketcham, "James Madison and Religion: A New Hypothesis," in Alley, *Madison on Religious Liberty*, 177–78.

4. The Great Awakening is at once a conservative reaction to Enlightenment influences and an attempt to integrate humanist ideas into Christian cosmology. Its revivals began in America in the 1720s and continued into the 1740s. Patricia Bonomi writes that the Great Awakening began as a contest between clerical factions, which "widened into a controversy that tested the limits of order and introduced a new form of popular leadership that challenged deferential traditions." It recognized religion and politics as expressions of individual liberty and, in this, served as a "rehearsal" for the revolution. Patricia Bonomi, *Under the Cope of Heaven: Religion, Society, and Politics in Colonial America* (New York: Oxford University Press, 1986), 133, 153. Gordon Wood, however, perceives both its conservative and revolutionary traits, describing it as a quest for "order [in] disrupted lives" (*Radicalism*, 144–45) as well as a cause of further communal erosion.

5. Calvinism depended upon a tenuous balance between grace and works. Man received salvation from the grace of God, in which act he was but a powerless recipient. However, his covenant with God required that he worship God and adhere to God's teachings in his earthly behaviors. Different dissenters deviated from orthodoxy in their emphasis of one component of this grace and works duality over another. Ann Hutchinson argued that as man receives grace directly from God, the role of ministers is largely irrelevant. Her emphasis of grace over works, known as Antinomianism, not only dissented from Puritan orthodoxy but also challenged the hierarchical authority of the New England theocracy. Conversely, there were dissenters who emphasized, first, that a man's actions or works were indicative of God's grace within him and, later, that by behaving as Jesus taught, man could, by performance of his covenental duties, merit salvation. This relative human-centeredness in Calvinist doctrine is known as Arminianism.

6. McLoughlin, *Isaac Backus*, 186 (quotation).

7. Miller, *Jonathan Edwards* (Westport, CT: Greenwood Press, 1973); Alan Heimert, *Religion and the American Mind: From the Great Awakening to the Revolution* (Cambridge: Harvard University Press, 1966), 59–95; Ahlstrom, *Religious History*, 281, 303–10. See also Stephen Stein, ed., *Jonathan Edwards' Writings: Text, Context, Interpretation* (Indianapolis: Indiana University Press, 1996); George M. Marsden, *Jonathan Edwards: A Life* (New Haven: Yale University Press, 2003).

8. "The Testimony of the Presidents, Professors, Tutors, and Hebrew Instructor of Harvard College in Cambridge Against the Reverend Mr. George Whitefield, and His Conduct" (Boston, 1744; Presbyterian Historical Society Library, Philadelphia).

9. McLoughlin, *New England Dissent*, 1:924; McLoughlin, *Isaac Backus*, 60 (quotations).

10. May, *Enlightenment in America*, 42, 54.

11. Christine L. Heyrman, *Commerce and Culture: The Maritime Communities of Colonial Massachusetts, 1690–1750* (New York: W. W. Norton, 1984); McLoughlin,

Isaac Backus, 233; Michael Crawford, *Seasons of Grace: Colonial New England's Revival Tradition in the British Context* (New York: Oxford University Press, 1991).

12. See for instance Bonomi, *Under the Cope of Heaven.*

13. Historians, Heimert writes, "have been so struck by the ironic unintended consequences of the Great Awakening in the unleashing of individualism that they have very nearly ignored the movement's direct intended ends of reasserting the community and reintegrating the collective" (*American Mind*, 212).

14. Mead, *Lively Experiment.*

15. May, *Enlightenment in America*, 10.

16. Ibid., 45; Walters, *American Deists*, 20; Handy, *Christian America*, 17; Gay, *The Enlightenment*, 22.

17. Locke quoted in Michael P. Zuckert, "Locke and the Problem of Civil Religion," in *The American Founding: Essays on the Formation of the Constitution*, ed. J. Jackson Barlow, Leonard Levy, Ken Masuge (New York: Greenwood Press, 1988), 91–120 (98). See also John Locke, *A Second Vindication of the Reasonableness of Christianity* (London: White-Hall, for A. and J. Churchill, 1697). Pastor Lemuel Briant quoted in Harry S. Stout, *The New England Soul: Preaching and Religious Culture in Colonial New England* (New York: Oxford University Press, 1986), 223–24. Stout asserts that although rational religion influenced Christian doctrine throughout the colonies it did so to a far less degree in New England.

18. The Rev. Noah Worcester quoted in McLoughlin, *New England Dissent*, 699–700; Charles Chauncy quoted in Ahlstrom, *Religious History*, 303.

19. Heimert, *American Mind*, 121–22, 136–44, 156–57.

20. Some historians contend that only about 4 percent of American people belonged to a church in 1776. See Levy, *Blasphemy*, 268. However, there is considerable debate among historians as to whether statistics reflecting church membership and attendance of religious services constitute accurate indicia of religiosity: see Patricia Bonomi and Peter Eisenstandt, "Church Adherence in the Eighteenth-Century British American Colonies," *William and Mary Quarterly*, 3rd ser., 39.2 (1982): 247; Rodney Starke and Roger Finke, "American Religion in 1776: A Statistical Portrait," *Sociological Analysis* 49 (1988): 39–51. For the predominance of women, see Elaine Forman Crane, "Religion and Rebellion: Women of Faith in the American War for Independence," in *Religion in a Revolutionary Age*, ed. Ronald Hoffman and Peter J. Albert (Charlottesville: University Press of Virginia, 1994); Ann Douglas, *The Feminization of American Culture* (New York: Noonday Press/Farrar, Straus and Giroux, 1977); Field, *Standing Order*, 59.

21. Marsden, *Religion and American Culture*, 43 44; McLoughlin, *New England Dissent*, 2:915; Levy, *Blasphemy*, 269 (Massachusetts); Isaac, *Transformation of Virginia*, 133, 135.

22. Nathan O. Hatch, *The Sacred Cause of Liberty: Political Religion in New England from the First to the Second Great Awakening* (New Haven: Yale University Press, 1977), esp. 1–60; also Ruth Bloch, *Visionary Republic: Millenial Themes in American Thought, 1756–1800* (Cambridge: Harvard University Press, 1985); Sacvan Bercovitch, *The American Jeremiad* (Madison: University of Wisconsin Press, 1978), 40–45. See also Friedman, *Inventors of the Promised Land.*

23. "Irenaeus" quoted in McLoughlin, *Isaac Backus*, 151.

24. Levy, *Blasphemy*, 269; Butler, *Awash in a Sea of Faith*, 214.

25. Congress quoted from Stokes and Pfeffer, *Church and State*, 83; Stiles quoted from Levy, *Blasphemy*, 269.

26. Motion reported in Stokes and Pfeffer, *Church and State*, 158. States enacting such provisions included North Carolina (1776), New York (1777), South Carolina

(1778), Delaware (1792), Maryland (1799), Georgia (1799), Kentucky (1799), and Mississippi (1817). James Madison, "Remarks on Mr. Jefferson's draught of a Constitution for Virginia," in *The Writings of Madison,* 9 vols., ed. Gaillard Hunt (New York: G. P. Putnam's Sons), 5:288.

27. In a letter written in 1800, Jefferson promised to use his power to thwart "schemes" of the clergy, whom he perceived to pose a tyrannical threat to republican government. Jefferson to Benjamin Rush, September 23, 1800, in *Writings* (ed. Bergh), 10:174–75. See also Jefferson, "Notes on Religion," October 1776, in Thomas Jefferson, *The Complete Jefferson,* ed. Saul K. Padover (New York: Tudor, 1943), 937–46; Jefferson, "No Politics in the Pulpit," March 13, 1815, in *The Complete Jefferson,* 953–55; Jefferson to Moses Robinson, March 23, 1801, and to Charles Clay, Esq., January 29, 1815, in *Writings* (ed. Bergh), 10:236, 12:232–34; Jefferson to Pierpont Edwards, July 21, 1801, in Thomas Jefferson, *The Writings of Thomas Jefferson,* ed. Paul Leicester Ford (New York: G. P. Putnam's Sons, 1897), 7:74–75.

28. McLoughlin, *Isaac Backus,* 131, 137, x, xi, 122–24 (Backus, 123), xi.

29. Adams quoted in Sweet, *Story of Religion,* 183–89.

30. Wood, *Creation,* esp. 91–92, 108–10, 117, 120, 143; Rakove, *Original Meanings,* 97–98 (quotation).

31. Francis Newton Thorpe, ed., *The Federal and State Constitutions, Colonial Charters and other organic laws of the state territories and colonies now or heretofore forming the United States of America,* 7 vols. (Washington, DC: Government Printing Office, 1909), 5:2788. See also Levy, *Establishment Clause,* 46, and *Constitutional Opinions,* 159.

32. Thorpe, *Federal and State Constitutions,* 5:3082.

33. Ibid., 5:3085, 3096. See also Levy, *Constitutional Opinions,* 157; May, *Enlightenment in America,* 197–202.

34. Thorpe, *Federal and State Constitutions,* 2:1689 (quotation); Levy, *Establishment Clause,* 47–48.

35. Thorpe, *Federal and State Constitutions,* 5:2597 (quotation); Benjamin Perley Poore, ed., *The Federal and State Constitutions, Colonial Charters and Other Organic Laws of the United States,* 2 vols. (Washington, DC: Government Printing Office, 1878), 1:278–87.

36. The full text may be found in Charles Kittleborough, ed., *The State Constitutions and the Federal Constitution: Organic Laws of the Territories and Other Colonial Dependencies of the United States of America* (Indianapolis: B. F. Bower, 1918), 654–55.

37. Hanson, *Necessary Virtue,* 192.

38. McLoughlin, *Isaac Backus,* 158–65, 223.

39. Ibid., 1388–89 (all quotations, emphasis added).

40. Franklin Hamlin Littell, *From State Church to Pluralism: A Protestant Interpretation of Religion in American History* (Chicago: Aldine, 1962), 15 (Whitefield); Poore, *Federal and State Constitutions,* 1:378 (parishes), 383 (quotation); Levy, *Constitutional Opinions,* 159, and *Establishment Clause,* 48.

41. Rakove, *Original Meanings,* 291.

42. Wood, "Interests and Disinterestedness," 77; Alan Kulikoff, *The Agrarian Origins of American Capitalism* (Charlottesville: University Press of Virginia, 1992); Nash, *Urban Crucible;* Appleby, *Capitalism and a New Social Order;* Wood, *Radicalism,* 128–44.

43. Robert H. Wiebe writes, "It promises no one good health, adequate leisure, a rising standard of living, or an equalization of rewards" (*Self-Rule: A Cultural History of American Democracy* [Chicago: University of Chicago Press, 1995], 9).

44. Friedman, *Inventors of the Promised Land,* 4–9; Washington quoted in Morris, "The Judeo-Christian Foundation," 109–14 (111).

3—"To Form a More Perfect Union"

1. The irony of the "Federalist" Marshall Court implementing the liberal policies sought by the Jeffersonian Republicans has been heretofore lost on most historians. Two exceptions are Charles F. Hobson, *The Great Chief Justice: John Marshall and the Rule of Law* (Lawrence: University Press of Kansas, 1996), and White, *Marshall Court.*

2. Thomas Fleming, *Duel: Alexander Hamilton, Aaron Burr, and the Future of America* (New York: Basic Books, 1999), 4–5 (Franklin and Hamilton). *Debates in the Federal Convention of 1787 as Reported by James Madison,* in *The Debates of the General State Constitutions on the Adoption of the Federal Constitution as Recommended by the General Convention in Philadelphia in 1787,* 5 vols., ed. Jonathan Elliot (Philadelphia: J. B. Lippincott, 1904) 5:7. Madison notes that at least part of the reason for the rejection of Franklin's motion was the fear among delegates that use of the prayer at that late date would signify a disillusionment with the proceedings. James Madison, "Federalist No. 10," in *The Federalist Papers,* ed. Clinton Rossiter (New York: New American Library, 1961), 79.

3. "The Northwest Ordinance," in *Liberty's Legacy,* ed. John C. Dann (published by the Ohio Historical Society as part of the Big Ten Conference's commemoration of the bicentennial). Madison described a 1785 bill proposing to set aside land "for the support of religion" in the unsettled western territories as "unjust in itself, so foreign to the authority of Congress . . . and smelling so strongly of antiquated bigotry." Madison to James Monroe, May 29, 1785, in *The Papers of James Madison,* ed. William T. Hutchinson et al. (Chicago and Charlottesville: University of Chicago Press and University Press of Virginia, 1962), 8:280.

4. Wood, "Interests and Disinterestedness."

5. Bernard Bailyn, ed., *The Debate of the Constitution: Federalist and Antifederalist Speeches, Articles, and Letters during the Struggle over Ratification,* 2 vols. (New York: Literary Classics of the U.S., 1993), 1:869. An anonymous letter to the *Virginia Independent Chronicle* dated October 31, 1787, noted a lack of moral virtue as a cause of national distress. Nowhere is virtue more important than in a republic, the writer contended, where people are responsible for their own governance. He called for the "legal establishment" of lay clerks trained by the Episcopal Church to revitalize religious training in the communities (Bailyn, *Debate,* 5:125–28). A letter signed by Denatus to the same newspaper on June 11, 1788, indicated objection to the proposed Constitution because of the failure of the drafters to provide for the education of the people in the essential tools of the republic—morality, religion, jurisprudence, and the art of war (5:260–67).

6. Quoted in Herbert J. Storing, *What the Anti-Federalists Were For: The Political Thought of the Opponents of the Constitution* (Chicago: University of Chicago Press, 1981), 23.

7. See, for example, Untitled editorial, *New Hampshire Recorder,* November 6, 1787.

8. The Rev. Thomas Reese, "An Essay on the Influence of Religion" (Charleston, 1788; microfiche in the Presbyterian Historical Society Library); New Hampshire polemicist quoted in Herbert Storing, ed., *The Complete Anti-Federalist,* 7 vols. (Chicago: University of Chicago Press, 1981), 4:242.

9. Madison to Jefferson, October 24, 1787, *Writings,* 5:30–31; Bailyn, *Debate,* 1:192–208.

10. Thomas Jefferson, *Reports of Cases Determined in the General Court of Virginia from 1730 to 1740, and from 1768 to 1772* (1774; Charlottesville, VA: F. Carr, 1903), 5; Jefferson, "Autobiography," 37. See also McGarvie, "In Perfect Accordance," 142–77, for a detailed analysis of Jefferson's attitudes regarding the role of law in shaping society.

11. Luther Martin, letter entitled "The Genuine Information," *Maryland Gazette,* December 12, 1787–February 8, 1788, in Bailyn, *Debate,* 1:655–56. Madison's notes dated Thursday, August 30, 1787, reflect that Mr. Pinckney of South Carolina made a motion to add to then article 20 of the Constitution: "but no religious test shall ever be required as a qualification to any office or public trust under the authority of the United States." Mr. Sherman "thought it unnecessary, the prevailing liberality being a sufficient security against such tests." Yet the notion passed, with only North Carolina dissenting. Madison, *Debates,* 5:498.

12. Caldwell quoted from Bailyn, *Debate,* 2:902. Handy notes that Christians who saw an advantage in a national religion were not rare in 1787. Handy, *Christian America,* 23. For "another speaker," see Madison, *Debates,* 4:212. See also Hanson, *Necessary Virtue,* 8–11, for attitudes on Catholicism. Calhoun quoted from Madison, *Debates,* 4:312. Reese, "Essay," n.p.

13. Madison, *Debates,* 2:44, 117–18; "Agrippa" [James Winthrop], letter to the *Massachusetts Gazette,* February 5, 1788, in Bailyn, *Debate,* 2:161; Madison, *Debates,* 2:119 (Colonel Jones).

14. Madison, *Debates,* 2:120 (Payson); Bailyn, *Debate,* 1:931 (Backus). Mark DeWolf Howe, without specific reference to Backus or Payson, notes that many evangelicals welcomed "a constitutional proscription of laws relating to religion . . . because of the deep conviction that the realm of spirit lay beyond the reach of government." Mark DeWolf Howe, *The Garden and the Wilderness: Religion and Government in American Constitutional History* (Chicago: University of Chicago Press, 1965), 18.

15. Bailyn, *Debate,* 2:902–9 (903), 193–95 (193), 1021.

16. Ibid., 919–20.

17. Publius [James Madison], "Federalist No. 52," February 8, 1788, in Bailyn, *Debate,* 2:182–86; H. Trevor Colbourn, *Whig History and the Intellectual Origins of the American Revolution* (Chapel Hill: University of North Carolina Press, for the Institute of Early American History and Culture, 1965), 49, 105, 122–45; Willi Paul Adams, *The First American Constitutions: Republican Ideology and the Making of the State Constitutions in the Revolutionary Era* (Chapel Hill: University of North Carolina Press, for the Institute of Early American History and Culture, 1980), 154–55 (quotations). For more on Priestley, see J. D. Bowers, "Avowing Ourselves Christians: Joseph Priestley, English Unitarianism, and the Development of an American Religion, 1774–1840" (Ph.D. dissertation, Indiana University, 2003).

18. "A Landholder" [Oliver Ellsworth], letter to the *Connecticut Courant (Hartford),* published December 17, 1787, in Bailyn, *Debate,* 1:521–25 (esp. 524). See also Samuel H. Parsons to William Cushing, January 11, 1788, in Bailyn, *Debate,* 1:748–53 (esp. 748).

19. James Madison, "Federalist No. 51," in *The Federalist Papers,* 320–25.

20. Congregationalists quoted from Leo Pfeffer, "The Deity in American Constitutional History," in *Religion and the State: Essays in Honor of Leo Pfeffer,* ed. James E. Wood Jr. (Waco, TX: Baylor University Press, 1985), 119–44 (121); "one delegate" quoted from Pfeffer, "Case for Separation," 52–94 (69–70). See also "Americanus" [John Stevens Jr.], letter to *Daily Advertiser (New York)* entitled, "On Montesquieu, A System Monger Without Philosophic precision and more on the Errors of Cato," in Bailyn, *Debate,* 1:487–93. Handy, *Christian America,* 8, 35 (quotation).

21. Bailyn, *Debate,* 1:807–10, 63–69.

22. Jefferson to Madison, December 20, 1787, ibid., 209–13; George Madison, "Objections to the Constitution," *Virginia Journal,* November 22, 1787, ibid., 345–49;

"Federalist Farmer" [Richard Henry Lee], letters to *The Republican (New York)*, November 8, 1787, ibid., 245; Mr. Spencer quoted in Madison, *Debates*, 4:152–54 (153). Some people of the time expressed considerable confusion over the modern social philosophy of the era. While arguing for protections of liberty, James Winthrop juxtaposed political freedom with economic freedom, failing to see, as Jefferson did, the interdependence between these two liberties. "Agrippa" [James Winthrop], letters entitled, "Cherish the Old Confederation Like the Apple of Our Eye," *Massachusetts Gazette*, January 11, 15, 18, 1788, in Bailyn, *Debate*, 1:762–73.

23. Jefferson to Madison, December 20, 1787, in Bailyn, *Debate*, 1:209–13.

24. "Centinel" [Samuel Bryan] to the *Freeman's Journal (Philadelphia)*, October 24, 1787, ibid., 77–91.

25. "Yet there is no restraint in form of a bill of rights, to secure (what Dr. Blackstone calls) that residuum of human rights, which is not intended to be given up to society, and which indeed is not necessary to be given up for any good social purpose—the rights of conscience, the freedom of the press, and the trial by jury shall be at mercy." Richard Henry Lee to Governor Edmund Randolph, October 16, 1787, published by the *Virginia Gazette*, December 6, 1787, ibid., 465–72.

26. William McLoughlin argues that dissenting sects contributed to disestablishment in their fight for toleration. The evangelicals' quest for the free practice of religion was oftentimes inconsistent with their desire for a Christian nation. McLoughlin, *New England Dissent*. William Warren Sweet, in his classic work *Story of Religion*, argues that the toleration springing from religious pluralism and the influence of the frontier precipitated disestablishment. Louis Hartz, in *Liberal Tradition*, finds that because of America's religious diversity the Founders did not have to replace a Christian worldview with a humanistic philosophy.

27. Cord, *Separation*; Mooney, *Public Virtue*; Neuhaus, *Naked Public Square*.

28. "Federalist Farmer," letters to *The Republican*, November 8, 1787, in Bailyn, *Debate*, 1:245–88 (245).

29. James Madison, speaking at the Virginia Ratifying Convention, said, "if there were a majority of one sect, a bill of rights would be a poor protection for liberty. Happily for the states, they enjoy the utmost freedom that multiplicity of sects which pervades America, and which is the best and only security for religious liberty in any society; for where there is a variety of sects, there cannot be a majority of any one sect to oppress and prosecute the rest" (*Debates*, 3:330). Noah Webster astutely observed that so long as the people are sovereign, no constitution is unalterable—one generation cannot control the opinions, privilege, and circumstances of the next. "On the Absurdity of a Bill of Rights," *American Magazine (New York)*, December 1787, in Bailyn, *Debate*, 1:669–72. See also speech of Governor Randolph at the Virginia Ratifying Convention (Bailyn, *Debate*, 2:709–17).

30. Bernstein, *Are We to Be a Nation*, 56.

31. For Pennsylvania, see Bailyn, *Debate*, 1:526; for New Hampshire, Stokes and Pfeffer, *Church and State*, 151; for North Carolina and New York, Stokes and Pfeffer, *Church and State*, 152; for Maryland, Bailyn, *Debate*, 2:536; for South Carolina, Bailyn, *Debate*, 2:578. Three states issued resolutions calling for amendments, providing that the powers not delegated to the national government are reserved to the states. These states were Massachusetts, New Hampshire, and South Carolina. Yet Virginia and North Carolina, in a reversal of the position they would take in the Civil War, claimed that the people, not the states, drafted the Constitution, and that other powers are reserved to them. In Virginia's case, this is a direct repudiation of Patrick Henry, who on

June 4, 1788, at his state's ratifying convention, asserted that the preamble drafted in Philadelphia beginning "We the people" was in error, for the constitutional convention, as a body of state delegates, lacked the authority to speak for the people but only for the various states. In fact, he trumpeted: "States are the characteristics, and the soul of a confederation. If the States be not the agents of this compact, it must be one great consolidated National Government of the people of all the States." Bailyn, *Debate*, 2:572.

32. Bailyn, *Debate*, 2:596; Pfeffer, "Case for Separation," 60.

33. Quoted in Rakove, *Original Meanings*, 36.

34. Reese, "Essay."

35. Rakove, *Original Meanings*, 96.

36. Stokes and Pfeffer, *Church and State*, 83–87; Cord, *Separation*, 41–46, 54–80; Fleming, *Duel*, 4.

37. See proclamations issued on October 3, 1789, and January 1, 1795, in James D. Richardson, *A Compilation of the Messages and Papers of the Presidents, 1789–1897*, vol. 1 (Washington, DC: Bureau of National Literature and Art, 1901). See also "Farewell Address," September 19, 1796, in W. B. Allen, ed., *George Washington: A Collection* (Indianapolis: Liberty Classics, 1988), 521; Fleming, *Duel*, 4–5. Relatively good reviews of Washington's religious beliefs and their effects on his public behavior are presented in Patrick J. Garrity and Matthew Spalding, *A Sacred Union of Citizens* (New York: Rowman and Littlefield, 1996), 78–80, 169–73; Paul F. Boller Jr., "George Washington and Religious Liberty," *William and Mary Quarterly*, 3rd ser., no. 17 (1960), 486–506.

38. Washington to the Ministers et al. of the Reformed German Congregation of New York, November 27, 1783, to the United Baptist Churches in Virginia, May 10, 1789, to the General Assembly of Presbyterian Churches, May 1789, to the Annual Meeting of Quakers, September 1789, to the Roman Catholics in the U.S.A., March 15, 1790, to the Hebrew Congregations of the City of Savannah, Georgia, undated, in Allen, *Collection*, 270–71, 531–32, 533, 533–34, 546–47, 549.

39. Washington to the Hebrew Congregation in Newport, August 1790, ibid., 547–48.

40. U.S. Congress, *American State Papers: Documents, Legislative and Executive of the Congress of the United States* (Washington, DC: Gales and Seaton, 1832–1862), 2:18. See also *U.S. Statutes at Large*, 8:155. It has been asserted that this language is not authentic; see Morton Borden, *Jews, Turks, and Infidels* (Chapel Hill: University of North Carolina Press, 1984), 76–79.

41. John Adams, Proclamation of March 23, 1798, in Richardson, *Compilation*; Jefferson, "Letter to Samuel Miller," January 23, 1808, in *Writings* (ed. Bergh), 11:428; Madison, Proclamations of July 9, 1812, July 23, 1813, November 16, 1814, in *The Papers of James Madison, Presidential Series*, 5 vols. (Charlottesville: University Press of Virginia, 1984); "Madison's Detached Memoranda," ed. Elizabeth Fleet, *William and Mary Quarterly*, 3rd ser., vol. 3 (July, 1946): 534–68.

42. Bernard W. Sheehan, *Seeds of Extinction: Jeffersonian Philanthropy and the American Indian* (Published for the Institute of Early American History and Culture by University of North Carolina Press, 1974), 19–21; Alexis de Tocqueville, *Democracy in America*, ed. J. P. Mayer, trans. George Lawrence (New York: Harper and Row, 1969), 293–94; Sheehan, *Seeds of Extinction*, 125–29.

43. Madison recounts his thoughts in the third person in his notes of the proceedings of May 31, 1787:

Mr. Madison said that he had brought with him into the convention a strong bias in favor of enemeration [sic] and definition of the powers of the national Legislature; but, also had doubts concerning its practability [sic] . . . But he should shrink from nothing which would be found essential to such a form of Gov't. as would provide for the safety, liberty, and happiness of the community. This being the end of all our deliberation, all the necessary means for attaining it must, however reluctantly, be submitted to. (Max Farrand, ed., *The Records of the Federal Convention of 1787*, 4 vols. [New Haven: Yale University Press, 1911, 1966], 1:53)

44. Ibid., 2:321–22, 325. Each of these proposals could have been the genesis of some congressional role in education. However, none was ultimately included in the Constitution. Seemingly all but the first, concerning a national university, and the last, addressing the promotion of business activities, died in committee. Furthermore, Madison's explanation of the language of the proposal establishing "public institutions, rewards, and immunities for the promotion" of various business activities indicates no intention to use that provision in support of education. In a letter to Professor Davis in 1832, Madison notes that the convention's rejection of this proposal was a repudiation of any government support for domestic business by direct positive action, which did not preclude indirect support through negative action such as duties and trade restrictions that were clearly provided for by the Constitution. Ibid., 3:520.

45. Lorraine Smith Pangle and Thomas L. Pangle, *The Learning of Liberty: The Educational Ideas of the American Founders* (Lawrence: University of Kansas Press, 1993), 147–50.

46. Farrand, *Federal Convention of 1787*, 2:616.

47. Ibid., 3:362 (quotation); Pangle and Pangle, *Learning of Liberty*, 149. For a decent general history of the proposed national university, see Edgar Bruce Wesley, *The University of the United States* (Minneapolis: University of Minnesota Press, 1935).

48. Ellwood P. Cubberly, ed., *Readings in the Public Education in the United States: A Collection of Sources and Readings to Illustrate the History of Education Practice and Progress in the United States* (Boston: Houghton Mifflin, 1934), 176.

49. Thomas E. Finegan, ed., *Free Schools: A Documentary History of the Free School Movement in New York State* (Albany: University of the State of New York, 1921), 60–65.

50. Cubberly, *Readings*, 122.

51. Newton Edwards and Herman G. Richey, *The School in the American Social Order* (Boston: Houghton Mifflin, 1947), 247–48.

52. The Massachusetts Constitution of 1780, chapter 5, section 2, in Kittleborough, *State Constitutions*, 654–55. Other New England constitutions are also available in the same source. See also Vera Butler, *Education as Revealed by New England Newspapers prior to 1850* (Philadelphia: Temple University, 1935); Maria Louise Greene, *The Development of Religious Liberty in Connecticut*, reprinted in the Civil Liberties in American History series, ed. Leonard W. Levy (New York: DeCapo Press, 1970); Ava Harriet Chadburne, *A History of Education in Maine* (Orono, ME: self-published, 1936); H. G. Good, *A History of American Education* (New York: Macmillan, 1956); Edwin Grant Dexter, *A History of Education in the United States* (New York: Macmillan, 1904).

53. Cubberly, *Readings*, 125.

54. Kelso, *Public Poor Relief*, 121 (quotation); Capen, *Poor Law of Connecticut*, 22, 41–44, 59.

55. Trattner, *Poor Law*, 19. See also Kelso, *Public Poor Relief*; Gross, "Giving in America."

56. Conrad Edick Wright, *The Transformation of Charity in Postrevolutionary New England* (Boston: Northeast University Press, 1992), 17–133.

57. Trattner, *Poor Law*, 39.

58. Brown, *Public Poor Relief*, 10–25, 26–28 (12). In 1759 North Carolina passed a law enabling elected vestrymen to raise taxes for the "provision of the clergy and support of the poor" (ibid., 26). In 1764 the law's scope was expanded to provide for building churches, schools, and outhouses. The established church functioned as a quasi-governmental organization to preach religion, educate the young, and care for the poor at public expense. In 1777 North Carolina repealed the laws establishing this social structure and enacted a law providing for the election of "seven freeholders as overseers of the poor" (ibid., 28). These men assumed all the duties of the church vestrymen but were public employees removed from any official connection to the church.

59. Martha Branscombe, *The Courts and the Poor Laws in New York State, 1784–1929* (Chicago: University of Chicago Press, 1943), 13–14 (citing *Colonial Laws of New York, 1773*, vol. 5, ch. 1600), 59–60.

60. Charles Lawrence, *History of the Philadelphia Almshouses and Hospitals* (New York: Arno Press, 1976), 17 (Penn), 18 (overseers), 19–21.

61. Ibid., 30–33.

4—God Is as Man Makes Him

1. Nelson, *Americanization*, 5.

2. Nisbet quoted in Wood, *Radicalism*, 305–6.

3. This concept enjoys tremendous popularity but is perhaps most strongly asserted by Jay Fligelman: "Central to the rationalist ideology of the American Revolution was the belief that in an ideal world all relationships would be contractual." *Prodigals and Pilgrims: The American Revolution against Patriarchal Authority* (New York: Cambridge University Press, 1982): 123. See also Tomlins, *Law, Labor, and Ideology*, and Grossberg, *Governing the Hearth*.

4. This illustration is drawn from a reading of colonial and postrevolutionary case law. As an example of colonial thought, as late as the mid-eighteenth century, an attorney contesting title to land held by the Van Rensselaers in New York argued that they already possessed "upwards of eleven hundred square miles surely enough for one family." See "Reasons in support of the objection of the inhabitants of King's District and others against granting the confirmation petitioned for by the Proprietor of Westenhook," February 22, 1775 (John Tabor Kempe Papers, New York Historical Society, box 5, miscellaneous). In colonial courts, arguments regarding the public welfare, wastefulness, and other equitable concepts oftentimes mitigated harsh contracts, even as to land. Conversely, by the 1790s in a case concerning a seller's failure to disclose pertinent facts in a real estate transaction, a Pennsylvania court could write: "The course of transacting business at large, will have due weight in matters of this nature; and courts of justice will be cautious of impeaching contracts, under the idea of a refined and over-strained morality, which seldom or never takes place in the ordinary affairs of life" (*Eichelberger v. Barnitz*, 1 Yeates 307 [Pa. 1793]). See also *Whitewell v. Wyer*, 11 Mass. 6 (1814). In *Fox v. Mackreth*, 2 Brown's Cha. Cases 420 (Pa. 1791), the court held that it "will not correct a contract merely because a man of nice honour would not have entered into it." See also Elizabeth V. Mensch, "The Colonial Origins of Liberal Property Rights," *Buffalo Law Review* 31.3 (Fall 1982), 703–4; Michael Grossberg, "Citizens and Families: A Jeffersonian Vision of Domestic Relations and Generational Change," in Gilreath, *Education of a Citizen*.

5. Horwitz, *Transformation*, 140; Jean Matthews, *Toward a New Society: American Thought and Culture, 1800–1830* (Boston: G. K. Hall, 1991), 24; Perry Miller, *The Life of the Mind in America: From the Revolution to the Civil War* (New York: Harcourt Brace and World, 1965), 109.

6. For a discussion on the independence of judges in the early republic, see Newmyer, *Chief Justice Story,* and Grossberg, *Governing the Hearth.* Words attributed to Jefferson in Wood, "Interests and Disinterestedness," 102.

7. Wood, *Radicalism*, 276–96, 325. See also Grossberg, *Governing the Hearth;* Tomlins, *Law, Labor, and Ideology;* Fred Konefsky, "As Best to Subserve Their Own Interests: Lemuel Shaw, Labor Conspiracy, and Fellow Servants," *Law and Labor History Review* 7.1 (Spring 1989): 219–39.

8. Horwitz, *Transformation;* Grossberg, *Governing the Hearth.*

9. Jefferson quoted in Horwitz, *Transformation,* 18.

10. Peter Charles Hoffer, *Law and People in Colonial America* (Baltimore: Johns Hopkins University Press, 1998), 142; Horwitz, *Transformation.*

11. Horwitz, *Transformation,* 1–17, 25, 99–108. The "will theory of contract law" denotes a legal theory studied in law school; the "will of the parties" is another legal term of art. "The early nineteenth century was the golden age of contract because it was the age of individualism and free will." Newmyer, *Chief Justice Story,* 150.

12. Hurst contends that the development of contract law in the early republic resulted in a "release of energy" contributing to the dynamic expansion of American commercial, industrial, and economic growth. Hurst, *Conditions of Freedom.* On the development of a liberal society in the early republic, identified by market economics and individual pursuit of self-interest, see Robert H. Wiebe, *The Opening of American Society: From the Adoption of the Constitution to the Eve of Disunion* (New York: A. A. Knopf, 1984); Sean Wilentz, *Chants Democratic: New York City and the Rise of the American Working Class, 1788–1850* (New York: Oxford University Press, 1984); Richard Bushman, *The Refinement of America: Persons, Houses, Cities* (New York: Random House, 1992); John M. Murrin, "Political Development in Colonial British America," in *Colonial British America: Essays in the New History of the Early Modern Era,* ed. Jack P. Greene and J. R. Pole (Baltimore: Johns Hopkins University Press, 1984), 414–56. It should be noted that not all historians see the early republic as an era of laissez-faire economics. See William J. Novak, *The People's Welfare: Law and Regulation in Nineteenth-Century America* (Chapel Hill: University of North Carolina Press, 1996); Barry Alan Shain, *The Myth of American Individualism: The Protestant Origins of American Political Thought* (Princeton, NJ: Princeton University Press, 1994); Oscar Handlin and Mary Flug Handlin, *Commonwealth: A Study of the Role of Government in the American Economy, Massachusetts, 1774–1861* (Cambridge: Harvard University Press, 1947, 1969).

13. Wood, *Creation,* 31; Charles Thomson to Thomas Jefferson, April 6, 1786, in *The Papers of Thomas Jefferson,* ed. Julian P. Boyd (Princeton, NJ: Princeton University Press. 1950), 9:380; *Niles Weekly Register,* no. 9, December 2, 1816, in Wood, *Radicalism,* 340; Davis quoted in Wood, *Radicalism,* 307.

14. Rush and Wirt quoted in Matthews, *New Society,* 11.

15. An excellent account of this process can be found in Lewis Perry, *Boats against the Current: American Culture between Revolution and Modernity* (New York: Oxford University Press, 1993).

16. McLoughlin, *New England Dissent,* 2:1001–13. McLoughlin writes that Baptists "deplored Jefferson's theological position" and "dissociated themselves from the deistic and anticlerical premises on which he based his stand" (ibid., 1013). *Newark*

Gazette, 20 September 1800, n.p. Robbins quoted in Edwin S. Scott Gaustad, "The Emergence of Religious Freedom in the Early Republic," in *Religion and the State: Essays in Honor of Leo Pfeffer,* ed. James E. Wood Jr. (Waco, TX: Baylor University Press, 1985), 25–42 (42n23). For Stockton, see Carl E. Prince, *New Jersey's Jeffersonian Republicans: The Genesis of an Early Party Machine, 1789–1819* (Chapel Hill: University of North Carolina Press, 1964, 1967), 57.

17. Ely quoted in Handy, *Christian America,* 50. Robert Handy notes that disestablishment affected the methods at the clergymen's disposal for achieving this goal but not the goal itself: "The means were to be voluntary and persuasive, but the goal of a Christian society was as clear as it had been in the days of legal establishment, even clearer." Ibid., 49.

18. Wood, *Radicalism,* 330; Madison to Jefferson, January 22, 1786, in *Writings,* 2:216.

19. Madison, "Report on the Resolutions . . . concerning the Alien and Seditious Acts," in *Writings,* 341–406 (384); Elizabeth Fleet, "Madison's Detached Memoranda," *William and Mary Quarterly,* 3rd ser., vol. 3 (October 1946): 534–68 (554). Madison also expresses opposition to public expenditure for chaplains in the armed services, congressional prayers, and days of thanksgiving.

20. Grossberg, "Citizens and Families," 3–27 (esp. 4).

21. Jefferson to Major John Cartwright, June 5, 1824, *Writings* (ed. Bergh), 16:42; Jefferson, "First Inaugural Address," March 4, 1901, ibid., 3:317.

22. See Edwin S. Gaustad, *Sworn on the Altar of God: A Religious Biography of Thomas Jefferson* (Grand Rapids, MI: Eerdmans, 1996); Charles B. Sanford, *The Religious Life of Thomas Jefferson* (Charlottesville: University Press of Virginia, 1984); Eugene R. Sheridan, "Liberty and Virtue: Religion and Republicanism in Jeffersonian Thought," in Gilreath, *Education of a Citizen,* 242–63.

23. Jacob Henry, "Speech in the North Carolina House of Democrats" (1809), reprinted in *Cornerstones of Religious Freedom in America,* ed. Joseph L. Blau (Boston: Beacon Press, 1949), 94, 93 (emphasis added); Stokes and Pfeffer, *Church and State,* 154–55.

24. Matthews, *New Society,* 3. The population grew from 2.8 million in 1780 to 9.6 million in 1820. Wood, *Radicalism,* 320–21; Horwitz, *Transformation,* 107–12; Arthur M. Schlesinger Jr., *The Age of Jackson* (New York: J. J. Little and Ives, 1945), 138.

25. Grossberg, "Citizens and Families," 6–17.

26. Ibid., 17.

27. "An Essay on Marriage or the Lawfulness of Divorce," *Pennsylvania Magazine* 1 (December supplement, 1775), 602; see also Nancy Cott, "Divorce and the Changing Status of Women in Eighteenth-Century America," in *The American Family in Social-Historical Perspective,* ed. Michael Gordon (New York: St. Martins Press, 1978); Grossberg, "Citizens and Families," 17, quoting Sir Henry Maine, *Ancient Law* (London: Dent and Sons, 1917), 140. For a description of changes in property laws affecting women in the early republic, see Marylynn Salmon, *Women and the Law of Property in Early America* (Chapel Hill: University of North Carolina Press, 1986).

28. Pangle and Pangle, *Learning of Liberty,* 79. See also "Washington's Speech to Both Houses of Congress," January 8, 1790, in *Writings of George Washington,* 39 vols., ed. John C. Fitzpatrick (Washington, DC: Government Printing Office, 1931–1944), 30:494; see also John Adams, "Observations on the Reconstruction of Government in Massachusetts During the Revolution," in *The Works of John Adams,* 10 vols., ed. Charles Francis Adams (Boston: Charles C. Little and James Brown, 1856), 4:259.

29. Benjamin Rush, "A Plan," in *Essays on Education in the Early Republic*, ed. Frederick Rudolph (Cambridge: Harvard University Press, 1965), 14–15.

30. Noah Webster, "On Education of Youth in America," Robert Coram, "Political Inquiries: to Which is added, a Plan for the General Establishment of Schools throughout the United States," in ibid., 44–45 (Webster), 141, 113.

31. Associated Presbytery in Pennsylvania, "A Solemn Warning by the Associated Presbytery in Pennsylvania" (Lancaster, PA: Francis Bailey, 1777), 10–11 [Phil. Lib.].

32. De Tocqueville, *Democracy in America* (ed. Mayer), 292; Richard Godbeer, *Sexual Revolution in Early America* (Baltimore: Johns Hopkins University Press, 2002); Trattner, *Poor Law*, 30. See also Robert A. Gross, *The Minutemen and Their World* (New York: Hill and Wang, 1976), 98–104, who notes not only the change in sexual practices during this time but also the change in law after the Revolution to accord women more legal right over their own decisions; see also Grossberg, *Governing the Hearth*. Griffin, *Their Brothers' Keepers*, 13 (drinking). See David W. Conroy, *In Public Houses: Drink and the Revolution of Authority in Colonial Massachusetts* (Chapel Hill: University of North Carolina Press, 1995); Robert P. Hay, *Freedom's Jubilee: One Hundred Years of the Fourth of July, 1776–1876* (Ph.D. dissertation, University of Kentucky, 1967), 122, 140.

33. Godbeer, *Sexual Revolution*, 234, 237, 303, 229 (young people).

34. McLoughlin, *Isaac Backus*, 212–13; Matthews, *New Society*, 52, 60; Godbeer, *Sexual Revolution*, 290.

35. Mathews, "Religious Experience of Southern Women," 196, 201.

36. Rush quoted in Friedman, *Crime and Punishment*, 73.

37. Louis B. Masur, *Rites of Execution: Capital Punishment and the Transformation of American Culture, 1776–1865* (New York: Oxford University Press, 1989), 44 (Bascom), 69 (Annan).

38. Ibid., 41, 42, 49, 7.

39. William White, *The Case of Episcopal Churches in the United States Considered* (Philadelphia, 1782); Miller, *Religious Liberty*, 94.

40. The term "civil religion" is used by Robert N. Bellah, most prominently in his essay "The Revolution and the Civil Religion," in *Religion and the American Revolution*, ed. Jerald C. Brauer (Philadelphia: Fortress Press, 1967). The term "religion of the republic" was coined by Sidney Mead and used repeatedly in his writings (*Lively Experiment* being the most significant). The expression "American Religion" is used in Harold Bloom, *The American Religion: The Emergence of the Post Christian Nation* (New York: Simon and Schuster, 1992).

41. Dwight quoted from Handy, *Christian America*, 21.

42. This example is borrowed from Marsden, *Religion and American Culture*, 33.

43. Miller, *Religious Liberty*, 92; Paul Tillich, "Freedom and the Ultimate Concern," in Cogley, *Religion in America*, 273; de Tocqueville, *Democracy in America* (ed. Mayer), 290–91, 293.

44. Handy, *Christian America*, viii; Hatch, *Sacred Cause of Liberty*, 11–12; John Reed, Sermon of December 12, 1787, for the ordination of the Rev. Kilborn Whitman, Boston (microfiche, now in the Presbyterian Historical Society Library, Philadelphia).

45. Hay, *Freedom's Jubilee*, 74–76.

46. Ibid., 193–94, 7.

47. "Extracts from the Minutes of the General Assembly of the Presbyterian Church in the United States of America, 1819" (Presbyterian Historical Society Library, Philadelphia), 172; "Narrative of the State of Religion," in ibid., 316; James M.

Banner Jr., *To the Hartford Convention: The Federalists and the Origins of Party Politics in Massachusetts, 1789–1815* (New York: A. A. Knopf, 1970), 27 (Tappan), 176 (Sanders).

48. Handy, *Christian America,* 21. Horace Bushnell wrote, "we will not cease till a Christian nation throws up its temples of worship on every hill and plain, till knowledge, virtue, and religion, . . . have filled our great country with a manly and happy race of people, and the bonds of a complete Christian commonwealth are seen to span the continent" (*Barbarism, the First Danger: A Discourse for Home Missions* [New York: Printed for the American Home Missionary Society, 1847], 32).

49. In 1784, Isaac Backus wrote, "It is readily granted that piety, religion, and morality are essentially necessary for the good order of civil society" (McLoughlin, *Isaac Backus,* 150).

50. Samuel McClintock, "A Sermon Preached before the Honorable the Council and the Honorable the Senate and House of Representatives of the State of New Hampshire," June 3, 1784, in Ellis Sandoz, ed., *Political Sermons of the Founding Era, 1730–1805,* 2 vols. (Indianapolis: Liberty Fund, 1998), 1:797.

51. Charles G. Finney, "Oration in Temperance," in *Lectures to Professing Christians* (London: Milner, 1837), 90; Lyman Beecher, "A Reformation of Morals Practicable and Indispensable" (1812), in Handy, *Christian America,* 44; Colin Wells, *The Devil and Doctor Dwight: Satire and Theology in the Early American Republic* (Chapel Hill: University of North Carolina Press, 2002), 173–74.

52. Unsigned letter to the *Connecticut Courant,* April 6, 1803, 1.

53. Backus quoted in McLoughlin, *New England Dissent,* 2:753. Similarly, in "An impartial statement of the Scripture Doctrine in respect of Civil Government and the duties of subjects," *Treatises on Various Theological Subjects Published at Different Times and Now Collected into Volumes,* 4 vols. (Middleton, CT: Clark and Lyman, 1816), 4:381–404, the Rev. Thomas Scott, D.D., could write: "It is the evident doctrine of scripture, that government is the appointment of God, to be a restraint on man's selfishness, and to preserve a measure of order in the world, notwithstanding human depravity; . . . God as Author of our rational nature, and the supreme Ruler of the World, is the Fountain of all subordinate authority; by whatever second causes he hath been pleased to confer it."

54. Edwards quoted in Handy, *Christian America,* 56; Unsigned letter to the *American Mercury,* October 22, 1801, 1; *The Works of Jesse Appleton,* 2 vols. (Andover, MA: Gould and Newman, 1837), 2:243.

55. The Rev. Samuel Brown Wylie, *Two Sons of Oil: The Faithful Witness for magistracy and ministry upon a scriptural basis* (Philadelphia: Greensburg, McCorkle, 1806); McLoughlin, *New England Dissent,* 1:1019–20.

56. The Rev. Jaspar Adams correspondence contained in "The Protestant Establishment," in Alley, *Madison on Religious Liberty,* 252–53.

57. Edwards and Richey, *American Social Order;* Dexter, *History of Education;* Good, *History of American Education;* Greene, *Religious Liberty;* R. Laurence Moore, "Bible Reading and Nonsectarian Schooling: The Failure of Religious Instruction in Nineteenth-Century Public Education," *Journal of American History* 86.4 (March 2000): 1581–99; Bernard Bailyn, *Education in the Formng of American Society* (New York: Vintage Books, 1960).

58. Pangle and Pangle, *Learning of Liberty,* 99; Collins quoted in Wood, *Radicalism,* 330; Butler, *Education,* 244.

59. Handy writes, "Evangelical Protestants hoped to prepare the way for the triumph of Christian civilization both by building up their own churches as aggressively

as they could and by extending their own influence in the nation through voluntary societies designed to achieve specific ends" (*Christian America*, 42–43).

60. McLoughlin, *New England Dissent*, 2:711; "On the Religious Education of Children," *Religious Instructor*, 1.1 (September 1810), 26–32. The *Religious Instructor* was published by the ministers of the Presbyterian Church from offices in Carlisle, PA. In its first issue, these ministers enunciated their purpose "to promote the cause of evangelical religion." The periodical cited participation in revivals, religious organizations, and missions. Later Alexander Campbell, leader of the Disciples of Christ, published the *Millenial Harbinger*. In its first issue in January of 1830, Campbell expressed its purpose: "This work shall be devoted to the destruction of Sectarianism, Infidelity, and Anti-Christian doctrine and practice. It shall have as its object the development and introduction of the political and religious order of society called THE MILLENNIUM, which will be the consummation of that ultimate amelioration of society proposed in the Christian scriptures."

61. "Some thoughts on the Death of the Witnesses," *Religious Instructor*, 1.8 (April 1811): 292–303.

62. Nord, "Systematic Benevolence," 240–44 (quotation). Kathleen Smith Kutolowski, "Freemasonry and Community in the Early Republic: The Case for Antimasonic Anxieties," *American Quarterly* 34 (1982): 543; Richard D. Brown, "The Emergence of Voluntary Associations in Massachusetts, 1760–1830," *Journal of Voluntary Action Research* 2 (1973): 64. "Senek, M. A.," to the *American Mercury*, January 31, 1791, p. 2.

63. Alexander quoted in Randall Balmer and John R. Fitzmier, *The Presbyterians* (Westport, CT: Greenwood Press, 1993), 49; McLoughlin, *Isaac Backus*, 213.

64. Anne E. Boylan, *Sunday School: The Formation of an American Institution, 1790–1880* (New Haven: Yale University Press, 1988), 16–17, 142.

65. The Rev. Timothy Dwight, "A Discourse on Some Events of the Last Century," in McLoughlin, *New England Dissent*, 2:918 ("modern liberality"); Dwight, "A Discourse," in Smith, Handy, and Loetscher, *American Christianity*, 1:530–39 (538, "take your side"); the Rev. Nathaniel Emmons, "Religious Instructors Useful to Civil Society," in *The Works of Nathaniel Emmons, D.D.*, 2 vols., ed. Jacob Ide (Boston, 1842), 1:237, 240–41 (quotation).

66. Jeremy Belknap, "A Sermon Delivered in Boston, May 26, 1796," in Banner, *To the Hartford Convention*, 157; the Rev. John Eliot, "A Sermon Preached . . . at the Ordination of the Rev. Mr. Joseph McKean," ibid., 156; Elis Smith, "A Discourse on Government and Religion Delivered at Gray, Maine, July 4, 1810" (New York Historical Society), 38–39.

67. See McLoughlin, *New England Dissent*, 2:709–11, for more detail regarding these doctrinal variations; for liberal ideology, see Grossberg, *Governing the Hearth;* for Leland, see McLoughlin, *New England Dissent*, 2:935; Sparks quoted in Matthews, *New Society*, 33.

68. Salem minister quoted in Field, *Standing Order*, 59.

69. Nathan O. Hatch, *The Democratization of American Christianity* (New Haven: Yale University Press, 1989), 35–39, 171, 115; Wood, *Creation*, 215; Nathan O. Hatch, "The Second Great Awakening and the Market Revolution," in *Devising Liberty*, ed. David Thomas Konig (Palo Alto: Stanford University Press, 1995), 246.

70. Russell E. Richey, *Early American Methodism* (Indianapolis: Indiana University Press, 1991), 83 (quotation). See also McLoughlin, *New England Dissent*, 2:720 et seq. A contrary interpretation should be noted. George M. Thomas, *Revivalism and Cultural Change: Christianity, Nation-Building, and the Market in the Nineteenth-Century*

United States (Chicago: University of Chicago Press, 1989) develops the thesis that Methodism reinforced the importance of individual initiative and responsibility for one's own salvation and thereby encouraged autonomy in business and social relationships. Nathan O. Hatch argues that the Second Awakening and the growth of the free market were integrated movements, although he also sees the growth of sectarian churches during the era as an expression of dissent from mainstream American culture and its embrace of free-enterprise individualism. See Hatch, "Second Great Awakening."

71. McLoughlin, *New England Dissent,* 2:752–53, 756.

72. Ibid., 761–62, 753–54; McLoughlin, *Isaac Backus,* 99 (quotation).

73. "Minutes of the Stonington, CT. Baptist Association, 1813," in McLoughlin, *New England Dissent,* 2:1016. For other indications of antimasonic sentiments prior to 1820, see Paul E. Johnson, *A Shopkeeper's Millenium: Society and Revivals in Rochester, New York, 1815–1837* (New York: Hill and Wang, 1978), 66–70.

74. McLoughlin, *New England Dissent,* 2:714–19.

75. Christine L. Heyrman, *Southern Cross: The Beginnings of the Bible Belt* (Chapel Hill: University of North Carolina Press, 1997), 8–9, 172, 312n14, 322n70, 18 (frivolities).

76. Ibid., 4, 41, 3, 20. Heyrman finds self-abasement a common evangelical characteristic across denominations or sects.

77. Ibid., 5–6; Wayland quoted in Handy, *Christian America,* 31–32.

78. Handy, *Christian America,* 27–28; Gaustad, "Emergence of Religious Freedom," 25 (quotation).

79. Dwight quoted in Sidney E. Mead, *Nathaniel William Taylor, 1756–1858: A Connecticut Liberal* (Chicago: University of Chicago Press, 1942), 46.

80. Ibid., 142–44; Thomas Jefferson, "Autobiography," in *The Complete Jefferson,* 956.

81. Channing quoted in Mead, *Nathaniel Taylor,* 178.

82. For more on the New Divinity Movement, see Mead, *Nathaniel Taylor.*

83. *Barnes v. Parish of Falmouth,* 6 Mass. 401 (1810) (emphasis added). The town was still a part of Massachusetts before Maine became a state in 1820.

84. *Baker v. Fales,* 16 Mass. 487 (1821).

5—Revolutionary-Era Disestablishment

1. McGarvie and Mensch, "Law and Religion." The synopsis of the Clarke matter is drawn from the development and interpretation of John Clarke, his bequest, and its influence upon Rhode Island society in James, *John Clarke and His Legacies.*

2. Howard S. Miller, *The Legal Foundations of American Philanthropy, 1776–1844* (Madison: State Historical Society of Wisconsin, 1961), 5–6, 47–48.

3. McGarvie and Mensch, "Law and Religion." The synopsis of the Muhlenberg matter is drawn from the development and interpretation of the Muhlenberg church, its legal status, and its mission in Leonard R. Riforgiato, *Missionary of Moderation: Henry Melchior Muhlenberg and the Lutheran Church in English America* (Lewisburg, PA: Bucknell University Press, 1980).

4. John Webb Pratt, *Religion, Politics and Diversity: The Church-State Theme in New York History* (Ithaca: Cornell University Press, 1967), 3–7; John F. Wilson, ed., *The Colonial and Early National Periods,* vol. 1 of *Church and State in America: A Bibliographical Guide* (New York: Greenwood Press, 1986), 10 (1638); see also George L. Smith, *Religion and Trade in New Netherland: Dutch Origins and American Development* (Ithaca: Cornell University Press, 1973); Pratt, *Religion, Politics, and Diversity,* 11 (quote from 1640).

5. Wilson, *Colonial and Early National Periods,* 10–11 (quotation); Pratt, *Religion, Politics, and Diversity,* 20.

6. Elizabeth Mensch, "Religion, Revival, and the Ruling Class: A Critical History of Trinity Church," *Buffalo Law Review* 36.3 (Fall 1987): 427-572; Michael Kammen, *Colonial New York: A History* (New York: Oxford University Press, 1975).

7. Eban Moglen, "Settling the Law: Legal Development in Provincial New York" (Ph.D. dissertation, Yale University, New Haven, 1992); Levy, *Constitutional Opinions,* 153 (quotation). The Articles of Capitulation agreed to at the time of the Dutch surrender provide at article 8 that the "Dutch here shall enjoy the liberty of their consciences in Divine Worship and church discipline."

8. Both Levy and Pratt cite this language: Levy, *Constitutional Opinions,* 153; Pratt, *Religion, Politics, and Diversity,* 34.

9. Levy, *Constitutional Opinions,* 153; see also Pratt, *Religion, Politics, and Diversity,* 26, 34. The assembly enactment provided that "no congregation shall be disturbed in their private meetings in the time of prayer, preaching, or other divine service. Nor shall any person be molested, fined, or Imprisoned for differing in Judgment in matters of Religion who profess Christianity" (Mensch, "Religion, Revival, and the Ruling Class," 438–39). Pratt, *Religion, Politics, and Diversity,* 36–49; Ahlstrom, *Religious History,* 204, 215–16; Levy, *Constitutional Opinions,* 153–54.

10. Edwin G. Burrows and Mike Wallace, *Gotham: A History of New York City to 1898* (New York: Oxford University Press, 1999), 91–102. Maryland responded similarly to its government's delay in recognizing the new monarchs (see also Carr and Jordan, *Maryland's Revolution*).

11. Ibid., 103–4.

12. Mensch, "Religion, Revival, and the Ruling Class," is an excellent history of Trinity Church; Botein, *Early American Law and Society,* 19.

13. Pratt, *Religion, Politics, and Diversity,* 159–60; the Rev. William Berrian, *An Historical Sketch of Trinity Church, New York* (New York: T & J Swords, 1847), 86, Pointer, *Protestant Pluralism,* 14, 53–54; E. Clowes Chorley, "The Beginnings of the Church in the Province of New York," *Historical Magazine of the Protestant Episcopal Church* 13 (March 1944): 5–25.

14. Berrian, *Trinity Church,* 34 (quotation). The SPG and Trinity Church together founded the Trinity Church School, sharing the cost of the teachers's salary. In 1748 Trinity Church began work on a "Charity School" to both educate and clothe poor children. Concerts were held to raise money for the project. Ibid., 69, 50, 57, 90–97. See also the *Weekly Post* of October 21, 1754, p. 131; Finegan, *Free Schools,* 19. In 1762 there were ten Anglican schools in New York, two Dutch schools, one French and one Hebrew school. In the early 1700s Trinity Church in New York City had undertaken substantial efforts to educate, feed, and clothe "the poor children of this place . . . as objects worthy of charity." Berrian, *Trinity Church,* 50, 57. Yet efforts by this wealthy church dwarf those of other Anglican churches in the state.

15. *A Narrative of a New and Unusual American Imprisonment of Two Presbyterian Ministers: And Prosecution of Mr. Francis Makemie, One of Them, for Preaching One Sermon at the City of New York, Written by a Learner of Law, and Lover of Liberty* (London, 1707), at Episcopal Church Library, New York; Pointer, *Protestant Pluralism,* 54.

16. Burrows and Wallace, *Gotham,* 124–25.

17. Journal of Madam Sarah Kemble Knight, quoted in Klein, "New York in the American Colonies," in Irwin H. Polishook and Jacob Judd, eds., *Aspects of Early New York Society and Politics* (Tarrytown, NY: Sleepy Hollow Restoration, 1974), 20; Pointer, *Protestant Pluralism,* 54–55.

18. Burrows and Wallace, *Gotham*, 141.

19. Ibid., 140–43.

20. Ibid., 145–46.

21. Jordan D. Fiore "Jonathan Swift and the American Episcopate," *William and Mary Quarterly*, 3rd ser., no. 11 (July 1954): 425–33.

22. Pratt, *Religion, Politics, and Diversity*, 67–71. Milton M. Klein, ed., *The Independent Reflector on Weekly Essays on Sundry important Subjects More particularly adapted to the Province of New York, by William Livingston and others* (Cambridge: Belknap Press of Harvard University Press, 1963), 173 ("liberal education"), 202 ("Divinity"), 195 ("Should the college"), 204 ("Nursery").

23. Burrows and Wallace, *Gotham*, 181.

24. Good summaries of the role of Trinity Church in the formation of King's College and the discontent it caused can be found in Levy, *Constitutional Opinions*, 154–55; Pointer, *Protestant Pluralism*, 56–66; Edward Countryman, *A People in Revolution: The American Revolution and Political Society in New York, 1760–1790* (Baltimore: Johns Hopkins University Press, 1981), 87–88. See also David C. Humphrey, *From King's College to Columbia, 1746–1800* (New York: Columbia University Press, 1976).

25. Pointer, *Protestant Pluralism*, 64.

26. Burrows and Wallace, *Gotham*, 208–9 (208).

27. Klein, "New York in the American Colonies," 16, 65–69; Pratt, *Religion, Politics, and Diversity*, 90; Countryman, *A People in Revolution*, 179–81, 186.

28. Burrows and Wallace, *Gotham*, 213, 220, 221, 227, 229.

29. Pointer, *Protestant Pluralism*, 82; Thorpe, *Federal and State Constitutions*, 5:2636–37.

30. Pratt, *Religion, Politics, and Diversity*, 114–15 (Livingston); Thorpe, *Federal and State Constitutions*, 5:2636. See also Stokes and Pfeffer, *Church and State*, 72–73.

31. Pratt, *Religion, Politics, and Diversity*, 54, 99.

32. Thorpe, *Federal and State Constitutions*, 5:2636.

33. Mensch, "Religion, Revival, and the Ruling Class," 472.

34. Ibid.

35. The story of this case and all quotations are taken from *Rutgers v. Waddington*, Judge J. Doane, August 27, 1784, in Richard B. Morris, ed., *Select Cases of the Mayor's Court of New York City, 1674–1784* (Washington, DC: American Historical Association, 1935), 302–26. The case is also published in Julius Goebel, *The Law Practice of Alexander Hamilton: Documents and Commentary* (New York: Columbia University Press, 1964), 1:392–419.

36. Mensch, "Religion, Revival and the Ruling Class" (quotation, 476).

37. Pratt, *Religion, Politics, and Diversity*, 100.

38. *Laws of the State of New York, 1777-1801* (Albany, 1886–1887), 1:647–49 (647).

39. Ibid., 1:661–62 (661).

40. Ibid., 1:613–18 (613).

41. Ibid., 1:637. This law was repealed in 1801 by Chapter 113 of the Laws of the State of New York.

42. Burrows and Wallace, *Gotham*, 238; *Laws of . . . New York*, 1:686–90.

43. Burrows and Wallace, *Gotham*, 274. Robert Wiebe has suggested that the differences between Hamilton and Jefferson were over means, not ends. *Opening of American Society*, xiii.

44. Dutch Reformed General Body quoted in Pointer, *Protestant Pluralism*, 89; Lewis quoted in Richard W. Pointer, "Religious Life in New York during the Revolutionary War," *New York History* 66.4 (October 1985): 357–73 (362).

45. Matthews, *New Society,* 16 (lawyer); Abíl Abbott, "A Discourse Delivered at North Coventry, July 4, 1799" (Hartford, CT, 1799), 8.

46. Christine Stansell, *City of Women: Sex and Class in New York, 1789–1860* (New York: A. A. Knopf, 1986), 14–15; Linda K. Kerber, *Women of the Republic: Intellect and Ideology in Revolutionary America* (New York: W. W. Norton, 1980).

47. Stansell conversely argues in *City of Women* that liberal republicanism subjugated women. James Fordyce, *Sermons to Young Women,* 2 vols. (London: T. Cadell and J. Dodsley, 1786), quoted excerpts from sermons nos. 9, 10 (2:74–75, 116–17).

48. Curtis D. Johnson, *Islands of Holiness: Rural Religion in Upstate New York, 1790–1860* (Ithaca: Cornell University Press, 1989), 106.

49. Johnson, *Islands of Holiness,* 24–25; Abraham Beach, "A Thanksgiving Discourse," delivered at Trinity Church, New York, 1784 (Episcopal Library), 38.

50. An Address to the Members of the Protestant Episcopal Church in the United States of America, New York, 1792 (New York Historical Society). New York's pastors were not alone in drawing this distinction. The Rev. Samuel Wales preached on May 12, 1785, that "security in happiness is not the lot of humanity" and "the consequences of outward prosperity have been more often fatal to the Christian cause than those of adversity" (Sandoz, *Political Sermons,* 1:839–63 [840, 842]).

51. *Colonial Laws of New York, 1773,* vol. 5, ch. 1600, cited in Branscombe, *Courts and Poor Laws,* 13–14.

52. Branscombe, *Courts and Poor Laws,* 59–60.

53. Stansell, *City of Women,* 4; Burrows and Wallace, *Gotham,* 333.

54. Burrows and Wallace, *Gotham,* 21. See also Benjamin Joseph Klebaner, *Public Poor Relief in America, 1790–1860* (New York: Arno Press, 1976).

55. Johnson, *Islands of Holiness,* 15; Pratt, *Religion, Politics, and Diversity,* 206.

56. Nathaniel Emmons quoted in Griffin, *Their Brothers' Keepers,* 7, 37.

57. Berrian, *Trinity Church,* 181–82. A traveler to the city in 1794 confirms that the fundraising at church services was intended to support the needy of the congregation, the charity school, and maintenance of the church building and its minister. Journal entry, Sept. 28, 1794, in William Strickland, *Journal of a Tour in the United States of America, 1794–1795* (New York Historical Society, 1971), 63.

58. In 1702 the colonial legislature passed a law "for the encouragement of a grammar free school in the city of New York." The school opened in 1704 but its charter was not renewed in 1707. After that time, New Yorkers depended upon church charity schools and private tuition academies. Finegan, *Free Schools,* 7, 22.

59. "Committee Report to Board of Regents of University of New York," ibid., 25–26.

60. Cubberly, *Readings,* 114–17.

61. Chapter 242 of the Laws of New York, June 19, 1813, in Finegan, *Free Schools,* 34.

62. Edd Doerr, *The Conspiracy that Failed: The Inside Story of the Campaign to Scuttle Church-State Separation in New York* (Washington, DC: Americans United for Separation of Church and State, 1968), 18–19 (quotation); Pratt, *Religion, Politics, and Diversity,* 167; "Report of the Commissioners Appointed by the Governor of New York," in Finegan, *Free Schools,* 36–43.

63. "Reasons of the Trustees of the Public School Society for Their Remonstrances Against the petition of the Roman Catholic Benevolent Society" (New York: Mahlon Day, 1831; now in New York Historical Society), 6.

64. In re: "The Commissioners of the Common Schools of the Town of Windham," April 13, 1835, *Decisions of the Superintendent of the Common Schools of the State of New York* (Albany: Croswell, Van Benthuysen, and Burt, 1827), 231.

65. "Reasons of the Trustees," 4.

66. Ibid., 2.

67. Ibid., 2–3, 6.

68. Convention minutes from October 5, 1785, in William Stevens Perry, ed., *Journals of the General Conventions of the Protestant Episcopal Church in the United States, 1785–1835*, 2 vols. (Claremont, NH: Claremont Manufacturing Company, 1874), 1:23–24; Pointer, *Protestant Pluralism*, 137–38 (petition); William Linn, pastor of the Dutch Reformed Church in New York City, "The Blessings of America," sermon of July 4, 1798 (New York Historical Society), 23–24.

69. Pratt, *Religion, Politics, and Diversity*, 122–23, 136; Charles Nisbet to Charles Wallace, October 31, 1797, Nisbet Correspondence, New York Public Library, Manuscripts Collection, New York.

70. Pointer, *Protestant Puritanism*, 138–39.

71. See for example, Perry, *General Conventions of the Episcopal Church*, 1:23, 279.

72. Johnson, *Shopkeeper's Millenium*, 3 ("foreordained"); Perry, *General Conventions of the Episcopal Church*, 1:321; Alexander McLeod, *Messiah, Governor of the Nations of the Earth*, sermon preached at the Reformed Presbyterian Church in New York City (New York: T & J Swords, 1803), 8; Alexander Proudfit, "An Address to the Rising Generation as a New Year's Gift for January 1, 1816" (New York Historical Society), 15.

73. See McLeod, *Messiah*, 15, where he asserted of God: "Not a motion or change in the physical or moral world which he did not forsee, and to which he did not give a place in his eternal arrangements." John M. Mason, "A Funeral Oration on the Death of General Washington," Brick Presbyterian Church, New York, February 22, 1800 (now in the Presbyterian Historical Society Library, Philadelphia), n.p.

74. "Memorial to the General Conference of the Methodist Episcopal Church by the New York Methodist Conference," 1808, in *Journals of the General Conference of the Methodist Episcopal Church, 1808*, 77.

75. John M. Mason, "A Voice of Warning to Christians on the Ensuing Election of a President of the United States" (now in the Presbyterian Historical Society Library, Philadelphia), n.p.

76. McLeod, *Messiah*, 33–34.

77. Jefferson, "Notes on the State of Virginia, Query 18," in *Writings* (ed. Bergh), 2:220.

78. In "A Voice of Warning," Mason writes: "Fellow Christians, —a crisis of no common magnitude awaits our country. The approaching election of a President is to decide a question not merely of preference to an eminent individual, or particular views of policy, but, what is infinitely more, of national regard or disregard to the religion of Jesus Christ."

79. McLeod, *Messiah*, 25.

80. "Minutes of the General Assembly of the Presbyterian Church in the United States of America, Philadelphia" (N.d. [1807]; Presbyterian Historical Society Library, Philadelphia), 1:485.

81. See Richard Twomey, "Jacobins and Jeffersonians: Anglo-American Radical Ideology, 1790–1810," in *The Origins of Anglo-American Radicalism,* ed. Margaret Jacob and James Jacob (London and Boston: Allen and Unwin, 1984), 284–99; Appleby, *Capitalism and a New Social Order.*

82. Johnson, *Shopkeeper's Millenium*; Mary Ryan, *Cradle of the Middle Class: The Family in Oneida County, New York, 1790–1865* (New York: Cambridge University Press, 1983); James Lazerow, "Religion and the New England Mill Girl: A New Perspective on an Old Theme," *New England Quarterly* 60.3 (September 1987): 429–53.

83. *People v. Melvin*, 2 Wheel. Cr. Cas. 262 (1810). See also Tomlins, *Law, Labor, and Ideology*, 138–42.

84. Johnson, *Shopkeeper's Millenium*, 84–85 ("free spirit"); *Working Man's Advocate*, October 30, 1833, cited in Schlesinger *Age of Jackson*, 138–39.

85. Joel Barlow, *Advice to the Privileged Orders in the Several States of Europe: Resulting from the Necessity and Propriety of a General Resolution in the Principle of Government* (Ithaca: Cornell University Press, 1956), 24–25. He added, "The existence of any kind of liberty is incompatible with the existence of any kind of church. By liberty I mean the enjoyment of equal rights, and by church I mean any mode of worship declared to be national or declared to have any preference in the eye of the law" (ibid., 28).

86. Wood, *Radicalism*, 331.

87. Mason, "A Voice of Warning," 570; John Henry Hobart, *The Corruptions of the Church of Rome Contrasted with certain Protestant Errors in a Charge, delivered to the Clergy of the Protestant Episcopal Church in the State of New York, Trinity Church, October 1817* (New York: T & J Swords, 1818), 12–13; Benjamin Moore, "The Charge of the Right Rev. Benjamin Moore, Bishop of the Protestant Episcopal Church in the State of New York, Delivered to the Convention of Said Church on the 5th day of October, 1803" (New York, 1803), 4.

88. David Mouton and Mordecai Myers, "Report of the Select Committee of the New York State Assembly on the Several Memorials Against Chaplains to the Legislature" (New York, 1832; now in the New York Historical Society).

89. Johnson, *Islands of Holiness*, 22–45.

90. Ibid., 22–23.

91. Ibid., 23, 33–34, 25 (quotation).

92. Johnson, *Shopkeeper's Millenium*, 80 (quotation), 84–85.

6—Southern Republicanism and Constitutional-Era Disestablishment

1. A. F. Thornton Miller, *Juries and Judges versus the Law: Virginia's Provincial Legal Perspective, 1783–1828*, In the Constitutionalism and Democracy series, ed. Kermit Hall and David O'Brien (Charlottesville: University Press of Virginia, 1994); Erskine Clarke, *Our Southern Zion: A History of Calvinism in the South Carolina Low Country, 1690–1990* (Tuscaloosa: University of Alabama Press, 1996), 29–38; Jon Butler, *The Huguenots in America* (Cambridge: Harvard University Press, 1983); Robert A. Baker and Paul J. Craven Jr., *Adventure in Faith: The First 300 Years of the First Baptist Church, Charleston, S. Carolina* (Nashville, TN: Broadman Press, 1982), 68; Timothy S. Huebner, *The Southern Judicial Tradition: State Judges and Sectional Distinctiveness, 1790–1890* (Athens: University of Georgia Press, 1999), 5. Judge Roane quoted in *Curries' Administrators v. Mutual Assurance Society*, 14 Va. 315, 347–48 (1809), in Huebner, *Southern Judiciary*, 5–6.

2. Clarke, *Our Southern Zion*, 29–38; Butler, *Huguenots in America*; Baker and Craven, *Adventure in Faith*, 68.

3. B. James Ramage, "Local Government and Free Schools in South Carolina," in *Local Institutions*, ed. Herbert B. Adams (Baltimore: Johns Hopkins University Press, 1883), 12:9.

4. Clarke, *Southern Zion*, 44–46 (46). Although the Lords Proprietor did not sign the new bill until 1707, the date of the law was made retroactive to November 30, 1706.

5. Ahlstrom, *Religious History*, 196–99. See also Charles S. Bolton, *Southern Anglicanism: The Church of England in Colonial South Carolina* (Westport, CT: Greenwood Press, 1982). Baker and Craven, *Adventure in Faith*, 85–86; Littell, *From State Church to Pluralism*, 14.

6. Edward McCrady, *A Sketch of St. Philip's Church, Charleston, South Carolina, from the Establishment of the Church of England under the Royal Charter of 1665 to the Present Time* (Charleston, SC: Lucas and Richardson, 1897; now in South Carolina Historical Society, Charleston), 12.

7. Anne King Gregorie, *Christ Church, 1706–1759: A Plantation Parish of South Carolina Establishment* (Charleston, SC: Dalcho Historical Society, 1961), 5; Ramage, "Local Government," 10 ("business"); the Rev. Frederick Dalcho, *An Historical Account of the Protestant Episcopal Church in South Carolina* (Charleston, SC: E. Thayer, 1820), 53 (oath).

8. McCrady, *Sketch of St. Philip's Church*, 17–18, 21–23.

9. Godbeer, *Sexual Revolution*, 121–22.

10. The first church school, with a limited enrollment, was started in 1711. Mc-Crady, *Sketch of St. Philip's Church*, 10.

11. John Furman Thomason, *The Foundation of the Public Schools of South Carolina* (Columbia, SC: The State Company, 1925), 56. In 1710 and 1712, the colonial assembly created a public school system, which failed, however, through lack of funds. Legislative funding was provided in 1722 but the funding was little used. In the 1740s and 1750s, editorials to *The Gazette (Charleston)* called for developing public schools and libraries to encourage "a gentlemanly deportment" in the young men of the city. No action was taken. Ibid., 4–5, 59.

12. Godbeer, *Sexual Revolution*, 121–22, 129 (Woodson), 136 (Johnston, Le Jau), 137.

13. Clarke, *Southern Zion*, 40, 47.

14. Albert J. Raboteau, *Slave Religion: The "Invisible Institution" in the Antebellum South* (New York: Oxford University Press, 1978), 92. See also Eugene D. Genovese, *Roll Jordan Roll: The World the Slaves Made* (New York: Random House, 1976); John W. Blassingame, *The Slave Community: Plantation Life in the Antebellum South* (New York: Oxford University Press, 1979); Mechal Sobel, *The World They Made Together: Black and White Values in Eighteenth-Century Virginia* (Princeton, NJ: Princeton University Press, 1987); William D. Pierson, *Black Legacy: America's Hidden Heritage* (Amherst: University of Massachusetts Press, 1993). Alexander Garden quoted in Clarke, *Southern Zion*, 69–70.

15. Baker and Craven, *Adventure in Faith*, 112; Ahlstrom, *Religious History*, 269–86. McCrady, *Sketch of St. Philip's Church*, asserts that Hart assumed his position in 1749. The Hart Family Papers, archived in the Manuscript Room of the South Caroliniana Library in Columbia, establish the date as 1752.

16. Oliver Hart's diary, entry undated but for year 1754, Oliver Hart Papers, South Caroliniana Library, Manuscripts Collection, Columbia, SC ("Revival"); Oliver Hart, sermon of June 5, 1963, First Baptist Church of Charleston, SC, Hart Papers (quotations). The Circular Church on Meeting Street in Charleston, religious home of William Tennant III, was arguably a Congregational church. Yet, after the Adopting Act of 1729, the distinction between many Congregationalists and Presbyterians was largely muted. Tennant himself was raised and ordained a Presbyterian. He oversaw the Circular Church as it became a truly ecumenical Christian body. When Hart was denied permission to speak in another Charleston church in 1780, he wrote, "Bigotry seems to be a Part of some Men's Religion. What they may gain by it I cannot tell" (Hart diary, August 18, 1780).

17. William Tennant, letters to the *South Carolina Gazette and Country Journal*, 1774, in "The Writings of Reverend William Tennant, 1740–1777," ed. Newton B. Jones, *South Carolina Historical Magazine* 61.3 (1960): 129–45 (129); William Tennant's remarks to the Assembly, September 11, 1776, in "Writings," *South Carolina Historical Magazine* 61.4 (1960): 189–209 (201).

18. Hart wrote to "My dear brother," on July 5, 1788:

the Providence of God hath appeared evidently in our Favour . . . With joy I often look forward and contemplate the rising glories of this continent; its inhabitants nourished by the most free, generous, and perfect form of government ever modeled; and cherished by the best of Rulers, chosen by ourselves, whose interests and inclination will conspire to make the ruled happy. When Peace, like the swelling tide shall flow over the mountains and cover the whole land. When Religion, freed from its Shackles, Learning, and Virtue, encouraged and prompted, shall spread far and wide. Wisdom and Knowledge shall increase, and every peasant be qualified for a Senator. Every man shall sit down peaceably under his own Vine and his own Figtree; — and the Trade, Favour, and Protection of America will be courted by all nations under Heaven. This is the Prize for which we are contending. (Hart Papers)

19. David Ramsay, "An Oration on the Advantages of American Independence," delivered in Charleston, July 4, 1778, in Clarke, *Southern Zion*, 89; Elizabeth Mensch, "Religion, Revival, and the Ruling Class", 481.

20. Walter Edgar, *South Carolina: A History* (Columbia: University of South Carolina Press, 1998), 226–27.

21. Hart to Henry Laurens, March 19, 1776, Hart Papers; Clarke, *Southern Zion*, 132.

22. Tennant, "Writings," *South Carolina Historical Magazine* 61.4 (1960), 194–95 (all quotations).

23. Ibid., 196–97.

24. Edgar, *South Carolina*, 229–30.

25. Hart to Richard Furman, February 1777, Hart Papers; Baker and Craven, *Adventure in Faith*, 169.

26. Constitution of South Carolina, article 28; see also Thorpe, *Federal and State Constitutions*, 2:801, 6:3251, 3258–59. Gregorie, *Christ Church*, 55–57.

27. Gadsden quoted in Edgar, *South Carolina*, 230.

28. Hart diary, March 19, 1777, Hart Papers; Hart to Joseph Hart, March 24, 1778. He also expressed a desire to compare the language in the South Carolina Constitution to that of Pennsylvania.

29. George C. Rogers, *Evolution of a Federalist: William Loughton Smith of Charleston, 1758–1812* (Columbia: University of South Carolina Press, 1962), 130; Stokes and Pfeffer, *Church and State*, 78–79 (constitution); Thomason, *Foundation of Public Schools*, 68–69.

30. Hay, *Freedom's Jubilee*, 172–73.

31. Smith quoted in Fred J. Hood, *Reformed America: The Middle and Southern States, 1783–1837* (Tuscaloosa: University of Alabama Press, 1980), 32–33.

32. Correspondence of Attorney Thomas Waites and his legal associate on behalf of his client, Claremont Episcopal Church, May 15, 17, 1825, Thomas Waites Papers, South Caroliniana Library, Manuscript Collection, Columbia, box 1, personal papers.

33. Eugene D. Genovese and Elizabeth Fox-Genovese, "The Social Thought of Antebellum Social Theologians," in *Looking South: Chapters in the Story of an American Region*, ed. Winfred B. Moore Jr. and Joseph F. Tripp (New York: Greenwood Press, 1989), 32; Hood, *Reformed America*, 27–29.

34. Heyrman, *Southern Cross*, 321–22n70; the Rev. Frederick Dalcho, "An Address" on the need for Christian education, ca. 1795 (South Carolina Historical Society, Charleston).

35. Alan Gallay, "The Great Sellout: George Whitefield on Slavery," in Moore and Tripp, *Looking South*, 22.

36. Edgar, *South Carolina: A History*, 254. One example of the growing power of the "yahoos" is the relocation of the capital to Columbia in 1786. Editorial, *Gazette of the State of South Carolina*, September 7, 1786 (Library Society of Charleston); *Journals of the House of Representatives (South Carolina) 1789–1790*, ed. Michael E. Stevens (Columbia: University of South Carolina Press, 1984), xv.

37. "Extract of a letter from an American gentleman in France," dated October 14, 1789, *City Gazette (Charleston, South Carolina)*, January 5, 1790.

38. Pierce quoted in Genovese and Fox-Genovese, "Antebellum Southern Theologians," 31–40 (32); Reese, "Essay"; Baker and Craven, *Adventure in Faith*, 206 (Furman).

39. "Scrupulosus" to the *City Gazette (Charleston, South Carolina)*, March 20, 1789, 2.

40. The *City Gazette or the Daily Advertiser (Charleston, South Carolina)*, Saturday, February 21, 1789, 2 (quotation); "Report and Resolution No. 109," *Journals of the House of Representatives*, in *City Gazette or the Daily Advertiser*, April 24, 1789, 4.

41. Letter titled "The Reflector No. 1," addressed to the Printers of the *City Gazette*, in *City Gazette (Charleston, South Carolina)*, April 5, 1790, 2; Letter titled "The Reflector No. 2," addressed to the Printers of the *City Gazette*, April 9, 1790, 2.

42. Edmund S. Morgan, *American Slavery, American Freedom: The Ordeal of Colonial Virginia* (New York: W. W. Norton, 1975). An excellent updating of Morgan's thesis, including an analysis of gender as a historical determinant of the ideological construction is Stephanie McCurry, *Masters of Small Worlds: Yeoman Households, Gender Relations, and the Political Culture of the Antebellum South Carolina Low Country* (New York: Oxford University Press, 1995).

43. The 1790 Constitution of South Carolina can be found in Thorpe, *Federal and State Constitutions*, 6:3664. The first publication of the new constitution appeared in three installments in the *City Gazette (Charleston, South Carolina)*, from Monday through Wednesday, June 7–9, 1790. See also Francis Marion Hutson, ed., *Journal of the Constitutional Convention of South Carolina* (Columbia: Historical Commission of South Carolina, 1946), May 10–June 3, 1790; James Lowell Underwood, *The Constitution of South Carolina*, 2 vols. (Columbia: University of South Carolina Press, 1989); Fletcher M. Green, *Constitutional Development in the South Atlantic States, 1776–1860: A Study in the Evolution of Democracy* (New York: De Capo Press, 1971).

44. Act No. 1500 of 1791, in South Carolina Statutes at Large, 5:175; Act No. 2344 of 1824, in South Carolina Statutes at Large, 6:241, section 3.

45. For development of this point, see Gross, "Giving in America."

46. Thomason, *Foundation of Public Schools*, 111–16, 67.

47. Ibid., 68, 6, 128–31.

48. Frederick Dalcho, "The Evidence from Prophecy for the Truth of Christianity and the Divinity of Christ In a Course of Catechetical Instruction" (undated, but

published prior to 1819; now in South Carolina Historical Society, Charleston). See also Gregorie, *Christ Church, 1706–1859*, 70. Frederick Dalcho, "An Address delivered in St. Michael's Church before the Charleston Protestant Episcopal Sunday School Society at their Seventh Anniversary, May 16, 1826" (South Carolina Historical Society, Charleston); Thomason, *Foundation of Public Schools*, 72 (Synod); Clarke, *Our Southern Zion*, 116–19 (Charter).

7—The *Dartmouth College* Case

1. McLoughlin, *New England Dissent*, 2:835–38; William H. Marnell, *The First Amendment: The History of Religious Freedom in America* (Garden City, NY: Doubleday, 1964), 129.

2. McLoughlin, *New England Dissent*, 2:838–41.

3. "An Act for Regulating Townships, Choice of town Officers, and Settling forth Their Power," *Laws of New Hampshire* (1719), 22:342.

4. McLoughlin, *New England Dissent*, 2:842–43. By 1795 there were forty-one Baptist churches in New Hampshire.

5. Ibid., 834–44. See also Johnson, *Islands of Holiness*, 17.

6. Thorpe, *Federal and State Constitutions*, 4:2471–72.

7. McLoughlin, *New England Dissent*, 2:845.

8. Ibid., 849.

9. Ibid., 851–54.

10. *Muzzy v. Wilkins* 1 NH (Smith), 1, 13–14 (1803).

11. For information on the debates over the teaching of morality and the form it would take, see Storing, *Complete Anti-Federalist*, 5:50, 125, 128, 260–67; Jurgen Herbst, *From Crisis to Crisis: American College Government, 1636–1819* (Cambridge: Harvard University Press, 1982), 242; Farrand, *Federal Convention of 1787*, 3:362; Storing, *What the Anti-Federalists Were For*, 23; Adams, "Observations on the Reconstruction of Government," 4:259; "Washington's Speech to Both Houses of Houses of Congress, January 8, 1790," in *Writings of George Washington*, ed. John C. Fitzpatrick (Washington, DC: Government Printing Office, 1931–1944; hereinafter cited as *Writings*), 30:494; Isaac Kramnick, "The Great National Discussions: The Discourse of Politics in 1787," in *The New American Nation, 1775–1820*, ed. Peter S. Onuf (New York: Garland Publishers, 1991), 5:384; Benjamin Rush, "A Plan," in Rudolph, *Essays on Education*, 141; Frederick Rudolph, *The American College and University: A History* (New York: Random House, 1962), 42. For more of Washington's sentiments on a national university, and on education in general, see "Farewell Address," September 17, 1796 (40:214–38), Washington to John Armstrong, April 25, 1788 (29:464), to George Steptoe Washington, March 23, 1789 (30:245), to Alexander Hamilton, September 1, 1796 (35:198), to the Commissioners of the Federal District, January 28, 1795, November 27, 1796 (34:106, 35:146), to John Adams, November 15, 1794 (34:22); all in Washington, *Writings*. See generally Wesley, *University of the United States*, which provides more general information on the proposed national university. See Jefferson to Madison, December 20, 1787, in Jefferson, *Papers*, 12:442 (regarding Jefferson). Jefferson's support for governmental action in support of education is an isolated example of his departure from an ideological preference for minimalist government. See John Lauritz Larson, "Jefferson's Union and the Problem of Internal Improvements," in *Jeffersonian Legacies*, ed. Peter S. Onuf (Charlottesville: University Press of Virginia, 1993), regarding Jefferson's conception of the role of government in addressing public works.

12. Herbst, *From Crisis to Crisis*, 177–78.

13. Ibid., also 182, 196–98; Edwards and Richey, *American Social Order*, 252; George B. Wood, *Early History of the University of Pennsylvania from its Origin to the Year 1827* (Philadelphia: J. B. Lippincott, 1896), 71–117; Edward Potts Cheyney, *History of the University of Pennsylvania, 1740–1940* (Philadelphia: University of Pennsylvania Press, 1940), 117–69.

14. John Whitehead, *The Separation of College and State* (New Haven: Yale University Press, 1973), 21.

15. Ibid., 24–31; Herbst, *From Crisis to Crisis*, 167–69; McLoughlin, *New England Dissent*, 2:891.

16. Jefferson, "Autobiography," 1149–51. See also "A Bill for the More General Diffusion of Knowledge," ibid., 1048 (quotation).

17. Herbst, *From Crisis to Crisis*, 163–64, 185, 212 (quotation).

18. Dumas Malone, *Jefferson and His Time: Jefferson the President, First Term, 1801–1805*, 6 vols. (Boston: Little, Brown, 1981), 4:235, 282, 365–425.

19. Balmer and Fitzmier, *The Presbyterians*, 49–51; Prince, *New Jersey's Jeffersonian Republicans*.

20. Matthews, *New Society*, 27.

21. Edward C. Elliott and M. M. Chambers, eds., *Charters and Basic Laws of Selected American Universities and Colleges* (New York: Carnegie Foundation for the Advancement of Teaching, 1934), 587 (quotation); Whitehead, *College and State*, 36–45; Greene, "Development of Religious Liberty," 379; Herbst, *From Crisis to Crisis*, 151–54, 162, 175.

22. Ezra Stiles, "Plan for a University," in *The Literary Journal of Ezra Stiles* (New York: Scribners, 1801), 163.

23. See Herbst, *From Crisis to Crisis*; Mead, *Nathaniel Taylor*; Whitehead, *College and State*.

24. For an excellent limited biography on Dwight, see Wells, *The Devil and Dr. Dwight*. See also Kenneth Silverman, *Timothy Dwight* (New York: Twayne, 1969); Stephen Berk, *Calvinism versus Democracy: Timothy Dwight and the Origins of American Evangelical Orthodoxy* (Hamden, CT: Archon Books, 1974); also John R. Fitzmier, *New England's Moral Legislator: Timothy Dwight, 1752–1817* (Indianapolis: Indiana University Press, 1998).

25. Wright, *Transformation of Charity*, 81; Mead, *Nathaniel Taylor*, 22–29, 43–53, 142–60; Bruce Kucklick, "Jonathan Edwards and American Philosophy," in *Jonathan Edwards and the American Experience*, ed. Nathan Hatch and Harry Stout (New York: Oxford University Press, 1988), 246–59; Winthrop S. Hudson and John Corrigan, *Religion in America: An American Historical Account of the Development of American Religious Life* (Upper Saddle River, NJ: Prentice Hall, 1992), 147–60. Edmund S. Morgan argues, however, that Yale was not in a state of irrelegion and infidelity when Dwight arrived there in 1795. See Edmund S. Morgan, "Ezra Stiles and Timothy Dwight," in *Proceedings of the Massachusetts Historical Society, 1960–1963* (Boston: Massachusetts Historical Society, 1963), 72:100–117.

26. Whitehead, *College and State*, 16–20; Wright, *Transformation of Charity*, 81.

27. Herbst, *From Crisis to Crisis*, 212–14; Charles C. Calhoun, *A Small College in Maine: Two Hundred Years of Bowdoin* (Brunswick, ME: Bowdoin College, 1993), 5–31; Balmer and Fitzmier, *The Presbyterians*, 50.

28. Herbst, *From Crisis to Crisis*, 213, citing "Harvard College, No. 1," and *Boston Patriot and Daily Chronicler*, October 2, 1819, 2, and "Harvard College, No. 3," *Boston Patriot and Daily Chronicler*, October 26, 1819, 1.

29. Ibid., 207.

30. Ibid., 222–24 (224).

31. Ibid., 207–8.

32. Ibid., 193–94.

33. Ibid., 170, 201–9.

34. James Axtell, "Dr. Wheelock's Little Red School House," in *The European and the Indian: Essays in the Ethnohistory of Colonial North America* (New York: Oxford University Press, 1981), 87–109 (91).

35. *Trustees of Dartmouth College v. Woodward,* 17 U.S. (4 Wheat) 518, 522 (1819); (hereinafter *Dartmouth*).

36. Ibid., 524.

37. Ibid., 536.

38. Whitehead, *College and State,* 34–36; Albert J. Beveridge, *The Building of the Nation,* vol. 4 of Albert J. Beveridge, *The Life of John Marshall,* 4 vols. (1919; Baltimore: Johnson Reprint, 1980), 223; Steven J. Novak, "The College in the Dartmouth College Case: A Reinterpretation," *New England Quarterly* 47 (1974): 550, 563.

39. Novak, "Dartmouth College Case," 553–54.

40. Ibid., 552–56, 563 (quotation).

41. Ibid., 552–56, 559.

42. Hay, *Freedom's Jubilee,* 199.

43. Novak, "Dartmouth College Case," 562.

44. Ibid., 563 (quotation); Eldon C. Johnson, "The Dartmouth College Case: The Neglected Educational Meaning," *Journal of the Early Republic* 3:45, 49 (quotation).

45. McLoughlin, *New England Dissent,* 2:882–83.

46. Ibid., 891–92.

47. Ibid., 888.

48. Beveridge, *Building of the Nation,* 225–30; President Francis Brown, "Sermon Before the Ecclesiastical Convention of New Hampshire," June 3, 1818, at the Convention of Congregational and Presbyterian Ministers in the State of New Hampshire (now in the Presbyterian Historical Society Library, Philadelphia), 12.

49. McLoughlin, *New England Dissent,* 2:883.

50. Ibid., 890–91.

51. Johnson, "Dartmouth College Case," 51, 52.

52. McLoughlin, *New England Dissent,* 2:888, 895; Beveridge, *Building of the Nation,* 230 (quotation).

53. *Dartmouth,* 539.

54. Ibid., 540–44.

55. Ibid., 533, 543, 544.

56. Ibid., 540–50.

57. The action was initially brought in New Hampshire state court. A special verdict found for the defendant (Woodward) on the condition that the legislature's actions were "legal and not repugnant to the Constitution of the United States." The Superior Court found the statutory actions lawful and issued a verdict for Woodward. The sole issue on appeal to the Supreme Court was the constitutionality of the legislative action. Marshall gave the opinion of the Court in which the state court decisions were reversed. Washington wrote a separate concurrence in which Johnson and Livingston concurred. Story's separate concurrence emphasized his findings in *Terrett v. Taylor.* Duvall dissented without written opinion. The Supreme Court argument was well attended in large part because of the fame of Daniel Webster, representing the

college. A good review of the lower court trials and Webster's argument before the Supreme Court is provided by Richard Current, "The Dartmouth College Case," in *Quarrels that Have Shaped the Constitution*, ed. John A. Garraty (New York: Harper and Row, 1964), 15.

58. Brown, "Sermon," 19–20 (all quotations).

59. *The Principles and Practices of the Patriots of the Revolution Being an Appeal to Reason and Common Sense* (Philadelphia: S. Roberts, 1819; now in the New York Historical Society), unpaginated. Elsewhere in the text, the unknown author cites Jefferson for assertions that "We must now place the manufacturer by the side of the agriculturalist," and "experience has now taught me that manufactures are now as necessary to our independence as to our own comfort."

60. See Bernard Schwartz, *A History of the Supreme Court* (New York: Oxford University Press, 1993), 50–51.

61. *Fletcher v. Peck*, 10 U.S. (6 Cranch) 87 (1810).

62. Jefferson's opinion actually examining an early form of the proposed sale may be found in Jefferson, *Writings* (ed. Ford), 6:55–57. Hamilton's opinion, written March 25, 1796, is in Robert Goodloe Harper, *Case of the Georgia Sales on the Mississippi Considered with a Reference to Law Authorities and Public Acts and an Appendix Containing Certain Extracts, Records, and Officials Papers* (Philadelphia: Printed for Benjamin Davies, 1797).

63. *Fletcher v. Peck*, 10 U.S. (6 Cranch) at 133–34; Beveridge, *Building of the Nation*, 223.

64. *Terrett v. Taylor*, 13 U.S. 43, 49 (1815).

65. Ibid., 43–47. The lower court ruled in favor of the trustees. Terrett and the other overseers for the poor, the defendants in the original action, appealed. As Justice Story's reasoning differed from that of the lower court, he instructed that the circuit court decision be reformed so as to conform to the Supreme Court decision.

66. Ibid., 49–50 ("citizens"), 50–51 ("principle"), 52 ("statutes").

67. *Dartmouth*, 629–30 ("act of incorporation"), 632 (private property), 634 ("eleemosynary").

68. Ibid., 601–2 ("education"), 634.

69. Ibid., 635, 636 (emphasis added).

70. Ibid., 642.

71. *Trustees of Philadelphia Baptist Association v. Hart's Executors*, 17 U.S. (3 Wheat) 1 (1819) (hereinafter *Hart*).

72. *Dartmouth*, 637.

73. Ibid., 712.

74. Ibid., 647.

75. Novak, "Dartmouth College Case," 45; Johnson, "Dartmouth College Case," 49.

76. *Hart*, 1.

77. Miller, *Legal Foundations*, xi, 26. See also Edith L. Fish, "American Acceptance of Charitable Trusts," *Notre Dame Law Review* 28.219 (1953). See also Peter Dobkin Hall, *The Organization of American Culture, 1700–1900: Private Institutions, Elites, and the Origins of American Nationality* (New York: New York University Press, 1982).

78. *Hart* (Story concurring).

79. Miller, *Legal Foundations*, 647 (quoting *Dartmouth*).

80. Ibid., 24.

81. This viewpoint, though reached independently, is consistent with the one expressed by Professor Nelson in his analysis of Marshall's judicial decision-making. See Nelson, "The Eighteenth-Century Background," 893.

82. Miller, *Legal Foundations;* Irvin Wylie, "The Search for an American Law of Charity, 1776–1844," *Mississippi Valley Historical Review* 46 (1959): 203; Stanley Katz, "Legal Change and Legal Autonomy: Charitable Trusts in New York, 1777–1893," *Law and History Review* 3 (Spring 1985): 51–89.

83. *Inglis v. Trustees of the Sailor's Snug Harbor,* 28 U.S. (3 Pet.) 99 (1830).

84. *Vidal v. Philadelphia (Girard's Will Case),* 43 U.S. (2 How.) 127 (1844).

85. Ibid., 201.

86. For details on the legislative process, see Barry Levy, *The Establishment Clause: Religion and the First Amendment* (New York: Macmillan, 1986), 40; Marnell, *The First Amendment,* 132; McLoughlin, *New England Dissent,* 2:858.

87. Loetscher, *Facing the Enlightenment and Pietism,* ix–x.

88. Herbst, *From Crisis to Crisis,* 242 ("increase"), 219. See also Donald Tewksbury, *The Founding of American Colleges and Universities before the Civil War: With Particular Reference to the Religious Influences Bearing upon the College Movement* (New York: Bureau of Publications, Teachers College, Columbia University, 1932), 16, 28.

89. Ernst Christian Helmreich, *Religion at Bowdoin College: A History* (Brunswick, ME: The College, 1981), 1, 5.

90. Calhoun, *Small College in Maine,* 20, 31.

91. Ibid., 31.

92. Ibid., 76.

93. *Eastern Argus,* October 7, 1817, n.p.

94. "Provisions of the Act of Separation of June 19, 1819," as cited in *Allen v. McKean,* 1 Fed. Case 489, 491 (C.C.D. Me. 1833) (No. 229). The Act of Separation was incorporated into the Constitution of Maine, effective March 15, 1820.

95. Jeremiah Perley, *The Debates, Resolutions, and Other Proceedings of the Convention of the Delegates Assembled at Portland on the 11th and Continued until the 29th Day of October, 1819, for the Purpose of Forming a Constitution for the State of Maine,* ed. Charles E. Nash (printed by A. Shirley, 1820), 281.

96. Ibid., 282, 283.

97. Ibid., 278 (emphasis added), 279. The text of Mr. Shepley's substitution reads: "The legislature of the State shall have the right to grant any further powers to alter, limit, or restrain any of the powers vested in such Literary Institution, as shall be judged necessary to promote the interests thereof."

98. Ibid., 285, 282, 283.

99. Ibid., 290.

100. Ibid., 278, 279 (emphasis added).

101. Bowdoin College, *General Catalogue of Bowdoin College and the Medical School of Maine, 1784–1894: Including a Historical Sketch of the Institution During its First Century Prepared by George Thomas Little, the Librarian* (Brunswick, ME: Bowdoin College, 1894), ii–iii.

102. Ibid., iii–xix; *Allen v. McKean,* 491. A good discussion of the role of Supreme Court justices on circuit is presented in G. Edward White, "The Working Life of the Marshall Court, 1815–1835," *Virginia Law Review* 70:1 (1984). See also Newmyer, *Supreme Court Justice Joseph Story.*

103. *Allen v. McKean,* 496.

104. Ibid., 497–504.

105. Calhoun, *Small College in Maine,* 92 (both quotations).

106. Ibid., 90–92.

107. Joan Marans Dim and Nancy Murphy Cricco, *The Miracle on Washington Square: New York University* (New York: Lexington Books, 2001), 19–24.

108. This is a term used repeatedly by Sydney Mead in his writings. See generally Mead, *Lively Experiment.*

109. De Tocqueville, *Democracy in America;* see also Brown, "Emergence of Voluntary Associations," 66–88.

110. Gross, "Giving in America," n.p.

Conclusion

1. Henry Adams, *History of the United States of America during the Administrations of Thomas Jefferson and James Madison,* rev. ed. (Englewood Cliffs, NJ: Prentice-Hall, 1963).

2. Norton, *Alternative Americas.*

3. Hamburger, *Separation.*

Bibliography

Primary Sources

Unpublished Documents

"America's Deliverance and Duty." Sermon preached at First Baptist Church in Charleston, SC, July 4, 1802. South Carolina Historical Society, Charleston.

Barlow, Joel. "Advice to the Privileged Orders in the Several States of Europe: Resulting from the Necessity and Propriety of a General Resolution in the Principle of Government." Ithaca: Cornell University Press, 1956.

Bearch, Abraham. "A Thanksgiving Discourse." Delivered at Trinity Church. New York, 1784. Episcopal Church Library, New York.

Brown, President Francis. "Sermon Before the Ecclesiastical Convention of New Hampshire." At the Convention of Congregational and Presbyterian Ministers in the State of New Hampshire. Presbyterian Historical Society Library, Philadelphia.

Dalcho, Frederick. "An Address" on the need for Christian education, ca. 1795. South Carolina Historical Society, Charleston.

———. "The Evidence from Prophecy for the Truth of Christianity and the Divinity of Christ In a Course of Catechetical Instruction." Undated, but published prior to 1819. South Carolina Historical Society, Charleston.

———. "An Address delivered in St. Michael's Church before the Charleston Protestant Episcopal Sunday School Society at their Seventh Anniversary, May 16, 1826." South Carolina Historical Society, Charleston.

"Extracts from the Minutes of the General Assembly of the Presbyterian Church in the United States of America, 1819." Presbyterian Historical Society Library, Philadelphia.

Gallager, Rev. S.F. Presentation "An Oration of the Anniversary of the Orphan Establishment in Charleston, South Carolina." Delivered on October 18, 1798. South Carolina Historical Society, Charleston.

Journals of the General Conference of the Methodist Episcopal Church, 1808.

Journals of the General Conventions of the Episcopal Church. Episcopal Church Library, New York.

Journals of the General Conventions of the Protestant Episcopal Church in the United States, 1785–1835. 2 vols. Claremont, NH: Claremont Manufacturing Company, 1874.

Linn, William. "The Blessings of America." Sermon, July 4, 1798, by the pastor of the Dutch Reformed Church in New York City. New York Historical Society.

Mason, John M. "A Funeral Oration on the Death of General Washington." Brick Presbyterian Church, New York, February 22, 1800. Presbyterian Historical Society Library, Philadelphia.

————. "A Voice of Warning to Christians on the Ensuing Election of a President of the United States." Presbyterian Historical Society Library, Philadelphia.

"Minutes of the General Assembly of the Presbyterian Church in the United States of America. Philadelphia." Presbyterian Historical Society Library, Philadelphia.

Nisbet, Charles. Correspondence. New York Public Library, Manuscripts Collection, New York.

Oliver Hart Papers. South Caroliniana Library, Manuscripts Collection, Columbia, South Carolina.

Proudfit, Alexander. "An Address to the Rising Generation as a New Year's Gift for January 1, 1816." New York Historical Society.

"Reasons in support of the objection of the inhabitants of King's District and others against granting the confirmation petitioned for by the Proprietor of Westenhook," Feb. 22, 1775, in John Tabor Kempe Papers, New York Historical Society, box 5, miscellaneous.

Reed, John. Sermon of December 12, 1787, for the ordination of Rev. Kilborn Whitman, Boston. Microfiche. Presbyterian Historical Society Library, Philadelphia.

Reese, Rev. Thomas. "An Essay on the Influence of Religion." Charleston, 1788. Microfiche (88 pages) in the Presbyterian Historical Society Library, Philadelphia.

Smith, Elis. "A Discourse on Government and Religion Delivered at Gray, Maine, July 4, 1810." New York Historical Society.

Thomas Waites Papers. South Caroliniana Library, Manuscripts Collection, Columbia.

Newspapers

American Mercury (Hartford, CT)
Virginia Independent Chronicle
Boston Recorder
City Gazette (Charleston, SC)
Connecticut Courant
Eastern Argus (Portland, ME)
Gazette of the State of South Carolina
Millenial Harbinger
Newark Gazette
New Hampshire Recorder
New York Times
The Pennsylvania Magazine
The Religious Instructor (Carlisle, PA)
Weekly Post (New York)

Law

CASES AT LAW

Allen v. McKean, 1 Fed. Case 489, 491 (C.C.D. Me. 1833) (No. 229).
Baker v. Fales, 16 Mass. 487 (1821).
Barnes v. Parish of Falmouth, 6 Mass. 401 (1810).
Cantwell v. Connecticut, 310 U.S. 296 (1940).
In re: "The Commissioners of the Common Schools of the Town of Windham," April 13, 1835, *Decisions of the Superintendent of the Common Schools of the State of New York*. Albany: Croswell, Van Benthuysen, and Burt, 1827.

Curries' Administrators v. Mutual Assurance Society, 14 Va. 315 (1809).

DeJonge v. Oregon, 299 U.S. 353 (1937).

Eichelberger v. Barnitz, 1 Yeates 307 (Pa. 1793).

Fletcher v. Peck, 10 U.S. (6 Cranch) 87 (1810).

Fox v. Mackreth, 2 Brown's Cha. Cases 420 (Pa.1791).

Gitlow v. New York, 268 U.S. 652 (1925).

Inglis v. Trustees of the Sailor's Snug Harbor, 28 U.S. (3 Pet.) (1830), 99.

Marsh v. Alabama, 326 U.S. 501 (1946).

Muzzy v. Wilkins 1 NH (Smith), 1 (1803).

Near v. Minnesota, 283 U.S. 697 (1931).

People v. Melvin, 2 Wheel. Cr. Cas. 262 (1810).

Rutgers v. Waddington (N.Y. 1784).

Terrett v. Taylor, 13 U.S. 43 (1815).

Trustees of Dartmouth College v. Woodward, 17 U.S. (4 Wheat) 518 (1819).

Trustees of Philadelphia Baptist Association v. Hart's Executors, 17 U.S. (3 Wheat) 1 (1819).

Vidal v. Philadelphia (Girard's Will Case), 43 U.S. (2 How.) 127 (1844).

Walz v. Tax Commission, 397 U.S. 664 (1970).

Whitewell v. Wyer, 11 Mass. 6 (1814).

STATUTORY LAW AND GOVERNMENT PAPERS

Charters and General Laws of the Colony and Province of Massachusetts Bay. Boston, 1814.

Elliott, Edward C., and M. M. Chambers, eds. *Charters and Basic Laws of Selected American Universities and Colleges*. New York: Carnegie Foundation for the Advancement of Teaching, 1934.

Grimke, John Fauchereaud, ed. *The Public Laws of the State of South Carolina*. Philadelphia: Aitken and Son, 1790.

Jefferson, Thomas, ed. *Reports of Cases Determined in the General Court of Virginia from 1730 to 1740; and from 1768 to 1772*. 1774; reprint, Charlottesville, VA: F. Carr, 1903.

Journals of the House of Representatives. "Report and Resolution No. 109."

Kittleborough, Charles, ed. *The State Constitutions and the Federal Constitution: Organic Laws of the Territories and Other Colonial Dependencies of the United States of America*. Indianapolis: B. F. Bower, 1918.

Laws of the State of New York, 1777–1801. Albany, 1886–1887.

"The Northwest Ordinance." In *Liberty's Legacy*, ed. John C. Dann et al. Columbus: Ohio Historical Society, June 1987.

Poore, Benjamin Perley, ed. *The Federal and State Constitutions, Colonial Charters and Other Organic Laws of the United States*. 2 vols. Washington, DC: Government Printing Office, 1878.

Statutes at Large of South Carolina. Columbia: A.S. Johnston, 1836–1841.

Thorpe, Francis Newton, ed. *The Federal and State Constitutions, Colonial Charters and other organic laws of the state territories and colonies now or heretofore forming the United States of America*. 7 vols. Washington, DC: Government Printing Office, 1909.

Underwood, James Lowell, ed. *The Constitution of South Carolina*. 2 vols. Columbia: University of South Carolina Press, 1989.

U.S. Congress. *American State Papers: Documents, Legislative and Executive, of the Congress of the United States.* Washington, DC: Gales and Seaton, 1832–1862.

U.S. *Statutes at Large.* Washington, DC: Government Printing Office, 1937. 50 volumes.

Published Works

Abbott, Abil. "A Discourse Delivered at North Coventry, July 4, 1799." Hartford, CT, 1799.

Adams, Charles Francis, ed. *The Works of John Adams.* 10 vols. Boston: Charles C. Little and James Brown, 1856.

Adams, John. "Observations on the Reconstruction of Government in Massachusetts During the Revolution." In Adams, *The Works of John Adams.*

Allen, W. B., ed. *George Washington: A Collection.* Indianapolis: Liberty Classics, 1988.

Associated Presbytery in Pennsylvania. "A Solemn Warning by the Associated Presbytery in Pennsylvania." Lancaster, PA: Francis Bailey, 1777.

Bailyn, Bernard, ed. *The Debate of the Constitution: Federalist and Antifederalist Speeches, Articles, and Letters during the Struggle over Ratification.* 2 vols. New York: Literary Classics of the U.S., 1993.

Beecher, Lyman. *Autobiography, Correspondence, et al.* New York: Harper and Bros., 1864.

Beverley, Robert. *The History and Present State of Virginia.* Chapel Hill: University of North Carolina Press, 1947.

Bushnell, Horace. *Barbarism, the First Danger: A Discourse for Home Missions.* New York: Printed for the American Home Missionary Society, 1847.

Butler, Vera. *Education as Revealed by New England Newspapers prior to 1850.* Philadelphia: Temple University, 1935.

Cubberly, Ellwood P., ed. *Readings in the Public Education in the United States: A Collection of Sources and Readings to Illustrate the History of Education Practice and Progress in the United States.* Boston: Houghton Mifflin, 1934.

Dalcho, Rev. Frederick. *An Historical Account of the Protestant Episcopal Church in South Carolina.* Charleston, SC: E. Thayer, 1820.

Edwards, Jonathan. *A Faithful Narrative of the Surprising Work of God in the Conversion of Many Hundred Souls in Northampton and Neighboring Towns.* London: C. Whittingham for W. Button, 1737.

———. *Some Thoughts Concerning the Present Revival of Religion.* Lexington, KY: Joseph Charless, 1742.

———. *A Treatise Concerning Religious Affections.* Boston: S. Kneeland and T. Green, 1746.

Emerson, Ralph Waldo. "The Essence of the Christian Religion." In *The Complete Works of Ralph Waldo Emerson.* 12 vols. Reprint New York: AMS Press, 1979.

Emmons, Rev. Nathaniel. "Religious Instructors Useful to Civil Society." In *The Works of Nathaniel Emmons, D.D.* Edited by Jacob Ide. 2 vols. Boston, 1842.

Farrand, Max, ed. *The Records of the Federal Convention of 1787.* 1911. 4 vols. New Haven: Yale University Press, 1966.

Finegan, Thomas E., ed. *Free Schools: A Documentary History of the Free School Movement in New York State.* Albany: University of the State of New York, 1921.

Finney, Charles G. "Oration in Temperance." *Lectures to Professing Christians,* London: Milner, 1837.

Fordyce, James. *Sermons to Young Women.* 2 vols. London: T. Cadell and J. Dodsley, 1786.

Goebel, Julius. *The Law Practice of Alexander Hamilton: Documents and Commentary.* New York: Columbia University Press, 1964.

Harper, Robert Goodloe. *Case of the Georgia Sales on the Mississippi Considered with a Reference to Law Authorities and Public Acts and an Appendix Containing Certain Extracts, Records, and Officials Papers.* Philadelphia: Printed for Benjamin Davies, 1797.

Henry, Jacob. "Speech in the North Carolina House of Democrats" (1809). Reprinted in *Cornerstones of Religious Freedom in America,* ed. Joseph L. Blau. Boston: Beacon Press, 1949.

Hobart, John Henry. *The Corruptions of the Church of Rome Contrasted with certain Protestant Errors in a Charge, delivered to the Clergy of the Protestant Episcopal Church in the State of New York.* Trinity Church, October 1817. New York: T & J Swords, 1818.

Hutson, Francis Marion, ed. *Journal of the Constitutional Convention of South Carolina.* 1790. Columbia: Historical Commission of South Carolina, 1946.

Jefferson, Thomas. "Autobiography." In *The Complete Jefferson.*

———. *The Writings of Thomas Jefferson.* Edited by Paul Leicester Ford. New York: G. P. Putnam and Sons, 1892–1899.

———. *The Writings of Thomas Jefferson.* 20 vols. Edited by Albert Ellery Bergh. Washington, DC: Thomas Jefferson Memorial Association, 1903–1907.

———. *The Complete Jefferson.* 1905. Edited by Saul K. Padover. New York: Tudor, 1943.

———. *The Papers of Thomas Jefferson.* Edited by Julian P. Boyd. Princeton, NJ: Princeton University Press, 1950–present.

———. *The Portable Thomas Jefferson.* Edited by Merrill D. Peterson. New York: Penguin Books, 1975.

Klein, Milton M., ed. *The Independent Reflector on Weekly Essays on Sundry Important Subjects More particularly adapted to the Province of New York, by William Livingston and others.* Cambridge: Belknap Press of Harvard University Press, 1963.

Locke, John. *A Second Vindication of the Reasonableness of Christianity.* London: White-Hall, for A. and J. Churchill, 1697.

Madison, James. *The Writings of Madison.* 9 vols. Edited by Gaillard Hunt. New York: G. P. Putnam's Sons, 1904.

———. *Debates in the Federal Convention of 1787 as Reported by James Madison.* In *The Debates of the General State Constitutions on the Adoption of the Federal Constitution as Recommended by the General Convention in Philadelphia in 1787.* 5 vols. Edited by Jonathan Elliot. Philadelphia: J. B. Lippincott, 1904.

———. *The Federalist Papers.* Edited by Clinton Rossiter. New York: New American Library, 1961.

———. *The Papers of James Madison.* Edited by William T. Hutchinson et al. Chicago and Charlottesville: University of Chicago Press and University Press of Virginia, 1962.

———. *The Papers of James Madison, Presidential Series.* 5 vols. Charlottesville: University Press of Virginia , 1984.

McLeod, Alexander. *Messiah, Governor of the Nations of the Earth.* Sermon preached at the Reformed Presbyterian Church in New York City. New York: T & J Swords, 1803.

Moore, Benjamin. "The Charge of the Right Rev. Benjamin Moore, Bishop of the Protestant Episcopal Church in the State of New York, Delivered to the Convention of Said Church on the 5th day of October, 1803." New York, 1803.

Morris, Richard B., ed. *Select Cases of the Mayor's Court of New York City, 1674–1784.* Washington, DC: American Historical Association, 1935.

Mouton, David, and Mordecai Myers. "Report of the Select Committee of the New York State Assembly on the Several Memorials Against Chaplains to the Legislature." New York, 1832.

A Narrative of a New and Unusual American Imprisonment of Two Presbyterian Ministers: And Prosecution of Mr. Francis Makemie, One of Them, for Preaching One Sermon at the City of New York. Written by a Learner of Law, and Lover of Liberty. London, 1707. Episcopal Church Library, New York.

Penn, William. *No Cross, No Crown.* Mt. Rainier, MD: AudioLogos, 1994.

Perley, Jeremiah. *The Debates, Resolutions, and Other Proceedings of the Convention of the Delegates Assembled at Portland on the 11th and Continued until the 29th Day of October, 1819, for the Purpose of Forming a Constitution for the State of Maine.* Edited by Charles E. Nash. Printed by A. Shirley, 1820.

Perry, William Stevens, ed. *Journals of the General Conventions of the Protestant Episcopal Church in the United States, 1785–1835* 2 vols. Claremont, NH: Claremont Manufacturing Company, 1874.

Powers, Edwin. *Crime and Punishment in Early Massachusetts, 1620–1692: A Documentary History.* Boston: Beacon Press, 1966.

The Principles and Practices of the Patriots of the Revolution Being an Appeal to Reason and Common Sense. Philadelphia: S. Roberts, 1819. New York Historical Society.

"Reasons of the Trustees of the Public School Society for Their Remonstrances Against the petition of the Roman Catholic Benevolent Society." New York: Mahlon Day, 1831. New York Historical Society.

Richardson, James D. *A Compilation of the Messages and Papers of the Presidents, 1789–1897.* Washington, DC: Bureau of National Literature and Art, 1901.

Sandoz, Ellis, ed. *Political Sermons of the Founding Era, 1730–1805.* 2 vols. Indianapolis: Liberty Fund, 1991.

Scott, Thomas, D.D. *Treatises on Various Theological Subjects Published at Different Times and Now Collected into Volumes.* 4 vols. Edited by Thomas Scott. Middleton, CT: Clark and Lyman, 1816.

Shoepf, Johann D. *Travels in the Confederation, 1783–1784.* 2 vols. Translated and edited by Alfred J. Morrison. Philadelphia: W. J. Campbell, 1911.

Stevens, Michael E., ed. *Journals of the House of Representatives (South Carolina) 1789–1790.* Columbia: University of South Carolina Press, 1984.

Stiles, Ezra. "Plan for a University." In *The Literary Journal of Ezra Stiles.* Microfiche. New York: Scribners, 1801.

Storing, Herbert J., ed. *The Complete Anti-Federalist.* 7 vols. Chicago: University of Chicago Press, 1981.

Strickland, William. *Journal of a Tour in the United States of America, 1794–1795.* New York Historical Society, 1971.

Tennant, Reverend William. "The Writings of Reverend William Tennant, 1740–1777." Edited by Newton B. Jones. *South Carolina Historical Magazine* 61, nos. 3, 4 (1960).

"The Testimony of the Presidents, Professors, Tutors, and Hebrew Instructor of Harvard College in Cambridge Against the Reverend Mr. George Whitefield, and His Conduct." Boston, 1744. Presbyterian Historical Society Library, Philadelphia.

Washington, George. *Writings of George Washington.* 39 vols. Edited by John C. Fitzpatrick. Washington, DC: Government Printing Office, 1931–1944.

Webster, Noah. "On Education of Youth in America," In Rudolph, *Essays on Education,* 44–45.

White, William. *The Case of Episcopal Churches in the United States Considered.* Philadelphia, 1782. Pamphlet in the Episcopal Library, New York.

The Works of Jesse Appleton. 2 vols. Andover, MA: Gould and Newman, 1837.

Wylie, Rev. Samuel Brown. *Two Sons of Oil: The Faithful Witness for magistracy and ministry upon a scriptural basis*. Philadelphia: Greensburg, McCorkle, 1806.

Secondary Sources

Adams, Henry. *History of the United States of America during the Administrations of Thomas Jefferson and James Madison*. Rev. ed. Englewood Cliffs, NJ: Prentice-Hall, 1963.

Adams, Willi Paul. *The First American Constitutions: Republican Ideology and the Making of the State Constitutions in the Revolutionary Era*. Chapel Hill: University of North Carolina Press for the Institute of Early American History and Culture, 1980.

Ahlstrom, Sydney E. *A Religious History of the American People*. New Haven: Yale University Press, 1972.

Alley, Robert S., ed. *James Madison on Religious Liberty*. Buffalo, NY: Prometheus Books, 1985.

Andrews, Charles. *The Colonial Period of American History*. New Haven: Yale University Press, 1938.

Andrews, Kenneth. *Trade, Plunder, and Settlement: Maritime Enterprise and the Genesis of the British Empire, 1480–1630*. New York: Cambridge University Press, 1984.

Appleby, Joyce. *Capitalism and a New Social Order: The Republican Vision of the 1790s*. New York: New York University Press, 1984.

———. *Liberalism and Republicanism in the Historical Imagination*. Cambridge: Harvard University Press, 1992.

Axtell, James. "Dr. Wheelock's Little Red School House." In James Axtell, *The European and the Indian: Essays in the Ethnohistory of Colonial North America*. New York: Oxford University Press, 1981.

Bailyn, Bernard. *The Ideological Origins of the American Revolution*. Cambridge: Harvard University Press, 1967.

Baker, Robert A., and Paul J. Craven, Jr. *Adventure in Faith. The First 300 Years of the First Baptist Church, Charleston, S. Carolina*. Nashville, TN: Broadman Press, 1982.

Balmer, Randall, and John R. Fitzmier. *The Presbyterians*. Westport, CT: Greenwood Press, 1993.

Banner, James M., Jr. *To the Hartford Convention: The Federalists and the Origins of Party Politics in Massachusetts, 1789–1815*. New York: A. A. Knopf, 1970.

Banning, Lance. *The Jeffersonian Persuasion: Evolution of a Party Ideology*. Ithaca: Cornell University Press, 1978.

Bellah, Robert N. "The Revolution and the Civil Religion." In *Religion and the American Revolution*, ed. Jerald C. Brauer. Philadelphia: Fortress Press, 1967.

Bercovitch, Sacvan. *The American Jeremiad*. Madison: University of Wisconsin Press, 1978.

Berk, Stephen. *Calvinism versus Democracy: Timothy Dwight and the Origins of American Evangelical Orthodoxy*. Hamden, CT: Archon Books, 1974.

Bernstein, Richard B. *Are We to Be a Nation? The Making of the Constitution*. Cambridge, MA: Harvard University Press, 1987.

Berrian, Rev. William. *An Historical Sketch of Trinity Church, New York*. New York: T & J Swords, 1847.

Beveridge, Albert J. *Beveridge, The Building of the Nation*. Vol. 4 of Albert J. Beveridge, *The Life of John Marshall*. 4 vols. 1919. Baltimore: Johnson Reprint, 1980.

Billias, George Athan, ed. *Selected Essays: Law and Authority in Colonial America*. Barre, MA: Barre Publishers, 1965.

Blassingame, John W. *The Slave Community: Plantation Life in the Antebellum South.* New York: Oxford University Press, 1979.

Bloch, Ruth. *Visionary Republic: Millennial Themes in American Thought, 1756–1800.* Cambridge: Harvard University Press, 1985.

Bloom, Harold. *The American Religion: The Emergence of the Post-Christian Nation.* New York: Simon and Schuster, 1992.

Boller, Paul F., Jr. "George Washington and Religious Liberty." *William and Mary Quarterly,* 3rd ser., no. 17 (1960): 486–506.

Bolton, Charles S. *Southern Anglicanism: The Church of England in Colonial South Carolina.* Westport, CT: Greenwood Press, 1982.

Bonomi, Patricia. *Under the Cope of Heaven: Religion, Society, and Politics in Colonial America.* New York: Oxford University Press, 1986.

Bonomi, Patricia, and Peter Eisenstadt. "Church Adherence in the Eighteenth-Century British American Colonies." *William and Mary Quarterly,* 3rd ser., 39.2 (1982): 240–62.

Borden, Morton. *Jews, Turks, and Infidels.* Chapel Hill: University of North Carolina Press, 1984.

Botein, Stephen. *Early American Law and Society.* New York: A. A. Knopf, 1983.

Bowdoin College. *General Catalogue of Bowdoin College and the Medical School of Maine, 1784–1894: Including a Historical Sketch of the Institution During its First Century Prepared by George Thomas Little, the Librarian.* Brunswick, ME: Bowdoin College, 1894.

Bowers, J. D. "Avowing Ourselves Christians: Joseph Priestley, English Unitarianism, and the Development of an American Religion, 1774–1840." Ph.D. dissertation, Indiana University, 2003.

Boyer, Paul. *Urban Masses and Moral Order in America, 1820–1920.* Cambridge: Harvard University Press, 1978.

Boylan, Anne E. *Sunday School: The Formation of an American Institution, 1790–1880.* New Haven: Yale University Press, 1988.

Branscombe, Martha. *The Courts and the Poor Laws in New York State, 1784–1929.* Chicago: University of Chicago Press, 1943.

Breen, Timothy. *Puritans and Adventurers: Change and Persistence in Early America.* New York: Oxford University Press, 1980.

Bremner, Robert. *American Philanthropy.* 1960. Chicago: University of Chicago Press, 1988.

Brewer, Holly. *Constructing Consent: The Legal Status of Children and American Revolutionary Ideology.* Chapel Hill: University of North Carolina Press, 2000.

———. "Beyond Education: Republican Revision of the Laws Regarding Children." In Gilreath, *Education of a Citizen.*

Brooks, Van Wyck. *The Flowering of New England.* Cleveland: World Pub., 1st reprint ed. 1946.

Brown, Richard D. "The Emergence of Voluntary Associations in Massachusetts, 1760–1830." *Journal of Voluntary Action Research* 2.64 (1973).

Brown, Roy M. *Public Poor Relief in North Carolina.* New York: Arno Press, 1976.

Buckley, Thomas E. *Church and State in Revolutionary Virginia, 1776–1787.* Charlottesville: University Press of Virginia, 1977.

———. "After Disestablishment: Thomas Jefferson's Wall of Separation in Antebellum Virginia." *Journal of Southern History* 61.3 (August 1995): 445–80.

Burrows, Edwin G., and Mike Wallace. *Gotham: A History of New York City to 1898.* New York: Oxford University Press, 1999.

Bushman, Richard. *The Refinement of America: Persons, Houses, Cities.* New York: Random House, 1992.

Butler, Jon. *The Huguenots in America.* Cambridge: Harvard University Press, 1983.

———. *Awash in a Sea of Faith: Christianizing the American People.* Cambridge: Harvard University Press, 1990.

Calhoun, Charles C. *A Small College in Maine: Two Hundred Years of Bowdoin.* Brunswick, ME: Bowdoin College. 1993.

Capen, Edward Warren. *The Historical Development of the Poor Law of Connecticut.* Privately published. Ph.D. dissertation, Columbia University, New York, 1905.

Carr, Lois Green, and David Jordan. *Maryland's Revolution of Government, 1689–1692.* Ithaca: Cornell University Press, 1974.

Carr, Lois Green, Russell R. Menard, and Lorena S. Walsh. *Robert Cole's World: Agriculture and Society in Early Maryland.* Chapel Hill: University of North Carolina Press, 1991.

Carr, Lois Green, Philip D. Morgan, and Jean B. Russo, eds. *Colonial Chesapeake Society.* Chapel Hill: University of North Carolina Press, 1988.

Chadburne, Ava Harriet. *A History of Education in Maine.* Orono, ME: self-published, 1936.

Cheyney, Edward Potts. *History of the University of Pennsylvania 1740–1940.* Philadelphia: University of Pennsylvania Press, 1940.

Chorley, E. Clowes. "The Beginnings of the Church in the Province of New York." *Historical Magazine of the Protestant Episcopal Church* 13 (March 1944).

Clark, J. C. D. *Revolution and Rebellion: State and Society in England in the Seventeenth and Eighteenth Centuries.* New York: Cambridge University Press, 1986.

Clarke, Erskine. *Our Southern Zion: A History of Calvinism in the South Carolina Low Country, 1690–1990.* Tuscaloosa: University of Alabama Press, 1996.

Clayton, Mary Kupiec. "Who Were the Evangelicals? Conservative and Liberal Identity in the Unitarian Controversy in Boston, 1804–1833." *Journal of Social History* 31.1 (1997): 86–107.

Coalter, Milton J., Jr. *Gilbert Tennant, Son of Thunder: A Case Study of Continental Pietism's Impact on the First Great Awakening in the Middle Colonies.* Westport, CT: Greenwood Press, 1986.

Cogley, John, ed. *Religion in America.* New York: Meridian Books, 1958.

Cohen, Bernard. *Science and the Founding Fathers: Science in the Political Thought of Jefferson, Franklin, Adams, and Madison.* New York: W. W. Norton, 1995.

Colbourn, H. Trevor. *Whig History and the Intellectual Origins of the American Revolution.* Chapel Hill: University of North Carolina Press, for the Institute of Early American History and Culture, 1965.

Conroy, David W. *In Public Houses: Drink and the Revolution of Authority in Colonial Massachusetts.* Chapel Hill: University of North Carolina Press, 1995.

Coram, Robert. "Political Inquiries: to Which is added, a Plan for the General Establishment of Schools throughout the United States." In Rudolph, *Essays on Education,* 141.

Cord, Robert L. *Separation of Church and State: Historical Fact and Current Fiction.* New York: Lambeth Press, 1982.

Corwin, Edward S. "The Supreme Court as National School Board." *Law and Contemporary Problems* 14 (Winter 1949).

Cott, Nancy. "Divorce and the Changing Status of Women in Eighteenth-Century America." In *The American Family in Social Historical Perspective,* ed. Michael Gordon. 2nd ed. New York: St. Martins Press, 1978.

Countryman, Edward. *A People in Revolution: The American Revolution and Political Society in New York, 1760–1790*. Baltimore: Johns Hopkins University Press, 1981.

Crane, Elaine Forman. "Religion and Rebellion: Women of Faith in the American War for Independence." In *Religion in a Revolutionary Age*, ed. Ronald Hoffman and Peter J. Albert. Charlottesville: University Press of Virginia , 1994.

Crawford, Michael. *Seasons of Grace: Colonial New England's Revival Tradition in the British Context*. New York: Oxford University Press, 1991.

Crothers, A. Glenn. "'One Undivided Current': Politics, Society and the Religious Settlement in Virginia." *Southern Historian* 14 (1993): 5–17.

Current, Richard. "The Dartmouth College Case." In *Quarrels that Have Shaped the Constitution*, ed. John A. Garraty. New York: Harper and Row, 1964.

Cushing, John D. "Notes on Disestablishment in Massachusetts, 1780–1833." *William and Mary Quarterly* 26.2 (1969): 169–90.

Dexter, Edwin Grant. *A History of Education in the United States*. New York: Macmillan, 1904.

Doerr, Edd. *The Conspiracy that Failed: The Inside Story of the Campaign to Scuttle Church-State Separation in New York*. Washington, DC: Americans United for Separation of Church and State, 1968.

Douglas, Ann. *The Feminization of American Culture*. New York: Noonday Press/Farrar, Straus and Giroux, 1977.

Dreisbach, Daniel L. "Thomas Jefferson and Bills Number 82–86 of the Revision of the Laws of Virginia, 1776–1786: New Light on the Jefferson Model of Church-State Relations." *North Carolina Law Review* 159 (November 1990): 69.

Edgar, Walter. *South Carolina: A History*. Columbia: University of South Carolina Press, 1998.

Edwards, Newton, and Herman G. Richey. *The School in the American Social Order*. Boston: Houghton Mifflin, 1947.

Feldman, Stephen M. *Please Don't Wish Me a Merry Christmas: A Critical History of the Separation of Church and State*. New York: New York University Press, 1997.

Field, Peter S. *The Crisis of the Standing Order: Clerical Intellectuals and Cultural Authority in Massachusetts, 1780–1833*. Amherst: University of Massachusetts Press, 1998.

Fiore, Jordan D. "Jonathan Swift and the American Episcopate." *William and Mary Quarterly*, 3rd ser., no. 11 (July 1954): 425–33.

Fish, Edith L. "American Acceptance of Charitable Trusts." *Notre Dame Law Review* 28.219 (1953).

Fitzmier, John R. *New England's Moral Legislator: Timothy Dwight, 1752–1817*. Indianapolis: Indiana University Press, 1998.

Fleet, Elizabeth. "Madison's Detached Memoranda." *William and Mary Quarterly*, 3rd ser., vol. 3 (October 1946): 534–68.

Fleming, Thomas. *Duel: Alexander Hamilton, Aaron Burr, and the Future of America*. New York: Basic Books, 1999.

Fligelman, Jay. *Prodigals and Pilgrims: The American Revolution against Patriarchal Authority*. New York: Cambridge University Press, 1982.

Fogleman, Aaron Spencer. *Hopeful Journeys: German Immigration, Settlement, and Political Culture in Colonial America, 1717–1775*. Philadelphia: University of Pennsylvania Press, 1996.

Foster, Charles I. *An Errand of Mercy: The Evangelical United Front, 1790–1837*. Chapel Hill: University of North Carolina Press, 1960.

Foster, Stephen. *Their Solitary Way: The Puritan Social Ethic in the First Century of Settlement in New England*. New Haven: Yale University Press, 1971.

Friedman, Lawrence J. *Inventors of the Promised Land*. New York: A. A. Knopf, 1975.

Friedman, Lawrence J., and Mark D. McGarvie, *Charity, Philanthropy, and Civility in American History*. New York: Cambridge University Press, 2003.

Friedman, Lawrence M. *A History of American Law*. New York: Simon and Schuster, 1973.

———. *Crime and Punishment in American History*. New York: HarperCollins, 1993.

Gallay, Alan. "The Great Sellout: George Whitefield on Slavery." In Moore and Tripp, *Looking South*.

Garrity, Patrick J., and Matthew Spalding. *A Sacred Union of Citizens*. New York: Rowman and Littlefield, 1996.

Gaustad, Edwin Scott. "A Disestablishment Society: Origins of the First Amendment." *Journal of Church and State* 11.3 (1969): 409–25.

———. "The Emergence of Religious Freedom in the Early Republic." In *Religion and the State: Essays in Honor of Leo Pfeffer*, ed. James E. Wood Jr. Waco, TX: Baylor University Press, 1985.

———. *Liberty of Conscience: Roger Williams in America*. Grand Rapids, MI: Eerdmans, 1991.

———. *Sworn on the Altar of God: A Religious Biography of Thomas Jefferson*. Grand Rapids, MI: Eerdmans, 1996.

Gay, Peter. *The Rise of Modern Paganism*. Vol. 1 of *The Enlightenment: An Interpretation*. New York: Random House, 1966.

Genovese, Eugene D. *Roll Jordan Roll: The World the Slaves Made*. New York: Random House, 1976.

Genovese, Eugene D., and Elizabeth Fox-Genovese. "The Social Thought of Antebellum Southern Theologians." In Moore and Tripp, *Looking South*.

Gilreath, James, ed. *Thomas Jefferson and the Education of a Citizen*. Washington, DC: Library of Congress, 1999.

Ginzberg, Lori. *Women and the Work of Benevolence: Morality, Politics, and Class in the Nineteenth-Century United States*. New Haven: Yale University Press, 1990.

Godbeer, Richard. *Sexual Revolution in Early America* (Baltimore: Johns Hopkins University Press, 2002).

Good, H. G. *A History of American Education*. New York: Macmillan, 1956.

Green, Fletcher M. *Constitutional Development in the South Atlantic States, 1776–1860: A Study in the Evolution of Democracy*. New York: De Capo Press, 1971.

Greene, Maria Louise. *The Development of Religious Liberty in Connecticut*. 1095. Reprinted in the Civil Liberties in American History series, ed. Leonard W. Levy. New York: DeCapo Press, 1970.

Gregorie, Anne King. *Christ Church, 1706–1759: A Plantation Parish of South Carolina Establishment*. Charleston, SC: Dalcho Historical Society, 1961.

Greven, Philip. *The Protestant Temperament: Patterns of Child Rearing, Religious Experience, and the Self in Early America* New York: A. A. Knopf, 1977.

Griffin, Clifford S. *Their Brothers' Keepers: Moral Stewardship in the U.S., 1800–1865*. New Brunswick, NJ: Rutgers University Press, 1960.

Gross, Robert. "Giving in America: 'From Charity to Philanthropy.'" Lecture to Planned Giving Institute at the College of William and Mary. Oct. 4, 1993; subsequently published in Friedman and McGarvie, *Charity, Philanthropy, Civility*.

———. *The Minutemen and Their World*. New York: Hill and Wang, 1976.

Grossberg, Michael. *Governing the Hearth: Law and the Family in Nineteenth-Century America*. Chapel Hill: University of North Carolina Press, 1985.

———. "Legal History and Social Science: Friedman's History of American Law, the Second Time Around." *Law and Social Inquiry* 13 (1988): 359.

———. "Citizens and Families: A Jeffersonian Vision of Domestic Relations and Generational Change." In Gilreath, *Education of a Citizen.*

Hall, Kermit L. *The Magic Mirror: Law in American History* New York: Oxford University Press, 1989.

Hall, Peter Dobkin. *The Organization of American Culture, 1700–1900: Private Institutions, Elites, and the Origins of American Nationality.* New York: New York University Press, 1982.

Hall, Timothy L. *Separating Church and State: Roger Williams and Religious Liberty.* Urbana-Champaign: University of Illinois Press, 1998.

Hamburger, Philip. *Separation of Church and State.* Cambridge: Harvard University Press, 2002.

Handlin, Oscar, and Mary Flug Handlin. *Commonwealth: A Study of the Role of Government in the American Economy, Massachusetts, 1774–1861.* 1947. Cambridge: Harvard University Press, 1969.

Handy, Robert S. *A Christian America: Protestant Hopes and Historical Realities.* New York: Oxford University Press, 1971.

Hanley, Thomas. *The American Revolution and Religion.* New York: Catholic University of America Press, 1971.

Hanson, Charles P. *Necessary Virtue: The Pragmatic Origins of Religious Liberty in New England.* Charlottesville: University Press of Virginia, 1998.

Hart, D. G. "The Failure of American Religious History." *Journal of the Historical Society* 1.1 (Spring 2000).

Hartz, Louis. *The Liberal Tradition in America.* New York: Harcourt Brace Jovanovich, 1991.

Hatch, Nathan O. *The Sacred Cause of Liberty: Political Religion in New England from the First to the Second Great Awakening.* New Haven: Yale University Press, 1977.

———. *The Democratization of American Christianity.* New Haven: Yale University Press, 1989.

———. "The Second Great Awakening and the Market Revolution." In *Devising Liberty,* ed. David Thomas Konig. Palo Alto: Stanford University Press, 1995.

Hay, Robert P. *Freedom's Jubilee: One Hundred Years of the Fourth of July, 1776–1876.* Ph.D. dissertation, University of Kentucky, 1967.

Heimert, Alan. *Religion and the American Mind: From the Great Awakening to the Revolution.* Cambridge: Harvard University Press, 1966.

Helmreich, Ernst Christian. *Religion at Bowdoin College: A History.* Brunswick, ME: The College, 1981.

Henderson, Joe M. *Fighting Poverty in the U.S.: Past, Present and Future Roles of the Church and the State.* Ph.D. dissertation, School of Theology at Claremont, 1984.

Herbst, Jurgen. *From Crisis to Crisis: American College Government, 1636–1819.* Cambridge: Harvard University Press, 1982.

Heyrman, Christine L. *Commerce and Culture: The Maritime Communities of Colonial Massachusetts, 1690–1750.* New York: W. W. Norton, 1984.

———. *Southern Cross: The Beginnings of the Bible Belt.* Chapel Hill: University of North Carolina Press, 1997.

Hobson, Charles F. *The Great Chief Justice: John Marshall and the Rule of Law.* Lawrence: University Press of Kansas, 1996.

Hoffer, Peter Charles. *Law and People in Colonial America.* Baltimore: Johns Hopkins University Press, 1998.

Hood, Fred J. "Revolution and Religious Liberty: The Conservation of the Theocratic Concept in Virginia." *Church History* 40.2 (1971): 170–81.

————. *Reformed America: The Middle and Southern States, 1783–1837*. Tuscaloosa: University of Alabama Press, 1980.

Hoopes, James. *Consciousness in New England: From Puritanism and Ideas to Psychoanalysis and Semiotic*. Baltimore: Johns Hopkins University Press, 1989.

Horwitz, Morton J. *The Transformation of American Law, 1780–1860*. Cambridge: Harvard University Press, 1977.

Howe, Mark DeWolf. *The Garden and the Wilderness: Religion and Government in American Constitutional History*. Chicago: University of Chicago Press, 1965.

Hudson, Winthrop S., and John Corrigan. *Religion in America: An American Historical Account of the Development of American Religious Life*. Upper Saddle River, NJ: Prentice Hall, 1992.

Huebner, Timothy S. *The Southern Judicial Tradition: State Judges and Sectional Distinctiveness, 1790–1890*. Athens: University of Georgia Press, 1999.

Hughes, J. R. T. *Social Control in the Colonial Economy*. Charlottesville: University Press of Virginia, 1976.

Humphrey, David C. *From King's College to Columbia, 1746–1800*. New York: Columbia University Press, 1976.

Hurst, James Willard. *Law and the Conditions of Freedom in the Nineteenth-Century United States*. Madison: University of Wisconsin Press, 1956.

Innes, Stephen. *Creating the Commonwealth: The Economic Culture of Puritan New England*. New York: W. W. Norton, 1995.

Isaac, Rhys. *The Transformation of Virginia, 1740–1790*. Chapel Hill: University of North Carolina Press, 1982.

James, Sydney V. *Colonial Rhode Island: A History*. New York: Scribners and Sons, 1975.

————. *John Clarke and His Legacies: Religion and the Law in Colonial Rhode Island, 1638–1750*. Edited by Theodore Dwight Bozeman. University Park: Pennsylvania State University Press, 1999.

————. *The Colonial Metamorphosis in Rhode Island: A Study of Institutions in Change*. Hanover: University Press of New England, 2000.

Johnson, Curtis D. *Islands of Holiness: Rural Religion in Upstate New York, 1790–1860*. Ithaca: Cornell University Press, 1989.

Johnson, Eldon L. "The Dartmouth College Case: The Neglected Educational Meaning." *Journal of the Early Republic* 3 (1983): 45–53.

Johnson, Paul E. *A Shopkeeper's Millennium: Society and Revivals in Rochester, New York, 1815–1837*. New York: Hill and Wang, 1978.

Kammen, Michael. *People of Paradox: An Inquiry Concerning the Origins of American Civilization*. New York: Random House, 1972.

————. *Colonial New York: A History*. New York: Oxford University Press, 1975.

Katz, Stanley. "Legal Change and Legal Autonomy: Charitable Trusts in New York, 1777–1893." *Law and History Review* 3 (Spring 1985): 51–89.

Kelso, Robert W. *The History of Public Poor Relief in Massachusetts, 1620–1920*. Mont Clair, NJ: Patterson Smith, 1969.

Kerber, Linda K. *Women of the Republic: Intellect and Ideology in Revolutionary America*. New York: W. W. Norton, 1980.

Ketcham, Ralph. "James Madison and Religion: A New Hypothesis." In Madison, *On Religious Liberty*.

Kimball, Gertrude S. *Providence in Colonial Times*. Boston: Houghton Mifflin, 1912.

Klebaner, Benjamin Joseph. *Public Poor Relief in America, 1790–1860*. New York: Arno Press, 1976.

Klein, Milton M. "New York in the American Colonies." In *Aspects of Early New York Society and Politics*, ed. Irwin H. Polishook and Jacob Judd. Tarrytown, NY: Sleepy Hollow Restoration, 1974.

Kloppenberg, James T. "The Virtues of Liberalism: Christianity, Republicanism, and Ethics in Early American Political Discourse." *Journal of American History* 74 (1987): 9–33.

Konefsky, Alfred S. "As Best to Subserve Their Own Interests: Lemuel Shaw, Labor Conspiracy, and Fellow Servants." *Law and Labor History Review* 7.1 (Spring 1989): 219–39.

Konig, David Thomas. *Law and Society in Puritan Massachusetts: Essex County, 1629–1692* Chapel Hill: University of North Carolina Press, 1979.

Kramnick, Isaac. "The Great National Discussions: The Discourse of Politics in 1787." In *The New American Nation, 1775–1820*, 12 vols., ed. Peter S. Onuf. New York: Garland, 1991.

Kramnick, Isaac, and R. Lawrence Moore. *The Godless Constitution: The Case against Religious Correctness*. New York: W. W. Norton, 1996.

Kucklick, Bruce. "Jonathan Edwards and American Philosophy." In *Jonathan Edwards and the American Experience*, eds. Nathan Hatch and Harry Stout. New York: Oxford University Press, 1988.

Kuenning, Paul P. *The Rise and Fall of American Lutheran Pietism: The Rejection of an Activist Heritage*. Macon, GA: Mercer University Press, 1988.

Kulikoff, Alan. *The Agrarian Origins of American Capitalism*. Charlottesville: University Press of Virginia, 1992.

Kutolowski, Kathleen Smith. "Freemasonry and Community in the Early Republic: The Case for Antimasonic Anxieties." *American Quarterly* 34.543 (1982).

Larson, John Lauritz. "Jefferson's Union and the Problem of Internal Improvements." In *Jeffersonian Legacies*, ed. Peter S. Onuf. Charlottesville: University Press of Virginia, 1993.

Lawrence, Charles. *History of the Philadelphia Almshouses and Hospitals*. New York: Arno Press, 1976.

Lazerow, James. "Religion and the New England Mill Girl: A New Perspective on an Old Theme." *New England Quarterly* 60.3 (September 1987): 429–53.

Lemon, James T. *The Best Poor Man's Country: A Geographical Study of Southeastern Pennsylvania*. Baltimore: Johns Hopkins University Press, 1972.

Levy, Barry. *The Establishment Clause: Religion and the First Amendment*. New York: Macmillan, 1986.

———. *Quakers and the American Family: British Settlement in the Delaware Valley*. New York: Oxford University Press, 1988.

Levy, Leonard W. *Constitutional Opinions: Aspects of the Bill of Rights*. New York: Oxford University Press, 1986.

———. *The Establishment Clause: Religion and the First Amendment*. New York: Macmillan, 1986.

———. *Blasphemy: Verbal Offense against the Sacred, from Moses to Salman Rushdie*. New York: A. A. Knopf, 1993.

Littell, Franklin Hamlin. *From State Church to Pluralism: A Protestant Interpretation of Religion in American History*. Chicago: Aldine, 1962.

Loetscher, Lefferts A. *Facing the Enlightenment and Pietism: Archibald Alexander and the Founding of Princeton Theological Seminary.* Westport, CT: Greenwood Press, 1983.

Lucas, Paul R. *Valley of Discord: Church and Society along the Connecticut River, 1636–1725.* Hanover, NH: University Press of New England, 1876.

Maier, Pauline. *American Scripture: Making the Declaration of Independence.* New York: A. A. Knopf, 1997.

Malone, Dumas. *Jefferson and His Time: Jefferson the President, First Term, 1801–1805.* 6 vols. Boston: Little, Brown, 1981.

Mann, Bruce. *Neighbors and Strangers: Law and Community in Early Connecticut.* Chapel Hill: University of North Carolina Press, 1987.

Marans Dim, Joan, and Nancy Murphy Cricco. *The Miracle on Washington Square: New York University* New York: Lexington Books, 2001.

Marnell, William H. *The First Amendment: The History of Religious Freedom in America.* Garden City, NY: Doubleday, 1964.

Marsden, George M. *Religion and American Culture.* San Diego: Harcourt Brace Jovanovich, 1990.

———. *Jonathan Edwards: A Life.* New Haven: Yale University Press, 2003.

Marty, Martin E. *Righteous Empire: The Protestant Experience in America.* Two Centuries of American Life series, ed. Harold Hyman and Leonard Levy. New York: Dial Press, 1970.

Masur, Louis B. *Rites of Execution: Capital Punishment and the Transformation of American Culture, 1776–1865.* New York: Oxford University Press, 1989.

Mathews, Alice E. "The Religious Experience of Southern Women." In *The Colonial and Revolutionary Periods,* vol. 2 of *Women and Religion in America,* 3 vols., ed. Rosemary Radford Ruether and Rosemary Skinner Keller, 2:193–232. San Francisco: Harper and Row, 1981.

Matthews, Jean V. *Toward a New Society: American Thought and Culture, 1800–1830.* Boston, G. K. Hall, 1991.

May, Henry F. *The Enlightenment in America.* New York: Oxford University Press, 1976.

McConnell, Michael W. "The Origins and Historical Understanding of Free Exercise of Religion." *Harvard Law Review* 103 (1990): 1409–517.

McCoy, Drew. *The Elusive Republic: Political Economy in Jeffersonian America.* New York: W. W. Norton, 1982.

McCrady, Edward. *A Sketch of St. Philip's Church, Charleston, South Carolina, from the Establishment of the Church of England under the Royal Charter of 1665 to the Present Time.* Charleston, SC: Lucas and Richardson, 1897. South Carolina Historical Society, Charleston.

McCurry, Stephanie. *Masters of Small Worlds: Yeoman Households, Gender Relations, and the Political Culture of the Antebellum South Carolina Low Country.* New York: Oxford University Press, 1995.

McGarvie, Mark. "In Perfect Accordance with His Character: Thomas Jefferson, Slavery, and the Law." *Indiana Magazine of History* 95.2 (June 1999), 142–77.

McGarvie, Mark, and Elizabeth Mensch. "Law and Religion in Colonial America." In *Cambridge History of Law in America,* ed. Michael Grossberg and Christopher Tomlins. Forthcoming, 2005.

McGlone, Robert E. "Deciphering Memory: John Adams and the Authorship of the Declaration of Independence." *Journal of American History* (Sept. 1998): 411–38.

McLoughlin, William G. *Isaac Backus and the American Pietistic Tradition.* Library of American Biography series, ed. Oscar Handlin. Boston: Little, Brown, 1967.

————. *New England Dissent, 1630–1883.* 2 vols. Cambridge: Harvard University Press, 1971.

Mead, Sidney E. *Nathaniel William Taylor, 1756–1858: A Connecticut Liberal.* Chicago: University of Chicago Press, 1942.

————. *The Lively Experiment: The Shaping of Christianity in America.* New York: Harper and Row, 1963.

————. *The Nation with the Soul of a Church.* New York: Harper and Row, 1975.

————. *The Old Religion in the Brave New World: The Jefferson Memorial Lectures.* Berkeley and Los Angeles: University of California Press, 1977.

Mensch, Elizabeth V. "The Colonial Origins of Liberal Property Rights," *Buffalo Law Review* 31.3 (Fall 1982).

————. "Religion, Revival, and the Ruling Class: A Critical History of Trinity Church." *Buffalo Law Rev* 36.3 (Fall 1987).

Miller, A. F. Thornton. *Juries and Judges versus the Law: Virginia's Provincial Legal Perspective, 1783–1828.* Constitutionalism and Democracy series, ed. Kermit Hall and David O'Brien. Charlottesville: University Press of Virginia, 1994.

Miller, Glenn T. *Religious Liberty in America: History and Prospects.* Philadelphia: Westminster Press, 1976.

Miller, Howard S. *The Legal Foundations of American Philanthropy, 1776–1844.* Madison: State Historical Society of Wisconsin, 1961.

Miller, Perry. *The Life of the Mind in America: From the Revolution to the Civil War.* New York: Harcourt Brace and World, 1965.

————. *Jonathan Edwards.* Westport, CT: Greenwood Press, 1973.

Moglen, Eban. "Settling the Law: Legal Development in Provincial New York." Ph.D. dissertation, Yale University, New Haven, 1992.

Mooney, Christopher F. *Public Virtue: Law and the Social Character of Religion.* Notre Dame: University of Notre Dame Press, 1986.

Moore, R. Laurence. "Bible Reading and Nonsectarian Schooling: The Failure of Religious Instruction in Nineteenth-Century Public Education." *Journal of American History* 86.4 (March 2000).

Moore, Winfred B., Jr., and Joseph F. Tripp. *Looking South: Chapters in the Story of an American Region.* New York: Greenwood Press, 1989.

Morgan, Edmund S. *The Puritan Dilemma: The Story of John Winthrop.* Library of American Biography series, ed. Oscar Handlin. Boston: Little, Brown, 1958.

————. "Ezra Stiles and Timothy Dwight." In *Proceedings of the Massachusetts Historical Society, 1960–1963,* vol. 72. Boston: Massachusetts Historical Society, 1963.

————. "The American Revolution Considered as an Intellectual Movement." In *Paths of American Thought,* ed. Arthur M. Schlesinger Jr. and Morton White. Boston: Houghton Mifflin, 1963.

————. *American Slavery, American Freedom: The Ordeal of Colonial Virginia.* New York: W. W. Norton, 1975.

————. "The Labor Problem at Jamestown, 1607–18." In *Shaping Southern Society: The Colonial Experience,* ed. Timothy H. Breen. New York: Oxford University Press, 1976.

Morris, Richard B. "The Judeo-Christian Foundation of the American Political System." In Madison, *On Religious Liberty.*

Murrin, John M. "Political Development in Colonial British America," In *Colonial British America: Essays in the New History of the Early Modern Era,* eds. Jack P. Greene and J. R. Pole. Baltimore: Johns Hopkins University Press, 1984.

Nash, Gary. *The Urban Crucible: The Northern Seaports and the Origin of the American Revolution.* Cambridge: Harvard University Press, 1979.

———. "Social Development." In *Colonial British America: Essays in the New History of the Early Modern Era,* ed. Jack P. Greene and J. R. Pole. Baltimore: Johns Hopkins University Press, 1984.

Nelson, William E. "The Eighteenth-Century Background of John Marshall's Constitutional Jurisprudence." *Michigan Law Review* 76 (1978): 893.

———. *Americanization of the Common Law: The Impact of Legal Change on Massachusetts Society, 1760–1830.* Athens: University of Georgia Press, 1994.

Neuhaus, Richard John. *The Naked Public Square: Religion and Democracy in America.* Grand Rapids, MI: Eerdmans, 1984.

Newmyer, R. Kent. *Supreme Court Justice Joseph Story: Statesman of the Old Republic.* Chapel Hill: University of North Carolina Press, 1985.

Niebuhr, Reinhold. "A Note on Pluralism." In Cogley, *Religion in America,* 42–51.

Noonan, John T., Jr. *The Lustre of Our Country: The American Experience of Religious Freedom.* Berkeley and Los Angeles: University of California Press, 1998.

Nord, David Paul. "Systematic Benevolence: Religious Publishing and the Marketplace in Early Nineteenth-Century America." In *Communication and Change in American Religious History,* ed. Leonard I. Sweet. Grand Rapids, MI: Eerdmans, 1993.

Norton, Ann. *Alternative Americas: A Reading of Antebellum Political Culture.* Chicago: University of Chicago Press, 1986.

Novak, Steven J. "The College in the Dartmouth College Case: A Reinterpretation." *New England Quarterly* 47 (1974): 550.

Novak, William J. *The People's Welfare: Law and Regulation in Nineteenth-Century America.* Chapel Hill: University of North Carolina Press, 1996.

Pangle, Lorraine Smith, and Thomas L. Pangle. *The Learning of Liberty: The Educational Ideas of the American Founders.* Lawrence: University of Kansas Press, 1993.

Perry, Lewis. *Boats against the Current: American Culture between Revolution and Modernity.* New York: Oxford University Press, 1993.

Pfeffer, Leo. "The Case for Separation." In Cogley, *Religion in America.*

———. "The Deity in American Constitutional History." In *Religion and the State: Essays in Honor of Leo Pfeffer,* ed. James E. Wood Jr. Waco, TX: Baylor University Press, 1985.

Pierson, William D. *Black Legacy: America's Hidden Heritage.* Amherst: University of Massachusetts Press, 1993.

Pocock, J. G. A. *The Machiavellian Moment: Florentine Political Thought and the Atlantic Republican Tradition.* Princeton, NJ: Princeton University Press, 1975.

Pointer, Richard W. "Religious Life in New York during the Revolutionary War." *New York History* 66.4 (October 1985).

———. *Protestant Pluralism and the New York Experience: A Study of Eighteenth-Century Religious Diversity.* Indianapolis: Indiana University Press, 1988.

Pratt, John Webb. *Religion, Politics and Diversity: The Church-State Theme in New York History.* Ithaca: Cornell University Press, 1967.

Prince, Carl E. *New Jersey's Jeffersonian Republicans: The Genesis of an Early Party Machine, 1789–1819.* Chapel Hill: University of North Carolina Press, 1967.

Raboteau, Albert J. *Slave Religion: The "Invisible Institution" in the Antebellum South.* New York: Oxford University Press, 1978.

Rakove, Jack N. *Original Meanings: Politics and Ideas in the Making of the Constitution.* New York: Random House, 1997.

Ramage, B. James. "Local Government and Free Schools in South Carolina." In *Local Institutions,* ed. Herbert B. Adams. Baltimore: Johns Hopkins University Press, 1883.

Richey, Russell E. *Early American Methodism*. Indianapolis: Indiana University Press, 1991.

Riforgiato, Leonard R. *Missionary of Moderation: Henry Melchior Muhlenberg and the Lutheran Church in English America*. Lewisburg, PA: Bucknell University Press, 1980.

Roeber, A. G. *Palatines, Liberty, and Property: German Lutherans and Colonial British America*. Baltimore: Johns Hopkins University Press, 1993.

Rogers, George C. *Church and State in 18th-Century South Carolina*. Charleston, SC: Dalcho Historical Society, 1959.

———. *Evolution of a Federalist: William Loughton Smith of Charleston, 1758–1812*. Columbia: University of South Carolina Press, 1962.

Rothermund, Ditmar. *The Layman's Progress: Religious and Political Experience in Colonial Pennsylvania, 1740–1770*. Philadelphia: University of Pennsylvania Press, 1961.

Rudolph, Frederick. *The American College and University: A History*. New York: Random House, 1962.

———, ed. *Essays on Education in the Early Republic*. Cambridge: Harvard University Press, 1965.

Ruether, Rosemary, and Rosemary Skinner Keller, eds. *Women and Religion in America*. 3 vols. San Francisco: Harper and Row, 1981.

Ryan, Mary. *Cradle of the Middle Class: The Family in Oneida County, New York, 1790–1865*. New York: Cambridge University Press, 1983.

Salmon, Marylynn. *Women and the Law of Property in Early America*. Chapel Hill: University of North Carolina Press, 1986.

Sanford, Charles B. *The Religious Life of Thomas Jefferson*. Charlottesville: University Press of Virginia, 1984.

Schlesinger, Arthur M., Jr. *The Age of Jackson*. New York: J. J. Little and Ives, 1945.

Schwartz, Bernard. *A History of the Supreme Court*. New York: Oxford University Press, 1993.

Shain, Barry Alan. *The Myth of American Individualism: The Protestant Origins of American Political Thought*. Princeton, NJ: Princeton University Press, 1994.

Shalhope, Robert E. *Toward a Republican Synthesis: The Emergence of an Understanding of Republicanism in American Historiography*. In *William and Mary Quarterly*, 3rd ser., no. 29 (1972).

Sheehan, Bernard W. *Seeds of Extinction: Jeffersonian Philanthropy and the American Indian*. Published for the Institute of Early American History and Culture by University of North Carolina Press, 1974.

Sheridan, Eugene R. "Liberty and Virtue: Religion and Republicanism in Jeffersonian Thought," In Gilreath, *Education of a Citizen*.

Silverman, Kenneth. *Timothy Dwight*. New York: Twayne, 1969.

Singleton, Gregory H. "Protestant Voluntary Organizations: The Shaping of Victorian America." *American Quarterly* 27 (1975): 549–60.

Singleton, Marvin K. "Colonial Virginia as the First Amendment Matrix: Henry, Madison, and the Assessment Establishment." In Madison, *On Religious Liberty*.

Skaggs, Donald. *Roger Williams' Dream for America*. New York: P. Lang, 1933.

Smith, George L. *Religion and Trade in New Netherland: Dutch Origins and American Development*. Ithaca: Cornell University Press, 1973.

Smith, H. Shelton, Robert J. Handy, and Lefferts A. Loetscher, eds. *American Christianity: An Historical Interpretation with Representative Documents*. New York: Scribner, 1963.

Sobel, Mechal. *The World They Made Together: Black and White Values in Eighteenth-Century Virginia*. Princeton, NJ: Princeton University Press, 1987.

Stansell, Christine. *City of Women: Sex and Class in New York, 1789–1860*. New York: A. A. Knopf, 1986.

Starke, Rodney, and Roger Finke. "American Religion in 1776: A Statistical Portrait." *Sociological Analysis* 49 (1988): 39–51.

Stein, Stephen, ed. *Jonathan Edwards' Writings: Text, Context, Interpretation.* Indianapolis: Indiana University Press, 1996.

Stoeffler, F. Ernest, ed. *Continental Pietism and Early American Christianity.* Grand Rapids, MI: Eerdmans, 1976.

Stokes, Anson Phelps, and Leo Pfeffer. *Church and State in the United States.* New York: Harper and Row, 1964.

Storing, Herbert J. *What the Anti-Federalists Were For: The Political Thought of the Opponents of the Constitution.* Chicago: University of Chicago Press, 1981.

Stout, Harry S. *The New England Soul: Preaching and Religious Culture in Colonial New England.* New York: Oxford University Press, 1986.

Sweet, William Warren. *The Story of Religion in America.* New York: Harper and Bros., 1950.

Tewksbury, Donald. *The Founding of American Colleges and Universities before the Civil War: With Particular Reference to the Religious Influences Bearing upon the College Movement.* New York: Bureau of Publications, Teachers College, Columbia University, 1932.

Thomas, George M. *Revivalism and Cultural Change: Christianity, Nation-Building, and the Market in the Nineteenth-Century United States.* Chicago: University of Chicago Press, 1989.

Thomas, John. *Alternative America: Henry George, Edward Bellamy, Henry Demarest Lloyd and the Adversary Tradition.* Cambridge, MA: Belknap Press, 1983.

Thomason, John Furman. *The Foundation of the Public Schools of South Carolina.* Columbia, SC: The State Company, 1925.

Tillich, Paul. "Freedom and the Ultimate Concern." In Cogley, *Religion in America.*

Tocqueville, Alexis de. *Democracy in America.* 1838. New York: Penguin Books, 1984.

———. *Democracy in America.* Edited by J. P. Mayer, translated by George Lawrence. New York: Harper and Row, 1969.

Tolles, Frederick. *Meeting House and Counting House: The Quaker Merchants of Colonial Philadelphia, 1682–1763.* Chapel Hill: University of North Carolina Press, 1948.

Tomlins, Christopher. "A Mirror Cracked? The Rule of Law in American History." *William and Mary Law Review* 32.2 (Winter 1991).

———. *Law, Labor, and Ideology in the Early American Republic.* New York: Cambridge University Press, 1993.

Trattner, Walter I. *From Poor Law to Welfare State: A History of Social Welfare in America.* New York: Macmillan, 1989.

Tushnet, Mark. *The American Law of Slavery, 1810–1860: Considerations of Humanity and Interest.* Princeton, NJ: Princeton University Press, 1981.

Twomey, Richard. "Jacobins and Jeffersonians: Anglo-American Radical Ideology, 1790–1810." In *The Origins of Anglo-American Radicalism,* ed. Margaret Jacob and James Jacob. London and Boston: Allen and Unwin, 1984.

Walters, Kerry S. *The American Deists: Voices of Reason and Dissent in the Early Republic.* Lawrence: University of Kansas Press, 1992.

Weber, Max. *The Protestant Ethic and the Spirit of Capitalism.* 1930. London: Allen and Unwin, 1948.

Wells, Colin. *The Devil and Doctor Dwight: Satire and Theology in the Early American Republic.* Chapel Hill: University of North Carolina Press, 2002.

Wesley, Edgar Bruce. *The University of the United States.* Minneapolis: University of Minnesota Press, 1935.

White, G. Edward. "The Working Life of *the Marshall Court*, 1815–1835." *Virginia Law Review* 70.1 (1984).

———. *The Marshall Court and Cultural Change, 1815–1835*. Vols. 3 and 4 in the History of the Supreme Court of the United States series, ed. Paul A. Freund and Stanley N. Katz. New York: Macmillan, 1988.

Whitehead, John. *The Separation of College and State*. New Haven: Yale University Press, 1973.

Whitehead, John S. , and Jurgen Herbst. "How to Think About the Dartmouth College Case." *Hist. Educ. Q.* 26 (1986): 333.

Wiebe, Robert H. *The Opening of American Society: From the Adoption of the Constitution to the Eve of Disunion*. New York: A. A. Knopf, 1984.

———. *Self-Rule: A Cultural History of American Democracy*. Chicago: University of Chicago Press, 1995.

Wilentz, Sean. *Chants Democratic: New York City and the Rise of the American Working Class, 1788–1850*. New York: Oxford University Press, 1984.

Wilson, John F., ed. *The Colonial and Early National Periods*. Vol. 1 of *Church and State in America: A Bibliographical Guide*. New York: Greenwood Press, 1986.

Witte, John Jr. "The Essential Rights and Liberties of Religion in the American Constitutional Experiment," in *Notre Dame Law Review* 71 (1996): 371–445.

Wolf, Christoph. *Johann Sebastian Bach: The Learned Musician*. New York: W. W. Norton, 2000.

Wolf, Stephanie G. *Urban Village: Population, Community, and Family Structure in Germantown, Pennsylvania*. Princeton, NJ: Princeton University Press, 1976.

Wood, George B. *Early History of the University of Pennsylvania from its Origin to the Year 1827*. Philadelphia: J. B. Lippincott, 1896.

Wood, Gordon S. *The Creation of the American Republic, 1776–1787*. New York: W. W. Norton, 1969.

———. "Interests and Disinterestedness in the Making of the Constitution." In *Beyond Confederation: Origins of the Constitution and America's National Identity*, ed. Richard Beeman et al. Published for the Institute of Early American History and Culture, Williamsburg, Va. Chapel Hill: University of North Carolina Press, 1987.

———. *The Radicalism of the American Revolution*. New York: A. A. Knopf, 1992.

———. Untitled lecture presented at Indiana University, Bloomington, Indiana, Fall 1995.

Wood, Gregory A. *The French Presence in Maryland, 1524–1800*. Baltimore: Gateway Press, 1978.

Wright, Conrad Edick. *The Transformation of Charity in Postrevolutionary New England*. Boston: Northeastern University Press, 1992.

Wylie, Irvin. "The Search for an American Law of Charity, 1776–1844." *Mississippi Valley Historical Review* 46 (1959): 203.

Zuckerman, Michael. "Holy Wars, Civil Wars: Religion and Economics in Nineteenth-Century America." *Prospects* 16 (1991): 205–40.

Zuckerman, Michael, ed. *Friends and Neighbors: Group Life in America's First Plural Society*. Philadelphia: Temple University Press, 1982.

Zuckert, Michael P. "Locke and the Problem of Civil Religion." In *The American Founding: Essays on the Formation of the Constitution*, ed. J. Jackson Barlow, Leonard Levy, Ken Masuge. New York: Greenwood Press, 1988.

Index

Mark Douglas McGarvie, J.D., Ph.D., is Assistant Professor of History and Law at the University of Richmond, where he also directs the first-year law skills program. He completed a postdoctoral Golieb Fellowship in legal history at New York University School of Law in 2002. He is coeditor of *Charity, Philanthropy, and Civility in American History,* which won the Skystone Ryan Research Prize for 2004.

McGarvie and his wife, Blythe, live in Williamsburg, Virginia.